The Cheyenne Nation

The Cheyenne Nation

A SOCIAL AND DEMOGRAPHIC HISTORY

John H. Moore

UNIVERSITY OF NEBRASKA PRESS
LINCOLN AND LONDON

The paper in this book meets the minimum requirements of American National Standard for
Information Sciences—Permanence of Paper for Printed Library Materials, ANSI Z39.48—1984.

LIBRARY OF CONGRESS CATALOGING-IN-PUBLICATION DATA

Moore, John H., 1939–
    The Cheyenne Nation.

    Bibliography: p.
    Includes index.
    I. Cheyenne Indians.   I. Title.
E99.C53M82 1987   976.6'00497   87-5856
ISBN 0-8032-3107-5 (alk. paper)

This book is respectfully dedicated to the memory of
Gene Weltfish

Contents

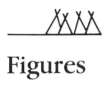

Figures

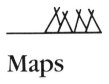

Maps

Plates

Tables

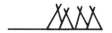

Foreword

PETER NEWCOMER

By the time most graduate students in anthropology have taken their Ph.D. orals, at least once they have probably had to write about or discuss "Maitland's dictum": "Anthropology will become history or it will become nothing." I don't know who Maitland was or whether he ever said this, but I certainly remember puzzling over it. What is the point? What good would a string of names and dates do for our understanding of unchanging peoples? But that was before I had any idea of what historical understanding of *our* society could do for *us,* either. As I look back, I can see that for nineteenth-century thinkers "history" meant the *scientific study* of a developmental or evolutionary *process.* It was not a list of events that followed each other in an order one had to memorize.

That is probably what Maitland wanted our science to become: not a collection of miscellaneous ethnological exotica in the style of pre-Darwinian naturalist biology, and certainly not a static functionalism in the service of the empire, but a dynamic mode of understanding social life as it moves and changes over time. In this, "social change" would not form the last chapter in the standard ethnographic plan, but rather would be the assumption the anthropologist begins with. "Change" in this scheme of things is not some outside stimulus to which a culture responds; it is an autochthonous movement that relieves pressure inside the social system, in the process establishing new structures, new possibilities, new patterns of stress and antagonism.

Anyone can see that a deterministic, mechanical "science" has no place in historical analysis. If social development were amenable to such a method of study, neither the past nor the present would show the diversity that exists. No, the regularities we are looking for are to be found not at the level of data, of "the facts," but rather at the level of *process,* in the same way they are in biology. This kind of science has succeeded in rendering itself truly historical. In it we have a unitary process (evolution by means of natural selection) that explains a bewildering diversity of fact. This is what we need, too, in anthropology. But how do we get there? This is what *The Cheyenne Nation* is about: the struggle to establish a *method*.

Somewhere in the development of our science we got off the track. Nineteenth-century anthropologists had the intention of speculating about the nature of the process by which human evolution was achieved, but their data were so spotty and so badly damaged in transit that no critical standards were ever established by their polemics. Then came the British Empire, indirect rule, and the anthropologist as spy. It was not that the various flavors of functionlism were better science than the evolutionary speculation they replaced. The ascendancy of a static methodology in anthropology was part of a similar movement toward pragmatism all over the social sciences: behavorism in psychology, marginalism in economics, and the statistical method in sociology were some correlatives in related fields. They prevailed because they answered the imperial need of the time, the need for control.

Functionalism is no longer fashionable in anthropology, but its assumptions still lie at the core of our thinking; our anthropology is as functionalist as our commonsense physics is Newtonian: deeply, unconsciously, in profound ignorance of alternatives.

It is only recently that any modification has been made to these theoretical structures. They were erected because the old social science could not serve our purposes, which are the opposite of those of the British Empire and the Bureau of Indian Affairs. Vietnam changed us and the world. It made us see social change as inevitable and as desirable. To participate in it intelligently, we had to find a method of grasping it intellectually, not as an occasional result of accidental outside forces, but as generated internally, by forces at work at all times in all societies. These are the assumptions made by a Marxist methodology. This book is a Marxist history. It sees the unfolding of history as a struggle, a process that moves forward by fits and starts, an alternation between episodes of conspicuous change and states of apparent rest. The Cheyenne nation "bounces through history in a series of national identities." Method—the promotion of a method that allow us to see this—is the real program of *The Cheyenne Nation*.

This goal is achieved not at the level of abstract recommendation, however, but by dint of some of the most arduous and painstaking research I have ever read through. To give us this book, John Moore winnows early travel accounts, amateur linguistic records, hand-drawn maps and diagrams, firewood calculations, the distribution of grasses, 150 years of oral history as related by mutual enemies, bad ethnography, and just plain racism. He makes it look easy.

His first technical precept is respect for the people and their knowledge. The first chapter has a lot of funny material on the errors of fieldworkers who would not credit what the Cheyennes told them. Funny, that is, until one recognizes the racism and special pleading for static functionalism that lie behind it.

His technical conclusion is that "instead of focusing on documents as a basic structure of history, we should use them as supplements to oral history." As a general rule, the oral history will make sense only if you have a fundamental understanding of what is going on. If you do not then you will be tempted to "correct" your informants. A great deal of bad ethnography has come out of this practice, as Moore makes clear. As one Cheyenne said, those old ethnographies are "like taking a child to a baseball game. When you take the child home, he can tell you something about what happened at the game, but it will sound very strange, for the child did not truly understand what the people were doing or why they were doing it." Right. But Moore was many times in loco parentis to these "child ethnographers" and was still able to decipher the rules of the game. "The rules" remain crucial because in all the flow and flux, we must still deal with *structure*. The objective is to *relate* the structure to the process of change, to derive each from the other in their motion.

The book begins by setting a structural problem, the arrangement of social groups in the Cheyenne ceremonial camp circle. How did these groups come into being, and what is their relationship to each other, considering that "the ceremonial circle is the tribe's symbolic tipi"? And we are off, into fields of statistics, thickets of misinformation, and all the hard work of finding the truth.

Out of the ceremonial circle comes the notion of the Cheyenne nation as a *tribal nation,* not merely as it exists in the ethnographic present, but in the process of its creation, and through the changes it undergoes. This kind of nation is different from the nation-state, with its exploitation and its bureaucracy. It is basically an alliance of *bands,* the "functioning economic and domestic units" of the Cheyennes, that forms this new thing. But in creating the tribal nation, the component bands "are themselves trans-formed in the process. Bands do not merely create a representation of themselves at a higher level, but instead create a social species of a different order entirely."

The new social formation probably came into being in the Black Hills about 1740. It solved many problems for the Cheyennes. The prophet Sweet Medicine is given credit for this momentous and complex social invention: "He was a real person and a political genius. He created a multidimensional charter for the Cheyenne nation by initiating or legit-imating the central institutions of the new nation. He forbade warfare among the bands by defining interband killing as murder and requiring exile for the Cheyenne murderers and the ritual cleansing of the sacred arrows. He defined the relations of the military societies to the national collectivity, defined the residence bands as 'sacred,' placed the manhao into the tribal circle, and created a new kind of political and judicial institution, the Council of Forty-four. He made a rule that war chiefs had to resign from their military societies to be peace chiefs."

But the story of the Cheyennes is not the biography of Sweet Medicine; it has much more to do with the conditions and the context in which this remarkable man lived. It was these material conditions that made his vision, his diplomacy, and his "greatness" possible. *The Cheyenne Nation* shows how it became possible at one point in Plains history for something like the Cheyenne nation to be created and how Sweet Medicine was there to work upon it, which he did, leaving his name and his traces everywhere in it.

That nation still lives, as John Moore's book demonstrates so vividly, and is still actively changing, as all healthy living things must do.

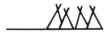

Acknowledgments

You should have good reasons before intruding on the business of another culture. This is especially true when its people have been victimized and oppressed by your own society. Merely being curious is not, I think, a good enough cause to bother them with your questions. My own purposes in knocking on Cheyenne doors over the past fifteen years have been twofold. First, I have had scientific goals, which I will explain in the first chapter; secondly, I have had other motives that are, I hope, benevolent.

My major professor at New York University, Tom Beidelman, was the first to encourage me to begin fieldwork with the Cheyennes. He pointed out that though the Cheyennes had been widely reported in the literature, very little was understood about them. What we had was Indian lore; what we needed was ethnology. My first interest was in religious symbolism, not for any good reason, but because everyone else was doing it. At the end of a long interview in Oklahoma in 1970, however, the arrow keeper at that time, Jim Medicine Elk, asked me a very good question: "You see how it is with us, John. You have lived in our homes and you know we have nothing—a little land, poor houses, and often no food. You ask me questions about our religion and I am glad to answer, but I wonder why you do not interest yourself in something that will have some benefit for our people."

Within the next few years Jim died, and my closest friend among the Northern Cheyennes, Henry Tall Bull, also died. Henry, the blossoming tribal historian of the Northern Cheyennes, had diabetes. Admitted to a white man's hospital for treatment, he experienced diabetic convulsions. According to the family, the hospital staff had difficulty controlling him and had him arrested in the middle of the night. After a winter night spent unconscious and unclothed on a jail bed, Henry developed complications. The family arrived at the hospital in the morning, learned what had happened, and bailed him out, but he died soon afterward. And I resolved that my next stint of research among the Cheyennes would have some practical purpose.

When I moved to the University of Oklahoma in 1977, I had my opportunity. At the instigation of Edward Red Hat, the new arrow keeper, assisted by Laird Cometsevah, a traditional chief, and Karl Schlesier, an anthropologist at Wichita State University, the Southern Cheyennes had founded the Southern Cheyenne Research and Human Development Association, with Laird as executive director. This association was to be the public arm of the traditional chiefs and headsmen, completely independent of the official tribal government. Laird Cometsevah became my best friend among the Southern Cheyennes and remains so. With him, I wrote a series of health-related proposals to various funding agencies, all of which were refused. In 1979, however, two particular proposals, to the National Institutes of Health and to the National Science Foundation, were carried into the sacred arrow tipi and blessed. And so the research reported in this book was funded by NSF Project BNS-8014119 and NIH Project 1-HD-14910.

Over the next two years, I am proud to say, thousands of dollars in research money was channeled into Cheyenne hands for interviews, library and archival research, and to organize the data we were collecting. This book represents the bulk of the research, the sociological and historical part, but other significant publications will include our results from the analyses of mortality, fertility, and epidemic disease. The most important result of this research beyond the present book, however, is the Sand Creek Project.

Since the early 1970s a group of Cheyenne volunteers had been working to collect genealogies of the descendants of the people attacked at the Sand Creek Massacre in 1864. The United States government had long since agreed to pay indemnities, but in later years it claimed the descendants could no longer be identified. As part of our funded research project, we collected genealogies and other information, which we entered onto the mainframe computer at the university, using George Collier's KINPRO-GRAM. So far, we have identified over three thousand descendants by genealogical methods. To identify others, I attempted to trace the histories of the bands present at Sand Creek, which resulted in the information included here as chapter 7. The primary workers in the Sand Creek Project, in addition to Laird, have been Colleen Cometsevah, Ruby Bushyhead, Terry Wilson, and Emma Red Hat. Colleen, especially, served as linguist and interpreter. The Sand Creek Descendents Association, reorganized in 1983, is chaired by Bobby Big Horse. Our attorneys are Steven Chestnut of Seattle, Washington, and Kurt Blue Dog of Madison, Wisconsin.

The elders who supplied information for all our research, genealogical and otherwise, are cited throughout this book. But I should also mention here certain men and women who were movers and organizers as well as informants. I especially wish to thank my brothers Wayne Red Hat and Luther Black Bear, also Willie Fletcher, Terry Wilson, Ed Burns, Jr., Everett Yellowman, Jennie Black, Kathryn Bull Coming, Agnes Hamilton, Al Tall Bird, William Tall Bull, Ted Rising Sun, Irene Tall Bull, Lyman Weaselbear, Lenora Hart, Roy Nightwalker, Eugene Black Bear, Joe Antelope, and Alfrich Heap of Birds. I am also saddened and mindful of our grandparents who helped with this project but died before it could be completed: Edward Red Hat, Walter Hamilton, Roy Bull Coming, John Greany, John Black Owl, Katie Osage, Jim Medicine Elk, and Alex Brady.

Of my colleagues, Karl Schlesier has been a constant source of support and encouragement. Donald Berthrong has kindly shared ideas and documents. Also, I should thank Margot Liberty and Father Peter Powell for their help at various times. Especially helpful in reading the manuscript and offering suggestions were Ray Wood, Helen Tanner, Patricia Albers, Donald Berthrong, Peter Newcomer, and Fred Eggan. For their criticisms, I wish to thank Ray DeMallie and Ives Goddard. For their theoretical discussions that have helped structure the whole manuscript I thank Pat Albers and Loretta Fowler. Their recent works are included in the References. Above all, I wish to acknowledge my teacher and friend James O'Connor, who taught me the principles of historical materialism I have tried to use in this book.

In our department, several graduate students were employed to implement what we called the "Cheyenne Ethnohistory Project." The assistant director of the project was Robert Nespor, who wrote his dissertation on Cheyenne agriculture. Others in the project were Rebecca Bateman, who worked for two years coding and organizing the Sand Creek data, and J. J. Chen-Chou, who worked on fertility and mortality, as well as Dan Swan, Dick Sattler, Jane Johnson, Dori Penny, Stan Johnson, Wayne McGuire, Steve Greymorning, and Monireh Rahmani. My special thanks go to Greg Campbell, who began as a graduate student but has become a colleague in Cheyenne studies. Our chairman at that time, John Dunn, consistently helped smooth over the rough spots in administering the grants. Mary McClain, manager of the university's Information Processing Service, oversaw the processing of the manuscript. My thanks to all of them.

Of the archivists and librarians around the country who helped with my research, I especially wish to thank Vyrtis Thomas of the National Anthropological Archives and Shelley Arlen of the Western History Collections of the University of Oklahoma. Also, I should mention Lynn Taylor of the Denver Public Library, Catherine Engel of the Colorado Historical

Society, David Bosse of the Newberry Library, Richard Ryan of the Clements Library, University of Michigan, James Paulauskas of the National Archives, Beverly Bishop and Deborah Bolas of the Missouri Historical Society, Sarah Hirsch of the Gilcrease Institute, Ruth Christensen of the Southwest Museum, Marsha Gallagher of the Joslyn Art Museum, and Beth Carroll of the American Philosophical Society.

I must also thank the many farmers, ranchers, stockmen, and county agents who shared with me their practical experience and knowledge of Plains environments. Especially I thank Robert Goodwin of Durham, Oklahoma, Ezra Blackmon of Freedom, Oklahoma, Guy Wilkins of Weatherford, Oklahoma, Burl Scherler of Sheridan Lake, Colorado, Rodney Johnson of Eads, Colorado, Ross Campbell of Pueblo, Colorado, Robert David and Merlyn Queen of Las Animas, Colorado, Robert Dawson of Chivington, Colorado, and also Mike Kinsey, William Sorenson, O. L. Lennen, and Jerri Zweygardt of Colorado. In Nebraska I consulted with Jack Russell of Benkelman, Mike Brown of Kimball, Allen Jones of Trenton, Russell Leiding of North Platte, and also Willie Holmes and Robert Ellis. In South Dakota, the following people provided information and guidance: Tom Quinn of Rapid City, Darrell Vig of Sturgis, Mike Knutson of Lisbon, and Roy Housman of McIntosh. I must also thank Edrian Ivers of Center, North Dakota, David Pratt of Hardin, Montana, and Al Destefano, L. C. Young, and Keith Covington of Cheyenne, Wyoming. My special thanks to my longtime friend Charles Rambow, custodian of the Cheyennes' sacred mountain near Sturgis, South Dakota.

I thank my wife Shelley for reading the entire manuscript and correcting it for style and clarity. All along, her help and support gave me the time for this writing. Thanks also to my son Jeremy, who sat without complaint through endless meetings and interviews. I appreciate his patience.

I must also extend some apologies here to the Southern Arapaho people, who have been excluded from this study although they have spent nearly two hundred years as the friends and allies of the Southern Cheyennes. I have excluded them for two reasons. First, current hostilities, centered on the business committee, tend to prevent an outsider from having friendly relationships with both nations at once. And second, I have refrained from inquiring into Arapaho culture so that I could keep a clear head concerning what was Cheyenne tradition and what was not. Thus this book adopts a Cheyenne perspective on history and social organization. The Arapahos, I am sure, view Cheyenne history quite differently. At this time, Loretta Fowler is undertaking field research with the Southern Arapahos that will help correct this imbalance.

Also my research has been more thorough concerning the Southern Cheyennes than the Northern Cheyennes of Montana. This has largely been a product of the sponsorship I received from the Southern Cheyennes in Oklahoma and of my physical proximity to them. I hope that Greg Campbell's field research in Montana will soon remedy this deficiency.

1 ⋀⋀⋀

Tribes and Nations

Life is struggle, and history has been called a record of the struggles of person against person, nation against nation, and class against class. But all too often tribal societies are thought to be exempt from conflict. They are pictured as romantic, idyllic groups in which culture is homogeneous, all members know their place, and custom is law. Frequently we are told that a tribe has occupied the same territory "since time immemorial" and that for it "time has stood still."[1]

I assert, however, that there is profound conflict and contradiction in tribal society, and that we cannot understand even the simplest facts about a society, its structure, and its history unless we know the nature of its struggles. That is, I make the ambitious claim that we can say nothing for sure about a tribal society unless we know the circumstances of its origin, its history of conflict, its current differences of opinion, and the future it has planned for itself. Far from being disruptive and dysfunctional to the development of a society, conflict and factionalism are beneficial and even constitute an adaptation to a geographical and political environment. Beyond that, if we now perceive tribal soccietes as pacific, homogeneous, bounded, and highly structured, it is mostly the fault of anthropologists. Too often they have seen variability and reported normality, have seen open conflict and reported only its resolution, have witnessed vast complexity and reported a simple and fantastic crystallography of social structure.[2]

To present a more realistic picture of the condition of a tribal society, I have selected the Cheyenne Indians for illustration—not because the nation is so little known to history, but because it is so very well known. Because of certain colorful and dramatic episodes in the past, and because of their central geographical position in the Great Plains, the Cheyennes are perhaps the best known of any Native American tribe, certainly in the popular mind. For example, one model of Chevrolet truck is called the Cheyenne, as was a popular television series of the 1960s. At least three motion pictures have been made concerning Cheyenne history—*Cheyenne Autumn, Little Big Man,* and *Centennial.* There are even pulp Westerns and romance novels on Cheyenne themes that bear such titles as *Cheyenne Raiders, Sweet Medicine's Prophecy,* and *Little Flower's Desire.*[3]

The Cheyennes are also well known historically, having been the life work of the distinguished historian Donald Berthrong.[4] Among anthropologists, George Grinnell and James Mooney have published the most and the best ethnography, but as we shall see, the unpublished field notes of Mooney, Truman Michelson, and such lesser luminaries as Ben Clark and Lt. Heber Creel also have much to offer. A more romantic perspective on recent Cheyenne culture has been represented in books by Father Peter Powell.[5] Bibliographic listings for "Cheyenne" in standard sources run toward a thousand entries—books, articles, manuscripts, field notes, and government records.[6]

Because of this wealth of material, it is possible to create and test certain hypotheses about conflict and change in Cheyenne society. My perspective in this book—and my problem, then—is the very opposite of the problem faced by a fieldworker who travels to some remote area and becomes the world's only expert on a little-known, exotic society. The world is full of Cheyenne experts. Scarcely a summer passes that some visiting scholar, student, or Indian hobbyist does not drop by my office and set me straight on some aspect of Cheyenne society and history. But if this were not the case there would be no one for me to argue with, using my dialectical model of Cheyenne society, and no one to understand my arguments once they were set out. So it is into this fertile field that I undertake to plant my own views and those of my fellow researchers and informants.

The fundamental theory I wish to present is that tribal nations of the world, such as the Cheyennes, are just like more complex nations in having an "ethnogenesis." Nations and tribes all undergo a period in which they consolidate themselves, in terms of their population, language, and culture, and begin life as a homogeneous collection of people. The "Cheyennes" are not a group that has existed from time immemorial; they sprang into being at a particular time, for some particular reasons. The basic purpose of this book is to explain when this happened and what the reasons were. At the same time I will emphasize that attempts toward homogeneity are never completely successful, and that throughout its history the Cheyenne nation has exhibited significant variability in culture, language, and social structure.

It is disturbing that, despite the abundance of material on the

Cheyennes, certain fundamental empirical questions about their history, migrations, and social structure are still unanswered. For example, there is the basic problem of how many Cheyennes there ever were. One must wonder why the population estimates have been so variable from the time of Lewis and Clark to the first reservation censuses in the 1870s. There is also the issue of Cheyenne bands—their number and names. Although we know the names of the more important bands, there is no suggestion in the ethnography of where even these were situated in time and space or how large they were. Also, we know little about their seasonal movements and historical migrations. Most often the published accounts make no attempt to distinguish one band from another.

Beyond that, we have little idea of the internal structure of a band or even if all bands were the same. We do not know what kinds of relationships existed among the members of a band. Were they related by blood, by marriage, or only by friendship and convenience? And though much has been written about Cheyenne tipis and Cheyenne horses, no one can say with certainty how many people lived in a Cheyenne tipi or how many horses they had. Much of this volume, then, will be devoted to answering these basic empirical questions in a reliable, scientific manner. But the book is intended to be more than ethnography. I shall continually discuss broader and more important theoretical questions concerning the general nature of "tribes" and "nations"—issues I shall address in detail after I explain my research methods.

Methods of Research

The methodology I bring to bear is one I recommend as appropriate for our times. We are perhaps the last generation of fieldworkers who can elicit any new knowledge about aboriginal Plains cultures, and we are the first generation to use computers to sort through great masses of census and administrative data. So the research exhibited here is best seen as a three-cornered dialogue among written sources, modern informants, and computer output. In this approach the ethnologist takes the role of moderator, developing new data and new questions. It is now only the oldest Cheyennes who can talk knowledgeably about such subjects as the internal arrangement of a tipi, Indian horse husbandry, or kinship systems of the past. Although many younger Cheyennes, in Oklahoma as well as Montana, speak their language fluently, they are more likely to talk about powwows, rock stars, or the latest Superbowl than about the legacy of the past. Modern Cheyenne culture is vibrant, alive, and constantly generating new ideas about powwows, Indian music, or peyote meetings, but information on aboriginal society is steadily diminishing as elders born at the turn of the century pass away.

I have worked with Cheyenne informants every summer since 1969, and throughout the year since I moved to Oklahoma in 1977. My most intensive fieldwork was done during a two-year period funded by the National Science Foundation and the National Institutes of Health, from September 1980 to August 1982. During that time I conducted hundreds of hours of interviews and drove over fifty thousand miles. I interviewed perhaps fifty elders on many occasions, individually and in small groups.

My competence in the Cheyenne language is nothing to brag about. The best compliment I ever received on my linguistic ability was from an elderly Cheyenne woman who listened to my serious efforts for several sentences. When I finished she paused, looked at the ground like a proper Cheyenne lady, and said politely, "You know, John, I can really tell you're trying to speak Cheyenne." I frowned a little, stifled a grin, then had to laugh out loud. She still teases me about it. Yet my understanding of Cheyenne is sufficient that informants persist in speaking to me in their native language. That is, they are confident enough I understand them that they will not switch to English but will continue to explain things in Cheyenne. In seeking to understand the political and kinship systems, especially, this has been a tremendous advantage, as you will see in chapters 7 and 8.

To elicit responses from informants (Cheyennes dislike the term "informant" because of the implications of "police informant," so I usually say "elders"), I have been lavish in my use of early government records, maps, and excerpts from the field notes of other anthropologists. Enough time has passed so that elders are intensely interested in these documents. At an earlier date, when these documents represented people informants knew personally, they may have been too quick or too slow to criticize others' opinions. But time has cooled some family jealousies and dimmed some memories. Modern elders most often are thrilled and delighted to see written statements made by their ancestors or to find familiar names in government records.

I have been wary, of course, of putting answers into the mouths of informants by using published and unpublished ethnography. My own experience, however, has shown that Cheyennes do not take published ethnography very seriously. Traditionalist elders are most often put off or exasperated by the past attempts of white people to understand their culture. As my friend Laird Cometsevah put it, "You see, in the past these white people would go to ceremonies and things and write down what they saw. They didn't get it wrong, exactly, they just didn't understand what was going on." Another Cheyenne told me that "these old books are like taking a child to a baseball game. When you take the child home, he can tell you something about what happened at the game, but it will sound very strange, for the child did not truly understand what the people were doing or why they were doing it."

When I showed government documents to informants, there was constant feedback between their comments and the computer printouts we generated at the University of Oklahoma in Norman. For example, Ed Red Hat once told me he heard that many Seiling people had married into the Clinton "bunch," and he pointed to two names on the Clinton list. So we were able to run a genealogical match of the two groups and discovered, in this case, that these two couples were exceptional and there was no general pattern of that sort. Ed Red Hat's early memories of Indian gardens at Thomas and Seiling, however, were confirmed by government records and were important for Robert Nespor's analysis of early reservation agriculture.[7]

Many of these old documents jarred the memories of our informants, expecially when they were interviewed in groups. One person might recall something that would prompt another to elaborate. In this way we were able to trace, for example, the histories of the individual bands far beyond anything done even eighty years ago. This kind of data on early reservation life is still available and was not collected in the classic period of Cheyenne ethnography, 1880–1910.

You will notice that throughout this book I give remarkable credence to the recollections and opinions of informants. This is not something I decided in advance; I have been driven to it by experience. The observations of informants have so often proved out against documentary and other "more reliable" evidence that I finally came to bestow my initial confidence on them rather than on other sources.

I first began to suspect that informants knew more than fieldworkers when I investigated Cheyenne ethnobiology in 1970 for my doctoral dissertation. Early in my research, Roy Nightwalker told me that the green and the white dragonflies painted on the bodies of dancers during the ceremonies were actually the same creature—that green dragonflies turned white as the summer progressed. I dutifully recorded this, thinking it was only a queer belief until I read in James Needham's *Handbook of the Dragonflies of North America* that the American green darner was "canescent," exuding a waxy substance over the summer that gradually turned it white.[8]

On another occasion Alex Brady of Montana told me that eagles were known for their fleetness of foot and could run down jackrabbits on the open plains. Once again I skeptically recorded the information, and it was not a month later that I watched a nature program on television about golden eagles and saw an eagle run down a jackrabbit while the narrator said, "It is a little known fact that eagles, by a combination of flying and running, can keep pace with a jackrabbit, even changing directions as the rabbits twist and dart around trees and bushes." After that I kept a respectful silence as informants told me about fulgurite, fossils, the birthing of beavers, and the family behavior of short-eared owls.[9]

As I began to collect oral history, then, and to read the oral histories collected by Mooney and Michelson, I was not surprised to find the elders were frequently more accurate and more specific than the ethnologists. Nonetheless, there has been a lot of uninformed second-guessing of informants by fieldworkers, which is one reason the ethnohistory of North America is so confused. For example, in one section of a narrative Truman Michelson collected from Tall Bull in 1910, Michelson wrote next to "Mississippi River" in the text, "must mean Missouri River."[10] The ethnologist was skeptical that the informant could refer to episodes so far back in history, so he muddled the narrative by "correcting" it. It is largely because of such misinformed tinkering with the reports of informants that our history of Plains tribes is so full of mistakes. It would perhaps have been better for previous scholars to publish their ethnohistorical texts "as is" rather than trying to create summaries, replete with errors.

Perhaps the most skeptical of all ethnologists was Robert Lowie, famous for his ethnography of the Crow Indians. In 1915 he said, "I cannot attach to oral traditions any historical value whatsoever under any conditions whatsoever. We cannot know them to be true except on the basis of extraneous evidence, and in that case they are superfluous."[11] This pronouncement, of course, very conveniently relieved him of the obligation to verify any historical statements his informants had made, and his published writings indicate he never tried to do so.

It is convenient for ethnohistorians, as well as ethnologists, to deny the value of oral histories, since that absolves them from doing any fieldwork at all. One good example from Cheyenne studies is a scholar who has published two collections of ledger drawings and a comprehensive history of the Cheyenne military societies.[12] Though she traveled all over the country to visit libraries and collect documents, she apparently never found it necessary or advisable to talk to Cheyennes about the issues that interested her. This led to a lot of naive speculation in her writings, and some outright mistakes. One was called to my attention in 1981 when I served as consultant to the Kiowas, Comanches, Plains Apaches, Cheyennes, and Arapahos for a reenactment and renewal of the Alliance of 1840.[13] As I collected various tribal accounts of events in the great alliance camp, one Cheyenne elder told me that her grandfather had drawn a picture of the event and that she had "seen it in a book." The picture turned out to be plate 2 in a collection of drawings by Howling Wolf, and the elders of the five tribes had a fine time naming the people and events in the picture, which shows the activities of the second day of the alliance, when the Kiowas gave horses to the Cheyennes.[14] But the editor never asked such informants to comment on the picture and merely speculated in print that it represented "the coming of the first horses owned by Cheyennes." That is, she substituted a made-up history for the facts, thereby introducing errors in Cheyenne history to confound future scholars.

Of course it is a lot of work to do fieldwork, worry over the documentary sources, and explore archives for the field notes of previous generations of ethnographers. But that is the requirement for our generation. Although the number of facts to be collected from informants concerning aboriginal times is diminishing, we have an increased capacity to find archival deposits and to analyze vast bodies of data from early reservation records. In an article in *Science,* I have shown how such data can be approached and analyzed using computers.[15]

And now we have a new problem to address—how to interpret the field notes of other ethnologists. We have reached the time when much of the information on aboriginal culture is in the form of unpublished field notes. Most of the original fieldworkers are dead, and we can no longer ring them up and ask them to elaborate on some question of language or kinship. So it is all the more necessary to proceed on a broad front, with this three-cornered dialogue among informants, written sources, and the great mass of administrative documents from early reservation times. Each point of the triangle can help illuminate questions from the other two sources.

Although many sophisticated computer analyses of census lists and other early records were done as part of our funded research of 1980–82, only a few of these will be reported here. Essentially, I have included only some simple analyses that have a direct bearing on Cheyenne social structure and history. I regard these as quantitative tests of the social and historical theories asserted by informants, suggested in unpublished field notes of other fieldworkers, or devised by myself and my fellow researchers. So it is appropriate to explain what kinds of theories these are and what we seek to establish by our analyses.

Tribes

Many of the issues discussed in this book revolve around the concepts of "tribe" and "nation." Although the concept of tribe, as usually understood, has little value in describing a society like the Cheyennes, I believe the concept of "tribal nation" is very useful. That is, I wish to amalgamate theories of tribe with theories of nationhood. But what do we mean by these two concepts, tribe and nation?

Morton H. Fried's thoughtful book *The Notion of Tribe* provides a convenient point of departure, since he lists several traits that tribes are universally supposed to exhibit but do not. [16] Like Franz Boas and Robert Lowie before him, and like his contemporary Marvin Harris, Fried likes to puncture theories by finding exceptions to general rules, in this case to the alleged general characteristics of all "tribes." [17] Also like these others, Fried takes the exceptions not as proving the rule, but as disproving it, and he offers no theory to replace the one he has demolished. Like the others, he leaves a conceptual vacuum where we ought to have an important theoretical idea. [18]

Although Fried raises many important issues about tribes, I will address only four of them here—concerning biology, economics, language, and ideology. As I discuss these issues, I will try to set a framework for the idea of the tribal nation that salvages some of the most useful "tribal" traits Fried discusses.

Although my ideas are derived from orthodox Marxism, I do not wish to belabor sectarian Marxist issues. Instead, I will argue in more general language and try to appeal to logic rather than political sentiment. The relevant theoretical sources, however, are cited. Especially, I wish to acknowledge the parallel development of certain Soviet theorists whose concern is with the "ethnos" and "ethnogenesis"—Julian Bromley, Vasili Kozlov, and Israel Gurvich. [19] But as an American, I should more properly discuss the theories of other Americans—Morton Fried in particular.

First of all, Fried argues that tribes are not biological entities, or "isolated breeding populations," as he puts it. He argues that since the idea of biological unity is pivotal to the whole notion of tribe, and since such unity does not exist, the concept is seriously undermined. In agreement with Fried, I will show that the Cheyennes have polyglot biological origins, just like every other nation on earth. But if we cannot define a tribe as a biologically homogenous group, we can still define a tribe or nation as a lawmaking group that *decides* about matters of marriage and mating, whatever the biological consequences might be. In the Cheyenne case, we will see that marriage outside the band, or even outside the nation, was highly recommended. That is, the Cheyenne nation was predicated not on *preserving* the biological separateness of the population, but on *extending* and *hybridizing* the nation with other groups. Far from being a handicap or detriment to national strength, marriage with foreign trading partners, such as Mandans, Anglos, and Arikaras, and with important military allies, such as the Teton Sioux and Arapahos, was reasonable and important. Hybrid bands created by large-scale intermarriages, such as the Masikotas, Wotapios, and Dog Soldiers, played an important role in Cheyenne history. They made the nation stronger, not weaker. The Cheyennes were no less a tribe for having encouraged these marriages.

Second, there is economics. Fried entertains, I believe, the naive idea that domestic exchange within a tribal society is more important than extrasocietal economics—foreign trade. Although it is sometimes difficult to tell when Fried is presenting his own ideas and when he is setting up, for criticism, the ideas of others, he nonetheless seems to argue that tribal domestic units are self-sufficient and therefore have no need to trade with other families within the alleged "tribe." But I will show that the Cheyenne bands had productive specialties—horses, robes, guns, pelts—that were traded among the bands as gifts accompanying marriages and tribal ceremonies.

Trade with other nations was also important for Cheyennes, and certainly it is true that there is no society in the world in which foreign trade is unimportant. Malinowski himself, discussed by Fried, was one of the first to point out the significance of long-distance trade for tribal societies: the Kula Ring encompassed hundreds of miles of the open Pacific.[20] In North America, trade for essential items—flint, bow wood, and such—goes back at least to 10,000 B.C., and it begins much earlier in the tribal societies of the Old World.[21] Just as domestic economy is an important internal organizing force of a society, so opportunities for foreign trade can force the mobilization or reorganization of the entire society, with radical and far-reaching consequences for internal organization. With the Cheyennes, we will see how bands, families, and the national structure were organized and reorganized over several centuries to suit the changing demands of the internal and external economy.

Third, there is language. Fried is correct, and certainly it must be obvious, that tribal and linguistic boundaries do not coincide anywhere in the world. I will present several North American examples in succeeding chapters. But it does not follow that language does not define the nation.[22] Even among tribal nations there is consistently a dominant national language. Insofar as national unity requires meetings, conferences, and shared ceremonies, there will be pressure toward the emergence of a single national language, as a convenience. That tribal nations are often caught by ethnographers in the process of developing a national language, or of splitting into two nations of the same language, does not mean linguistic unity is unimportant in the life of the nation. With the Cheyennes, we will see the emergence and submersion of dialects and languages in response to the changing demands of national existence.

Last and perhaps most important, there is the role ideology plays in the life of a nation. By "ideology" Fried apparently means a belief in abstractions that have, in practice, no particular social or political consequences. He specifically cites and quotes so-called charter myths for various tribes and clans around the world. But Fried neglects the fact that "beliefs" in practical matters concerning law, proper marriages, and rules for membership in voluntary associations are also matters of ideology. Perhaps the greatest contribution of structural functionalism to general anthropology has been the recognition that abstract beliefs are intimately related to patterns of practical action. It is ethnocentric to think that "ideology" is as divorced from reality in tribal societies as it sometimes appears to be in Western societies.

In the context of ideology Fried asks sarcastically, "If a bunch of people got together and said they were a tribe, wouldn't they be a tribe?" Oddly enough, this is precisely the definition of a nation used seriously by Rupert Emerson: "a body of people who feel that they are a nation." In his important book, Emerson added another definition of "nation" that is broad enough to include tribal nations.[23] "The ideal model of the nation . . . is a single people, traditionally fixed on a well-defined territory, speaking the same language and preferably a language all its own, possessing a distinctive culture, and shaped to a common mold by many generations of shared historical experience." To this I would add that a tribal nation writes its own charter, both in mythical or symbolic terms and in all kinds of practical and explicit ways. The tribal nation defines its rules of citizenship and the duties of its citizens. It creates special roles by sex, age, rank, and status and defines citizenship by participation in and respect for those roles. Always there is a national religion. And most important, a tribal nation forbids warfare among its member groups and requires them all to cooperate in making war against enemies of the nation.

Among the Cheyennes, member bands were assigned places in the ceremonial circle. Their presence at the ceremonies symbolized a renewal of their charters as member bands. Citizens had to marry in a legal manner, had to join a military society if they were male, and had to respect the peacekeeping role of the chiefs. The list of duties and responsibilities goes on and on, and all together these laws, customs, beliefs, and norms tended to integrate the discrete bands into a tribal nation—and still do. As long as this nation or any nation functions, it continues the attempt to integrate and homogenize the language, legends, laws, economic behavior, and social

practices of its citizens, all of which are legitimated in the major ceremonies. So I believe Fried is quite wrong when he concludes, "The tribe is
not a consistent, coherent ritual group." At least he is wrong about the
Cheyennes.

I think Fried's theory is also incorrect when applied to other Plains
Indians who practiced the Sun Dance. Politically, the Sun Dance was
nothing less than a statement of who was in and who was out of the national
alliance at any one time, and of who the current allies and enemies might
be. Member bands of the Plains nations camped in their regular places,
guests in a special place. Enemy scalps and representations of enemies were
flaunted and reviled during the ceremonies. As national membership
changed and new patterns of alliance were designed, Sun Dance ritual was
retooled to show the new arrangements. In exhibiting these traits, the
Kiowas are as good an example as the Cheyennes.[24]

Nations

As a scientific concept, "nation" has its main origin outside anthropology.
As applied to tribal peoples, the concept is mostly a product of the twentieth century, evolving from what have been called "national minority
questions" in modern nation-states. In one recent application of national
theory, the Bureau of Indian Affairs, through its Branch of Federal Ac-
knowledgment, has developed general guidelines for evaluating the "Indian status" of various unrecognized groups around the country. The present
process is in sharp contrast to government procedures of the nineteenth
century, when societies as diverse as the Cherokees, Cheyennes, and Paiutes
were equally designated "tribes" and administered in a manner that often
ignored their radical cultural and political differences.[25]

In the mid-twentieth century, as former colonies of European powers
gained their independence after World War II, the United Nations encouraged the study of relationships between new nation-states and the national
minorities within their boundaries, particularly in Africa.[26] Even earlier,
the Soviet Union had to decide on questions of political autonomy for ethnic
minorities after the revolution of 1917. Some of these "minorities," however, were huge by North American standards, numbering millions of people
in the cases of the Kazakhs, Uzbeks, and Georgians.[27]

Scholarly questions about "nation" were first raised, in a serious and
practical manner, concerning new European nations in the nineteenth century. As the Hapsburg empire became fragmented, hot political questions
arose about where the boundaries of the new European nations should be
drawn. What, exactly, was Hungary? Where did it begin and end? Was

multilingual and multicultural Switzerland a "nation" in the same sense that France was? All these questions were debated against a backdrop of the restoration of the French monarchy, the revolutions of 1848, the Franco-Prussian War, and the creation of national boundaries that finally precipitated the "Balkan Crisis" before World War I.

In any event, out of these arguments and political debates of the nineteenth century, and out of the efforts of various countries in the twentieth century to solve practical questions of "nation," there have emerged some definitions of nation that I believe are useful for understanding tribal peoples whether or not these tribal nations are within a larger political unit. Here I will define four of the most important characteristics that tribal nations must exhibit: citizenship, territory, political unity, and shared language. These overlap the characteristics Fried has criticized, but they are not the same.

Nations charter themselves, actively and explicitly, and define their own membership. It is not done by anthropologists or historians. The "charter myths" of a tribal nation most often designate the legitimate members of the national body, usually by band, village, or clan, as we shall see in chapter 4. Such lists of member groups constitute one definition of membership in the nation. If one's group is mentioned in the mythic charter, one is a citizen.

Citizens of tribal nations are also defined by the roles and duties they must fulfill. Perhaps there is an obligation to appear at the annual ceremonies, as with the Cheyennes, or there may be a standardized initiation into adulthood. There are all kinds of explicit, symbolic, and ceremonial ways, sanctioned by the collective nation, by which individuals can say they are citizens.

I am not arguing, however, that everyone within the nation must agree about the conditions and obligations of citizenship. Among the Cheyennes, complaints have always been received from bands who found it difficult to attend the ceremonies and therefore did not consider that particular requirement a condition of citizenship. It therefore became the business of the military societies to enforce attendance, by coercion before the ceremonies or punishment afterward.[28]

But this difference of opinion about the obligations of citizenship does not undermine the idea that a nation is defined by its citizens. As long as there are compelling reasons for maintaining a nation, there will be continual actions to bring people into conformity with their defined roles and duties. When the reasons for maintaining the nation are less compelling for some, then there is disagreement and polarization, perhaps fomenting a schism into two new nations with differing definitions of citizenship.

This process of forcing conformity and resisting it is normal for nation building and growth. The modern United States is no less a nation for having differences of opinion about income tax, bilingual education, or immigration policy, nor is it less a nation for having historically broken off from Great Britain or having prevented a schism by fighting the Civil War. These processes are entirely normal for a nation-state, just as they are for a tribal nation such as the Cheyennes. The nationhood lies in the original charter and in the attempt to maintain and expand that charter, whatever its nature. And I contend that a notion of citizenship is consistently a part of all national charters, including those of tribal nations. In general, tribal nations and nation-states are much more similar than anthropologists and historians at present acknowledge.

Another consistent theme defining tribal nations is shared territory. Nations tend to have among themselves an explicit reckoning of where each nation lives, exclusively. The various treaties between the United States and tribal nations are the best illustration I know of that tribal nations have always maintained sophisticated notions of territory. This is not to say, however, that all neighboring nations will accept the territorial claims of a particular group, and certainly wars were continually fought among North American tribes about who belonged where. But still, no tribal nation in North America pleaded "no opinion" when asked the limits of its territory.

Within their own national territories, however, nations have varied in their ideas of real property and usufruct. The eastern, horticultural nations of North America recognized the exclusive rights of villages and clans to farm particular areas. Nomadic bands of Cheyennes, however, were free to travel, visit, and hunt anywhere in the shared national area, though each band had a "usual range" centered on some good wintering area. Allies also were welcome in national territory as long as they did not claim it as their own.

Like everything else, territorial claims change through time. The progression of Cheyenne claims can be read in the series of treaties signed between 1828 and 1868.[29] Part of the Cheyenne national charter was to invade the central plains, expel other tribes, and hunt there exclusively. They claimed such new territory by right of conquest.[30] In this they were no different from "civilized" nation-states, which also claim a bounded area for the exclusive domicile of their citizens, wherein they exercise political control.

Nations are also war-making units—they act collectively. In fact, failure to participate in a national war when called upon, or making war without national sanction, is usually grounds for being expelled from any nation. Cheyenne national unity was exhibited most forcefully in their war against the southern tribes, particularly the Kiowas, in 1838. When all the Cheyenne bands were gathered, the attack began. Although the Arapahos and Oglala Sioux were staunch Cheyenne allies for most of the war period, their presence was not required for the Cheyennes to declare all-out war or, to use their own vernacular, to "move the arrows" against an enemy. Declarations of war could be made only by the representative units of the citizens, the chiefs and headsmen. When other nations fought alongside the Cheyennes they were allies, not citizens.

Conversely, just as a tribal nation makes war together, the members do not make war among themselves; they preserve political unity. They define as "murder" any killing within the nation. Murders are crimes and are punished by national law. In the Cheyenne case, their sacred arrows not only were the focus of war making, but were and are also the means of restoring order after a murder. In this case the arrows must be renewed after a murder, to restore cosmological order and reinforce the national principle that Cheyenne citizens may not kill one another.[31]

Last, there is language. Insofar as a nation has internal relationships for marriage, politics, and ceremonies, a common language is a convenience. And we will see with the Cheyennes that as long as the nation was strong and undivided, the Cheyenne language prevailed over other languages and dialects. Captives, adoptees, and incorporated tribes rapidly became Cheyennized in the period between 1790 and 1864. But as a segment of the Cheyennes was attracted toward the Sioux and toward a new territory shared with them on the Republican River, they became progressively Siouanized, threatening to split the Cheyenne nation. In the 1860s, a hybrid and bilingual Dog Soldier nation began to emerge, with new definitions of citizenship, territory, and politics, but this emergence was aborted by the events of 1869.

In sum, nations, like all social institutions of whatever size, have a beginning and an end. But neither the beginning nor the end of a nation's history is determined by chance. Rather, both are controlled by conditions of political economy that can be described in scientific terms. A nation is like a biological individual. It is *born* from the shared needs of possibly diverse people who group together out of self-interest. A nation has a *maturation* during which it tends toward uniformity of behavior and toward a homogeneity of the traits discussed above. But inevitably nations, like all social institutions, *die,* and they are fragmented into diverse groups that ultimately become other nations, with different languages, religions, and political structures. But only the nation dies; the people and their culture do not. They become part of other societies and other cultures. The central institutions of any nation thus are best understood in light of the conditions of political economy that brought about the nation's birth and those that divide the nation and threaten to destroy it.

Where Do Nations Come From?

Despite temptation, I have not called this book *Birth of a Nation* or *The Evolution of Cheyenne Society*, although national and evolutionary theory are prominent here. I rejected the first title, of course, because it had been preempted by a racist film classic, but I rejected the second for reasons that deserve some discussion.

Historians have used the word "evolution" in a manner that seems unusual to me, and perhaps to other anthropologists as well. For example, there is the book *Slavery and the Evolution of Cherokee Society* by Theda Perdue (1979). By "evolution" this author means nothing more than change or development, of the sort discussed by many other historians. This use tends to distort the definition of evolution that has been built up by anthropologists and biologists over the past 150 years. By "evolution" most biologists and anthropologists mean *regular, universal,* and *structured* change, not merely the history of a particular biological species or a particular society.[32]

Anthropologists use the word "evolution" in a broadly comparative sense, as part of a special vocabulary. That is, we try to describe the changes in one society using concepts that can also be applied to other societies. We try to construct *general laws* of evolution that apply everywhere. We try very hard not to create a taxonomy in which every society is unique. It defeats the purpose of evolutionary thinking to describe each societal change as a singular and incomparable event. Still, I have heard scholars at the annual Frontiers Symposium in Oklahoma claim that events on the Roman frontier in England, the Brazilian frontier in South America, and the United States frontier were each unique and are absolutely incomparable.[33] They even scoffed at one historian's suggestion that the interactions between Romans and Picts could have anything at all in common with the interactions of Spaniards and Aztecs, or Russians and Uzbeks.

Evolutionary theorists begin with the opposite idea. We are trying to describe particular events in a manner that makes comparison easy instead of difficult. Therefore we offer definitions of tribe, nation, band, and clan. We have a special vocabulary for kinship, which I will present in chapters 8 and 9. We talk about exogamy, endogamy, and agnatic and uterine tendencies. We do this to make comparisons possible. We have as a goal precisely what some people scoff at: we wish to state, as precisely as possible, how the events in North America in 1700 were comparable to events in China in

800 or in Roman Britain in 200. We wish to discover whether the same *principles of evolution* were in operation.

Evolutionary principles are applied in this book to understanding the origins and development of a particular nation. My theory in general is that nations begin by the conscious and explicit charter of their citizens and develop through periods that sometimes integrate the citizenry and sometimes divide it. Attempts to integrate and homogenize a nation are never completely successful. Throughout its life, a nation is characterized by difference of opinion and by variation in social and political structures, and these variations are vital to its continued existence. In the Cheyenne case, it was the polarity between a "peace faction" and a "war faction" that helped preserve them through the difficult years of the nineteenth century. At intervals, however, some faction of any nation can seize upon existing differences to charter a new nation, as the "Dog Soldiers" attempted to do. Such events are as normal for a tribal nation like the Cheyennes as for a complex nation-state like the United States of America. My use of the term "tribal nation" in this book, then, is intended to help bridge the supposed evolutionary gap between "tribes" and more complex "nations" that have a state structure. Tribal nations and nation-states both exhibit *national* behavior, as described above. This is not to say I see no differences between, say, the Cheyennes, the Aztecs, and the Victorian British. The differences are obvious—social classes, complex division of labor, a standing army, sedentism, and public works, to name a few. But one of the differences is *not*— and I cannot emphasize this too strongly—that "tribes" are simple, homogeneous, and stable polities while "nations" have parties, factions, treaties, revolutions, and a colorful "history." I maintain that the Cheyennes are a nation not only in the sense of citizenry, territory, politics, and language, but also in having an origin, a development, periodic crises, and even revolutions. Tribal history everywhere is every bit as colorful as English history, if we but knew it. And despite all appearances, the Cheyennes are not, as some authors allege, a "people without history."[34] That we are usually ignorant of tribal history does not mean it never happened.

In setting forth my own theories, from an orthodox Marxist perspective, I also wish to refute the idea that tribal nations were caused by—or arose as a response to—civilized nations. Julian Steward is considered the author of this theory, though he is nowhere very explicit about it.[35] Steward and Leslie White, between them, spawned a whole generation of interconnected scholars who were centrally interested in cultural evolution. These scholars have created elaborate taxonomies of societal "types" and have postulated how societies might move from one type to another.[36] Few of them, however, have had any actual field experience with tribal societies, and of course none of them could be very knowledgeable about *all* the societies used as examples. As a consequence, they have been very uncritical in their use of ethnographic examples and have tended to place particular societies in awkward or inappropriate slots in their taxonomies. It is the taxonomy *itself* that has maintained their interest, as they vault around the world looking for examples. In seeking their examples, they look at no one society in great depth, nor do they usually sample a large group of societies in any organized manner. A typical result is a book like *Primitive Social Organization* (1962), in which Elman Service offers page after page of apparently profound theories of evolution that are uniformly unquantified, undocumented, and unproved. To prove even one of his theories would require a small army of scholars and a research budget in the millions of dollars. As it is, Service's theories carry no more weight than the wild and imaginative theories of such nineteenth-century evolutionists as Lubbock, McLennan, and Spencer.[37]

In his elegant essay "The Two Cultures," C. P. Snow has contrasted the work habits of scientists with the methods of scholars in the humanities.[38] One of the differences is the high status of "data" or empirical evidence in the sciences and its low status in the humanities. Rather than appealing to evidence, humanists such as Service most often appeal to prejudice or sentiment or call attention to the intrinsic beauty of their formulations. Sometimes they appeal to nothing more important than the fact that they know each other and share assumptions. So "schools of thought" in the humanities often merely consist of scholars of the same training and temperament rather than being a scientific collective sharing the results of their experiments.[39]

Anthropology is a discipline poised between science and the humanities and comprises scholars of both persuasions. The cultural evolutionists mentioned above, I believe, are best understood as a community of humanists, with a shared perspective on human society and its development. To support their theories, they do not "sample" for data in any scientific way, nor do they "control" for other variables. They resemble the practitioners of the "comparative method" Franz Boas critized for reporting only those traits and ethnographic examples that tended to support their conclusions.[40]

An important exception to this criticism is the (then) cultural evolutionist Marshall Sahlins, in his book *Social Stratification in Polynesia* (1958). For this book Sahlins examined the geographical situations of Polynesian societies that occupied different places in the taxonomies of cultural evolution. From their distribution in the Pacific, Sahlins sought to explain how the more complex Polynesian societies developed from simple ones. But even with all his attention to data, Sahlin's theories at best qualify only as speculative history, not real history observed and reported directly by participants. Also, Sahlins conducted no fieldwork personally, but relied exclusively on secondary sources. As a consequence, he was in no position to criticize his sources or improve his data.

So one purpose of this book on the Cheyennes is to refute certain theories of evolution, expecially concerning the origins of tribal nations, by looking deeply into the history of one society. Rather than appealing to readers' predilections or pointing out the beauty of my theory, I wish to call attention to the bare empirical facts. I want readers to judge for themselves whether the Cheyennes were masters of their own fate, originating and chartering their nation without outside influence, or whether Morton Fried is correct in saying that it is always the pressure and example of an outside "civilized" nation that causes tribal nations to be founded.

Fried's original statement of his theory—a rather reckless one I think— is as follows:

> It seems to me that the so-called "tribal" groups . . . are not social organizations whose integrity recedes into a remote past. Rather, there are clues indicating that the tribalism displayed is a reaction to more recent events and conditions. That such tribalism can be made to play a major political role in a real present is not a modern discovery. Long before recent European colonialism, not to say neocolonialism, the Roman, the Chinese, and other expanding state societies had grasped the essentials of divide and rule. What is more, in the relations between these states and simpler organized societies it was understood, within the complex cultures, that effective manipulation demands a certain minimum of organization within those simple societies. There have been examples in which "tribes" have been consciously synthesized to advance a scheme of external political control. It is not beyond belief that groups within former colonial powers would consciously or unconsciously do whatever they could to create and maintain factionalism.[41]

If I may interpret Fried, he says that tribes—what I have called tribal nations—are groups explicitly organized by members of a "civilized" society to suit their own convenience. I believe that in part this statement of the theory represents Fried's regional bias as a scholar specializing in China. While it may be true that the Han Chinese organized Mongols and Manchus into "buffer" groups on their northern border, this was not necessarily a widespread practice or the only way "tribes" came into existence.[42] In a later statement of his theory, Fried is more careful and more modest, as follows: "The precipitation of tribes, it seems to me, was triggered by the emergence of the state, but did not really get into high gear until the emergence of the ancient empires and, later in a greater burst, after the appearance of colonialism and imperialism." Just previous in this same article Fried says, "What is more, with reference to this particular problem, we must attempt to think of the society of the time prior to the emergence of the world's earliest pristine states *as it was in the absence of all states*."[43]

In postulating what the condition of the world might have been before there were organized, literate states, Fried is in the same position as the child who wants to know whether the refrigerator light stays on when the door is closed. Since only organized states had writing and kept records, we cannot hope to know whether tribes or nations existed before that, since the archeological record, of itself, will not at present yield to that kind of inquiry. Suppose we have an excavation report from a prehistoric campsite or village that may have been a tribal nation. How can we know its political or linguistic relationship with the campsite or village over the next hill? Evidence of trade will not tell us, since trade is conducted equally with friends and enemies, and cultural similarities also tell us nothing about nationhood. The Middle Missouri is a perfect example of how some very similar archeological remains can represent radically different ethnic groups. Without historical records, I doubt anyone could correctly reconstruct the political history of the Middle Missouri—the patterns of alliance and enmity—from archeological data alone.[44]

To answer questions about the origins of nations, we must use the records left by literate peoples, and those concerning the Cheyennes give us a rare opportunity to peer into the closed refrigerator and see if the light is on. Because there are two hundred years of records on the Cheyenne nation as a free society, including the circumstances of its inception, we have a chance to understand general principles of nation formation by reference to a well-documented example.

Existing Cheyenne ethnography, however, as interpreted by scholars, is not always helpful in understanding Cheyenne history. Although the facts are most often there, the interpretations frequently tell us more about the ethnographers than about the Cheyennes. The most general and most damaging error in classic Cheyenne ethnography is the idea that the Cheyennes were everywhere and always the same—that is, that a Cheyenne band on the Republican River in 1860 was culturally the same as a Cheyenne band in the Black Hills in 1805. Throughout the period of classic fieldwork, 1890–1935, the Cheyennes were consistently described as a stable, integrated, homogeneous society, remarkable for the chastity of the women and the ruling authority of the Council of Forty-four. In two previous articles I have criticized this notion in a preliminary way, pointing out the conflict between the chiefly faction with its "uterine" or female-centered social tendencies and the "agnatic" or male-centered tendencies of the military societies.[45] Generally speaking, the classic ethnographers did not see this conflict, paid little attention to the origins and charter of the Cheyenne nation, and tended to reduce Cheyenne history to the simplistic picture of a stable, structured society, frozen in time and interacting with other societies in a consistent and predictable manner. We can understand how this simplistic picture came into being if we learn a little more about these early writers.

The Ethnographic Fieldworkers

Of the classic ethnographers, George Dorsey was probably the most casual in his fieldwork. A leisured gentleman, Dorsey was president, at different times, of both the Adventurer's Club and the Geographical Society of Chicago. He was a lieutenant commander in World War I and an adviser to Woodrow Wilson at the peace conference in Paris.[46] He undertook his Southern Cheyenne fieldwork under the sponsorship of the Field Museum, which also published his results—*The Cheyenne*—a detailed description of Cheyenne ceremonies, the ceremonial camp, and the selection of chiefs.[47]

I suggest that Dorsey had very structured ideas of how his own society operated and that he projected these theoretical ideas onto society in general and the Cheyennes in particular. We can ascertain something of Dorsey's general philosophical notions about human society from the popular books he wrote, especially *Why We Behave Like Human Beings* (1925), *Hows and Whys of Human Behavior* (1929), and *Man's Own Show: Civilization* (1931). In this last book, Dorsey explained his own hopes for "civilizing" the Indians, in which the Christian churches would take a leading role, and he also characterized tribal societies as being determined by environment, led by despots, and in the blind grip of superstition. In general, Dorsey was a Spencerian evolutionist in his theories and an empiricist in his metaphysics.[48] Concerning his notions of social order and harmony, we should look at his 1929 book the *Hows and Whys of Human Behavior*. Ironically, Dorsey wrote the following lines in New York City at a time when fifty thousand workers rioted in Union Square protesting the executions of Sacco and Vanzetti and twelve thousand furriers were involved in some of the bloodiest labor battles in American history. Nonetheless, Dorsey wrote: "Can we say that a girl who has put in ten years at a typewriter without having advanced in position in any respect whatsoever, has a 'vocation'? We can. Thousands of young and middle-aged clerks, messengers, stenographers, chauffeurs, waiters, chorus girls, nurses, school-teachers, elevator operators, street-cleaners, policemen, doormen, janitors, *et cetera*, pursue their vocations as zealously as do the great bankers, lawyers, doctors, actors, journalists, merchants, artists, and scientists, theirs. They have found their life work, they are enjoying their bent, they are content."[49]

Dorsey was equally blind to conflict in Cheyenne society. I have quoted an example of Dorsey's thought from another book because it represents, I believe, his unguarded philosophical opinions. In general I believe that no kind of ethnographic scholarship can be completely understood in its own terms. That is, each scholar works within a particular historical and personal context that largely determines what he or she chooses to write about, and what is written. In Dorsey's case his background and his general opinions were such that we would fully expect him to write a certain kind of ethnography about the Cheyennes. And he did. His descriptions of Cheyenne legend and ceremony exhibit the dead hand of tradition and the rote performance of rituals with no explanation of meaning or motivation. It is Dorsey, more than any other ethnographer, who is criticized by modern Cheyennes. Although painters continue to use *The Cheyenne* as a reference for Sun Dance designs, they find his text confused and perplexing.[50] We find no explanation in Dorsey's book of what the paints, for example, are supposed to represent. He described the tribal circle in great detail, but with no idea that there was any rational priority or order in the camping arrangement, or any history of development. Noting some variability in the camp circle, he apparently attributed it to the foggy memory of elders.

It is sometimes said that all great minds are masses of contradiction. How ironic it is to find, then, that George Dorsey, who gave us our most mechanistic and stodgy descriptions of Cheyenne culture, should have written these lines: "The common assumption that primitive cultures are set in cast-iron molds is not justified. Their simplicity only seems so to our ignorance. They are in truth enormously complex, and, psychologically speaking, as rich, full, and complete as ours. There is something doing all the time. These cultures inevitably change."[51] But when it came to actually doing ethnography, Dorsey could not manage a single dynamic theory. He never practiced what he preached.

George Grinnell also had some strong ideas about Indians that he presented not in his ethnography, but in other works. Although his fieldwork among the Cheyennes was more extensive than Dorsey's, he remained outspokenly patronizing and even racist in his ideas about savages and civilized men. An aristocrat and a Spencerian evolutionist like Dorsey, Grinnell had some disturbing views of Indian intelligence: "The Indian has the mind of a child in the body of an adult. The struggle for existence weeded out the weak and the sickly, the slow and the stupid, and created a race physically perfect, and mentally fitted to cope with the conditions which they were forced to meet, so long as they were left to themselves.

When, however, they encountered the white race, equipped with the mental training and accumulated wisdom of some thousands of years, they were compelled to face a new set of conditions. The balance of nature which had been well enough maintained so long as nature ruled, was rudely disturbed when civilized man appeared on the scene."[52]

So here we have Grinnell's opinions in a nutshell, stated explicitly. Like a host of other historians and anthropologists, he considered Indian societies to be simply hanging around in some kind of stable and undisturbed state of nature until white people arrived. Much of what is seen among Indians, he observed, is merely their reaction to a superior culture. There is still a hint of this attitude of superiority in Fried's idea that there were no tribes until there were civilized states to show them how to get organized. I believe that the cultural evolutionists' lack of personal experience with tribal peoples has led them to seriously underestimate their capabilities to actively control their evolution, as they constantly devise novel solutions to new problems. Quick intelligence and social innovation are not confined to "civilized" peoples. It was just as clever for the Cheyennes to devise new family types, new soldier societies, or a strategy of "structured dispersion" to avoid epidemics as it was for civilized people to invent Masonic orders, Prussian regiments, or a Ford assembly plant.[53]

Compared with Dorsey and Grinnell, the last classic fieldworker, James Mooney (plate 1), comes off as far superior, both as an ethnographer and as a compassionate human being. Whereas Dorsey and Grinnell worked in the field only a few summers, Mooney's fieldwork encompassed two decades. Those who have read Mooney's field notes regard him as having probably the most energy and the worst handwriting of any ethnographer sent out by the Bureau of American Ethnology. To solve the mystery of Mooney's handwriting, I used grant money to employ Wanda Downs in my project, to read Mooney's notes and type out passages relevant to the problems being discussed here. The results of this distillation of Mooney's manuscripts are sprinkled over the next nine chapters.

As far as I know, Mooney never wrote any pandering, popular books like those by Dorsey and Grinnell.[54] Throughout the work he did publish, Indian people consistently have a dignified and respected position. He neither maintained patronizing romantic images, like Grinnell or like Peter Powell in our time, nor developed any racist stereotypes for explaining Indian behavior. Twice he materially assisted Indians in their struggles against the government, and once he may have saved many lives. Asked to write an official report on the Ghost Dance, fear of which caused the massacre of the Big Foot band at Wounded Knee, Mooney reported that the ceremony was harmless.[55] Later Mooney provided research assistance for an

Plate 1.   James Mooney, ethnologist for the Bureau of American Ethnology.
Portrait 55-D, National Anthropological Archives, Smithsonian Institution.

effort to have the Native American Church—the peyote religion—toler-
ated and accepted by the Bureau of Indian Affairs. For his efforts in promot-
ing "heathen religion," he was investigated by a congressional committee
and forbidden to visit any reservations.[56] I suspect that Mooney, an Irish
nationalist himself, was predisposed to sympathize with oppressed minority people and their efforts to maintain a separate religion. I have great
respect for James Mooney as an ethnographer and as a person, as the
following pages will show.

   To Mooney's credit, he also noticed the dynamic aspect of the Cheyenne
ceremonial circles and reconstructed a speculative history of change in his
major monograph, *The Cheyenne Indians.*[57] Mooney had no training in
kinship, however, and he could not explain how or why the circle changed

as it did. Like Dorsey and Grinnell, Mooney was a victim of his own times, before British anthropology had developed the formidable research tools Fred Eggan brought to the study of Cheyenne ethnography. Unlike Dorsey and Grinnell, Mooney had no particular drum to beat concerning tribal society in general or the mentality of "savages." He merely reported as best he could, limited as he was by the techniques of the day. But his basic decency and humanism permeate all his writings.

Of the modern ethnographers, I will have much to say in chapter 9 about Fred Eggan. Some readers might wonder why I have not given much attention to E. Adamson Hoebel, whose writings have introduced thousands of people to Cheyenne ethnography. There are two reasons. First, Hoebel and I have already been conducting a lively debate in the pages of scholarly journals about some of the ethnographic issues raised in this introduction.[58] Not wanting to be repetitive, I have raised these issues here not against Hoebel, but against Dorsey and Grinnell. Second, though we must credit Hoebel for his pioneering work in the anthropology of law and his pedagogy in general, he did not really contribute much original fieldwork. It consisted, I believe, of two summers' experience.[59] Therefore his published work and field notes have not been as useful here as the work of other people. But let me at least summarize the three articles in which we have debated some central ethnographic issues.[60]

In 1974 I published an article in the journal *Ethnohistory* arguing that the "classic" ethnographers of the Cheyennes, including Mooney, Grinnell, Dorsey, and Hoebel, had erred in presenting the Cheyennes as a stable, tightly integrated society dominated by council chiefs. Alternatively, I presented a dialectic model of Cheyenne society that emphasized the tension existing between a "uterine" faction, led by the council chiefs, and an "agnatic" faction, led by the soldier chiefs. I argued that the early part of the nineteenth century was characterized by the dominance of the council chiefs, which was gradually undercut by the emergence of the soldier chiefs as leaders of the so-called Dog Soldiers, the dominant faction after 1864.

In his response, not published until 1980, Hoebel argued that "Moore's representation of the classic writers' picture of Cheyenne sociopolitical organization is, in the face of the whole evidence, a highly selective and over-simplified caricature." He also argued that the basic social unit of the Cheyennes was not matrilocal and matrilineal—"uterine," as I had argued—but also included affines, which made the group "bilateral." Speaking of himself and Llewellyn, Hoebel said, "Llewellyn and Hoebel place their heaviest emphasis on structural-functional analysis, but definitely do not overlook the trend toward increasing power of the military societies viz-à-viz the peace chiefs and the tribal council. . . . Moore's contribution is to highlight and bring into sharp focus the importance of historical change in the shift of dominant power from the peace chiefs to the military societies between 1840 and 1878."

In my response the next year, I argued that I was "proceeding from an evolutionary theoretical perspective, while Hoebel is intent on reducing evolutionary processes to specific historical events." Hoebel's approach I characterized as "historical reductionism," which I claimed obscured the operation of the motor of history—group conflict—and failed to detect general and widespread historical trends. In the same 1981 article, I also criticized Hoebel's analysis of kinship and his accuracy in reporting certain events.

This book, then, is in many ways a continuation of my debate with Hoebel. Here I will marshal a great amount of additional data to support what I have already maintained about Cheyenne society and about the early ethnohistory of the Plains. But in addition I am raising some new issues and broadening my horizons geographically and historically. The historical events I debated with Hoebel concerning the rise of the Dog Soldiers constitute only one episode in the historical period covered here.

So these are the basic themes of the book—evolution, change, innovation, conflict, and the origin of nations. Throughout, I have tried to describe such matters for the Cheyennes in a language that will allow comparisons anywhere in time and space. My purpose is to set up the Cheyennes as one example of a process of nation building among tribal societies that I consider universal. I hope other ethnographers will supply more examples of the same kind of process, also using the language of comparative science. But I realize that some may read this book out of a particular interest in the romantic side of Cheyenne culture. So be it. There is no way I could write this story without making it a great adventure.

2

The Tribal Circle

When Cheyenne elders explain their social structure to other people, or discuss it among themselves, they use diagrams of the ceremonial circle. This has been true from the time of the earliest ethnographers—Gatschet, Hewitt, and Ben Clark—to the present.[1] The use of a ceremonial diagram for this purpose, however, does not imply that the elders are merely describing an aspect of their religious life. Rather, they are using a uniquely Cheyenne system of graphic symbols—a kind of native sociology—to describe in general the relationships among the most significant units of their society. These significant units are called *manhao* in Cheyenne, a word that has been variously translated into English as bands, clans, camps, and "bunches." These are the units arranged in circles on the diagrams drawn by Cheyenne informants, and interpreting these diagrams correctly is the most serious task facing anyone who wishes to understand Cheyenne history and social structure.

In this chapter I will take an organized approach to the twenty or so diagrams of camp circles collected by ethnographers and tribal historians over the years, with the goal of getting the bands correctly identified.[2] Without a basically correct "grammar and dictionary" of Cheyenne social structure, no other important tasks in history or ethnology can be easily attempted. The fundamental problem of interpretation is that some of the existing diagrams are very detailed, while others are very sketchy. Also, some names of bands appear on nearly every diagram, while others appear only once or twice. All together, the diagrams include bands with nearly a hundred different names, some in Cheyenne and others in English.

Although the *nature* of these bands is very important, we will put off that question for the moment to simplify our inquiry. That is, we will not yet ask whether these bands are unilineal clans, cognatic groups, ramages, sodalities, associations, or whatever. For the time being we will only try to make identifications among the bands and to sort them out. And here, as in so many ethnographic enterprises, we will find that the scientific key lies in the native language. Where the English translation of a band name is garbled or ambiguous, the native language most often is crystal clear.

Our final goal in this chapter will be to construct some sort of "correct" model of the tribal circle based on empirical evidence. As it is, the tribal circles described by different informants appear to be so contradictory that previous ethnographers have felt they had to believe some informants and disbelieve others. And so discussions raged among Mooney, Dorsey, Hyde, and Grinnell about whose informants were "reliable" and whose were not.[3]

I am taking a rather different approach, assuming that *all* the informants are correct and that the differences in the tribal diagrams mostly represent difficulties in translation and differences in perspective. I believe that if we account for these linguistic and cognitive differences, we will be able to construct, on a statistical basis, something like an "agreed-upon" structure that would not have offended any informant. I am arguing, then, that there is some kind of "true" structure underlying the apparent variability, which we can discover by searching the documents exhaustively, by being careful in translating the Cheyenne language, and by relying on statistics to discover patterns that we cannot detect by casual inspection.

More than anyone else, it was James Mooney who recognized the importance of interpreting the tribal circles and who also recognized that the circles must be understood as dynamic rather than static structures. In his classic monograph written for the American Anthropological Association in 1907, Mooney presented several versions of the Cheyenne camp circles collected during his fieldwork in 1900–1905. His last diagram represents an attempt to reconstruct, back through time, what he calls the "probable earliest arrangement" of the tribe. In his accompanying narrative and list of "divisions," Mooney categorized five of the bands as "original," five more as "secondary," meaning they were offshoots from the "original" groups, and nine others as "pseudodivisions." So he said essentially that there were three kinds of bands.

When he separated his "divisions" into three "kinds" or categories, Mooney provided the first of three important clues we need to interpret these diagrams correctly. For we see that there are qualitative linguistic differences among the bands he placed in his three categories. The first or "original" group consists of bands with names it is difficult or impossible to explain in Cheyenne or to translate accurately, whereas the two following groups are progressively easier to translate. Only one of the names on the first list has a regular translation with which all Cheyennes concur, according to Mooney: Omisis is "Eaters." The next most regular translation on the list is for Hevhaitaneo, usually rendered Hair Rope People, though sometimes simply Hairy People or Fur People. There is considerable debate, however, about whether the name refers to "hairy" buffalo robes or to a kind of "hair rope" used to catch horses, and there is also the question whether this "rope," if that is the correct translation, is made from buffalo beards or from horse tails.[4] At this point in our inquiry, however, the issue is not how to translate the names correctly, but only whether the names are difficult or easy to translate.

From the balance of Mooney's "original" names, Masikota and Heviksnipahis are also difficult to understand precisely, even in Cheyenne, while Sutaio is impossible. Masikota is said to have something to do with flexing, but the same element, *masi,* is also used in Cheyenne in indicate insects with flexed legs, such as grasshoppers and crickets, and also human corpses with flexed legs. Heviksnipahis seems to have something to do with beavers or choking, but it might also be related to words for aorta or burning. Sutaio is a very old word indeed, since it was originally applied to a separate tribe incorporated into the Cheyennes, perhaps even before the "Cheyennes" can be called a nation. I can find no record of anyone's ever attempting to translate it. Also, the name Cheyennes call themselves, Tsistsistas, has no regular translation.

We can better understand the puzzle about Cheyenne band names if we look at analogous problems in English. The word "English" itself, for example, is the name both of a language and of a people. If you ask an ordinary Englishman what the word "means," however, few will know that it means anything, much less try to identify the linguistic roots. If pressed, an Englishman might venture to say, incorrectly, that the word has something to do with angles or perhaps angels. But because English has been a written language for a long time, we can look at a dictionary and discover that the root of English means "fishhook," referring to the shape of the Angles' original tribal territory in what is now Holstein in Germany.[5]

If we pick sociological names of more recent vintage in English, we can get more accurate responses. For example, most Americans can identify terms such as Know-Nothings, Tories, or Whigs, and most could probably supply some additional information and perhaps a supporting story. And when we get to very recent sociological names, like Yuppies, Communists, or Fundamentalists, nearly anyone can supply a meaning and an etymology.

If we approach Mooney's list of Cheyenne band names in the same spirit, we can predict that his list of "secondary" names, those bands known to be derived from others, should contain names that are intelligible both in Cheyenne and in translation. And sure enough, Mooney reports that the Oivimanas are the "Scabby band," the Hownowas "Poor People," the Oktogonas "Bare Shins," the Hisiometaneos "Ridge People," and the Wotapios "Eaters," this last term derived from the Sioux word *wota,* "eat." From Mooney's discussion we also learn about the origins and individual histories of the bands, facts that were hard to find for the "original" bands. When we get to Mooney's "pseudodivisions" we are in the area of recent history, as we find some bands named after chiefs from reservation times. Here, however, I will not go further into the histories and relationships of these bands, saving that for chapter 7. But so far we have discovered, both from Mooney's list and by analogy, one basic principle—that bands of recent origin have names that are more intelligible and more easily related to known historical episodes than are the names of older bands. This is our first clue toward untangling the whole puzzle.

The second clue we need was provided at a gathering of Southern Cheyenne informants in 1980, by Minnie Red Hat and her daughter-in-law Emma Red Hat. After I had made some awkward inquiries about alternative names for bands, Minnie set out to explain to me that there were different "kinds" of names applied to Cheyenne bands. First of all there were "ceremonial names," old names mentioned in songs and prayers and referring to locations in the tribal circle. Then there were "clan" names, referring to the kinds of "clans" men belong to, such as the Dog Soldiers or Bowstrings. And last there were "nicknames," some taken from chiefs' names and others used only to tease. After some urging, Minnie finally supplied some "teasing nicknames" that were in vogue when she was a child. "Owl Eyebrows," she said, and laughed. "Greasy Pants," she said, and everybody laughed. And then Minnie supplied the crucial clue that sometimes nicknames could turn into serious names. She gave the examples of Hevhaitaneo, "The Hair Rope People," and Oivimana, "the Scabby People," both names of Mooney's "sacred" bands.

Minnie Red Hat's suggestion about the transformation of names, along with the apparently dynamic nature of the names found on Mooney's list, led me to analyze a third set of clues—historical documents. In short order, a set of passages was collected from published and manuscript sources that spelled out more specifically the principles by which Cheyenne bands were named.

The first passage comes from Rev. Rodolphe Petter, a Mennonite missionary who lived for many years among the Cheyenne people beginning about 1892. As an aid to fellow missionaries, Petter produced a dictionary, a grammar, and various readings in Cheyenne.[6] Even though Petter made no pretense of being a social scientist or an ethnographer, his dictionary is nonetheless a gold mine of important cultural facts. Concerning "bands," one entry in his English-Cheyenne dictionary, Petter demonstrated that he understood very well the dynamic nature of Cheyenne social structure. Just before presenting a long list of what he called "family names" and discussing them, he wrote the following sentences, crucial for our purposes.

Different names were given to certain groups of Cheyenne families, sometimes in reference to the camping order in the tribal circle and often times because of a local particularity or prominent family traits. Some such names have even arisen since I was with the Cheyennes. For instance a part of the Hotamhetaneo living in the neighborhood of Fonda, Oklahoma are called the "Veenoto," because of one Cheyenne who did not cut his eyebrows. Another instance is a family group, whose head man was an "Eseomhetan," but who were called "Eezenehetaneo"—Swampmen, because they camped near a swamp. Another family group was called "Otatavoha"—Bluehorse, from an old man of this name, who died but a few years ago. The three names came up since I came to the Southern Cheyenne. Other band names I know to also be of recent dates, e.g., Anskovenenes (Narrow-nose-bridge), and Pen-et'ka. What has happened within thirty or forty years must have happened before too. Even the band Heveksenxpaess is not very old.

Petter's mention of the Blue Horse band gives us a unique opportunity to test some ideas about the evolution of band names. As it happens, Blue Horse lived until allotment, though he was a very old man at that time, his age listed as ninety-four on the preliminary list of 1891. Blue Horse is also listed in another unique document, not as an old man, but as an active and energetic band leader of the prereservation period. This second document is the biography of a Cheyenne woman who bore the poetic name Rising Fire.[7]

The biography of Rising Fire, entitled *Hoistah, an Indian Girl* is a rare book by any measure. Published in 1913, the book is based on an oral narrative from Hoistah herself. The oral narrative was apparently not collected personally by the editor of the volume, Stephen M. Barrett, since Barrett was born in 1865 and Hoistah died about 1875,[8] but somehow Barrett gained access to the manuscript after he arrived in Oklahoma in 1904, and he embellished it for publication.

The importance of Hoistah's biography comes mostly from the fact that she was born about 1795 and witnessed many of the important events in the evolution of Cheyenne society in the nineteenth century. It is certainly the oldest published Cheyenne narrative in existence, and it may be the oldest authentic narrative from the whole Plains area, excluding the episodic and ambiguous histories presented in winter counts. In her narrative Hoistah recounts the visit of Lewis and Clark, the period of Cheyenne corn farming, the nomadic period, and the final migration to Oklahoma Territory.

It is hard to doubt the basic authenticity of *Hoistah*, despite Barrett's embellishments. Essentially, Barrett put some of the narrative into dialogue form and added some photographs from a later period to "illustrate" the biography. But the special details of domestic and political life provided by Hoistah are absolutely authentic. In 1913 these had not been published anywhere and could not have been made up by a non-Indian. Also, the book does not contain the usual myths about Indians fostered by the "Indian lore" books of the period. In addition, even Hoistah's errors are the sort a Cheyenne woman would make, errors in perception of the kinds of activities—ceremonial and political life—from which Cheyenne women were mostly excluded. It is with an eye both to Hoistah's accuracy and to her inaccuracy, then, that we look at her description of the ceremonial circle. She describes arrangements for a Sun Dance about 1830, in a valley of the Cheyenne River near the Black Hills.

> The opening of the circle to the eastward was about a quarter of a mile wide. Immediately to the south of this opening a place was indicated for the sacred Aorta Band and the Dog-Warrior Band. At the north of the entrance a space was reserved for the Hive Band and the Buffalo-Bull Warrior Band; on the western rim of the circle were spaces for the Fur-Men Band, and for the Sutai or adopted people. Between these several centres lesser bands were to be located. There were places for all, even the outlaws.
>
> The ancient order of the Sacred Arrow-Medicine led by Lame Bull came early the next morning, and before night Blue Horse had led in his band of Fox Warriors, and in turn all the different bands, sacred and military, had arrived and their tepees were placed within the mighty circle—more than six hundred tepees.

Several key passages in this section authenticate the narrative. First of all, the translations of the band names are correct but nonstandard, representing someone's independent attempts to translate Cheyenne words. Second, Hoistah's ideas about band identity and organization fly in the face of the conventional ethnology of that period, though they agree with *Cheyenne* ideas. If the narrative were inauthentic and borrowed from Mooney and Dorsey, a strict difference would have been noted between "bands" and "military societies," but Hoistah fearlessly calls them all bands. Although she notes, just as Minnie Red Hat did, that there were different kinds of bands, in this case Hoistah calls them "sacred and military."

We will return in a later chapter to this important question of the different "kinds" of Cheyenne bands, but let us trace at this point what happens to Blue Horse's "band of Fox Warriors." In fact, the identification of the band as Foxes immediately enables us to lay bare the whole process of band metamorphosis, at least for this one group. The "Fox Soldiers," by one name or another, are known from several of the camp circles collected by Mooney and Truman Michelson. An alternative name for the Fox Soldiers is Flint Men or Moiseyo in Cheyenne, according to Grinnell, Mooney, and Petersen.[9] And so this group, whether known as Flint Men, Fox Men, or Blue Horse's band, is listed on several of the diagrams of tribal circles from prereservation times. But what happened to them afterward?

Since Blue Horse lived until allotment, we can find him and his descendants taking trust land near Seiling, Oklahoma. According to Katie Osage, an informant born in 1895, this group continued to camp in a distinct place in the tribal circle until 1914, at which time the elders decided that it was confusing to try to continue the old band order at the annual Sun Dance and that thereafter people would camp as "communities," taking their names from the nearest white settlement. Therefore on the 1936 tribal circle reconstructed by Katie Osage, Roy and Kathryn Bull Coming, and the Red Hat family (fig. 1), we find Blue Horse's descendants listed under "Seiling

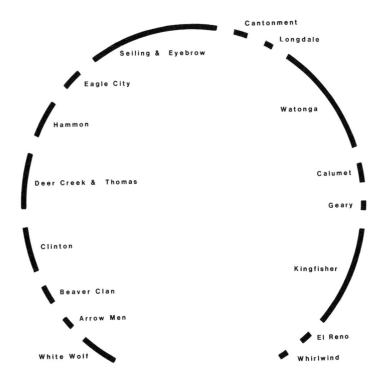

Figure 1. Tribal circle about 1936. The length of the circumferential segments indicates the sizes of the groups in that year. West is at the top.

bunch." And on the camping diagram prepared for distribution in modern times, at the 1978 Sun Dance, we find that "Area #2," in the northwest, is reserved for the Seiling people (see fig. 37 on p. 333).

There has also been at least one attempt in modern times to provide a new nickname for the Seiling people. According to other Cheyennes in the area, some of the Seiling people were known as the "Butcher band" for a few years in the 1960s. This was the result of a Sunday traffic accident involving a cattle truck. Because many cattle were killed or injured in the accident, local people, including several carloads of dressed-up Cheyennes, were invited to butcher the animals and take them home. After the jokes subsided about people in their Sunday best jumping out of their cars and hacking up cow carcasses, the people involved were sometimes called out at giveaways as the "Butcher band." However, the name did not stick because after a few years the people no longer responded to the call.

So for one group, at least, we have a fairly complete longitudinal profile of band evolution from 1830 until 1978. But we still do not know the specifics of band metamorphosis, either the personnel or what caused it. All we can say at this point is that from a group called the Fox or Flint People, all or some became known first as Chief Blue Horse's band and then the Blue Horse band. And then all or some of these people became known as the Seiling bunch or the modern-day Seiling community. Although it is good to have this amount of documented continuity through time, we should not expect too much from analyzing the historical profile of a single band. As in all puzzles, you cannot see the whole picture merely by looking at one piece. But at this point we at least know we are dealing with some kind of evolutionary process or metamorphosis of bands, and we know that at any one time a band might be known by several names. We also know that one kind of name, and possibly one kind of band, is known by the chief's name. Another kind of name, such as "Seiling people," is geographic in nature. And the oldest names apparently are neither place-names nor chiefs' names but are more complex in their etymological structure. But to get more information both about the individual bands and about their relationships, we have to consider the whole tribal circle.

One of our goals should be to simplify our problem by finding alternative names for the same band. If we can by this method reduce the total number of named bands from nearly a hundred to a manageably small number, we might have better success in discovering a relatively simple underlying structure for the tribal circle. As we have seen, alternative names can be used at the same time, such as Fox people and Flint people, and sometimes there is an old or obsolescent name in use at the same time as a new name, such as Blue Horse band and Seiling bunch. And sometimes there is a temporary nickname, like "Butcher band." Whether or not such names represent a permanent reorganization, we need to know what the equivalencies are. Some of the differences between tribal circles provided by different informants may simply be a matter of nomenclature, not structure. But we should expect some variability, because we know that during the time represented in the diagrams, 1805–1914, these bands were moving through periods of cultural and political turmoil.

For the present we will consider only the tribal circles that are supposed to represent the preallotment period, before 1892. This puts manageable limits on the number of names we must consider. In addition, we will consider only those tribal circles that were intended to be comprehensive. We will exclude fragmentary documents and descriptions of only part of the tribe—only Northern Cheyennes, only Southern Cheyennes, and so forth. We will also exclude the various attempts of Mooney and Grinnell to construct synthetic "actual" diagrams, based on "reliable" informants (and possibly only on their own intuition). This is to increase the reliability of the results, to decrease the size of the sample, and for statistical reasons that I will explain in a moment.

To increase the number of complete tribal circles to be included in the sample, I have searched in the Smithsonian anthropological archives, the Southwest Museum archives in Los Angeles, and many other places. The largest number of additional diagrams comes from the unpublished field notes of Truman Michelson, an ethnologist for the Bureau of American Ethnology from 1910 to 1915. His six diagrams, plus Mooney's five and one from Grinnell make a total of twelve to be analyzed. Our first task is to list all the names from the diagrams and determine which of the band names are actually alternative names for the same band.

Table 1 represents the results of my attempts to merge band names. On the table I have placed the band names in the same order as Mooney did, added some additional names from Michelson's diagrams, and deleted several of Mooney's bands that do not appear on his pre-1892 diagrams. I have also added the Hotametaneos (Dog Soldiers) as a full-fledged band and numbered the whole list down the left column. In merging names, I have not only drawn on documentary sources, but also have relied on modern Cheyennes for assistance. The particular informants for this section have been Laird Cometsevah, John Greany, John Black Owl, Susie Black Owl, and Walter R. Hamilton. Methodologically, I went as far as I could with documentary sources and then showed my lists to these Cheyenne informants.

The band names on table 1 represent a standardized spelling, mostly derived from Mooney, but augmented from Petter's dictionary. In the next

Table 1   Cheyenne Band Names Mentioned by Selected Informants

BAND NAME	ENGLISH VERSIONS	NUMBER OF MENTIONS
1 Heviksnipahis	Aorta, Windpipe, Burnt, Beaver	12
2 Hevhaitaneo	Hairy, Hair Rope, Buffalo Beard	9
3 Masikota	Crickets, Grasshoppers, Drawn-up	8
4 Omisis	Eaters	12
5 Sutaio		11
6 Wotapio	Eaters, Half-Cheyennes, Cheyenne-Sioux	7
7 Oivimana	Scabby, Hives, Scalpers	7
8 Hisiometaneo	Ridge, Pipestem	8
9 Oktogona	Bare-Legged	10
10 Hownowa	Poor, Red Lodges	3
11 Anskowinis	Narrow Nose	1
12 Moiseo	Monsoni, Flint, Foxes, Blue Horse, Flies	5
13 Moktavhetaneo	Black Lodges, Utes	3
14 Nakoimana	Bear	2
15 Tsistsistas	Arrows, Cheyennes, Sand	3
16 Totoimana	Shy, Bashful, Prairie	5
17 Hotametaneo	Dog Soldiers	3
18 Oivimana	Northern Scalpers, Northern Scabbies	4
19 Voxpometaneo	White River	2
20 Ononeo	Rees	2

column are English translations of the names and some alternative Cheyenne names for the same bands. These names and the standard names constitute all the names used on the twelve diagrams. The last column lists the number of times each band is mentioned on the twelve diagrams. This gives us some idea of the relative importance of the different bands. We would predict that the oldest or largest bands would be mentioned most often.

With the expansion of the sample to twelve diagrams, and with the careful translation and merging of names, it is instructive to compare this improved list to Mooney's. First of all, it is clear from the improved list that three pairs of names are "nested" one inside another, and two are duplicated. The nested names include, most importantly, the name Cheyennes call themselves—Tsistsistas. According to classic informants, this not only is the tribal name but is also the name of a particular band. One of Michelson's informants, Grasshopper, even listed himself as a member of that band, also called the Arrow band, the Sand People, or the Cheyennes proper. This is apparently the same group as Hoistah's "ancient order of the Sacred Arrow-Medicine," a group that according to modern informants, ultimately took allotments near Bessie, Oklahoma, south of Clinton. Descendants of this band still call themselves Tsistsistas or "Arrow People" and still camp near the southern part of the opening of the tribal circle at ceremonies.

The names for two other bands are also nested inside a more general usage. Hevhaitaneo refers to a particular southern band, but it is also a term used by the Northern Cheyennes to refer to all the Southern Cheyennes. Conversely Omisis, as used by Southern Cheyennes, can mean either the whole of the Northern Cheyennes or else the Omisis proper, excluding the Sutaios and fragments of other bands that ultimately settled in Montana.

One duplicated name is "Eaters," which has a Cheyenne form, Omisis, and a Siouan form, Wotapio. Some informants have given only the name "Eaters" on their tribal circles, so it is not clear which they meant. The other duplicated name is Oivimana, used both to designate a large southern band centered at Watonga, Oklahoma, and a smaller Northern Cheyenne band. This northern group was fissioned off from the southern group in 1882, when the Indian agent complained that eighty-two Southern Cheyennes had gone to Montana "without authority."[10]

Before we look at the corrected tribal diagrams and embark on a statistical analysis, one other important matter must be disposed of. We must discuss certain matters of *perspective,* cultural and personal, that bear on the way the diagrams are arranged. First of all, we should note that Cheyenne cardinal directions are not the same as map directions. East, for Cheyennes, does not parallel the equator but is the direction of the sunrise at the time of the Sun Dance in early June. The other cardinal directions are also rotated clockwise in Cheyenne thinking, so that some ethnologists have said that the Cheyennes are oriented toward the "semicardinal" directions. Of course from a Cheyenne perspective it is Anglos, not Cheyennes, who are oriented toward "semicardinal" directions. For the sake of simplicity in the following discussions, I will use Cheyenne directions rather than Anglo ones.

In addition to having a different conception of geography, individual Cheyenne informants also have tended to orient their personal band diagrams depending on whether they were members of an eastern, western, northern, or southern band. Peter Powell has noted quite accurately that from the standpoint of a modern Northern Cheyenne traditionalist, the cultural world is laid out toward the east and therefore the top of a native map is east.[11] Little Chief, however, in his elaborate drawing of the ceremonial circle, puts east to the left and south at the top. This reflects the position of his band at the northern perimeter of the circle—he drew the circle as seen from his band's position in the ceremonial camp.[12] Mooney's informants, who mostly represented southern bands, apparently put east to the right of their diagrams, though we cannot be sure that it was not Mooney himself who arranged the diagrams to correspond with usual map directions.

An informant's band membership also determined the amount of detail in the drawing. Obviously an informant would be more aware of the divisions and subgroups of his own or neighboring bands and would perhaps be unaware of the fine structure of bands he seldom saw. As we shall see, Lone Wolf, a Southern Cheyenne informant for Mooney, made fine distinctions among the subdivisions of southern bands but lumped all the northern bands into "Omisis." By contrast White Bull, a northerner, broke down the northern bands into seven groups for Michelson but left out five southern groups mentioned by Lone Wolf. So in analyzing the tribal circles, we must take into account not only the unique viewpoint of Cheyenne geography, but also the biased perspectives of particular informants.

Another cultural attitude to be taken into account is that the whole tribal circle, in the Cheyenne way of thinking, represents a tipi. In fact the "Sun Dance" is called in Cheyenne the Mohaewas, or Medicine Tipi Ceremony. In contrast to what some ethnologists have said, the medicine tipi referred to in the name is not just the arbor where the pledgers dance, but the whole tribal circle.[13]

It is important to understand tipi symbolism at this point because in the family tipi, just as in the tribal "tipi" or tribal circle, there are honored, less honored, and awkward positions. Nearest the opening of the tribal circle, analogous to the door of the tipi, are two honored positions. The subchiefs of the military societies and of the priestly orders, for example, are called the "doorkeepers" of their groups. And so the two positions nearest the door are respectable.

The south side of the tipi is where the family sits, wife and children, with the wife nearer the door. Similarly, in the tribal circle, we might expect to find the Hevhaitaneos, an original band, nearer the circle opening than Mooney's alleged derivative or "daughter" bands—Oivimanas, Hisiometaneos, and Wotapios. But we will see about this after our analysis is complete. The most respected sitting place in a tipi has been opposite the door, where the head of the household or honored guests usually sit. By analogy, it is the place opposite the circle opening that is reserved for the most honored guests of the Tsistsistas, the Sutaios or "Adopted People," as we shall see.

The least respected place is clockwise from the head of the household toward the door. In a tipi, this is where one puts in-laws and guests requiring little respect, such as teenagers. In the tribal circle, according to modern informants, this is the place to be avoided, for fear one's band might be teased as tribal "in-laws." Older informants say it was the penalty of latecomers to camp in that place, or that it was reserved for Arapahos. Even now, Arapahos are teased about this.

The ceremonial circle, then, is the tribe's symbolic tipi, and we should be able to detect some kind of underlying order in the circle, just as in the tipi. Also, as families move through time and there are births, deaths, and marriages, seating arrangements have to be changed. In the same way, we can expect that the "seating arrangements" of the bands in the tribal circle will change as historical circumstances dictate.

Table 2 lists the tribal circles as described by twelve Cheyenne primary informants listed by order of birth. [14] On the table we find the names of the informants, their dates of birth as determined from manuscripts or censuses, and a reference to the ethnographer who recorded the diagram and comments. Only Wolf Chief's information is in two sources. He described the Northern Cheyenne subgroups for Grinnell and added the rest of the circle for Michelson. [15]

The numbers in the last set of columns are the code numbers taken from table 1 and represent the order of the bands according to each informant, clockwise from the opening of the circle. Obviously some informants were more specific than others, with Wolf Chief offering the most names, sixteen, and Iron Shirt the fewest, three. Translating the numerical codes, with Iron Shirt as an example, table 2 says that he gave the names Heviksnipahis, Hevhaitaneo, and Omisis, in that order, as constituting the tribal circle. Wolf Chief's list begins with Heviksnipahis, Hevhaitaneo, Sutaio, Hotametaneo, and Omisis.

It is reassuring to note that after the name equivalencies have been independently established from documents and manuscripts (table 1), no band name appears twice on the list of any informant. If we had made a mistake in merging, we might have found a single erroneously merged band appearing twice on a list. For example, if we had erroneously merged 10, the Red Lodges, with 13, the Black Lodges, we would have had to face the awkward fact that a list might have band 10 appearing twice. As it is, however, there is good agreement between the tribal circles and the documentary sources used for name merging.

The problem involving the name "Eater" arises because some informants did not specify whether they meant Wotapio or Omisis. In table 2, however, they are all coded 4. Mysteriously, though, four of Michelson's informants, themselves members of southern bands, did not position the Eaters,

Table 2   Order of Bands According to Selected Informants

INFORMANT	BAND	REFERENCE	DATE OF BIRTH	CIRCLE REFERENCE
Mad Wolf	Hvk	Mooney B	1829	Mooney 1907
White Bull	Omi	Mic 2822	1830	Mic 2822
Big Jake	Hev	Mooney B	1834	Mooney 1907
Iron Shirt	Hev	Mic 2822	1835	Mic 2822
Lone Wolf	Mas	Mooney B	1838	Mooney 1907
Wolf Robe	Sut	Mooney C	1840	Mooney 1907
White Eagle	Hev	Mic 2811	1843	Mic 2822
Old She Bear	His	Mic 2822	1845	Mic 2822
American Horse	Hvk	Mic 2822	1847	Mic 2822
Howling Wolf	Hev	1917 Comp	1849	Mooney 1907
Wolf Chief	Omi	Mic 2822	1850	Grinnell 334 & Mic 2822
Grasshopper	Tsi	Mic 2822	1857	Mic 2822

Note: Listed order of bands is from table 1. First reference is to source for band identification. Mooney and Michelson manuscript numbers refer to the National Anthropological Archives, Smithsonian Institution; Grinnell's MS. 344 is in the Southwest Museum, Los Angeles; Howling Wolf's identification is from the 1917 Competency Interviews, National Archives. Informants are listed by seniority.

LISTED ORDER OF BANDS															
1	2	3	4	5	6	7	8	9	10	11	12	13	14	15	16
1	7	12	8	2	6	16	5	3	9	4					
1	2	5	17	4	12	6	9	18	16	13	20	19			
1	5	2	6	7	8	10	9	3	4						
1	2	4													
1	5	2	7	6	8	3	4	9							
1	12	5	6	8	7	2	13	9	14	3	4				
1	10	7	8	2	5	17	9	12	4	16					
1	8	3	9	5	17	4									
15	1	5	17	9	4										
1	8	15	5	2	7	6	13	3	4	11					
1	12	7	2	8	6	10	9	5	3	4	18	13	20	19	16
1	15	3	9	5	17	4	18								

as a southern group at all, but placed it as a northern one. The implication may be that the Wotapios are a subgroup of the Omisis rather than of the Hevhaitaneos. That is, they may be the "Eaters proper" in the same way that the Arrow People are the "Cheyennes proper." This is a rather radical suggestion, however, which we will keep in mind for the next chapter.

Before attempting to apply statistical methods to these lists of bands, perhaps we should recall our ultimate purpose. With quantitative analyses it is very easy to be seduced by the numbers, so that we come to look at relations among numbers rather than relations among people, in this case people organized into bands represented by numbered codes. Ultimately what we are trying to discover is an underlying order to the diagrams. Already we have found two methods of stripping away apparent disorder. First we merged names and identified nicknames, so that we have fewer distinct bands to deal with—twenty instead of fifty-nine on the twelve lists. The number codes of table 2 reflect this simplification. Next we have tried to account for the kind of variability in the diagrams that could be expected from differences in perspective, either tribal or individual. So now we are ready to move to quantitative methods, but once again for the same purpose, to strip away further layers of apparent variability and expose what we hope is a simple underlying structure.

The first problem we must solve statistically is caused by the fact that while some informants have given us very long lists, others have given short ones. Therefore while the second band listed by Iron Shirt represents the position opposite the door, halfway around, the second band listed by Wolf Chief is not even one-quarter of the way around the circle, since he listed a total of sixteen bands. So we have a problem of scaling—transforming the band positions mathematically so that the position opposite the door is the same on all diagrams, as well as the positions near the door, and all in between.

If we look at the individual lists supplied by informants as "strings" of bands, then we must scale the responses so that the center band of any string is given the same numerical value, no matter how long or short the string. To express the position of each band in the string, we should create a fraction in which the numerator is the band's position in the string and the denominator is the total number of bands in that particular string. For example, a band in position five on a string of ten bands will be given the value $5/10$, or .500. A band listed in position seven of thirteen would be calculated at $7/13$, or .485.

Calculating band position in this way, however, expresses not the position of the center of the band, but the border between one band and the next. For example, if the first of four bands is expressed as $\frac{1}{4}$, or .250, this is actually the boundary between band 1 and band 2. If we calculated other bands in the string this same way, we would get a value of .500 for the second band, which is not directly opposite the opening as its numerical value might imply, but is actually south of the "honored guest" position. To make the numerical values more precise, then, we should subtract ½ or .500 from each numerator of the fraction, to express the position of the center of the band. This will make the mathematical expressions more reflective of the actual physical structure and will help correct for the differences between long and short strings. For example, it makes a difference of .167 in the position of Heviksnipahis in Iron Shirt's short string.

Table 3 represents the results of scaling the strings of bands listed on the tribal diagrams in table 2. For each band on each string we now have a numerical value representing how far around the circle that band was situated. It is now possible to average the scores for any band to see if it has any regular and "correct" place, as Grinnell, Mooney, Dorsey, and others have always assumed. Several of the most important facts about Cheyenne social structure, however, can be determined merely by inspecting the columns of numbers.[16]

One apparent anomaly observed in the data is that several bands—the Hevhaitaneos, Hisiometaneos, Moiseos, Masikotas, and Hownowas— show one or two very low scores among other scores that tend to cluster. This anomaly is easily explained by modern informants. According to Sun Dance priests, this is due to the old practice of having the pledger's band camp in the doorkeeper's position for the year he has "put up" the ceremony. So to correct for this practice, I have thrown out "doorkeeper" scores in calculating a mean for the next graphic presentation, figure 2. Plotted against these means are the number of mentions for each band on the twelve diagrams in the sample. The largest, oldest, or most important bands, therefore, should appear farther to the right on the figure.

In looking at the figure, it is immediately clear that Mooney placed the four "original divisions" in the correct order on his diagram of "probable earliest arrangement"—Heviksnipahis, Hevhaitaneos, Masikotas, and Omisis. When we average the scores for these four bands, we get values of .075, .348, .706, and .870. But there is something odd about the Sutaios, Mooney's other original band. Its values do not cluster around a single position as do those of the other four bands. In fact, as we look at the raw scores, this band seems to cluster around two values, one low and one high. If we average these two clusters separately, we get means of .242 and .584.

When I asked modern informants why the Sutaios should appear in two positions on the tribal circle, they had a unanimous answer—that there

Table 3 Scores for Band Position According to Selected Informants

BAND NAME	INFORMANT												N	X̄	S
	Mad Wolf	White Bull	Big Jake	Iron Shirt	Lone Wolf	Wolf Robe	White Eagle	Old She Bear	American Horse	Howling Wolf	Wolf Chief	Grasshopper			
1 Heviksnipahis	.045	.038	.050	.167	.056	.042	.045	.071	.250	.045	.031	.062	12	.075	.066
2 Hevhaitaneo	.409	.115	.250	.500	.278	.542	.409			.409	.219		9	.348	.140
3 Masikota	.773		.850		.722	.875		.357		.773	.594	.312*	7	.706	.179
4 Omisis	.955	.346*	.950	.833	.833	.958	.864	.929	.917	.864	.656	.812	11	.870	.089
5 Suatio	.682	.192	.150		.167	.208	.500	.643	.417	.318	.531	.562	11	.397	.199
6 Wotapio	.500	.500	.350		.500	.292				.591	.344		7	.440	.110
7 Oivimana	.136*		.450		.389	.458	.227			.500	.156		6	.363	.140
8 Hisiometaneo	.318		.550		.611	.375	.318	.214		.136*	.281		7	.381	.146
9 Oktogona	.864	.577	.750		.944	.708	.682	.500	.750		.469	.438	10	.668	.170
10 Hownowa			.650				.136*				.406		2	.528	.173
11 Anskowinis										.955			1	.955	—
12 Moiseo	.227	.423				.125	.773				.094		5	.328	.280
13 Moktavhetaneo		.808				.625				.682			3	.705	.094
14 Nakoimana						.792					.781		2	.785	.008
15 Tsistsistas									.083	.227		.188	3	.166	.074
16 Totoimana	.591	.731					.955	.786			.969		5	.806	.159
17 Hotamhetaneo		.269					.591		.583			.688	4	.533	.182
18 Oivimana		.654									.719	.938	3	.770	.149
19 Voxpometaneo		.962									.906		2	.934	.040
20 Ononeo		.885									.844		2	.864	.029
Sutaio high cluster													5	.584	.077
Sutaio low cluster													6	.242	.104

Note: Numbers in italic constitute low cluster.

*"Doorkeeper scores," thrown out of calculations.

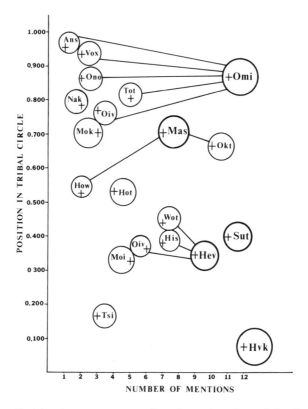

Figure 2.   Positional score versus number of mentions for each band.

were two groups of Sutaios in Oklahoma, as well as other Sutaios in Montana. The low value, they say, represents those Sutaios who were associated with and always camped near the Hisiometaneos, while the high values probably represent either the Sutaio family groups that camped with the Masikotas near Seiling or with an Omisis fragment near El Reno, or perhaps the Sutaio band associated with the Omisis in Montana. Unfortunately, our analysis does not enable us to discriminate clearly between the last three possibilities, because of variability among the "high" members of the sample. If and when other Northern Cheyenne diagrams are collected, this question can be settled.

Next we should look at the bands that just follow the primary bands, and right away we get a historical bonus. The three bands that allegedly split off from the Hevhaitaneos do in fact immediately follow that band in their numerical scores. Just after the Hevhaitaneos or Hair Rope People are the Oivimanas, with a score of .363, the Hisiometaneos with .381, and the Wotapios with .440. And so we have supported, quantitatively, the idea that daughter bands immediately follow the mother band in the tribal circle. After looking at additional evidence in the next chapter, however, we will have to revise our ideas about the Wotapios.

In his comments on the tribal circles, Mooney said that the Hownowas and Oktogonas also were derivative bands, in this case from the Masikotas. Looking at the numerical scores, we can see some support for this theory, and also for the significance of the Cheyenne tipi analogy. The numerical score for the Hownowa band is .528 when we disregard the one low score as doorkeeper, and the Oktogona score is .668, both farther from the door than their alleged parent band, Masikota.

When we look at the scores for bands toward the end of the string, we can once again see a pattern. In this case, a Northern Cheyenne informant, Henry Tall Bull, has provided the essential clue by identifying bands on the list as corresponding to modern Northern Cheyenne communities. Here again we find this confirmed by the numerical scores, as Oivimana, Voxpometaneo, and Totoimana are all farther from the door than their alleged mother band, Omisis. The tipi analogy might equate these bands with the children of a second wife, who would herself sit on the north side, with her children to her right.

Other minor bands from the diagrams we can neglect for now—Ononeo, Anskowinis, Moktavhetaneo, and Nakoimana. By the time of Grinnell's and Mooney's fieldwork, the Cheyennes had been on the reservation for thirty years, and we can expect some new bands to have formed, as Rodolphe Petter indicated. For historical purposes, we need to be most concerned with the "four original bands" we have been discussing— Heviksnipahis (Aorta), Hevhaitaneo (Hair Rope People), Masikota (translation unsure), and Omisis (Eaters).

Besides these and the Sutaios, we are left with two major bands, the Hotametaneos (Dog People) with a score of .533, and the Moiseos (Flint People) with a score of .328. And finally we must face the question whether these two remaining bands are *qualitatively different* from the others, and what these differences might be. Beyond that, we must now raise the rather sticky issue of dual organization as this general structural principle might have been institutionalized by the Cheyennes.

In two articles I have presented evidence for the polarization of Cheyenne society between a peace faction and a war faction in the nineteenth century.[17] To summarize my argument briefly, I have contended that the dominant structure of the early part of the century was the traditional hunting and trading band, organized around women and led by peace chiefs. After about 1830, however, the warrior societies became increasingly prominent within the tribe, finally emerging as discrete residence bands with their own territory and a reorganized political structure.

Historical sources are very clear about the status of the Dog Soldier band (Hotametaneo) as a separate, politically independent unit. Also, a story often repeated is that after the cholera epidemic of 1849, the Masikota band joined the Dog Soldiers en masse, and the Dog Soldiers thereafter camped in the traditional place of the Masikotas.[18] But there is a complex relationship between the Kit Foxes or "Fox Men," the Masikotas, the Moiseos or "Flint People," and the Dog Soldiers, which we can understand only after looking at their histories. For the moment it is enough to say that the Foxes, like the Dog Soldiers, apparently did have a regular place in the tribal circle. But was this an exclusive place, and why didn't all the informants note it?

By now we should have grown accustomed to the fact that living informants can supply answers where documents fail us. In this case, after hours of discussions with elders, we discover once again that we are not asking exactly the right question. Instead of asking, What is the correct place of the Fox Soldiers in the tribal circle? we should be asking, Is there a different way of looking at or drawing the tribal circle? As it happens, some of the first "tribal circles" offered to me by informants in the late 1970s were diagrams that most often contained only four "bands"—Bowstrings, Elks or Hoof Rattlers, Foxes, and Dog Soldiers. By the conventional wisdom of ethnologists, these were not bands, but military societies. Thinking that informants had misunderstood the question, I casually filed the responses—all of which, by the way, were identical: Bowstrings to the southeast, Elks southwest, Foxes northwest, and Dog Soldiers northeast. It was also noticeable that the diagrams were squares, not circles, with the soldier bands at the corners. Figure 3 shows the positions of the soldier bands from these diagrams.

After finishing the numerical analysis of the tribal circle, in 1981, and inquiring further among elders, the significance of those early diagrams was suddenly brought home to me—military societies, like conventional bands, had a usual position in the tribal circle. The societies, for their initiations just before the Sun Dance, construct arbors at the four corners of the ceremonial circle. After the circle fills up, however, these arbors are outside the circle, in the arrangement shown on the diagrams given to me in the 1970s. But because no informant had given me a diagram that contained both the circle of bands and the square of societies, I had never put two and two together.

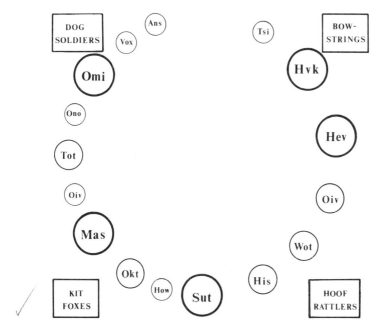

Figure 3.   Dualistic structure of the Cheyenne ceremonial camp.

In the middle of pondering this problem in early 1982, I received an
ethnographic surprise in the mail. My friend George Eager of the Museum
of the American Indian had sent me a just-identified drawing of a Cheyenne
tribal circle, dated about 1875 (plate 2). But this "circle" was a square, and
the groups identified were the military societies, not the traditional bands.
Here was confirmation, then, that this "squared" way of looking at things
was not just a recent innovation of the society headsmen, but was an ancient
part of Cheyenne tradition.

The reason the square and the circle appeared on the same drawing, in
this case, was that the artist had tried to telescope the events of several days
into one illustration. So he showed the military ceremonies and the Sun
Dance events simultaneously, although they are held several days apart.

Although I will consider the relations between bands and societies at
much greater length in later chapters, we must keep in mind for now that it
is possible to see Cheyenne society in at least two alternative ways, as shown
in figure 3. From one perspective, we can see a circle comprising the four
"original" bands facing each other around the opening, joined by the
Sutaios in the "honored guest" position and flanked by their daughter

Plate 2.   Little Chief's drawing of the Cheyenne ceremonial circle, about 1867.
Specimen 11/1706, Museum of the American Indian, Heye Foundation.

bands. Or we can see the structure as a square with an opening in the eastern
side and four military societies at the corners. This is what ethnologists have
called a dual organization—two ways of looking at the same structure. A
society headsman and a council chief might look at the same ceremonial
campground, and one might say he is looking at a square while the other
sees a circle. There is an ingrained cultural ambiguity.[19]
    Analyzing the situation further, one might wonder why only two of the
four Southern Cheyenne societies appear in the tribal circles given to Mooney and Michelson. Dogs and Foxes were given as bands, but not Bowstrings
or Elks. To explain this, living informants tell us that the Dogs and Foxes
were the militant bands in the war period, bands who kept to themselves
and ultimately settled in the area between Seiling and Longdale in
Oklahoma. With two societies withdrawn from the usual band structure,

the remaining bands would naturally comprise only members of the remaining two societies—Bowstrings and Elks. When I asked modern informants if these societies also had "geographic locations" on the Oklahoma
reservation, I was told that the "home territory" of the Bowstrings was
Watonga and Deer Creek, while the Elks lived mostly near Clinton and
Hammon. So we have two militant soldier societies associated with certain
reservation bands and two other societies associated with the other bands.

Cheyennes say that two sets of laws govern the soldier societies—one set
for the Dogs and Foxes, another for the Bowstrings and Elks. These two
pairs of societies, in modern times, share initiations and social events
among themselves. Informants maintain this has always been the case, even
in prereservation times. And we can see, in plate 2 and figure 3, that one
pair of societies, the Dogs and Foxes, is situated at the northern and western
sides of the "square," bracketing the traditional positions of the Masikota,
Oktogona, and Omisis bands. In the same drawing, we see the Bowstrings
and Elks bracketing the other bands, thereby reflecting the relationships
attested by modern informants. In this case we will see that the camp circle
reflects both the ceremonial relationships among the groups and also the
real geography of allotments taken in Oklahoma in 1892.

Figure 3, then, represents a sort of "master diagram" of Cheyenne social
structure based on information supplied by twelve informants from the
prereservation period, augmented by the information just discussed. The
positions of the bands in the diagram represent the actual numerical scores
of the bands calculated as I have described. The difference between this
diagram and similar "master models" attempted by classic ethnographers
is, I believe, a matter of empirical science, in that I have used explicit
criteria to select a sample of diagrams, to improve the data, and to make
calculations.[20] This is not a model that is intuitive or based on certain
"reliable" informants. Although other ethnologists might certainly quarrel
with my procedures, this model represents my present best conclusions. I
maintain that it is better to do ethnography this way, with explicit procedures for sampling and calculation, than to argue from highly *selective*
evidence, as humanistic historians and humanistic ethnologists tend to do.

We should not lull ourselves into believing, however, that this model
represents anything like a static or eternal structure of Cheyenne society.
The figure is at best a snapshot of Cheyenne social organization at the time a
certain twelve informants were interviewed. And judging from the ages of
the informants, we are probably not describing any structure that predates
1829, the earliest birth year for any informant.

If what we have is essentially a snapshot of Cheyenne society, it is one that
is still blurred, except that now it is blurred only by motion, not by error.

As the individual bands and the whole society pass from one stage of social evolution to the next in the nineteenth century, they present an ambiguous appearance. When the daughter bands of the Hevhaitaneos were first formed, for example, the members of Oivimanas and Hisiometaneos were for a time members of two groups simultaneously, one parent and one daughter. This ambiguity, as part of their history, is preserved in the diagrams we have constructed. Similarly, the history and past ambiguity of the daughter bands of the Masikota and Omisis bands are preserved on the diagrams. This ambiguity is something we should expect to find in any kind of vital, evolving social structure. But there is another kind of ambiguity in Cheyenne society, resulting from a dual organization between residence bands and military societies. The full significance of this kind of ambiguity we have yet to discover.

Figure 3 is a representation of Cheyenne society against which we will play off the various perspectives of Cheyenne informants, historians, and ethnologists to be considered in subsequent chapters. If we have constructed it properly, we should be able to extrapolate from it both forward and backward in time. Since it is a dynamic model, we should be able to see in it both the consequences of historical events and the play of contemporary social problems, if we know what to look for.

In the next chapter, we will attempt first to travel backward in time from the diagram, to the days of Lewis and Clark. For it is during this period that the history of the North American Great Plains is very troublesome to ethnohistorians. Early maps name bands that entirely disappear in a few years. Strange political situations are alleged to exist, and confusion abounds about the migrations, fissions, and fusions of the various Algonquian and Siouian groups.

It is perhaps surprising to discover that in attempting a very modest task—identifying Cheyenne bands properly—we have unwittingly prepared ourselves for a much more ambitious project—an analysis of early explorers' journals. Perhaps, with some additional preparation, even the maps of the seventeenth century will talk to us, for we now have some idea of what to look for in tracing the continuity of Cheyenne history back through time.

As we look backward, we should be attentive to early tribal traditions. According to Cheyenne elders, when the nation originally was formed, the different "clans" were *called together from the cardinal directions* to sit in their assigned places in the tribal circle. Even today, at the Sun Dance the camp crier summons each "clan" and band to come from its home community to the campsite. In the words of the arrow keeper, Edward Red Hat, in 1981: "In the old days when they had some ceremony at Bear Butte, the bands always camped around the mountain in the same order as they camped in the tribal circle. And the rest of the year, they camped around the Black Hills same way, Omisis north, Hevhaitaneos south, and Heviksnipahis east. It was always like that until the sickness and the fighting mixed them all up. But still, when we have ceremonies, we camp the same way they used to, long time ago, all around Black Hills."

3

The Early Documents

In this chapter I will show how the better understanding of the tribal circle achieved in chapter 2 can help us interpret documents describing the very early history of the Cheyenne people—during the origin and development of the nation. A knowledge of the band names will help, as will our discovery of the principles by which bands are named—alternate naming, nicknaming, and the "nesting" of names. Three sets of documents will be examined: the Lewis and Clark maps and journals; the narratives of traders and travelers, especially Frenchmen, from the period 1680–1804; and early maps, both published and hand drawn. We will proceed backward in time, building from the later to the earlier sources.

The previous chapter alerted us to at least five dynamic processes that operated to transform the social structure of Cheyenne bands. We can supply provisional names for these processes: fission, polarization, fusion, dispersion, and hybridization. Even with the limited information we have accumulated so far, we can provide definitions and sketchy examples for some of these processes. Fission is simply the splitting of one band into two or more bands, so that new or distinct names have to be supplied for the subgroups. We already have the example of the Arrow People or "Cheyennes proper," allegedly the mother band of all the Cheyennes. We may also have the "Eaters proper," though we do not yet know whether the mother band is the Omisis or the Wotapios, and we may also have the "Oivimanas proper" from later reservation years, from which the northern Oivimana band has hived off.

Two examples of polarization have already been suggested, for the Hevhaitaneos or Hair Rope People, and for the Hotamhetaneos or Dog Soldiers. In each case Cheyenne leaders were attracted to some geographical location and a new band was formed from people originating in several other bands. In the former case, the Hevhaitaneo band was formed from people who migrated south to trade at Bent's Fort and engage in the horse trade. In the latter case, the Dog Soldier band was formed from among those militants in each band who wished to resist United States encroachment.

The last three types of transformation all represent some kind of amalgamation. Fusion occurs when one band joins another, without intermarriage, and becomes merged with it, perhaps accompanied by the coining of a new band name. Dispersion occurs when a band becomes weakened or diminished in numbers and the members disperse by families to seek refuge with relatives in other bands. Hybridization is the generating of new bands by intermarriage with other bands or other ethnic groups. When Cheyennes married Sioux, for example, new bands of "Cheyenne-Sioux" were generated. Large-scale intermarriage with Sioux bands occurred at least three times in Cheyenne history. By the end of this chapter we will have a better idea of what happens to such hybrid groups and of the importance of these groups for Plains ethnohistory.

My basic purpose here is to identify the proto-Cheyenne bands that were later consolidated into the Cheyenne nation. The problem in finding these bands is that many of the documents we will look at are contradictory about the correct names for bands and about which bands belonged to which ethnic and linguistic groupings. So I will argue for what I consider the best candidates for recognition as proto-Cheyenne bands, though I realize there are other ways to interpret this same evidence.

Before taking up the specific documentary sources, we need to review the general events in the northern plains in the early historical period.[1] Essentially the pattern is for large movements of native groups around the Great Lakes and westward onto the northern plains. In addition to the Cheyennes, several other Algonquian peoples—such as the Blackfeet, Arapahos, and Atsinas—apparently migrated into the Great Plains at about the same time, from an original subartic homeland north of Lake Superior. The Sioux, including the Tetons, apparently came from the southeast, passing through the Great Lakes area and then onto the high plains. Identifying these Siouan and Algonquian tribal groups, and tracing their complex migrations and interactions, remains the single most important and most difficult problem in Plains ethnohistory. Some recent work by Ossenberg is helpful; he traces Cheyenne ancestry back to the Arvilla Complex, situated in central Minnesota about A.D. 800–1400.[2]

The specific historical framework for the period we are interested in, beginning about 1680, can be best understood if we focus on the Sioux who were more or less allied during much of their history. The bands and nations of this extensive group, comprising perhaps 100,000 people, gradually moved from the Great Lakes toward the headwaters of the Missouri in this period. Pushing them from the north were the well-armed Crees and Assiniboines, and later the Chippewas. All of these were being harassed by the Iroquois and other nations of the east, who were raiding down the St. Lawrence River and across the Great Lakes. Ultimately, of course, the prime movers in all of this were the European invaders from Britain and France, who had successfully established colonies on the east coast and were busily pushing Indians aside or organizing them into the fur trade.

At the time of the first French explorations in the seventeenth century, the Sioux migration westward from the Great Lakes had scarcely begun; early maps find them still near Lake Superior. By the time of Jonathan Carver, however, in 1766, some of the westernmost, or Teton, Sioux had moved all the way to the Missouri, and by the time of Lewis and Clark some had crossed the Missouri and were still moving west, later surrounding the Black Hills.

As we consider documentary sources from this period, we will move gradually backward in time, taking first Lewis and Clark, then the explorers' journals, and finally the maps—for our purpose is to extrapolate carefully backward from the information on Cheyenne bands presented in the previous chapter. As we look for additional information about the bands we have names for, we hope we will find further clues about Cheyenne social organization in earlier times, before there was a Cheyenne nation. In general, we hope to discover the origins of the Cheyennes by considering them as part of this massive move westward, in which everyone was continually caught up in various patterns of alliance or enmity with the Sioux or with the enemies of the Sioux.

Lewis and Clark

The Lewis and Clark expedition of 1803–5 produced much more ethnographic information than is generally supposed. Thomas Jefferson's instructions to Meriwether Lewis included the charge to "make yourself acquainted, as far as a diligent pursuit of your journey shall admit, with the names of the nations and their numbers." In addition, Jefferson gave Lewis and Clark a long list of questions to be answered for each tribe concerning commerce, culture, and the "moral and physical circumstances which distinguish them from the tribes we know."[3]

If we at present underestimate the ethnographic importance of Lewis and Clark, it is in part the result of the fragmented and sporadic publication of their journals and maps. Lewis committed suicide three years after the expedition returned, and much of the manuscript material he scattered has not yet been put back together. The most detailed map of the expedition, for example, did not appear in print until 1887, soon after it was discovered in the archives of the War Department.[4] Nearly every passing decade has seen the publication of some fragment of a map or a narrative, either by the leaders of the expedition or by some other member of the party.[5]

Lewis and Clark posted on their comprehensive map, in the area of the Black Hills, "Cheyenne Nation, 110 lodges and 300 warriors, rove." The accompanying narrative contains the answers to Jefferson's queries. To collect their answers in an organized way, Lewis and Clark pasted together a large chart, $34\frac{1}{2}$ by 27 inches, still preserved in the archives of the American Philosophical Society in Philadelphia. Since this chart contains much of what we know about the Cheyennes in this period, I reproduce here Jefferson's questions and the answers Lewis and Clark collected. I list only the questions that are salient for our purposes. I have preserved the style and spelling of the original.[6]

a. The Names of the Indian nations, as usually spelt and pronounc'd by the English.

    a. Cheyennes

b. Primitive Indian names of Nations and Tribes, English Orthography, the syllables producing the sounds by which the Inds themselves express the names of their respective nations.

    b. Shar-ha

c. Nick-names, or those which have generally obtained among the Canadian Traders.

    c. Chien (Dog)

d. The Language they speak if primitive marked with a * otherwise derived from, & approximating to.

    d. *Chyenne

e. Nos. of Villages.

    e. _____

f. Nos. of Tents or Lodges of the roveing bands.

    f. 110

g. Number of Warriours.

    g. 300

h. The probable Number of Souls, of this Numbr. deduct about $\frac{1}{3}$ generally.

    h. 1200

p. The names of the nations with whom they are at war.

    p. a Defensive War with Sioux or (Darcotas) and at war with no other that I know of

q.　The names of the nations with whom they maintain a friendly alliance, or with whom they may be united by intercourse or marriage.
　　q.　With the Ricaras, Mandans, Menatares, and all their neighbors in the plains to the S.W. on Chien R.
r.　The particular water courses on which they reside or rove.
　　r.　No Settled place they rove to the S.W. of the Ricaras, and on both Sides of the Cout Noir or black hills, at the heads of the Chien River, do not cultivate the Soil, they formerley lived in a Village and Cultivated Corn on the Cheyenne River, a fork of the red river of Lake Winipique, the Siouis drove them from that quarter across the Missourie, on the S.W. bank of which they made a Stand (a fort) a little above the ricares a few years, and was compelled to rove well-disposed inds.

In addition to the tabular data, Lewis and Clark added a paragraph reasserting that the Cheyennes formerly lived on the Sheyenne River in what is now North Dakota, and that they had a subsequent village on the Missouri "about 15 miles below the mouth of the Warricunne creek."[7] We will follow up these historical leads later, but for now we are interested in finding out more about Cheyenne social structure in the early 1800s. Our immediate interest is not merely in the group described as "Cheyennes," but also in other groups that are given a multitude of unfamiliar names by Lewis and Clark.

It was George Grinnell who first noticed that there was another Cheyenne band on the Lewis and Clark map, in addition to the "Chyennes" explicitly noted. From his familiarity with the language, Grinnell observed that Lewis and Clark's "Staetan" tribe was more likely the Cheyenne expression "Sutai-hetan," translated as "men of the Sutaio." So what is listed as a separate tribe was in fact, according to Grinnell, a Cheyenne "band."[8] And the question is raised whether other Cheyenne bands might also appear on the map, disguised as separate tribes. But before we go farther into this question, we had better try to reconstruct, as carefully as possible, the circumstances in which Lewis and Clark collected their information. In particular, we must know whether their information actually came from Cheyenne informants, or from someone else. Otherwise we cannot make sense of the names on the map, since different tribes had different names for each other.

The publication of Capt. William Clark's field notes in 1964, considered together with the journal kept by Sgt. John Ordway, published in 1916, allows us to reconstruct the ethnographic situation of Lewis and Clark rather precisely.[9] It was the winter of 1804–5 when the expedition camped on the upper Missouri near the village of the Mandan Indians, a camp they dubbed "Fort Mandan." During that winter, Lewis and Clark collected information necessary to fill up their chart and to construct their maps. This was supposed to be sent to Jefferson after the spring thaw of 1805.

Dug in for the winter and suffering from below-zero temperatures, Lewis and Clark nevertheless entertained a long list of chiefs, traders, and travelers who helped them in their ethnographic survey. Among these, according to Clark's field notes of 2 December were "Several Mandan Chiefs and 4 Chyannes Inds who Came with a pipe to the Mandans."[10] On the same day, Ordway recorded in his own journal "a nomber of the Shian or dog Indians came from the village to visit us. We gave them victuals and used them friendly."[11]

So we can confirm that there actually were Cheyennes among Lewis and Clark's informants, although the linguistic situation must have been complicated. In the first place, no member of the expedition could understand Cheyenne, although some Mandans, who were notoriously multilingual as traders, probably understood both Cheyenne speech and the universal sign language of the Plains.[12] Even today when Cheyennes do "sign talk," it is often accompanied by a spoken version of the same sentence. A listener, then, relies not only on his knowledge of sign language, but on whatever he can pick up from the spoken message. Modern "sign talkers" tell me, however, that because sign language has a conventional word order used by all tribes on the Plains, one speaks at the same time only if one's native language approximates the same order.[13] In sign language, for example, the subject normally comes before the verb and the object comes afterward, as in English and Cheyenne. Languages where the verb or object comes first are usually not spoken at the same time the signs are made simply because, psychologically, it is difficult to say one thing while signing another. The Mandan language, as it happens, has the normal word order of subject-object-verb, so it would not have been spoken by Mandans to accompany Mandan signs.[14] Most likely, then, the Cheyennes at Fort Mandan in 1804 were speaking to the Mandans simultaneously with signs and in Cheyenne and were being spoken to in the same manner by Mandans.

Since Captain Clark and Sergeant Ordway have told us explicitly that there were Mandans and Cheyennes present at the interview on 2 December, we are able to reconstruct that part of the linguistic situation. We can also infer French participation, not because they were mentioned as present, but from indirect evidence. To begin with, the "tribal" name given for the Cheyennes by Lewis and Clark is not the name used by the Mandans, Tamahonruckape, but the one used by the Sioux and French traders, Chyenne/Chien.[15] Since the Sioux were at war with the Mandans, we must assume that it was French and not Sioux people who were present at Fort Mandan. Although the journals are not explicit about a French trader being present on 2 December, these traders are noted as being in and out of the fort during the entire winter. In particular, much of the information may have come from "Mr. Tabbow," or Pierre Tabeau(x), whose journals have been published and will be discussed in the next section.[16] Also, several members of the Lewis and Clark expedition were native French speakers and may have relayed the French name to Clark.

The word represented by the spelling "Cheyenne" is originally a Sioux word, Saiyena, literally meaning "red speakers." Those dialects of Dakota, Lakota, or Nakota that were mutually intelligible the Sioux called "white talk," while speech they could not understand they called "red talk." Therefore the Cheyennes, as speakers of an Algonquian language not known to be related at all to Sioux, were called "red speakers."[17]

That the term "Cheyenne" happened to sound similar to the French word for dog, *chien,* created considerable confusion among early observers. When French traders referred to the "Cheyennes," by whatever spelling, an educated English speaker could not be sure whether they were representing an Indian word or translating it into French. The tribal designation "Crow," for example, was simply translated from native languages by French traders as *corbeaux* in French and as "crow" in English. How could English speakers be sure the French were not attempting the same kind of translation with *chien?*

As we reconstruct the linguistic route of Cheyenne information in 1804, then, it is passing from Cheyenne to Mandan to French to English, accompanied along the way by signs. But what was the actual substance of the communication and the form of the questions and answers? Obviously, since the information was passing through several different languages, only two of which (French and English) bear any similarity, we cannot assume that the ethnographic and geographic information emerged in English unscathed. And what about the constraints imposed by sign language, an extremely abbreviated though elegant way of speaking? Can we successfully account for all these linguistic constraints?

To begin our analysis, sociologically at least, we must realize that in Cheyenne the term for "tribe" and the term for "band" are the same, *manhao.* If one translates into Cheyenne the questions, What tribe are you? and What band are you? they come out exactly the same. A literal translation is something like, Of what blood are you? Similarly, if Lewis and Clark had asked, What tribes are situated on the Upper Platte? the question would appear in Cheyenne as Of what blood are the people on the Upper Platte? If a Cheyenne responded, The Beaver tribe lives on the Upper

Platte, or The Beaver band lives on the Upper Platte, the sentence comes out exactly the same in Cheyenne.

Sign language is no more specific. The dictionaries of sign language provide no word for "tribe," and W. P. Clark suggests that for "band" one should sign "chief-tipi-people" and then the possessive particle.[18] In short, sign language must be recognized as a practical shorthand that did not allow much room for sophisticated social analysis. Neither sign language nor Cheyenne allows a discrimination between "band" and "tribe," even though European travelers as well as modern anthropologists have been very interested in the difference. And even nineteenth-century French, we should note, used the word *tribu* to designate both nations and bands.[19]

On linguistic grounds, then, it is quite legitimate to look on Lewis and Clark's map and in their narratives for Cheyenne bands labeled "tribes." Even if we had no other reasons to suspect that these terms were being confused, certain peculiar aspects of the narrative text itself would tell us. In the first place, Clark noted only 110 lodges of Cheyennes in the chart sent to Jefferson, but Clark and Ordway say in their journals that the Cheyennes who visited on 2 December comprised 300 tipis. Even if we add the 40 lodges of "Staetan" to Clark's 110, we have still not got nearly the 400–600 lodges reported by other observers over the next several years.[20] There must be other bands.

If we look back at the word the Mandans used for Cheyennes, Tama-honruckape, we get our first confirmation that it is bands, not tribes, that are listed on Lewis and Clark's map and in their statistical summary. For we see that the Mandan word *mahon,* "arrow," is part of the term. From sign language we can confirm that "striped arrows" is an alternative sign language name for Cheyennes.[21] Early Mandan dictionaries are sketchy, however, and do not contain the full etymology for Tamahonruckape. Hollow's more recent dictionary (1970) provides the literal explanation: "his-arrow-stock-by hand-to be dirty."[22] We cannot be sure, however that the same etymology would have been offered two hundred years ago, if Mandan etymologies are anything like the Cheyenne etymologies of chapter 2.

If we deduce from this evidence that the "Chyenne" referred to by the Mandans was some group they called "Arrow-something" and not necessarily the whole nation, then we have a good idea, from the previous chapter, who these people might be. We already know that sometimes a term for part of a band is used to refer to the whole, and that the relative prominence of band subgroups can change through time. So we can theorize, at this point, that the "Chyennes" on Lewis and Clark's map may be the Arrow People/Heviksnipahis grouping, which clustered on the diagrams of the previous chapter. In this grouping on figure 2, a greater antiquity for the Arrow People is suggested by the fact that one informant, American Horse, placed the Arrow People in the tribal circle *before* Heviksnipahis, and from Petter's statement that Heviksnipahis was a recent band name.

If we are correct in deducing that these "Chyennes" are a major subgroup, or manhao, then it is of about the correct size, 110 lodges. This number of lodges comprises about 1,200 people, according to Lewis and Clark (600 people would be more accurate), enough for a band but not enough for the Cheyenne nation. As the manhao of Arrow People/Heviksnipahis, however, it not only is of the correct size, but is also in about the correct geographic location, from what we have been told by modern informants. This group is nearest Bear Butte on the Lewis and Clark map (see map 1), and we see

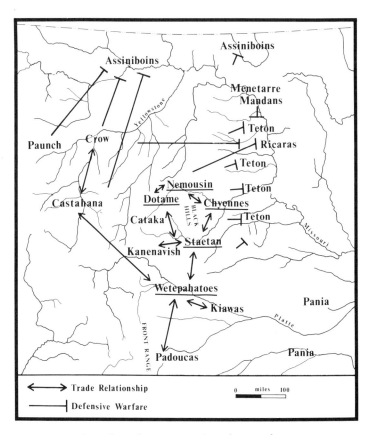

Map 1. Lewis and Clark's information replotted on modern map.

several other named groups circled westward around the Black Hills. But we will have to do a lot of deduction and discarding of hypotheses before we can identify these other bands as possibly Cheyenne.

One way of analyzing the Lewis and Clark reports in an organized way is to try to match all the tribes they list with all the non-Cheyennes we know were in that area at that time, and then see if what we have left over are Cheyennes. Such a task is possible because of the pioneering work in Plains ethnohistory done by Riggs, Hyde, Wood, and others.[23] From this work we have a fair idea of what groups were in the area at that time, especially along the Missouri, and what the populations were. So we should be able to match up Lewis and Clark's list of tribes with other ethnographic reports published later.

Table 4 reproduces parts of Lewis and Clark's list, on the left, and Riggs's later information, published in 1893, on the right. Here we discover that the Tetons, like their eastern cousins the Santees and Yanktons, are well accounted for, if we add a little additional information from some more recent sources. Buechel and Royal Hassrick tell us that the "Teton, sah-o-

Table 4   Comparison of Lewis and Clark's Tribal List with Riggs's 1893 Listing

LEWIS AND CLARK		RIGGS
"BANDS"	"SUBDIVISIONS"	
Teton (Bois Brulé)		Brulé
	Esahateaketarpar	
	Warchinktarhe	
	Choketartowomb	
	Ozash	
	Menesharne	
Teton, Okandandas		Oglala
	Sheo	
	Okandandas	Ogalala
Teton, Minnakineasso		Minnekonjoo
	Minnakineasso	Minikangye Wozupi
	Wanneewackatoonelar	
	Tarcoehparh	
Teton, Sahone		Hunkpapa
	Sahone	
	Tackchandeseechar	
	Sahonehontaparpar	

ne" includes not only the Hunkpapa, listed as "Sah-o-ne-hont-a-par-par," but also the Sans Arc, Two Kettles, and Blackfoot bands listed by Riggs.[24] So all the major "bands" listed by Lewis and Clark are accounted for, although we cannot match their "subdivisions" from Riggs. If these subdivisions are anything like the Cheyenne bands discussed in chapter 2, we should not be surprised to find them changing their structure and names rapidly through time.

With all the major Teton groups accounted for, we can turn to the riverine tribes, bearing in mind once again that our information is primarily Mandan and French in origin. As with our information on the Sioux, we can expect to find more detail concerning the tribes closer to Fort Mandan and more vagueness and "lumping" concerning tribes farther away. Since by 1804 Lewis and Clark had already passed through the territory of the Pawnees, the Arikaras, and the Siouan tribes of the Lower Missouri, they were very clear about the political relationships among these groups, though they were not so clear about linguistic affiliations. Similarly, Lewis and Clark had descriptions of tribes trading with the French from north of the Missouri—Crees, Chippewas, Assiniboines, and others—so that these too are well and accurately described. And from the Hidatsas (also known in the journals as Menetarees, Big Bellies, and Gros Ventres), a nearby riverine group, there is a good description of the Crow or "Raven" Indians who had separated from their Hidatsa cousins in the recent past.

By the time Lewis and Clark had completed the winter at Fort Mandan, they had collected excellent, detailed information about the Indian nations of the Middle Missouri. Additional data concerning the tribes between Fort Mandan and the Pacific Ocean were gathered over the next two years and ultimately published in their journals. But there still remained an area that was vaguely known, between the Missouri River and Mexico, and this is the area to which we must now turn.

So far in this analysis, we have systematically accounted for the tribes Lewis and Clark numbered from 1 to 27 and from 35 to 44 (table 5). If there are any additional Cheyenne bands on the list, they are most likely among the groups numbered 28 to 34. These are the nomadic tribes situated on the expedition map south and west of the Missouri, toward Mexico and the Rocky Mountains.

As we identify any of these groups as bands of a particular tribe, we will inevitably contradict some of the information presented by Lewis and Clark. That is, there is no way of creating a master classification of the groups that does not in some way violate some of the information given on their maps and tables, simply because that information is itself contradictory. The Castahana nation, for example, is said to be a "Padouca" or Co-

Table 5   Lewis and Clark's List of Indian Nations

NUMBER AND NAME FROM LIST		MORE RECENT DESIGNATION
1	Grand Osarge	Osages
2	Little Osarge	Osages
3	Kanzas	Kaws
4	Ottoes	Otos
5	Missouries	Missouris
6	Pania proper	Pawnees
7	Pania Loup	Pawnees
8	Pania Republicans	Pawnees
9	Mahar	Omahas
10	Poncare	Poncas
11	Ricaras	Arikaras
12	Mandans	Mandans
13	Shoes Men	Hidatsas
14	Big Bellies	Hidatsas
15	Ayauwais	Iowas
16	Saukees	Sacs
17	Renarz	Foxes
18–27	Sioux	Sioux
28	Chyennes	Cheyennes
29a	Wetapahato	
29b	Cayauwa	Kiowas
30a	Canenavich	Arapahos
30b	Staetan	
31	Cataka	Kiowa Apaches
32	Nemousin	Comanches?
33	Dotame	
34	Castahana	
35	Ravin	Crows
36	Paunch	Atsinas?
37–39	Assiniboins	Assiniboines
40	Knistanoes	Crees
41	Fall Indians	Atsinas
42	Cattanahaws	Blackfeet?
43	Blue Mud Indians	Shoshones?
44	Alitan	Comanches?

manche group that speaks a Siouan language. Comanche and Sioux, however, are unrelated languages. The Atsinas and the Hidatsas are both called "Gros Ventres" and "Menetarees" by Lewis and Clark at different times. Since contradiction is embedded in the data, the best we can hope for is to violate the data offered by Lewis and Clark as little as possible.

Two operations on the present data base will help us interpret it correctly. First of all, we notice that many of the questions answered in Lewis and Clark's statistical summary carry the entry "same as" followed by the name of some other tribe in the summary. In table 6 these "same as" correlations are entered in the hope that they will help inform us about which tribes shared territory, enemies, or trade or otherwise acted together.

For another thing, we notice that though Lewis and Clark are quite specific about rivers as home ranges of the tribes, the rivers on their map are rather contorted and inaccurate, having been drawn on the basis of hearsay information. In the hope of placing the tribes closer to their actual geographic arrangement, I have replotted the locations of the tribes in question on a modern map (map 1). Where two tribes were listed together in the summary but were placed north or west of each other on the map, I have retained this spatial arrangement on the revised map.

What we hope to find on the map, in addition to the "Chyennes" and "Staetan," are several more bands of Cheyennes, and perhaps several proto-

Table 6   Lewis and Clark's Tribes That Are Said to Be the "Same as" Another Tribe in Some Important Trait

TRIBE LISTED AS	SAID TO BE SAME AS												
	BR	MI	OG	CH	WE	KI	CAN	ST	CAT	NE	DO	CAS	CR
Brulé													
Minnecunjou		3											
Oglala	1												
Chyennes													
Wetapahoto				1									
Kiawa				1									
Canenavich				1	1	1							
Staetan				1	2	1							
Cataka				1	2		4	1		1	1		
Nemousin					1		2		3				
Dotame					1		2		2				
Castahana							1						
Crow												1	

Arapaho bands as well. We might also find some bands of Comanches, Kiowas, and Apaches, though these tribes were not actually seen by the explorers and lived farther from the regular trade routes. Also, we might hope to find the Cheyenne bands not yet fully integrated into a "nation" and the three proto-Arapaho bands not yet fully distinguished from the Atsinas.[25] So that alliances and enmities of these tribes toward other tribes can be noted, I have plotted on this same map locations of several contiguous groups, notably the Mandans and Tetons. To avoid cluttering the map, I have not plotted the trade relationships with the Mandans. According to Lewis and Clark, *everyone* traded with the Mandans except the Tetons.

All of the tribes in question, numbers 28–34, are said to be in alliance with each other, though variously at war with the Tetons and the Assiniboines, as plotted on the map. Three of the names listed were continuously (and correctly) applied to the same people right up to modern times. These are the Crows, Kiowas (Kiawas), and Cheyennes (Chyennes). In addition, the Kanenavish Indians are identified continuously in traders' and military reports as an Arapaho band. Leaving aside the "Paunch" Indians, who may or may not be Atsinas, there remains the identification of Lewis and Clark's "Wetepahatoes, Cataka, Dotame, Nimousin, and Castahana."

If we identify the Kanenavish Indians as Arapahos, it will be difficult to assert that any groups north of them are Kiowas or Comanches, since the home or core territories of bands constituting a nation are usually contiguous. If we look at other groups in the same area—Crows, Lakotas, Arikaras, Kiowas, Comanches—the component bands of a nation are consistently contiguous to one another. There is no reason to believe the Cheyennes or Arapahos were any different.[26]

Judging from other documents and traditions already cited, it is not likely that the Atsinas in 1804 were yet politically separated from the proto-Arapaho bands. We might expect them still to share allies and enemies with the other bands. This then is one argument for designating the Castahanas as Arapahos, because they are the only other of Lewis and Clark's bands who are said to be at war with the Assiniboines, the enemies of the Atsinas. Comparing the tabulated entries for these two groups, the Castahanas and the Atsinas, we find that they are alleged to speak the same language, identified as "Menatare (or big belly)." In the "same as" correlation, the only one listed for the Atsinas is "same as for the Castahanas." Another argument for the Castahanas being Arapahos is given in Lewis and Clark's comments: "Their territories are in common as above stated of the Canenavich," who we know more reliably are Arapahos.

So far we have evidence for three Proto-Arapaho bands—Atsina (Paunch), Kanenavish (Canenavich), and Castahana—and we have one more to look for. The most promising place to look is the band that is contiguous to all of them, the Catakas. Lewis and Clark considered this one and two others—Dotames and Nimousins—as being closely grouped geographically. However, they also tell us that one of these three, they do not say which, speaks a different language than the other two. That the odd band is Cataka is argued once again from the "same as" data in table 6, where we see a relationship between Cataka and Cananevich. We might consider this to be the other Arapaho band were it not for evidence that it is in fact the "Kiowa Apaches" under the name applied to them by the Pawnees.[27]

We are left, then, with three bands in addition to the Staetan that could be Cheyennes—the Wetepahatos, the Dotames, and the Nimousins. Taken all together, they make as good a contiguous cluster as the suggested proto-Arapaho bands. But we should still consider some additional evidence before moving to the linguistic evidence, which I believe makes their identity more certain.

The Wetepahatos are mentioned as coresident with the Kiowas. They are also said to frequent the Cheyenne River, which embraces the Black Hills, and to be horse traders. We might infer that their presence with the Kiowas was to facilitate the trade discussed by Lewis and Clark. Looking at the "same as" table, we can see that the relationships of the Wetepahato group are not so much with the Arapahos as with the cluster of other groups still unidentified. They are rather "non-Arapaho" in their behavior and affinities.

I suggest that Wetepahato and Wotapio are cognate band names, as is argued further in the Linguistic Appendix, on the basis that the spellings of these two words do not vary between themselves any more than do other various versions I list in the Appendix. Other kinds of information support an antiquity for the Wotapio band name back to the eighteenth century. Oral histories for the band, which will be considered in the next chapter, maintain that the band was named in the period before warfare with the Sioux, even before the Cheyennes migrated westward across the Missouri.

We are left with the Dotames and Nimousins as possible Cheyenne bands. I believe the combination of evidence from contiguity and from shared behavior as indicated on table 6 indicates that these bands too are Cheyennes. As far as I can determine, the name Dotame appears only in Lewis and Clark's report and in the journal of Tabeau, who may have given the name to Lewis and Clark.[28] I suggest that the word Dotame is phonetically the same as Totoimana, the Cheyenne "prairie people," for reasons elaborated in the Linguistic Appendix.

The remaining candidate to be a Cheyenne band has a name given at least three spellings by Lewis and Clark using variant vowels—Nimousin,

Nemosen, and Nemosin. Although it was alleged to be a Comanche name for themselves, Mooney found Lewis and Clark's versions so deviant from the others that he decided it was "apparently a misprint of Nemene or Nimenim."[29] I suggest, instead, that the name is merely "Northern Eaters," using the Cheyenne prefix for north, nao-, in the construction "naoomisis."[30] With the Wotapios withdrawn to the south, it was necessary to differentiate them, the Southern Eaters, from the Northern Eaters. The term Naomisis is still used to designate the "Eaters" who live in Montana.

A confirmation that all three of these bands—Wetepahato, Dotame, and Nimousin—may well be Cheyenne lies in their geographic arrangement, wrapped around the Black Hills. Just as Ed Red Hat said in 1981, they are in the same order on the ground as in the ceremonial circle. The Cheyennes/Heviksnipahis are just southeast of Bear Butte, in the door-keeper position, the Wetepahatos are south, the Staetans are in the guest position, and the Omisis and their subgroup, the Totoimanas, are at the north side of the opening. But where is the Masikota band, which is also supposed to be a major and original band? It is nowhere among these groups. This is a question we will save for a little later.

With this much experience with documents, then, it seems that so far the strategy suggested in the introductory chapter—of considering native tradition a valid framework against which documents are to be measured—is essentially sound. For it was the Cheyenne language, first of all, that cautioned us that there could be confusion between "bands" and "tribes." Cheyenne informants also suggested the connection between location in the camp circle and real geography. In the rest of this chapter we will examine other maps and documents within a framework suggested by Cheyenne informants, dealing with three additional questions: the location of Cheyenne farming, Cheyenne relations with the Sioux, and Cheyenne origins in the east. After examining documents relating to these episodes, we will be prepared in the next chapter to rewrite Cheyenne ethnohistory from a native perspective, considering European sources not as central, but as supplementary.

French Traders and Cheyenne Farming

It is only an Anglo-American myth that Lewis and Clark, in 1804, were blazing their way through a wilderness unknown to Europeans. In fact, the first French explorations and trade relations with tribes beyond the Great Lakes took place as early as La Salle in 1680.[31] From then until Lewis and Clark, there was a continuous involvement of French traders with the tribes between Lake Superior and the Upper Missouri. Although very few of these hundreds of traders kept journals, nevertheless we can see constant improvement in the published French maps of the area.[32] This first great period of exploration from Great Lakes trading stations lasted from about 1634 to 1673. French exploration from St. Louis began about 1764 and lasted until Lewis and Clark.

Between 1680 and 1803, this area was continually contested among the Great Powers—France, Britain, Spain, and later the United States. What information we have on the Indian tribes of this region, then, must be understood against the political situations that characterized the various decades. For example, little organized information comes from the French Canadians after the French and Indian War was lost in 1763. The new wave of French traders from the south was just getting established in the Middle Missouri area in 1790 when Louisiana was suddenly Spanish, and then French, and then American in 1803. But there were bursts of cartographic interest in the area as the French first sized up their possessions in the late 1600s, as the British Colonial Army tried to outflank the French in the 1760s, and as both Spanish and French agents in 1790 appraised the area for its potential for trade and colonization. In all cases the Cheyennes show up time and again—as trading partners, as potential allies, and as a military threat.

Those documents mentioning that Cheyennes farmed in the Black Hills were produced just before Lewis and Clark. All the writers were people interested in the fur trade, which had been steadily pushing up the Missouri under impetus from Pierre Chouteau.[33] Chouteau himself was mostly a supplier of expeditions, and he ultimately was displaced by John Jacob Astor's American Fur Company. But our best information comes from three trader-explorers who came from St. Louis to the Upper Missouri at the turn of the century—Tabeau, Truteau, and Perrin du Lac. We should use Perrin du Lac's information with caution, however, since he may merely have plagiarized the reports of others.

The Cheyenne oral tradition I wish to document here is one I have heard scores of times from Cheyenne elders—that the Cheyennes formerly raised corn in the Black Hills. Judging from such sources as Jablow, Holder, and Powell, one might suppose this assertion would be hard to verify.[34] But surprisingly, we see that all three French sources are explicit, and one is very lengthy, in stating that the Cheyennes were indeed corn farmers.

It may also be that some scholars do not consider it *possible* to farm in the Black Hills, so perhaps a few ecological facts are called for at the outset before we look in detail at the French documents. The basic problem in any Plains farming, of course, is water. Successful "dry" farming, or farming without irrigation, is possible with Indian varieties of maize only as far west as the fifteen-inch isohyetal line, marked on the accompanying map (map 2). West of that line, Indian crops were not successful often enough to justify the input of labor and seed.[35] The Black Hills area, however, is exceptional.

Like many elevated land masses, the Black Hills pushes up wet surface air into the colder upper atmosphere. As a consequence, rainfall condenses downwind of the elevated land mass, forming a rain shadow on the earth's surface. On the rainfall map of the northern Great Plains, we see a rain shadow just east of the Black Hills creating a farmable region—an island of rainfall—two hundred miles west of the fifteen-inch isohyet.

The soils and climate of the Black Hills also do not preclude corn farming. According to the *Atlas of American Agriculture,* the Black Hills are

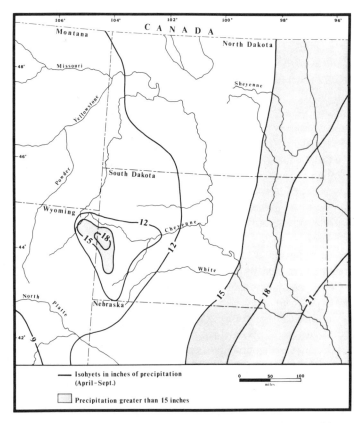

Map 2.   Rainfall in the Black Hills area. Redrawn from Baker 1936 by Mary Goodman.

mostly Laurel alluvium, a fertile type of soil.[36] The number of frost-free days, depicted on map 3, is also adequate for corn farming. With this ecological background, then, it is not so surprising to read in the French reports that the Cheyennes were farmers in the river valleys east of the Black Hills. The earliest observer, François Marie Perrin du Lac, put it as follows in 1802: "The Chaguyennes, although wanderers the greatest part of the year, sow near their cottages maize and tobacco which they sell to the Scioux. Many others come to reap at the beginning of autumn. They are, in general, good huntsmen and kill great numbers of castors, which they sell to the Scioux. Many other wandering nations that are allied to the Cha-guyennes hunt in the same country. They are the Cayowas, the Tocaninam-biches, the Tokiouakos, and the Pitapahatos."[37]

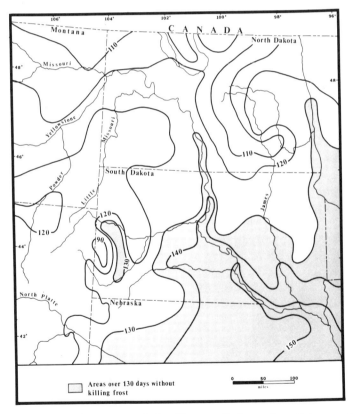

Map 3.   Frost-free days in the Black Hills area. Redrawn from Baker 1936 by Mary Goodman.

Concerning social organization, Perrin du Lac, like Lewis and Clark, described one group as the Cheyennes proper but mentioned two other groups. As he put it: "The Chaguyennes, who are continually wandering on both (banks of the Chaguyenne River) in pursuit of buffalowes, are divided into three hordes, the largest of which preserves the name Chaguyenne; the second is named Ouisy; and third, Chousa."

In Truteau's "Description of the Upper Missouri," written in 1796, there is similar information:

> Two leagues above the dwelling of the Ree issues forth the river of the Cheyenne (Chaguine) which some hunters have named the Fork. . . . About thirty leagues from its mouth, upon one of its tributaries called the River of the Bunch of Cherries, the Cheyenne built there some permanent huts, around which they cultivated little fields of maize and tobacco; but, further-more, this nation, which is divided into three bands or hordes, of which the largest bears the name of Cheyenne, the second is called Ouisy and the third is Chouta, wanders without cessation the length of this river and crosses in search of wild cows, even many chains of hills that separate, by several ranges, these vast prairies.[38]

In his narrative journal, written the previous year in the field, Jean-Baptiste Truteau gives more details of relationships between the Cheyennes and neighboring tribes.

> On the Southwest and to the West, on the branches of a large river (which I name the river of the Cheyennes) which empties into the Missouri about three miles above the second Ricara village, are situated several nations called the Cayoguas, the Caminanbiches, the Pitapahotos, etc., all of a different speech. The Cheyennes wander over the country along the river, a little below those first named. The vast country, not far from here, over which these different nations roam, abounds in beaver and otter, since they have never hunted these animals, not having had any intercourse with the white men. It would be easy, by means of the Cheyennes who are their friends, to extend our commerce with these nations and obtain from them fine furs.[39]

In other sections of his journal, Truteau relates some particular dealings with the Cheyennes, one of which is directly related to our purposes.[40] On 6 July 1795 Truteau entertained "three men of the Cheyenne Nation, from a village called Ouisay, which has not yet come here, . . . they reported that the Cayouguas, the Caminanbiches and the Pitapahotos of whom I spoke above, had drawn near and were camped just beyond them."

The third significant French journal from this period is that of Pierre

Antoine Tabeau, the trader mentioned by Lewis and Clark. It is to some extent a compendium of his own experiences and those of earlier traders. His journal is also the latest, 1803–5. In his remarks on the Cheyennes, Tabeau emphasizes both their strategic position for trade and their vacillating relationships with the Sioux. Here I extract a few sentences from a section Tabeau entitled "The Cheyennes and other Neighboring Nations":

> The commodities of the Ricaras attract almost all the year a large crowd of Sioux from whom the Ricaras have to endure much without deriving any real benefit. It is not so with the Cheyennes and many other wandering nations, whom they supply with maize, tobacco, beans, pumpkins, etc. These people visit them as true friends, and the advantage of the trade is almost equal. The Cheyennes, having themselves been farmers, put a higher value on the commodities, and with more difficulty, go without them. . . . Now that the Cheyennes have ceased to till the ground, they roam over the prairies west of the Missouri on this side of the Black Hills, from which they come regularly at the beginning of August to visit their old and faithful allies, the Ricaras. . . . The Ricaras, before this year, carried to the foot of the Black Hills tobacco and maize. They accompanied the Cheyennes and found, at the meeting place, eight other friendly nations—The Caninanbiches, the Squihitanes, the Nimoussines, the Padaucas, the Catarkas, the Datamis, the Tchiwak, and the Cayowa. The first two speak the same language, but all the others speak a different one. . . . With the exception of the Cheyennes, all these nations, although always at peace with the Ricaras, never approached the Missouri.[41]

From these three sources, then, we learn not only that the Cheyennes farmed in the Black Hills, but when they ceased to do so—just before Lewis and Clark. In addition, we have confirmed that the Cheyennes comprised three bands, although some of the names are different from those collected by Lewis and Clark. Clearly the "Chayennes" are the "Chyennes" of 1804, whom we have identified more particularly as the Tsistsistas proper and the Heviksnipahis, though there may be other bands in this group as well. Unfortunately, none of these earlier sources give us any information about population or number of lodges for each group.

Perrin du Lac and Truteau both gave three subgroups for the Cheyennes—Cheyenne proper, Ouisy, and Chouta/Chousa. It is tempting, then, to identify the Ouisys as the Omisis and the Choutas as the Sutaios and to assume that Lewis and Clark's Wetepahatos are either somewhere else or submerged in one of these bands. Also, it seems significant that Tabeau, who does not mention the Ouisys or Choutas, *does* mention the "Nimoussines" (Northern Eaters) and "Dotamis" (Totoimana) as separate tribes.

Perhaps these are alternative names for Cheyenne bands undergoing the kind of social change we examined in the previous chapter.

In this historical period we get the idea, both from Lewis and Clark and from the French traders, that Plains Indian political alliances were limited but broadening. Most notably, the Teton Sioux were less integrated politically than they were later. Although later they were able to field an army that twice defeated the United States—once in 1866 and again in 1876— in 1800 the Sioux nations maintained only intermittent patterns of alliance among themselves. [42]

As we follow the Cheyennes and the Siouan groups further back in time, we should note that the word "Dakota" (also Lakota and Nakota) is not originally a linguistic or an ethnic designation for a group of bands, but a political one. It means simply "the alliance." This immediately raises two questions: Who were the allies? and Who were the enemies? We should not, by any means, assume that each group was homogeneous in language and culture, for there are many North American examples to the contrary. The Kiowas, for example, included Apachean bands in their tribal circle who were full-fledged members of the nation, despite the fact that their origins and language were radically different. The Creeks and Seminoles were even more diverse, including bands consisting entirely of Red Stick Muskogees, Hitchitis, Mikasukis, Yuchis, escaped black slaves, Yamasees, and Alabamas at different times. The members of the Iroquois League also had important differences among themselves, especially the Tuscaroras. So language and politics are emphatically not the same thing. [43]

In the case of the Dakotas, the enemies were the Crees and the Chippewas. These tribes formed broad seasonal alliances symbolized by carrying the calumet among various villages. Smoking the pipe meant you were part of the alliance, at least for that season of warfare. [44]

The Cree and Chippewa alliances, like those of nearly every people at war, included dissident members of enemy groups. In fact, it is nearly universally true that war alliances take advantage of existing political splits to incorporate some of those enemy groups into the new alliance. Modern and familiar examples are those Ukrainians and Byelorussians who joined the Germans against the Russians in World War II, the Vichy French and Egyptians, who joined the Germans against the Allies, and the Austrians, Cyrenaicans, and Sicilians, who joined the Allies against the Axis. In the case of the Cree and Chippewa alliances, the Sioux who joined them became known as the Assiniboines.

Needless to say, the Assiniboines were not held in high regard by the rest of the Sioux, but were called by them *hohe*, or "outlaws." The Cree-Chippewa-Assiniboine alliances persisted a very long time against the Sioux, from about 1656 until peace was enforced by the United States government after 1850. But what about the other side of this coin? If there were Sioux who were split off from the rest by the opportunity of alliance, perhaps there were Algonquians who went the other way and were split off from other Algonquian groups by the opportunity of becoming part of the Dakota Alliance. And perhaps these alliance-minded Algonquians included the ancestors of the Cheyennes.

In this regard it is noteworthy that the Cheyenne name for the Assiniboines is exactly the same as that of the Dakotas—Hohe, "outlaws." That is, the Cheyennes have borrowed a Dakota word rather than using a native term. A friendly attitude between Cheyennes and Dakotas is also implied by the fact that the Dakotas do not call the Cheyennes any derogatory name, but merely Cheyennes, "red speakers." In return, the Cheyennes call the Dakota Ohoohomeo, "the people who were invited."[45]

The Cheyenne participation in the Sioux Alliance is made very explicit in the journal of Jonathan Carver, written over the winter of 1766–67 from his camp on the upper Minnesota River. As leader of a colonial reconnaissance force during the French and Indian War, Carver's job was to map the western flank of the possible war area and to count friends and enemies among the Indian tribes of the Upper Mississippi. He wrote:

> On the 7th of December, I arrived at the utmost extent of my travels toward the west where I met with a large party of the Naudowessie Indians, among whom I resided seven months. These constituted a part of the eight bands of the Naudowessies of the Plains and are termed the Wawpeentowahs, the Tintons, the Asrahcootans, the Mawhaws, and the Schians. The other three bands, whose names are the Schianese, the Chongousceton and the Waddapawjestin, dwell higher up to the west of the River St. Pierre on plains that, according to their account, are unbounded and probably terminate on the coast of the Pacific Ocean. The Naudowessie nation, when united, consists of more than two-thousand warriors. The Assinipoils, who revolted from them, amount to about three hundred; and leagued with the Killistinoies, live in a continual state of enmity with the other eleven bands.[46]

Looking at the band names supplied by Carver in 1766, we should note first that he references the Cheyenne information as "according to their account," implying that he actually talked to some Cheyennes. He says that the "Schianese" at that time lived on the River St. Pierre, now known as the Minnesota River. He also mentioned that they were corn farmers.

I suggest that Carver's Waddapawjestins, Chongouscetons, Schienese, and Schians are the ancestral bands of the Cheyenne nation. Of these, the most transparent identification can be made between the Waddapawjestins and the Wotapios, also known later as the Wetepahatos. I believe Waddapaw is the same as Wotapio, for reasons listed in the Linguistic Appendix. More troublesome, on a strictly linguistic basis, is any connection between Chongousceton and Chouta or Sutaio. The name Chongasketon appears in various forms not only in Carver's journal, but also on many of the French maps to be studied in the next section. Even though these may be two different names, I still believe they were being applied to the same band, for several reasons. In the first place, we find, in the reports of both Tabeau and Carver, the bracketing of three bands as closely allied. In Tabeau the third band is Chouta; in Carver it is Chongousceton. Second, as we move back through time, we find many examples of the Chongasketons as contiguous to the Cheyennes. That is, if we found Carver's bracketing of the three names merely to be anomalous, we might dismiss it. But the Cheyennes and the Chongasketons are listed together as far back as we care to go, as we shall see in the next section.

Carver's listing of two Cheyenne groups, the Schians and the Schianese, provides some fertile possibilities for discovering the workings of band fission in this period. For we find that another early traveler, Regis Loisel, also listed two Cheyenne groups, which he labeled Chayennes and the Chahuines or Chaoines.[47] It seems unlikely to me that both these travelers could have made the same mistake; it is more likely that there coexisted in the late eighteenth century two distinct groups called Cheyennes, one allied with the Sioux east of the Missouri and the other a more independent entity west of the Missouri. In fact, Carver emphasized the alliance by specifically stating that the "Shyanawh" were a band of the "Naudowessee."[48]

At this point I wish to suggest, only briefly, that the band called Schians or Shyanawh by Carver and Chayennes by Loisel is the Masikota band we have been looking for. I believe it split off from the Cheyennes proper by its association with the Oglala Sioux. It was known to Lewis and Clark as the Sheo (see table 4). Significantly, the Sheo band disappears as an Oglala subgroup at the same time as the Masikota band appears among the Cheyennes.[49] In the next chapter I will show how Cheyenne oral tradition supports this view.

In his journal, Carver suggests the intimacy of relationships between the Sioux and the Cheyennes in this period. This view is consistent with the accounts of T. S. Williamson, who noted in 1850 that "the Shiens, who Gallatin says have a language kindred to the Algonquin, were received as allies and though speaking a different language, were long, if they are not still counted as part of the Dakota nation. Hence their name, Sha-i-e-na in the Ihanktonwan dialect, being equivalent to Sha-i-api-in in the Isanyati. Both applied to those who speak a different language from the Dakotas, and applied especially to Shiens because all others speaking a different language were counted as enemies."[50]

Even earlier Lewis Hennepin, whose maps and journal will be discussed in the next section, noted that the term Nadowessie meant not just the people later called "Sioux" or "Dakota," but "also several other Nations which we include under the general Denomination of Nadoussians."[51] This word Nadoussians, in its various forms, is not what the people called themselves but what the Chippewas called the members of the Dakota Alliance, a name later shortened to "Sioux" by the French. The name means "serpents" and is still regarded as derogatory by many Dakota people.

So it does not violate the documents of the period to suppose that the Cheyennes, sometime before 1800, were members of the Dakota Alliance. It only violates prevailing ideas among some scholars that language, politics, and culture are all the same thing. But if it is a regular occurrence among modern nations, such as Belgium, Switzerland, Canada, and Yugoslavia—just to mention a few—that political unity can extend beyond the linguistic group, why should we be surprised to find that this was also the case in eighteenth-century North America? Certainly the Creeks, Seminoles, Kiowas, and Iroquois give us other examples of the same process and in the same period of history. I am arguing, then, that early travelers tended to assume that tribes that were politically allied therefore spoke the same language, which is not true.

The general impression we get from documents relating to this period, about 1766, is of a group of contiguous Algonquian bands, allied with the Dakotas, shifting west as part of a general movement. At this point the Cheyennes apparently did not yet constitute a separate nation politically but were part of an alliance dominated by Siouan-speaking peoples. The band names, although they are familiar to us, are not being consistently reported to Europeans. Although Carver in 1766 and Lewis and Clark in 1804 mention the Wotapios, the intermediate French sources do not. Neither the French nor Lewis and Clark mention the Chongasketons as such, though we do find references to the "Chousa" and the "Chouta," possibly the same group. Also, we have the name Ouisy from Truteau and Perrin du Lac, who explicitly gave it as the name of a Cheyenne subgroup. But perhaps maps from this and earlier periods will help clarify the problem of identifying the Chongasketons and also the Ouisys, or "Eaters." And we must still explain where the Masikotas came from, and the circumstances of their split with the Oglalas.

The Early Maps

Since libraries and manuscript collections are constantly being improved by cross-listing and microfilming, it is not surprising that many important maps overlooked in earlier times are now readily available to scholars. So the "new" insights and "fresh" interpretations offered here are only partly due to our looking from a different theoretical perspective, and arise largely because nowadays maps are easier to find and copy. Still, several explicit references to the Cheyennes in early times occur on maps that have long been in print or stored in major libraries. For example, if we wish to confirm the position of the Cheyennes in the days of Lewis and Clark, there is the excellent atlas edited by Carl Wheat, *Mapping the Transmississippi West,* published in 1954. On page 158 we find a reproduction of Soulard's 1795 map of the northern plains in which a "Chaguine" village is shown near the Black Hills. Collet's 1796 map, included in the same atlas, shows the "Chaguiene" on the Cheyenne River. Perrin du Lac's 1802 map shows the Cheyennes and also the "Chaguyenne River," while a map entitled simply "The Mississippi" shows the "Terre des Cheyen" in the Black Hills and also a village of the "Chiriteune ou Chequiene" on the north branch of the Cheyenne River. In addition, a map brought back from the field by Lewis and Clark and called by them "the Spanish Map" shows the "Chaguine Indians" on the Little Missouri in approximately the same period.[52]

When we go farther back in time, however, confirmations are supposedly much harder to find. Especially, it has been called "difficult" to document one of the most frequently debated assertions of Cheyenne oral tradition, that they once lived on the headwaters of the Mississippi near a large lake. Grinnell, Hyde, Will, and Wood all failed to confirm this assertion from early maps, although none of them denied it. Grinnell even lamented that these early positions of the tribe "would seem now impossible to learn."[53] But there exists a manuscript map of 1697, drawn by Lewis Hennepin, in which the "Nation du Chien" is represented clearly on the west bank of the Mississippi River near its source. On another map of the same period, this one a hand-drawn manuscript map in the Newberry Library produced by Jean-Baptiste Franquelin in 1697, we find the "Chaienaton" in approximately the same position. On an earlier map, in which Franquelin tried to present information collected by Louis Joliet in 1674, we find once again the "Chaiena" on a tributary of the Upper Mississippi, in modern Minnesota. In all three cases the nearest major body of water is "Lac de Buade" or "Chongasketon Lac," probably the present-day Leech Lake in Minnesota.[54]

So once again the oral tradition of the Cheyennes, that they once lived on the Mississippi near a large lake, has proved out. Another bit of oral history will help us put this period in better linguistic order. According to the Sutaio elders White Bull (born about 1820) and Coyote (born about 1830), the name given the Sutaios when they were a separate tribe was "Dog People."[55] According to modern informants, this was a nickname applied to the Sutaios because they had no horses and had to use dogs to pull their travois.

This helps clear away some of the confusion about the word Chien. It may be that the French in the 1660s were met on the Upper Mississippi not only by a group whom the Sioux called "Saiyenas" or "red speakers," but also by a very similar and neighboring band called the Dog People, which translates into French as Chien, a name that sounds very much like Saiyenas. The resulting confusion, then, was ultimately resolved politically, though not linguistically, when the Sutaios, or Dog People, were taken into the Cheyenne political structure in the early nineteenth century. The Sutaios did not persist in being called Dog People, in large part, because there was a preexisting soldier society among the Cheyennes of the same name, although as late as 1910 White Bull and Coyote remembered the name.

One other bit of confusion for this period has been created by the Jesuit scholar Jean Delanglez regarding the "Nation of Forts," a trader's nickname for the Chongasketons.[56] While it is true that the best translation for Chongasketon is "nation of forts," the original maps do not in fact say "nation of forts" in English, but rather *nation de hommes forts* in French. The French phrase, which translates as "nation of strong men," was shortened to *nation des forts* or "nation of the strong" on later French maps and was finally copied erroneously by an English publisher apparently unfamiliar with French as "nation of forts," a group alleged to be different from the Chongasketons. But if the maps cited in table 7 are put in chronological order, the origin of the error is much clearer.

Hennepin's original translation of Chongasketon was not "Nation of Forts," but rather "Dog Tribe." Delanglez and others have dismissed this as an error, but we should note that Hennepin's translation is consistent with the idea that the Chongasketons are Sutaios because Cheyenne oral tradition states that the Sutaios were originally called Dog People.[57] In Dakota, dog is *chonga* and people is *-ton*. That is, Hennepin, the mapmaker, and Cheyenne oral tradition, taken together, suggest that the Sutaios are the Chongasketons of early maps and that the other renderings of the name are perhaps based on a misunderstanding.

Whether or not one can make "dog people" out of Chongasketon, the group, or at least part of it, behaved very much like a proto-Cheyenne band throughout its period of existence. In the first place, Armand Lahontan, one of the first explorers to visit the "Sonkaskitons," said that they spoke an Algonquian, not a Siouan language.[58] La Salle, despite the assertion made by Delanglez, was ambiguous in his identification of the Chougasketons as Sioux when he wrote in 1680, if I may quote him in French precisely, that Lake Issati was inhabited by "les Issati, les Nadouessans, les Tintonha, les Oudebaton, les Chougasketon, et par d'autres peuples qui l'on comprend sous le mesme nom de Sioux ou de Nadouessious."[59]

From 1680 until the journals of Carver in 1766, whenever the Cheyennes

Table 7   Sources for Locations Plotted on Map 4

SOURCE	REFERENCE	LISTED AS	PLOTTED AS
Hennepin 1698	Karpinski 1931, atlas, 25	Chongaskabi or Nation of Forts	S
		Nation du Chien	C
		Oua de Batons or Gens de Rivières	O
Anonymous 1682	Newberry Library Map 4F G3300 .C3	Chongasketon	S
		Oudebatons	O
		Nation des Forts	C
de Fer 1705	Karpinski 1931, atlas, 33	Les Houetbatons or Gens de Rivière	O
		Les Songatskitons or Nation de Tracy	S
Moll 1709	Karpinski 1931, atlas, 34	The Houetbatons	O
		Tracy N.	S
Coronelli 1695	Karpinski 1931, atlas, 23	Oisa de Battons	O
Franquelin 1697	Newberry MS and Wedel 1974	Chaienaton	C
		Chongatsquiton or Nation des hommes forts	S
		Ouadebaton or Nation de la rivière	O

are mentioned, they are usually in company with the Chongasketons. I suggest that at some point the proto-Cheyenne part of the Chongasketons separated and migrated west, while the main body became known as the Sissetons. Perhaps there was a symbiotic relationship before the separation, with the proto-Cheyennes hunting and the proto-Sissetons farming. I will explain the workings of this kind of system in subsequent chapters. The group called Chongasketons consistently is reported alongside the Cheyennes afterward, while the Sissetons ultimately emerge as a Dakota group.

I believe the process evidenced on these early maps and documents is the same as the process we have seen from later times—a hybrid group undergoing fission. The name Chongasketon seems to be "nested" in the same manner as bands in chapter 2, with the name sometimes applied to the Cheyenne-speaking subgroup and sometimes used to designate the larger unit. The smaller Cheyenne-speaking group apparently kept the "Chongasketon" name for a while but ended up in the Cheyenne nation as the Sutaio band, while the Dakota-speaking Sissetons remained east of the Missouri. If one maintains the orthodox view that all the groups labeled Chongasketon were always Sissetons, one has to explain why Sissetons and Chongasketons are mentioned separately by Carver, and how the Sissetons came to migrate to the Minnesota River with the Cheyennes, as Carver noted, and then soon marched back to the Upper Mississippi under the name Sisseton.[60]

The "Ouadebatons," who are alleged by many to be the Wahpeton Sioux, are a parallel case to the Chongasketons, except that here the linguistic identification between the names is more compelling. In the Linguistic Appendix I present arguments that the Oudebatons are the same as the Wotapios. The problem lies in how the band names were spelled in French and in English.

According to Mooney's Cheyenne informants, the name Wotapio is a Lakota loanword meaning the "Eaters." But as time went on, I suggest the Lakota version was used by Cheyennes only for the southern subgroup, while the majority of the band were called by the Cheyenne translation, Omisis, "Eaters," or Naomisis, "Northern Eaters." Even today elders of the Wotapio band continue to speak the same dialect as the Northern Cheyennes, although their vocabulary does not exhibit the same differences as between Northern Cheyenne and Southern Cheyenne. But we will return to this "Wotapio problem" in later chapters.[61]

So it is not at all certain, and it is surely not explicit from the early documents, that the Chongasketons are the Sissetons and the Oudebatons are the Wahpetons. One might even wonder, on the basis of common sense, why early travelers would have noted the existence of small Siouan-speaking subgroups, but not large Algonquian groups who spoke a radically different language. There is certainly room in the early nomenclature of the Sioux for the Sissetons and the Wahpetons, without preempting the names Chongasketon and Oudebaton. Many names on the lists and maps of Le Sueur, Franquelin, Raudot, and Delisle have never been linked with known Siouan tribes and many are better candidates than the Chongasketons and Oudebatons, on both geographic and linguistic grounds.[62]

Apparently the alleged Siouan identities of these band names began with some casual and unsubstantiated allegations by various scholars. Rev. T. S. Williamson may have started it all when he said that Hennepin had entered the Sisseton Sioux as "Chongasketons" on his map and journals.[63] But Williamson presented no evidence whatever that this was what Hennepin meant. The authors of the Wahpeton and Sisseton articles in the *Handbook of American Indians* followed Williamson's example and submerged the Chongasketons and Oudebatons into the Sioux, once again without stating any reasons.[64] Later, in 1938, Grace Nute, who wrote an introduction for the edition of Hennepin's journal published by the Minnesota Society of the Colonial Dames of America, identified the Issati as Mdewakantons and the Chongasketons as Sissetons but cited no evidence.[65] From there, such identifications apparently passed on to the influential book of Delanglez, and thence to scores of other scholars. But there is no basis for it in the original maps and documents, and I believe there is more reason to suppose that the Chongasketons and Oudebatons are proto-Cheyenne groups who were later incorporated into the Cheyenne nation.

On linguistic grounds, the Cheyennes appear to be the northernmost of the Central Algonquians, or Great Lakes tribes, rather than the westernmost of the Northern Algonquians. That is, the Cheyenne and Sutaio languages are more like Sac, Fox, and Kickapoo than they are like Cree and Chippewa.[66] The geographic positions of the Cheyennes, Chongasketons, and Oudebatons on all these early maps is consistent with this model of history.

The early maps of the area west of Lake Superior often contain French nicknames applied to the tribes by traders and explorers, in addition to representations of native terms. Some maps have only the native names, some have only the French names, and some have both or a mixture. The most comprehensive list of equivalencies between native terms and French nicknames is supplied by Pierre Charles Le Sueur, written in the corner of Franquelin's 1697 map and reproduced in Wedel's 1974 article. My ultimate purpose here in analyzing these names, and some others, will be to construct a map with as many Cheyenne locations on it as possible, in the hope of reconstructing Cheyenne migrations in a comprehensive manner.

My strategy here will be to consider all early map identifications valid, in the hope of creating a comprehensive picture of Cheyenne locations and movements. That is, if a tribe listed on a map or document is identified as "Cheyenne," "Chongasketon," or "Oudebaton" by any mapmaker at all, I will accept it. The advantage of this procedure is to increase sample size and to remove the personal biases of scholars. The disadvantage, of course, is that I am disregarding perhaps valid objections offered by some scholars, and I might thereby be including some locations dismissed for good reasons. But I believe the advantages of this strategy outweight the disadvantages.

Map 4 represents by the letters C, S, and O the earliest locations of Cheyenne villages I have been able to identify with any certainty. The names plotted and the sources of the maps are listed in table 7. In general, each letter represents some mapmaker's independent attempt to show the location of a Cheyenne group, based on the mapmaker's own informants.

Beginning about 1710, the Cheyennes, Oudebatons, and Chongasketons disappear from the area of the Upper Mississippi. The circles on map 4 represent where they went according to various ethnohistorians.[67] Unfortunately this historical period, 1690–1760, furnishes very little cartographic or documentary information about the movements of nations in the area supposed to be occupied by the Cheyennes. The circles on the map are mainly archeological sites alleged by the Sioux to be fortified villages occupied by Cheyennes. Of historical documents, in addition to the journal of Jonathan Carver, the only one of consequence from this period was written by the Vérendrye brothers in 1743.[68] The Vérendrye account has been problematic for ethnohistorians because it refers to Indian groups only

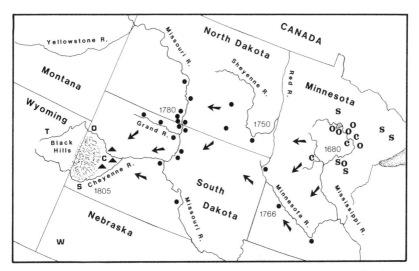

Map 4. Locations of Cheyenne villages, 1680–1805. Sites plotted as black dots are taken from Grinnell 1918; Wood 1971; Bushnell 1922; and Riggs 1893, 194.

by their French nicknames. But with the list of nicknames from Le Sueur, we may be in a position to evaluate the Vérendrye account.

Although the Vérendrye expedition was earlier than Carver's, it was farther west. Beginning at the village of the Mandans in the summer of 1742, the Vérendrye brothers made a long sweeping circle of the northern plains, meeting a variety of Plains tribes. Since there was some continuity of trading contact between the French and the Indians from 1680 to 1742, one might reasonably expect a consistency in the use of the nicknames listed by the Vérendryes. In fact, the purpose of the nicknames was to simplify the confusing mass of different names Plains tribes used for each other. However, when we compare the list of Vérendrye nicknames with Le Sueur's list published by Wedel, we find that none of them are exactly the same. The only Vérendrye nickname that has been alleged to be Cheyenne for any good reason is the "Gens de la Flèche Collée," or "Nation of the Glued Feathers." In a letter to George Grinnell in 1917, George Hyde said that he suspected this name had something to do with the Cheyenne Medicine Arrow ceremony.[69] To Hyde's speculation, we can also add the observations that "striped arrows" is a sign language name for the Cheyennes and that some word relating to arrows was used for the Cheyennes by the Mandans, the primary hosts of the Vérendryes.

In addition to the identification of the "Gens de la Flèche Collée" with the Tsistsistas, one other of the Vérendrye nicknames suggests a Cheyenne band. A nickname recorded forty years earlier for the Oudebatons is "Gens de Rivière." In 1742 one of the groups met by the Vérendryes was called the "Gens de la Belle Rivière." There is nothing in the description of this "Gens" to exclude them as possible Cheyennes, though the evidence is weak. And we shall see in the next chapter that Cheyenne oral history states that the Oudebaton and Tsistsistas bands had both crossed the Missouri toward the Black Hills before the Sutaios, which is consistent with the Vérendrye account. "Gens de la Belle Rivière" may also refer to the main body of Cheyennes, since "Belle Rivière" was a common name for the Cheyenne River.[70]

A better bet for a Cheyenne band is the Vérendryes' "Petits Renards." This is the common name in French both for the kit fox and the swift fox of the American plains, *Vulpes macrotis* and *Vulpes velox*. The Fox Society of the Cheyennes takes its name from this animal (the species are not discriminated in Cheyenne either), which is called *voxces* in Cheyenne. But the Teton Sioux, as we shall see in the next chapter, have maintained a Fox Society, which they say was founded by a Cheyenne. So we cannot be completely sure that the "Petits Renards" are the Fox Men, also known as the Flint Men on the camp diagrams of chapter 2.

An additional map from this period is, like the Vérendrye account, suggestive but problematic. A map of Senex, dated 1721, shows "Many Villages" along the Minnesota where the Cheyennes are supposed to be, according to ethnohistorians.[71] But instead of being labeled Chiens, Chongasketons, Oisas, Choutas, or Dotames, as we might expect, they are divided into two groups called the Eokoros and the Eskanapes. Both these names, as far as I know, are nowhere related to any names for Cheyenne groups, and they are alleged by Fletcher to be the Arikaras.[72]

The triangles on map 4 represent the positions of the Cheyennes in the Black Hills as reported by the French and Anglo explorers of 1785–1810. Since the Cheyennes were farmers in this period, it is worth mentioning that farming was difficult in that area before 1740. According to tree-ring data collected from the area of Cherry Creek, that region was much drier before that date. However, the tree rings are broader afterward, indicating a significant climatic change and the improved possibility of corn farming. Donald Lehmer has noted that villages in that area were "larger and more permanent" after the climatic shift.[73] The single initial letters around the Black Hills represent the positions of Cheyenne bands as described by Lewis and Clark.

The dates on the map represent my best guesses about when the Cheyennes lived at one place or another. For the farming sites between the Missouri and the Mississippi, I have made no attempt to determine which Cheyenne subgroups were responsible for building which villages. From the sizes of the villages, however, it is clear that the whole population could not have lived in one village. Although we will go further into the issue of population in chapter 5, we can develop some rough figures here. Figure 7 (chap. 5) shows four palisaded villages from this area and this period. If we calculate the population of each earthen lodge at about fifteen, then the population of each village was about nine hundred. Estimates of Cheyenne population in this period are about three thousand, which means that the nation probably occupied at least three villages at the same time. This agrees generally with the explorers' and mapmakers' accounts, which identify three groups of Cheyennes in this period.

My research, then, tends to support the theories of Wood, Grinnell, and Holder,[74] who see the Cheyenne bands as moving independently westward, although probably remaining contiguous to one another. And indeed, if one looks at the circles on the map, they look like stepping stones westward for the Cheyenne nation. In my research for this chapter, however, I have gone beyond previous researchers and actually found Cheyenne map locations for the earlier historical period, 1680–1730. I have pointed out how the social and political units of a later time correspond with map names.

Also, I contend that the Cheyennes before 1740 were not yet a nation but were merely a group of allied villages speaking similar languages.

My most general purpose in this chapter has been to criticize the orthodox taxonomy of band and tribal names from protohistoric times, which has been devised by assigning each antique name from a map or document to a specific tribal nation known from later times. I argue that this practice assumes, erroneously, that the composition and identity of nations have been unchanged from these times, an assumption we know to be incorrect for the Cheyenne example, from the data of chapter 2. Far from being frozen in time, these bands and nations were undergoing constant transformation by which they created and broke alliances and formed patterns of trade and intermarriage with other bands and tribes across ethnic and linguistic boundaries. Although in subsequent chapters I will cite other examples and specifically illustrate how these processes work, for the present I only hope I have shaken readers' confidence in the orthodox interpretation so that there is room for other ideas. This will allow me, in the next chapter, to show that Cheyenne oral tradition is within the range of possibility—to suggest that a different, more dynamic theory, emphasizing *process,* might be more appropriate overall.

Figure 4 is a schematic model of events among the proto-Cheyenne bands as I reconstruct their history in the eighteenth century. The pattern I am proposing, of alliance and intermarriage among bands, is a familiar one from later times, as we saw in chapter 2 and will see again in chapter 7. I argue that in this protohistoric period the effect of intermarriage among bands of different language was the creation of hybrid groups, which were ambiguous in their ethnicity and might ultimately join politically with either parent group. Further, I argue that it was the benefits to be derived from membership in the Cheyenne nation that ultimately drew three of these hybrid bands, the Wotapios (Eaters), the Masikotas (Sheos), and the Sutaios (Chongasketons), away from their Sioux allies and toward the Black Hills where the Cheyenne nation was founded.

In chapter 2 we learned that Mooney's informants at the turn of the century had asserted there were four "original bands" of the Cheyennes. In the same chapter, we corroborated that assertion statistically by an analysis of the various tribal circles collected from twelve informants. In this chapter we have learned the histories of these four original bands—the Arrow People or Cheyennes proper, the Omisis or Eaters, the Masikotas or Fox People, and the Sutaios, or adopted people. The origins of the other most important parent band, the Hevhaitaneos or Hair Rope People, we have not yet seen, since that happened early in the nineteenth century, after the events recounted above. But we have now accounted for all four of the bands

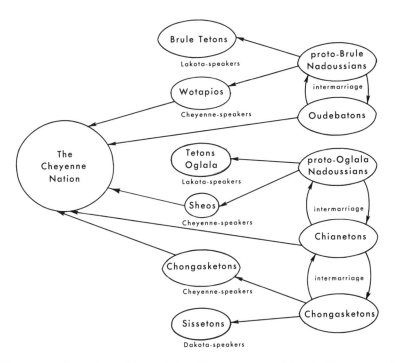

Figure 4. Schematic model of relationships among protohistoric Cheyenne and Sioux bands.

that are said to be very ancient and important. In the next chapter we will see how Cheyenne oral history supports the idea of separate origins for the ancient bands, and in subsequent chapters we will see how and why bands are formed, how they live, and how they interact and hybridize with other bands, even across ethnic and linguistic boundaries.

4

Oral History

In the oral tradition of the Cheyennes their history appears twice—once as sacred story and again as secular history. The sacred stories are full of abstract symbolism, moral lessons, and high purpose. As told by Cheyenne elders, these stories are similar to the statements any political or religious leaders might make about the founding of their nation. By contrast, the narratives of secular history, sometimes collected from the same elders, tend to contain just the bare facts—names, places, and times. In this chapter we will examine both these kinds of oral narrative to create an integrated view of Cheyenne history from their own perspective. First, to establish an overall framework of history, we will look at the sacred stories. As we proceed through them, I will add data from our second source, secular history, and from some other sources as well. My purpose will be to create a new historical synthesis, covering the period from earliest times to the Lewis and Clark journals—the same period covered in the previous chapter, but this time from a native perspective. In particular, we will be looking for the origins of the four bands James Mooney's informants said were "original."

When stories of religious importance are told by Cheyenne elders, they are accompanied by prayers and rituals and told only at night. They are also said to be "tied together"—that is, each discrete episode is preceded by a particular episode and followed by another. Creation stories, of course, have no preceding episode, and episodes of prophecy have no following episode. Taken all together, the Cheyenne sacred episodes constitute a lengthy cycle, comparable to the Gilgamesh Epic or the legend of King Arthur, which might require many hours of narration—more than one narrator can manage in one evening. For this reason, Cheyenne storytellers like to perform in groups, taking turns with the different episodes. Because of the length of the stories, the full cycle has never been collected all at once.

Perhaps the nearest to the whole cycle was collected by George Dorsey over four days in 1901 from Bushyhead and DeForest Antelope.[1] Apparently conditions were ideal for ethnography. Dorsey, like James Mooney who accompanied him, was involved in protecting the Cheyenne ceremonies from the missionaries and also from the army, which had threatened to disperse the participants. Both Mooney and Dorsey, then, were demonstrably friends of the Cheyennes and had the confidence of the priests, as attested by the photographs and field notes they collected. Also, some of the priests were worried that they might die before they communicated their knowledge to others.[2] Therefore in 1901–3 they were motivated, willing, and qualified to provide the full cycle of stories, published by Dorsey in 1905.

Most efforts at collecting Cheyenne oral traditions, however, have been much less successful. Frequently ethnographers were given hurried, abbreviated, or garbled versions of the sacred traditions. The general appearance of these fragments of sacred stories, which compose most of the published texts, indicates the same kind of hurried and awkward situation I have frequently seen in my own fieldwork. Although I have made no attempt to collect such stories, out of respect for Cheyenne privacy, they were often volunteered to me.

When the stories are told properly, it must be in a serious manner with accompanying prayers and ritual. For example, when Lt. Heber Creel's informant told him the Sweet Medicine story in 1881, he "made signs similar to Romish sign of the cross, which had to be imitated by his auditor."[3] If the sacred stories are told without ritual, then one is only *talking about* the stories, not telling them. When one talks about the stories, the episodes can be given informally in any order, and entire episodes can be skipped or transposed. Also, a person who *talks about* the stories need not be a qualified storyteller. He or she could be any Cheyenne who mentions something about the stories to an ethnographer.

Unfortunately, however, those who have published Cheyenne stories have most often not known the status of their storytellers or of the stories they collected, nor have they always communicated to readers the circumstances of collection. But if the Cheyenne stories were told then as they are now, and we have no reason to say they were not, we can judge as more accurate the full versions of the stories, collected under ritual conditions from qualified priests. Of the published versions of sacred stories, Dorsey's clearly fit these criteria the best, as do Grinnell's texts.[4] Of the rest, we can only say generally that the longer texts are the more reliable.

Unreliability in the texts is introduced when an informant tampers with the order of the episodes or transposes a major character from one story to another. In my own fieldwork, the order of episodes has often been juggled because of interruptions, or lack of time, or too much time. For example, a qualified storyteller in 1982 was hurrying an episode of the sacred stories he was telling me because he wanted to catch a ride with a relative. After another relative showed up and said the car had broken down, the informant went back and "tied" previous episodes of the cycle to the one already narrated, as if they happened afterward rather than before. Several of the published narratives and handwritten field notes of ethnographers show this same pattern of juggling, often with interposed awkward passages as the storyteller tried to create a smooth transition for episodes told out of their regular sequence.

The transposition of characters, another source of confusion, is caused more by political intent than by circumstances of time. An informant who is a council chief, a Sun Dance priest, or the headsman of a military society can succumb to the temptation to make his organization's role seem of the highest importance in the history of his nation. The greatest opportunity for this kind of variability is provided in stating the order in which Sweet Medicine created the soldier societies and the Chiefs' Society. Invariably, an informant will give his own society as having been founded first unless members of other societies are present at the narration. Several published narrative texts also exhibit this variability. A modern Bowstring headsman told me that the Bowstrings were created first, while a Dog Soldier says the Bowstrings were not created by Sweet Medicine at all but were formed much later from among "the survivors of a massacre."

Also, some informants will inject the names of particular culture heroes, such as Sweet Medicine or Erect Horns, back into the roles of usually nameless heroes, such as characterize the very early creation stories. In the story of the two young men, for example, to be discussed later, one informant told me the two young men were in fact Sweet Medicine and Erect Horns, the respective culture heroes of the Tsistsistas and Sutaios. Most versions of this story, however, have anonymous heroes, or else the heroes have names that reflect their roles in the story.

If I had not already criticized the documentary sources in the previous chapter, the Cheyenne sacred stories would seem fragmented and contradictory. In fact, the classic ethnographers of the Cheyennes were apparently dissuaded from interpreting or commenting on the stories by these very difficulties. Most often the sacred narratives were presented "as is," implying perhaps that they were so "mysterious" that no interpretation could be attempted. Compounding these problems, some published versions are not even attributed to any informant and carry no information about where they were collected or when. Seldom if ever are we told whether the stories were told formally or informally or what the social relationship was between the informant and the ethnographer.

Truman Michelson (plate 3) was an ethnologist for the Bureau of American Ethnology who began work among the Cheyennes in 1910, just after Mooney and Dorsey but who was contemporary with Grinnell and Hyde.[5] By 1910 Michelson was aware of the problems of tribal structure outlined by Mooney in 1907, so he was usually careful to record not only the names of his informants, but also their band affiliations and those of their parents and spouses.[6]

Michelson's initial experience with the Cheyennes in 1910 was brief, and he soon turned to his major interest, the Central Algonquians, especially the Foxes and Kickapoos, but he returned for another stint of fieldwork

Plate 3.   Truman Michelson, ethnologist for the Bureau of American Ethnology. Portrait 52-B, National Anthropological Archives, Smithsonian Institution.

among the Cheyennes in 1929–32. Only one of the oral narratives he collected was ever published, in part because Michelson died only a few years after completing his later fieldwork.[7]

One amazing fact about Michelson's texts is that three of them are asserted to be the origin stories of particular bands rather than of the whole tribe. Not surprisingly, in view of the previous chapter, these stories are for the Aortas (Heviksnipahis, Tsistsistas, or Cheyennes proper), the Eaters (Wotapios or Omisis), and the Sutaios (Chongasketons or Dog People), the same three groups noted separately on early maps and documents. Following, then, are the three unpublished versions of these stories collected by Michelson. I have selected Michelson's versions both because they are attributed to particular informants and because the stories deserve to be published somewhere and made accessible.

After relating the first two of the three origin stories, for the Aorta and Eater bands, I will then examine the story of the two young men, which represents the merging of these two bands before the coming of the Sutaio. Next I will relate the colorful Sutaio origin story, called "The Story of Lime," and then I will add some elements of secular history from Michelson's informants. After an analysis of the story of Sweet Medicine or Mutsiev, the bringer of the sacred arrows, I will add some comments about Siouan origins for certain Cheyenne bands and then attempt a new synthesis of Cheyenne ethnohistory—one that emphasizes oral traditions but remains true to the documentary sources of chapter 3. By the end of this chapter we will have identified all the "original" Cheyenne bands that were important to Mooney's informants, including the Masikotas.

White Bull, who gave the Aorta origin story to Michelson, was apparently not the medicine man of the same name, also known as Ice. Michelson's White Bull is identified only as a Northern Cheyenne, which tells us nothing conclusive about his band identity. Michelson's informants in Montana included members of several southern bands, in addition to members of the Omisis and Sutaio bands, who were the most numerous on the Tongue River reservation in 1910. Unfortunately White Bull was one of the first informants interviewed by Michelson, and the ethnographer was not as careful in recording biographical information as he was later. In any event, here follows White Bull's origin story, which I will end at the incident concerning the founding of the Aorta people. I use the handwritten version of the story here because Michelson's typed version incorporated some additional transcription errors.[8]

AORTA ORIGIN STORY

The Great Spirit created man in the daytime and woman in the nighttime. When they were created, they met each other. The man said, "Do you know

anything about how we were created? If you don't, I think I know about it."
The woman replied that she knew how humans could be reproduced. She
asked the man if he knew anything about that. At that time they both could
hardly understand what they were trying to talk about.

The woman thought the only way that humans could be reproduced was
from her breasts. The man did not realize what his penis was for. He thought
that he could reproduce by using his forehead. He began butting his head
toward her. But then the woman said, "I've got my vagina here and you have
your penis there." And then the man knew she was right.

Then the woman said, "Sometimes when I urinate, I make blood. It is
from there that humans can be created. That's the source of people." And the
man said, "Yes!" Then he told her he was the sun because he was created in
the day, and that's where his seeds come from. "And you," he said, "you were
created at night; you belong to the moon. I'm going to drop my seed into
you, and your vagina will be the source of my blood coming into the world."
He told her, "Look at my fingers; I have 10 fingers. By the end of ten new
moons, my seed will appear." And the man said, "When the child is born,
he'll be raised like I am."

After he said that, he told the woman that towards the north there was
always snow. "Once in twelve months that snow will come over our heads.
The Great Spirit created it for that purpose. And from the south, thunder
and lightning will bring the summer, which will bring happiness to our
dwellings. Then the woman said to him, "An animal will come from the
north under the leadership of a white bull. When these buffaloes appear,
what can you do to kill them?" The man said, "I will get some hard rocks and
crack them, and make sharp rocks for arrowheads to kill with." When the
man got the idea how to kill, he went out to cut bows and arrows.

When he got the bows and arrows, he had another idea as to what would
be best to put on these arrows. He went out; he saw all kinds of birds flying in
all directions coming to where he was. He thought. He asked one of the birds
if the bird had any objection to his using his wings. And the crow flew about
where he was and told him he did not object to having his wings put on the
arrows, so that the birds might feast with him whenever he shot the buffaloes
on the prairie. He was now all prepared to go out to kill.

"How can we dress the buffalo after he is killed?" the woman asked. He
said to her, "You go out; get a very large rock." She brought the rock to him.
He cracked two rocks together. He broke them in two. A great big arrowhead like a knife appeared there. He went out, made a kill, and used this
arrowhead for a knife. The woman said, "How can we cook? We have no way
to make fire." The man said, "You go out and get a white buffalo chip, and
bring it to me. I will start a fire." He had a hard stick about as long as his
forearm and a flat rock. He ground the buffalo chip fine and put it on the

rock. He placed the stick in the buffalo chip and rolled it between his hands for a long time. By and by the chip started burning. (That is the way we got fire.) He cut the rib out and placed it on a pole over the fire. He got a hard flat rock. He put sticks on top of the rock. (That's the way they used to cook.) That is the beginning of the workings of the mind.

At this time they were naked. The man went out and killed a bear. He cut off the front legs half way up and skinned it off to the bone. He rubbed this bone against the rock to make it flat on both sides. They stretched the buffalo hide out flat. And the woman scraped the hide with that bone and dried the hide in the sun. The man at the same time got sinew out of the buffalo and made bow strings out of them. (That is the beginning of easy times.) He also killed an elk. He cut off one horn to make a scraper. They put a sharp stone against this scraper. So the scraper was completed. After it was scraped thin, she put on brain with liver and rubbed them in. Then she left it outside to dry. She went out to draw water with a jug. She sprinkled the hide with water. The man said: "You go and dig out that soup-root (a high sticky brush on the hills)." She dug it out and chipped it fine, mixed it with water and rubbed it in the buffalo hide. She tied the hide to a tree and scraped it off with a stone knife. The man got a great hip bone and cut off the large end. He saw a lot of small holes. He began to scrape the hide with it: it dried the hide.

They tied one end to the top of a tree with sinew and another end to the bottom and placed the loose part against the tree. The woman began to work the hide against the sinew string. The hide was completed. "We can live this way," the man said. They cut out the shoulder blades of the buffalo and made arrowheads by cutting the bone with the stone knife. At that time everything came to be used that had never been used before. They used buffalo horns for dippers; and wooden buckets (cut off stumps of trees) began to appear. "That's the hardest part; now I can kill small animals, bears, antelopes, and deer so we can use them for clothes. We can scrape them the same way." And then they began to dress themselves with the skins of all kinds of small animals.

Then the woman said, "We have so many things. When we move how can we carry our things?" "Yes," he said, "I am going out and see if I can get some animals to live with us to carry our things." So he went out and looked about the country for animals. He looked around where he stood. He saw two very shaggy animals galloping towards him and another one besides. They came to where he was. These were animals of two kinds. He did not know that they were dogs. One of the smaller ones was very active and shy, the other two were very kind and gentle. That was the beginning of using dogs for carrying things on their backs. And the man said to the woman, "This will be our way of living, travelling around with those dogs everywhere we go."

They already had two children. The oldest was a boy; he was beginning to walk; the other, a girl, was beginning to crawl. They were going to make their first move. They put the little girl on a dog-travois. From the time they were created they had no combs. The woman said to her husband, "How can we comb our hair?" He said, "I'm going out to get something." So he went out and killed a porcupine, and he cut off his tail and brought it to her. He skinned the tail. He put a stick in the hollow skin. They used it to comb their hair.

The woman said, "We are very unclean; we must dress our faces some way. What can we do?" The man said, "You go out and think what you can get, and I will go out to think what we could dress our faces with." So they both went out. When the woman was out she saw a star falling and went to where it fell. She looked there and found a circle of mud. It was a very bright red color. She thought it would be just the thing for them. And the man saw the beauties of the earth where he looked about. He found paint and went back home with it. There they both brought what they wanted. This is the origin of the first time people painted.

His wife went with him to kill buffaloes. He killed a buffalo. They both had robes. The man was still naked. The woman had the skin of a deer hanging from her waist. The woman said, "You must leave the robe away from you where you are dressing the buffalo." He said, "Wait a little while; I have got a gee-string inside the buffalo's stomach." So he dressed the buffalo. As soon as he opened the buffalo he took out the entrails and found a piece joined to the spleen. He took it for a gee-string. On each side they cut the hump of the buffalo. They cut the cord out and used it to go around the man's waist as a gee-string with the other. Then he put his robe away, and dressed the beef. After this was done the man thought he would smoke. He cut a piece of the buffalo's aorta and dried it hard like a rock. Then the woman said to him, "What are you going to smoke in that pipe?" He said, "I know, there's a weed that grows on sand hills which I am going to get, and mix it with Cree tobacco." That shows the Indians were the first people to introduce tobacco. After he used the aorta pipe he used one of deer bone. The aorta pipe is the origin of the Aorta clan. Up to this time there was but one family.

The second origin story we will consider, the "Sacred Leader of the Eaters," was obtained by Michelson from Wolf Chief, who identified himself as an Eater, like his mother, father, and wife (plate 4). He gave his birth year as 1851, the year the Fort Laramie treaty was signed. This story is very brief compared with the Aorta story. Like the story of Aorta origins, it has anonymous heroes, implying that it happened long ago.[9]

SACRED LEADER OF THE EATERS
A great many years ago this story was told by the very old great-grandfathers that lived on the east of the Mississippi. There was a man who came from the

Plate 4.   Wolf Chief, informant for Truman Michelson. Negative no. 307-A by De Lancey Gill, 1908, National Anthropological Archives, Smithsonian Institution.

forests to this band. It was not known where he came from; later he wandered away from the tribe. About 40 years afterwards there was another boy who came to the same clan. He also did not know where he came from. The people thought he was trying to be a medicine man. They told him, "You're too young to be holy. This clan has got its own holy man." Like the other man, this one disappeared from this clan.

About 40 years after this second one, another came, but he was too small to teach the people about the miracles that should hereafter come to pass. The people said, "You are too small and you will not live long enough to teach these people. You will have to go on." And he disappeared from the tribe, like the other two. About 40 years after this third, there appeared a young man of age 30, with a wife of the same age. He came to this clan. The people were glad to see them both, asking them where they came from. The young man told them that they had come from the big forest east of the Mississippi, that they once were wild beasts from that forest, and had come to the clan to tell what they knew for the good of the people.

In addition to this brief story about Eater origins, there is other evidence of the antiquity and uniqueness of the band. Another of Michelson's informants told him that the Eaters, unlike more recent bands, originally had a special rainbow tipi with an eagle-feather shield.[10] The drawing in Michelson's notes shows a tipi with a shield hung in the same position as is Nimoyah, the "turner" associated with Northern Cheyenne religion practice. It may be that the rainbow tipi represents the original tribal symbolism of the Eaters, before they joined with the Aortas to become the Cheyennes. It would not be surprising to discover that part of this symbolism, the turner, was later incorporated into the sacred hat ceremonies, when the hat became the focus of Northern Cheyenne ceremonial attention after they came to live permanently in Montana in 1884.[11] According to Mrs. Vinnie Hoffman, a Cheyenne elder from Hammon, Oklahoma, a former nickname for the Wotapio band was "Rainbow People," Nononetan.

It is also significant to note that the Cheyennes have incorporated rainbow symbolism into their Sun Dance altar, making it different from the "Sun Dances" of surrounding nations. I believe this implies that the symbol came from a preexisting Cheyenne tradition rather than being borrowed with other aspects of the ceremony. The Sun Dance itself, of course, is an invention of the Plains Indians, having its origin no earlier than about 1650, when the various pedestrian peoples surrounding the Plains began to acquire horses and congregate along Plains rivers.

Another singular aspect of Cheyenne ceremonial life is the chiefs' medicine bundle, now kept in the sacred arrow tipi in Oklahoma. Although there are several versions of the origins of the bundle, there is essential agreement that the idea for having chiefs, for holding a chiefs' election ritual, and for maintaining a chiefs' bundle came from a captive woman born in another tribe.[12] Only a few versions of the sacred stories say that Sweet Medicine brought the chiefs' bundle or organized the Chiefs' Society. I mention the chiefs' bundle here only because it may represent a unique and aboriginal symbol of the Aorta grouping, like the rainbow tipi of the Eaters, perhaps dating from before the founding of the Cheyenne nation.

Further evidence for the separate origins of these two Cheyenne bands— Eaters and Aortas—comes from American Horse, born in 1847, as he related some comments on "secular history" to Michelson in 1910. Twice he said that there were two original groups of Cheyennes, not including the

Sutaios.[13] Some versions of the sacred stories also mention that there was originally more than one band of Cheyennes. And we should remember, from the previous chapter, that the words "band" and "tribe" are the same in Cheyenne. In a version of the sacred stories published by Grinnell,[14] Sweet Medicine speaks to the assembled people as follows: "I have traveled far over the prairie. I have seen other Cheyenne camps, and some camps of the Arapaho. They are scattered far and wide."

Linguistic evidence also supports the idea that the Eaters and the Aortas were originally separate tribes. Their dialects are too different to have diverged only in the past hundred years. For example, they have different sets of words for horse and dog, implying that they constituted separate language communities at the time when they first acquired horses, or heard about them. The Northern Cheyenne word for horse is *moehenoha,* "tame elk," while the Southern Cheyenne word is *nathoze,* meaning "my dog" and implying "my servant." The words for horse gear, however—bridle, saddle, halter—are the same in both dialects.

In any event, if we have evidence for the separate origins of these two tribal subgroups, as we do, then we should also expect to find a story in Cheyenne tradition that accounts for their joining into one group. Such a story should both reconcile their cultural differences and express their new and desirable relationships to one another. One episode of the sacred cycle that accomplishes both these tasks nicely is called "The Two Young Men." I believe this story symbolizes the formation of the Cheyenne nation from two preexisting subgroups, the Aortas and the Eaters.

In his preface to several long versions of this sacred story, George Grinnell interpreted it as expressing the meeting of the Cheyennes with the Sutaios. There are at least three reasons, however, why we must reject this idea. First of all, there are several other stories that express the coming of the Sutaios, and they say it was *after* Sweet Medicine. The meeting of the two young men, however, is said to be *before* Sweet Medicine.

Second, Grinnell apparently never heard the stories of the separate origins of the Aortas and the Eaters, nor did he ever figure out the maps and documents presented in the previous chapter. Therefore he had no reason to suspect there were more than two component bands for the founding of the Cheyenne nation. Third, most of the versions of "The Two Young Men" mention personal names for the heroes that have nothing to do with Sweet Medicine, the Cheyenne cultural hero, or with Erect Horns, the Sutaio hero.

The names of the heroes in the story, however—and I do not want to anticipate the next chapter too strongly—do suggest a situation that was very common among Plains tribes in that period: symbiosis between a hunting group and a farming group. The usual name of one hero is Corn Leaf or Tassel, while the other is usually named Red-Red-Red-Red. In Cheyenne the word for red and for blood are the same—*mae*—so the second hero's name might equally well be represented as Blood-Blood-Blood-Blood. That is, in most versions of the story the name of one hero suggests horticulture and the name of the other might suggest carnage or butchering.

Situations of symbiosis between farmers and hunters are prominent in Tabeau's account of Loisel's expedition up the Missouri about 1800.[15] Concerning the relations between the Lakotas and the Arikaras, he says: "the Sioux came from all parts loaded with dried meat, with fat, with dressed leather, and some merchandise. They fix, as they wish, the price of that which belongs to them and obtain, in exchange, a quantity of corn, tobacco, beans, and pumpkins that they demand."

Two Cheyenne bands are explicitly reported as being in this symbiotic situation in the same historical period—as nomadic hunters for a group of sedentary farmers. One of these is the "Ree band," so named because of their affiliation with the Arikaras, or Rees. This band later settled on Rosebud Creek in Montana after 1884. Their relations with the Rees are expressed in a story called "Half Sutaio, Half Ree" collected by Michelson.[16] The other band is unnamed but is mentioned in George Grinnell's manuscript 142 from the Southwest Museum in Los Angeles. According to two of Grinnell's informants, Standing All Night and Doll Man, one band of Cheyennes "dwelt permanently with the Mandans." Ben Clark also commented on the extent of intermarriage with Mandans and Rees in his manuscript dated about 1880.[17] So the ethnographic evidence supports the general idea that some Cheyennes were nomadic hunters while others were sedentary horticulturists—simultaneously.

It is my thesis that the story of the two young men in fact represents the amalgamation of a predominantly farming group, the Aortas, with a predominantly hunting group, the Eaters. Before discussing this idea further, however, we should look at one version of the story, collected by A. L. Kroeber in 1899.[18] The version is blessedly brief—apparently Kroeber's informant was tired, suspicious, or in a hurry—but it contains the essence of the story.

THE TWO YOUNG MEN

There was a large camp near a spring called old-woman's spring. The people were amusing themselves by games, and were playing the "buffalo-game" with rolling hoops. Two young men were standing by, watching. They were painted alike and dressed alike, and wore the same headdresses, and both wore buffalo-robes. Finally one of them told the people to call every one, and that all should watch him; that he would go into the spring, and bring back food that would be a great help to the people ever after. The other young man also said that he would bring them food. There was an entrance to the spring, formed by a great stone, and by this the two young men descended into the spring, both going at the same time. They found an old gray-headed woman sitting, and she showed them on one side fields of corn and on the other herds of buffalo. Then one of the young men brought back corn, and the other buffalo meat, and the people feasted on both. And that night the buffalo came out of the spring; and there have been herds of them ever since, and corn has been grown too.

Some other details of the story can be added from other versions.[19] Most important, when the young men appear, the one named Corn Leaf comes from the right end of the camp circle, the position of the Heviksnipahis, while the one named Red-Red-Red-Red comes from the other end of the circle, the position of the Omisis or Eaters. As we might expect, Corn Leaf is the hero who brings the corn, while Red-Red-Red-Red brings the buffalo meat. Concerning the association between the Omisis and buffalo meat, we should note that both Mooney's and Grinnell's informants gave as their explanation of the name "Omisis" the fact that the "Eaters" got their name from eating buffalo meat. No informant said they got their name from eating corn.

If we accept the idea that there was symbiosis between the Omisis and Aorta groups, new light is shed on the locations of the bands according to Lewis and Clark.[20] Looking back at map 1, one way of interpreting the band locations is that the Cheyennes proper or Aorta People were situated in the home camp, in the agricultural area east of the Black Hills, while the Omisis or Eater groups were in satellite hunting camps.

We can further hypothesize that the group known as Wotapio is at this point equivalent to the other Eater groups, like them living in a satellite hunting camp, in symbiosis with the Cheyennes on the Cheyenne River. Because of their more southerly location, however, the Wotapios were closest to the horse-rich areas of the central and southern plains. As the horse trade became important, then, they were swept into the center of it, along with some other subgroups of the Cheyennes proper. The sedentary Cheyennes, we should note, were themselves closer to the trade routes than were the other Eater bands. Ultimately, the Wotapios were considered part of the southern or Hevhaitaneo grouping, despite their Eater origins, and settled in early reservation times in what was called "West Camp," near Hammon, Oklahoma. As late as 1907 the Wotapio band petitioned the government for transfer to Montana, "so as to be with their relatives, the Northern Cheyennes."[21]

Linguistic evidence supports these ideas about Wotapio origins. Having entered the world of horsemanship alongside bands from the Cheyennes proper (Aortas or Heviksnipahis), the Wotapios' vocabulary evolved in the same manner as those of the other southerners, though spoken with a northern accent.[22] This situation has persisted until the present, according to modern informants. So, despite the fact that the Wotapios became a subgroup to the Southern Cheyennes, or Hevhaitaneos, their parent group was the Eaters, not the "Cheyennes" on the Lewis and Clark map. This separation of the Wotapios from the other Eater bands also explains why the informants quoted in chapter 2 were often undecided about whether the "Eaters" belonged in the Omisis position or as Wotapios among the Hair Rope People.

Even though the story of the two young men represents the alliance between two originally distinct groups—Aortas and Eaters—it does not do so in a very forceful manner. In some versions of the story the young men are merely and totally symbolic, having no names, no families, and no personal history before or after they formed the tribal circle. As a national charter, the story is somewhat lacking in the drama and force exhibited, for example, in the Old Testament or in Nordic, Greek, and Roman "charter myths." The same cannot be said, however, for the story of Sweet Medicine. For in this story "the marvelous boy" is killed, brought to life, and transformed into animals before he at last brings to the Cheyennes their greatest possession, the sacred arrows. Modern storytellers regard the Sweet Medicine saga as the political charter for their nation, while the story of the two young men is related as an episode of early, although sacred, history. I interpret this to mean that when the prophet Sweet Medicine came among the Cheyennes, the Eater and Aorta groups were already together but not organized into the formidable political force they became after Sweet Medicine brought the sacred arrows.

Published versions of the Sweet Medicine saga emphasize his experiences inside Nowahwas or Bear Butte in South Dakota and his presentation of four sacred arrows to the Cheyennes—two arrows to kill enemies and two to kill buffaloes. More than any other institution, the arrows represent the identity of the Cheyenne nation. First, the arrows require a ceremonial renewal when any Cheyenne dies at the hands of another Cheyenne. The performance of this ceremony, then, imposes a tremendous responsibility on the community of priests and on the relatives of the transgressor. The necessity for this ceremony emphasizes the seriousness of murder within the nation. Second, the arrows also represent the "ultimate weapon" of the nation in making war. Important attacks on enemy nations required the "moving of the arrows" against the enemy, which in turn required the presence of all bands and therefore of all citizens. As active symbols, then, the arrows defined citizenship both by mandating a ceremony at the murder of the Cheyenne and by requiring the presence of all member bands for full-scale warfare.

Although the acquisition of the sacred arrows is perhaps the most important episode of the Sweet Medicine story, here I will present two unpublished versions of the story that emphasize other episodes. I do this because Grinnell, Llewellyn, and Hoebel have already established the importance and function of the arrows, while the two versions below emphasize aspects of Sweet Medicine's character that are previously unreported. The first version tells about his transformation into birds and animals; the second emphasizes the several miracles he performed.

White Bull emphasized the miraculous powers of Sweet Medicine in the version he gave Michelson in 1910.

SWEET MEDICINE, FIRST VERSION

Mutsiev was found when all the men had gone on a buffalo hunt. He was with the young men. He killed a bull calf 2 years old. He dressed the buffalo, skinned the hide so he could have it for his robe. An old man came to him and asked him "I will have that buffalo for my robe." "No, I'm going to make use of it. I shall use it so that the people will know hereafter what is going to happen. I'm going to use it for a great miracle." But still this old man asked for it 4 times. Each time Mutsiev insisted that he could not have it. He cut off the hoof of the buffalo. When the old man reached for the skin, Mutsiev hit him on top of the head. He took the hide home.

The old man was missed. Everybody seemed to know Mutsiev had killed the old man. The old man's body was found. All the War Societies went to kill him. Every time they tried to catch him he disappeared. He turned into a coyote, a fly: nobody could catch him. The first time they tried to catch him they surrounded the lodge. A coyote ran out. Then the warriors went to a high bluff; they saw Mutsiev at the edge of the bluff. They began to surround him. As soon as they were close to him he turned into a deer and got away. Then he was seen again. They surrounded the place again. When they were nearly on the point of killing him he turned into an owl and flew away. The next time he turned into a blue-bird. Then they gave up.

Once again Mutsiev was seen, this time coming up a hill. He was carrying a cane in his arm. He was walking backward and forward. All the people looked to see him. He had a cane with feathers on it. The second time he appeared he had a bow and arrow with feathers at the ends of the bow and arrows, which had stone heads. There were 4 arrows. The third time he appeared he had a stick like a bow but curved at one end, signifying protection for the warriors called contaries. The fourth time he had a bow and arrow for the Foxes; the fifth time he had the skin of a buffalo head with horns on, and a shield. All the people looked on with surprise. They expected some great event was going to happen. This last was for the Bowstring Society. The sixth time he had feathers stuck into his head in all directions and he had a rattle; he was painted black all over. That signified the Dog Society. The seventh time he came back with a pipe. This was for the chiefs. He wanted to make peace. Then he disappeared for 4 years.[23]

A second unpublished version of the Sweet Medicine story is from Old She Bear, a man born in 1842 and interviewed in 1910 by Michelson.

SWEET MEDICINE, SECOND VERSION
At first, Indians were poor, and had nothing to eat. Food was scarce. A woman threw her baby in the river where there were logs, twigs and bushes. One old woman, who was so old that she had to use a cane, went to gather wood. She pulled the twigs out one by one and found the baby, all wrapped up (interrupted by prayer). The woman picked up the baby and fixed him up good. She wanted to have him for her benefit, so he could support her. Every day the baby grew. In ten days it could walk and it helped the old woman. That boy took care of her two horses. Every morning he would go after them. The Indians asked the old woman where she got that boy.

The boy told the old woman that he would take pity on the people. The people did not know where that boy came from. An old man asked everybody "Where does that boy come from?" They still did not know. The woman who threw her baby away did not show up. They were going to move camp. The old woman told the boy "Go after those two horses over there." Some black birds were sitting on the horses' backs. The boy told the old woman to make 4 arrows so he could shoot the black birds. He went toward the horses. She was watching him. Everybody was busy packing up camp. When she looked up he had disappeared. The two horses were hobbled. They came back by themselves to the old woman. At the foot of the hill there was a big flat rock. They went over where the boy was last seen. They found his tracks. They could not find him. He must have gone inside the hill. There was a stone in front of an opening. Nobody could lift that stone. The boy had gone in. The hill was a tipi inside. He saw a man and woman sitting down. They put him in the back of the lodge, as an honored guest. The man and woman gave him instructions what he should do when he got out in the world so he could help the people. As he listened, they told him how people were going to live in the future and how he had been thrown away; that they would have buffalo again and have a good hunting ground. They gave him this name "Mutsiev" and told him that he should tell all the people that was his name, so that all nations would know it. They gave him a buffalo robe with horns and hoofs on. It was painted red. And they told him to go out into the world to go back to his home, to help all the Indians.

After he got out, a big herd of buffalo was sent out too. "You will find the Arapahoes first, next the Sioux, next the Pawnees, and fourth you shall find your own people—the Cheyennes. And your name shall go over all the nations." He started off on his journey. He went over the hill, and down, toward some smoke. He looked down and saw tipis in a circle. He had been told not to stop at any of these places but to keep on his journey. He passed some hills. He looked down and saw a river. Everything looked blue. He saw the Sioux camped in a circle. He saw no one playing hoops. So he knew they were Sioux. Next he saw camps everywhere down the river. He thought they were not his people. He kept on journeying. He sat down, smoked, dressed up, painted. He had his robe turned inside out.

He saw two boys hunting birds. They were using arrows, shooting. The people saw him way off. They thought he was a buffalo. They wondered what it was. The Indians were nearly starved. Everybody was poor. The boys were coming close. They were naked, poor, dirty and skinny. Pretty soon Mutsiev spoke up and told the boys to come to him. The boys were afraid of him because he had the buffalo robe on. He told them not to be afraid. The boys came on each pushing each other forward. He told them to come have a feast. He told them his name.[24]

In the rest of this version Mutsiev brings food to the Cheyennes, organizes their political structure, and shows them the sacred arrows. He also organizes the ceremonies, including the Sun Dance.

Considering these two versions alongside those already published, a complete picture of Sweet Medicine emerges. All in all, we can see that he brought the Cheyennes every gift that was important to them in their years on the Plains. The arrows allowed the Cheyennes to kill buffaloes and to defeat their enemies. The Sun Dance and the Arrow Ceremony provided an expression of solidarity for the new nation. In some versions, Sweet Medicine also brings healing medicines, horses, and the idea for a tribal circle. But the most important gift Sweet Medicine brought, and the one most often emphasized in the stories, was the military societies.

On the face of it, it might seem strange that Sweet Medicine, instead of calling together the various *manhao* (tribes or bands) to form the nation, should call together the military societies. But in fact, the focal point of the Sweet Medicine saga is when he appears to the people in the costumes of the five major military societies. These are regarded as his "instructions" to the societies on how to dress and how to organize themselves.

To understand why it was societies and not bands that were called together, we have to understand something about the nature of these two types of organizations in Cheyenne society. First of all, a band could scarcely be called an "organization," since it had no formal structure but was merely a group of related people who traveled together for most of the year. Although the bands had "chiefs" present, these chiefs were not representatives of the band to the Council of Chiefs but were elected because of ancestry and character. A single band could have any number of chiefs.[25]

We have already seen in chapter 2 how loose and flexible the bands were in the nineteenth century. There was no agreement among the informants who described the tribal circle about exactly how many bands there were, or even what their names were. The band was a dynamic and impermanent domestic group, not a discrete, permanent political unit.

By contrast, the military societies were not only more permanent, but also highly political, both in their relations with other nations and in the internal affairs of the Cheyennes as well. Clearly, if a national political consensus was to be achieved by Sweet Medicine, the societies had to be consulted, not the bands. The saga makes this explicit, for there is no version of the story in which Sweet Medicine calls the bands together— always it is the societies.

As we saw in chapter 2, bands are almost the same as societies for some purposes. Informants have told ethnographers that societies "tend" to be situated or centered in certain bands. Ideally, the bands recruit husbands to live with their young woman and are therefore said to be "matrilocal," while society membership tends to be passed through the male line. In practice this means that while certain bands might tend to have a higher proportion of members of a particular society, all large bands, or "bunches," have at least some members of every society. In addition, since all men were supposed to be members of some society, when the societies were all called together so were the bands, since every man was involved. Both society and band membership were universal among Cheyenne men, although societies were the expression of *political* activity. I will discuss the general characteristics of these agnatic (male) and uterine (female) structures in chapter 6.[26] For the moment we need understand only that it was societies rather than bands that were the building blocks of Cheyenne society in the Sweet Medicine saga, because societies, not bands, were the most powerful expressions of political life.

The other expression of political life, the Council of Forty-four Chiefs, was and is an altogether different kind of organization. The council chiefs have been the domestic and juristic leaders of the tribe—the learned elders and arbitrators. Like the sacred arrows, the council symbolizes the unity and integrity of the nation. The restoration of order and harmony after a murder requires both the intercession of a chief and the renewal of the arrows. Traditionally, council chiefs have served conspicuously as arrow priests. No version of the Sweet Medicine story gives much importance to the council, but several versions do mention that the chiefs were founded at the same time as the societies. There is no version in which Sweet Medicine calls together the council chiefs as representative of the bands or of the tribe. Given the nature of the council, this is quite understandable.[27]

The Council of Forty-four can be best understood as a group that transcended the individual band and truly tied all the bands together in a novel manner. Soldier chiefs ("headsmen," more properly) were required to resign from their military societies to become council chiefs, whereupon they took up the pipe and bag as their symbols and wore a single feather, symbolizing the personal modesty they were supposed to exhibit. Plate 5 shows a group of chiefs assembled about 1909, with their pipes and bags. By contrast,

Plate 5. Group of chiefs in 1909. *Standing, left to right:* Harvey Whiteshield, Joi Hamilton, and Robert Burns. *Sitting:* Wolf Robe, Little Hand, Yellow Bear, White Eagle, and Mower. Photo no. 353 by De Lancey Gill, National Anthropological Archieves, Smithsonian Institution.

plate 6 is a very early photograph of a Crooked Lance Society headsman, Powder Face, dated about 1868. His appearance and demeanor are very different. Chiefs were charged with two duties only: peacemaking within the nation and foreign relations, especially trade, and treatymaking. The council chiefs were emphatically not the rulers of bands, and they had no power to make war. There is some confusion in Cheyenne ethnography on this latter point, which has been emphasized to me by many of the modern

Plate 6.   Powder Face, a Crooked Lance headsman, about 1868. The Denver Public Library, Western History Department.

chiefs. If the council met to consider an issue of foreign relations, they could either opt for peace or else take no action. In the latter case a military society could then take the decision from the council, opt for war, and try to mobilize the nation. If a consensus formed around the plans of a military society, then the nation went to war. But the chiefs' council could not declare war; they could only declare peace.[28]

With the coming of the Sutaios and their incorporation into tribal politics, the Sweet Medicine story presented problems to Cheyenne oral historians. With such a powerful and miraculous hero in the sacred tradition, how could he ever be reconciled in sacred literature to the arrival of another band and yet another political amalgamation? The story presented in Cheyenne tradition provides an ingenious solution—Sweet Medicine becomes involved in a fight to the death with the Sutaio leader, Erect Horns. When neither is able to prevail, the two tribes are united into a new and even more powerful nation.

Sutaio origins and the fight with Mutsiev are expressed in their most complete form in the story Michelson collected from Tall Bull in 1910. Tall Bull identified himself as a Sutaio and gave the following origin story for his people. I reproduce it here in its entirety because, as far as I know, the story has never appeared in print in any form.[29] The name "Lime" refers to the baked selenite powder used for white ceremonial paint.

LIME

There was a band of Sutaio near the Missouri River. A young man was elected from this band to a war-society to look after the people. This young man was very large in appearance. He became an influential man among the people. He was called Lime. He had two wives. One was old, the other younger. The younger one used to play with her husband as if he was a child. She tied him in a cradle. When she did that, she used to throw the rope over the trees so as to swing him. She did not know that Lime was holy. One day the older brother of Lime made a bow and arrow for him. Before that no one ever used bows and arrows. He taught him how to use them. After the bow and arrow had been made for him, Lime went out and looked about for something to shoot at. While looking about he found a very large rabbit: He shot him. It was so big that he couldn't take it home with him. He left the rabbit, and came home to get a dog and travois to bring the rabbit home.

On the following morning he went out again to find something to shoot at. While looking about he found an antelope and shot him. He was so big that he couldn't carry him home. He came back after a dog and travois and went out to bring him home. He called two or three war-societies to come and eat the antelope.

On the third morning he went out again to look out for something to kill. He found one deer and shot him and came home to get his dog and travois to bring it home. He called the people to eat at his lodge.

On the fourth day he went out again to shoot at something. He saw a moose and shot him. He killed him and came home, got his dog and travois to bring the moose home.

His brother came to his lodge again. His brother dressed him up, painted his face, and gave him a buffalo-robe. After he had dressed him, he told him to go out along the bank of the creek, to lie there, and to look for the best girl he could get. So he went and hid himself near the bank. There were young girls passing continually in front of the creek. By and by he saw a fine girl. He made a charge at her. He took his knife out and cut her into pieces. His brother had not told him to do that, but Lime misunderstood. He was only supposed to throw the girl down and touch her at the vulva with the knife.

Then a war-society came out of their lodge and complained of Lime to his brother. They told him that he had better let his brother go off some place; if he didn't, Lime might kill all the people, as he had already killed one person. His brother asked what he had done. They said: "He has killed the finest girl in the tribe. He tore her to pieces alongside the river."

The brother was surprised. He talked to Lime about making a canoe, and launching it into the water. After they had paddled across the river they left the canoe and walked in an unknown direction. While on the way they saw a buffalo. It came to him. His brother shot and killed it. He cut a large club and gave it to Lime. After they had dressed the buffalo, he told Lime to walk around keeping the flies off by waving the club. Thus he spoke to him.

The elder brother said he would look for another buffalo. But he went to where he had left the canoe. He went back to the tribe. When he came back he called all the war-societies to his lodge. He told them that he had taken his brother across the water and left him there to keep him away from the tribe.

He, the big brother who returned, was a big chief. He had two wives. A war society met to decide what punishment to mete out to the chief and two wives. They decided that they would have to be used as servants anytime when a society was smoking, or anything else. They tortured them for one whole year in every way. The three suffered for his brother's act. After one year the younger wife asked her husband: "Where did you leave your brother?" She asked him to go back with her to where he left his brother so that they might bring Lime back. The three, both the wives and the chief, sneaked away one night. They went where they had left the canoe. They got on it and crossed the river. When they crossed, they left the canoe and walked to where he had left his brother. They came to him at morning twilight.

The big brother came to where his younger brother had been left. When the elder brother came he found a big pile of bones on the spot where he had told his younger brother to scatter flies off the buffalo. He saw his brother still walking around it, in a deep trench worn by his feet. He listened. He heard a voice. The voice said: "My brother has left me here, and I hope that he is higher than the chief at this time because he has done this to me." The two women and the elder brother saw him still walking. He was still waving that club. The elder brother spoke down to him. He did not look at them. The older wife asked him to look up and have pity on them, that the tribe had tortured them for his sake. He did not look up. The younger one started to cry when she saw him. She said to him: "Lime, we are in a hard fix. They have almost taken our lives away for your sake." "Well," he said. He looked up and had pity on her. He climbed up. So the four started back to where they had left the canoe. Lime told them to look straight at his back. He started to walk on the water. He walked as if on ice. The three followed him. They all walked across. They came back to the tribe. They made a camp on the outskirts of the camp. Their lodge was made of tall grass. The younger brother said to his sisters-in-law: "Go out and cut off a club." They brought wood to him. He made a club. One night when the war-societies came together they asked one of the members to go out and see if the runaways were coming home. So he went out towards the end of the camp. He saw a fire a distance away from the lodges. He went to it. He peeked in. He saw Lime sitting at the back part of the lodge. He recognized him and went back to where the war-societies were. He made no report. He went to his own lodge; he called his wife and children to get ready to run off from the camp.

While the war-societies were waiting for a report, they sent another messenger to find if the runaways were coming home to the same place. He found Lime at the same place. He peeked in. He recognized him; he came back and made no report but went to his own lodge, alarmed his own family so they might get away. Lime said: "They know us now. We will go to the war-societies' place." They came to the lodge. The oldest brother went in first, his two wives next, and Lime last. Lime carried a club. The leader of one of the societies arose, got his buffalo robe, stretched it in the back of the lodge nearly in the centre so they might sit down. They were welcomed. "You mustn't sit there," Lime said to his sister-in-laws, "You sit at the entrance." The men of the war-societies became terrified and trembled. Lime said to them: "You must all sit down the same way." He told the younger wife to get up. He gave her his club to hit each man across the shins with all her might. She hit every one of them. She almost killed them.

He called the elder wife to get the club. He told the men, "Sit down properly." He said to the elder wife, "Now you go ahead and hit each one of them square on the head with all your might." She hit every one. They became senseless. While this was going on, someone peeked in the door. He saw that Lime was treating the leaders of the tribe very severely. He told the rest of the people. They became frightened and all ran off into the night.

The elder brother got up, told the war-societies to get the buffalo robe and spread it. He sat down on it. Lime told the people to fill the pipe and gave it to his brother. He called the last man in the row to take a piece of fire in his own hands as carefully as he could and to place it before his brother. He did so. Lime called on each to do that until morning. In the morning he turned them loose.

When the war-society men went to look for their lodges, their families were gone. The four—Lime, his brother, and the latter's two wives—crossed the Mississippi River. The band that had been frightened away joined the Cheyennes. They told the Cheyennes that they, the Sutaios, had a leader who never could be killed. The leader of the Cheyennes at the time was Mutsiev (Sweet Medicine).

Sweet Medicine and Lime wanted to meet each other. The whole band of Cheyennes came to the four. This was near the Mississippi River. There was a little island on the river on which the four lived. Lime had a vision: There was going to be a band of people coming to kill him. So he told the two women to cut a stick so that he could make a club. He made a club. When he finished it, he put red paint on it. He told his brother and sisters-in-law, "Day after tomorrow the enemy will be at hand." He gave them instructions. He said to them, "If Sweet Medicine cuts me in two, you should take my body to the river and put me together. I will then become just as good as ever. He will do that three or four times; you must do what I have told you each time. If I don't happen to get up in time when the enemy appears, you wake me up."

At daybreak they woke Lime up. They said, "Lime, get up; the enemy are at hand." So he got up. He dressed up and painted his face in good shape. They went out. They walked a little way to where the stream was. They looked toward the enemy. No one could count how many there were. The great leader stood far ahead of the rest of them. There was a high ridge where the enemy came. Sweet Medicine stood far ahead. He, Sweet Medicine, called out to him, "My friend, today we wish to know each other. I'm going to kill you today. You can do the best you can to deal with me or else you can kill me."

Lime said to him, "Remember today; I'm going to do the same. You must do the best you can to deal with me. I'm surely going to kill you." Sweet Medicine said, "I'm going to do it now." He raised his sword. It was made of hard rock. He waved it toward Lime. He cut Lime from his neck to his arm.

His brother and two sisters took him at once to the river. He was healed. He raised his club and waved toward Sweet Medicine. He knocked him down.

Sweet Medicine had told his people to cover him with a robe if Lime should kill him. They covered him with a robe. He was healed. Sweet Medicine raised his sword, waved it toward Lime; he cut him in two. Lime fell. His brother and sisters-in-law took him to the river. He was healed. He hit Sweet Medicine. He knocked him down. They covered him with a robe. Sweet Medicine cut Lime in two just below the juncture of his legs. His brother and sisters-in-law took him to the river. He was healed. He came back. He hit and knocked Sweet Medicine down. They covered him with a robe and he was healed.

They moved closer to each other, though still at a distance. Sweet Medicine said to Lime, "My friend, you must have come here to imitate me. I came to save the people hereafter in this world." Lime said to him, "I guess you have come to imitate me." Sweet Medicine said, "I know one trick. You shall know it today." Lime, "I too know one trick. You shall know it today." Sweet Medicine said, "I know this trick." A big shower came. The thunder was terrific over Lime. Lime said, "I know this trick too." A storm of snow came together with the shower. There was a big noise between the two. In four successive days there was a shower of rain and a storm of snow with it. On the morning of the fourth day Sweet Medicine surrendered to Lime. They came together and made peace. There was just the same thing in them. Neither could beat the other.

The Sutaio and the Cheyenne crossed the Mississippi and went East. Lime gave instructions to his brother and sisters-in-law: I am going on a distant journey. I'll be gone four days (He meant forty years). Then I will be back on the fourth day with my successor.

Another complete Lime story, which Michelson collected from Bull Thigh (plate 7), also in 1910, is very similar. But it begins by stating explicitly that the Sutaios formerly lived in bark wigwams. The story describes Lime as a Sutaio leader, and it takes the allied tribes, after the fight with Sweet Medicine, into the Black Hills.[30] Yet another of Michelson's stories collected from Badger,[31] explains how the Sutaios "lost" their buffalo, and a narrative from White Bull explains the circumstances surrounding the separation of the Cheyennes from the Sutaios in the first place.[32]

Along with the sacred Lime story, which explains Sutaio origins and the meeting with the Cheyennes in symbolic terms, Michelson's informants also related the secular history of the event, with places and times. Tall Bull, in addition to narrating the story of Lime, also told Michelson that the Sutaios had formerly planted corn on the Missouri River but hunted around

Plate 7. Bull Thigh, informant for Truman Michelson. Photo no. 45, 799, taken by Michelson in 1910, National Anthropological Archives, Smithsonian Institution.

the Black Hills.[33] When they moved permanently to the Black Hills, he said, they planted corn around Running Creek, a tributary of the Cheyenne River east of the Black Hills. White Bull added that the Sutaios remained east of the Mississippi after the Cheyennes moved west, in a time when neither had horses.[34] Grasshopper, interviewed in 1910, told Michelson that the Sutaios and the Cheyennes were once separated by the Mississippi.[35] Wolf Chief added that the Sutaios had divided into two groups before they crossed the Mississippi, but one group stayed east.[36] Ice said that both groups eventually crossed, one joining the Cheyennes at the mouth of the Yellowstone River, the other at the Cheyenne River.[37] It was also reported to Michelson that Left Hand Bull's great-grandfather, a Sutaio born about 1740–50, was born in "Canada."[38]

Taken all together, then, Michelson's informants were able to narrate Cheyenne history from much earlier times than Grinnell or Mooney would ever have suspected. Locations east of the Mississippi are about 1680–1700, according to the French maps described in chapter 2. However, we cannot improve much on Grinnell's investigation of the route taken by the Cheyennes before they reached the Black Hills.[39] Working with Lakota oral tradition, some living informants, and archeological evidence, Grinnell postulated that the Cheyennes moved from somewhere in the Great Lakes areas south to the Minnesota River, then west to the Sheyenne River, then farther west to the Great Bend of the Missouri in North Dakota, and then southwest to the Black Hills. One informant never interviewed by Grinnell, however—Bear Tongue—was more specific than Grinnell's informants, even including Sheyenne River sites in his narration. The following remarks were related by the interpreter Ben Clark, who talked with Bear Tongue sometime before 1887 but never published the interview:

> When we left this country (the Sheyenne River), we travelled Westward until we came to the Missouri River. There the Cheyennes remained a good while and were neighbors of the Mandan, Arikaras and Hidatsas. The Cheyennes married some of their women and some of the descendants of those unions still live and bear the names Ree Woman or Hidatsa Woman. Here they first heard of horses and of certain Indians who rode them, also of horses running wild on the plains to the southwest. This was the cause or one of the causes for another move. The Missouri was crossed and a southwest course pursued until the Black Hills country was reached between the forks of the Red Paint River (Cheyenne River). From here expeditions were made long distances south and west. The Shoshonis were visited and afterwards many battles were fought with them and also with the Crows. In the North Platte country they (the Cheyennes) fell in with the Arapahoes who had crossed the upper Missouri sometime before them, and in company with the Arapahoes, raids were made on the Utes in the mountains.[40]

Two of Michelson's informants also related the early "secular history" of the nation. Iron Shirt made a brief statement that "when the Rees raided their corn fields east of the Black Hills, the Cheyennes ceased to raise corn." Coyote, born in 1859, emphasized the period of Cheyenne history after they crossed the Missouri and before they arrived at the Black Hills. I include it here in its entirety because it is the very best narrative of secular history I have found anywhere, and it is so far unpublished.

The Cheyennes came from the north, straight north of the Black Hills. At that place there was corn. They brought it with them toward the Black Hills, and they followed a stream. Transportation was by dogs; horses were unknown. They decided to camp indefinitely at this stream. They used flint implements to cultivate the ground in small spaces, to plant the seed. The fall of that year they had a good crop of that corn. After putting it away in containers of hides, they decided to go on a buffalo hunt. They made some dugouts on the bank and stored the corn there. They sealed the dugout with logs. Then they went on a buffalo hunt. It was some months before they returned. Upon their return they discovered some one had been there and had stolen all their stored corn. They knew not who had done this but they assumed it was the white man. The Cheyennes considered this a serious loss, the same as losing a relative.

They drifted farther south and drifted for days, going in a southwestern direction. They came to a country heavily timbered with cedar—Nowahwus is the name of this big mountain. "Bear Mountain" is what the white men probably call it. All this time the Cheyenne were at war with all tribes, no matter who. There were a few in a party out hunting and came on an Indian not a Cheyenne. He was alone. They asked him by signs who he was. He replied in signs, used the index finger of his right hand on the right side of his nose, going up and down—Blue Cloud Indians. He asked the Cheyennes what tribe they were. The Cheyenne spokesman using the sign language crossed, or cut index finger with index finger. They shook hands. That sealed the friendship between these tribes. There would be no more war between these two. The party of Cheyennes on their return reported the incident to their chiefs—at that time there were no chiefs as today. At that time a man earned his chieftainship in battle or war. The chiefs said the children had shaken hands with the stranger. It was all right, from then on there would be no war with those people. This chief said if the Arapaho comes to my camp, he will not be molested, and they have been together up to the present day.

The Sutaio were in a band of their own, but they spoke practically the same language as the Cheyennes. But they were at war with them. They seemed to recognize that since the Arapaho had joined the Cheyennes, that they (the Sutaio) would be powerless to make war against the two tribes. They recognized the Cheyennes had the medicine arrows and that the Arapahoes had the sacred pouch (which contains the pipe, etc.). The Sutaio had the medicine cap. The medicine man of this tribe, through a vision, recognized that if the Sutaio were to survive they must be at peace with them. The Sutaio came and made friendship with the Cheyenne.

Years after, horses came into existence. The Sioux evidently knew where the Cheyenne were encamped but the Cheyenne were not aware that the Sioux were in the country. The Sioux evidently must have come from the north, for they only had dogs, while the Cheyennes were already well supplied with horses. The horses were found in the south by the Cheyennes. The Sioux came unannounced, without formalities. They were also recognized as friends thereafter. The Cheyennes gave them horses and other gifts. That practice is still in vogue. When they visit they always give each other presents. Then after a time the Sutaio moved northeast from the Cheyennes. From then these four peoples were allied, became powerful and fought with other tribes.[41]

Lakota Origins

From the narratives quoted and cited above, some of the essential foundations of Cheyenne society are clear. First of all, we find two groupings, the Aortas and the Eaters, who traveled southwest from the vicinity of the Mandans and were joined together at Bear Butte in the Black Hills by the prophet Sweet Medicine. The tribal circle they formed, according to sacred stories, had the Aortas on the south side of the opening and the Eaters on the north side. Later they were joined by the Sutaios, who took the guest position, opposite the door. At this point, then, we have identified three of the five "original" component bands mentioned by Mooney. However, we have not yet fully explained where the "Eaters" came from. Also, we have not yet, as promised, taken up the Masikota problem. To account for these aspects of Cheyenne history, we must look eastward, toward the Sioux.

When I speak of Teton origins for the Eater and Masikota bands, I do not mean to imply that the groups were originally Teton people, culturally or linguistically; I mean only that they were originally resident and intermarried with the Lakotas, as other Cheyenne bands were later resident and intermarried with the Rees and Mandans. Although Teton origins for the Eater band are well known, such origins for the Masikota band are not. In addition to searching out the Masikota evidence we need, we should also look at Teton affiliations for another band, the Moiseos (Fox or Blue Horse band), since the informants of chapter 2 also mentioned Siouan affiliations for that group.

We already know that the Siouan names "Wotapio" and "Ou de baton" for the Eater band go all the way back to the French maps of 1680. George

Bent has added the information that the band was descended from Cheyennes who had intermarried with the "Moiseyev" band of Tetons, a group last seen about 1814.[42] Mooney's informants gave "Monsoni" as a synonym for "Moiseo," although they disagreed about the origins of the band. Big Jake and some other informants alleged that the Eaters were affiliated with the Masikota.[43]

If one looks on the early maps for a Siouan group with a name like Moiseo, Moiseyev, or Monsoni, there are no good candidates. On Lahontan's map we find the "Monzoni," it is true, but north of Lake Superior near Hudson Bay, a group historians call Cree.[44] Marquette in 1673[45] and Thevenot in 1681[46] listed the Mouingouena/Moingouena in the correct place to be affiliated with the Eaters (Wotapios or Oudebatons), but the similarity in names does not seem very convincing.

In Cheyenne, the name Moiseyev means Flint People, but I am unaware of any Lakota band names that have this translation. Lewis and Clark give us nothing recognizable as Monsoni or "Flint People." So for the moment we will have to leave it a mystery who the Eaters' Siouan affiliates were, pending the discovery of new maps or documents or some more competent translations of Lakota band names.

Nevertheless, numerous Cheyenne informants have claimed that the Eaters began with Siouan affiliations and Siouan intermarriage, and we have no reason to believe they did not, even though we cannot identify the Lakota group in question. This scenario is consistent with the general idea that the Eaters, unlike the Aortas, emphasized hunting rather than agriculture and were engaged in symbiotic relationships with sedentary tribes. Various Siouan groups were agricultural in this period.[47]

One consequence of Sweet Medicine's charter for a Cheyenne nation was that the Eater bands became politically identified with other Cheyennes rather than with the Tetons. Apparently this had taken place by the time of Carver, in 1766. He reported that while the "Shians" were still part of the Dakota Alliance, the "Shianese, the Chongousceton, and the Waddapawjestin" (this last the parent band of the Wotapios proper, the Omisis, and other Eater bands) lived farther out on the Plains and were not part of the alliance.[48]

From Carver's evidence, it is reasonable to infer that the Cheyenne nation had already been formed by 1766, from the three groups he mentioned as "out on the Plains." In any event, we can infer that they were no longer part of the Dakota Alliance, except for the "Shians." We have already noted that the same picture emerges from Loisel's report of 1803, which mentions two groups of Cheyennes—one called Cheyennes and the other "Chahuines," listed next to the "Sioux."[49]

To solve the Masikota problem, I suggest that the group Carver called "Shians" and Loisel called "Chahuines" was the group that later joined the Cheyenne nation as the Masikota band. I argue that this was the last group to leave the Great Sioux Alliance and join the nation to which it was linguistically and ethnically related, the Cheyennes. Tabeau even listed a motivation for this breakup, saying that when a dispute arose between the Sioux and the Arikaras, the Oglalas and the "Chihants . . . sided each one with one of the opposing parties."[50] There are three additional lines of evidence for this derivation of the Masikotas from the Tetons, one from Lewis and Clark, another from linguistics, and the last from recent censuses and modern informants.

Concerning Lewis and Clark's information, if we had only Lewis's statistical summary to rely on, we would never find the Masikotas among the Siouan nations. In his summary Lewis noted only that there were two subgroups of the Oglalas, whom he gave as the Okandandas proper and the "Sheo."[51] In the actual field chart, however, now kept in the archives of the American Philosophical Society in Philadelphia,[52] there are some surprises. First of all, there is no mention of the "Sheo," but there is an interesting entry concerning the three bands of the Lakotas—the Oglalas, the Minneconjous, and the Soanes. In the column entitled "The names of the nations with whom they maintain friendly alliance or with whom they may be united by intercourse or marriage," we find the "Cheyennes." If we looked only at the Cheyenne side of the statistical summary, which appeared in the published report, this information would be entirely lost, for it is said that the "Cheyennes" were at war with the Teton Sioux. Lewis never summarized the additional tabulated data for the Tetons in the same way as for the other tribes, but instead inserted a long general passage castigating them as "the vilest miscreants of the savage race."

It is important to note that the Sheos, like the Staetans, Dotames, and Wetepahatos—all of these Cheyenne bands rather than tribes—disappear from prominence after Lewis and Clark. They are not in Riggs's list, Dorsey's list, or any later one. I suggest that they disappear from the Teton list because they have been added to the Cheyenne tribal circle. But this is not the only argument for deriving the Masikotas from the Tetons. There is also linguistic evidence.

Cheyenne informants have always been hard pressed to explain the meaning of "Masikota" in English. Most frequently, the complex idea is communicated that the word implies the legs of a corpse that are drawn up in death, as the grasshopper's or cricket's are in life. The lexeme -masi- carries this idea.[53] None of the Cheyenne ethnographic sources, however, have explained the meaning of the lexeme -kota-. The field notes of ethnographers indicate that informants were not asked. So to correct this gap in the ethnography, I undertook to inquire about the name Masikota from among the descendants of this band, who now live in the vicinity of Fonda, Oklahoma.

The consensus of my modern informants is that the suffix -*kota*- is used in Cheyenne merely to show that the name has Siouan origins.[54] It is a suffix Cheyennes recognize from La*kota* and Da*kota*. But the -*masi*- is a Cheyenne root, meaning "flexed corpse" as previously reported. This unusual idea is also represented by a single word in Lakota, according to Buechel's dictionary. He represents the word as *shiyo,* cognate with *sheo,* although he has garbled the definition somewhat. He says it refers to "the muscle in the front side of the upper part of a man's leg. In times past, men always died when that muscle was hurt badly."[55] On the face of it the definition seems erroneous, implying that a man could die from a blow to the leg. Cal Fast Wolf, a Dakota linguist and native speaker, tells me that the idea is the same in Lakota as in Cheyenne—the Cheyenne word is merely a translation.[56] Lewis and Clark's "Sheo" is simply the Lakota version of the band name for Masikota, the "Legs-Drawn-Up band."

Other linguistic evidence concerns the presence around Fonda of people with Lakota ancestry. One modern informant from that area, Katie Osage, tells me that some of the Masikota people "had grandmas who talked good Sioux." This can be confirmed from the census of 1891, which lists three women named "Sioux Woman" in that neighborhood. None of the other Cheyenne communities in Oklahoma had more than one "Sioux Woman," except Hammon. Hammon also had three "Sioux women," and that is where the Wotapio band settled, another band of historical Siouan affiliations. But we will consider these later migrations and transformations in a subsequent chapter.

One last band possibly derived from the Lakotas needs to be mentioned here, though briefly. Remember from chapter 2 that one of the discrete bands was called the Moiseos, nearly the same name as the Siouan group from which the Eaters were said to be derived. The evolution of this band into the Fox band and the Blue Horse band was traced briefly. To this evidence we need to add that the Oglalas have a Fox military society, nearly identical to the Cheyenne Kit Foxes, which they say came from the Cheyennes long ago. In fact, the Oglalas give a version of the Sweet Medicine story as their charter for the Kit Foxes.[57]

The question whether the Oglala Kit Foxes were derived from the Masikotas, or were part of them, or were merely neighbors we will leave aside for the moment. I will only note here that the Fox band, like the Eaters and the Masikotas, has some kind of historical Siouan affiliation. In chapter 7 we will explore the interactions among these bands and nations in the nineteenth century.

A New Synthesis

In this concluding section of the chapter, I wish to review briefly my major arguments and conclusions. To do this, I will refer to two figures. The first, figure 5, represents the prehistoric transformations of the Cheyenne tribal circle, according to Cheyenne informants. The second, figure 6, represents the perceptions of that structure by various European observers. As we can see, the last tribal circle and the last arrangement of tribal names represent exactly the same bands. My general argument throughout this chapter and the whole book is that there is no contradiction between the European sources and Cheyenne oral history regarding these major transformations, and in fact they are complementary in their historical coverage. I also argue, and demonstrate, that Cheyenne oral history is more complete, more precise, and more correct than European sources.

The first diagram in figure 5, about 1720, shows the arrangement of the tribal circle as it is legitimated by the sacred stories of the two young men and by the story of Sweet Medicine. These events occurred when the separate bands were formed into a nation, but before the arrival of the Sutaios, originally a separate tribe, from across the Mississippi.

The second diagram, about 1750, shows the position in the circle taken by the Sutaios, across from the opening in the "guest" position. The term "Eaters" has been used both in this diagram and in the previous one because no informant was able to say when the term Omisis first came into use. It may have been, all along, that the Oudebatons never called themselves that, but only the Siouan speakers did. The term "Aortas" is used on both these first two diagrams for the same reason. No informant could say when the terms Tsistsistas and Heviksnipahis were first used. Most likely the original term for this half of the tribe was Tsistsistas, since it is untranslatable and therefore probably older, while the term Heviksnipahis not only is translatable, but is also related to a secular story reported by Grinnell, in which the band was founded by a chief named Porcupine Bear.[58] The group's taboo on eating beavers, it is said, resulted from Porcupine Bear's illness when he did so.

The third diagram on figure 5, about 1800, represents the three divisions noted in the journals of Lewis and Clark. By this time the Eater bands had dispersed into the satellite camps noted by Lewis and Clark and were involved in a symbiotic relationship with the Aortas or Cheyennes proper. This was before the polarization of the Tsistsistas into the Hevhaitaneos, or

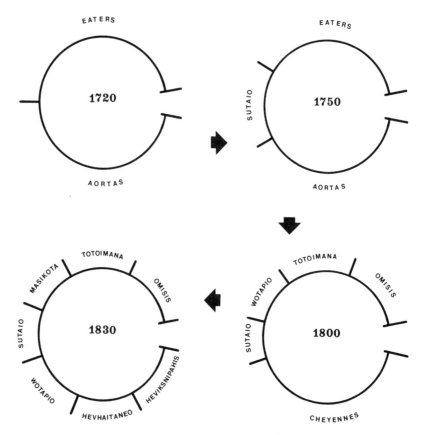

Figure 5.   Historical transformations of the Cheyenne tribal circle.

Hair Rope People, who went south to enter the horse trade, and the Heviksnipahis, who were left behind on the Upper Platte.

The fourth diagram of the figure represents two major transformations, about 1830. First of all, the Masikotas have assumed their place, having migrated from the territory of their Teton allies. Second, the polarization of the Tsistsistas has occurred, with the Hevhaitaneos migrating south of the Platte to the Arkansas, while the Heviksnipahis band remained between the forks of the Platte. We will examine these movements in more detail in chapter 7. The last transformation noted on this diagram is the geographical movement of the Wotapios proper to the south, reflected in their joining the other southern bands on the south side of the tribal circle. As mentioned in chapter 2, however, their "correct" position was still ambiguous in the minds of later informants, with some placing them in the traditional "Eater" position and others putting them as a subgroup of the Hevhaitaneos. I have also retained on the diagram the other subgroup of the Omisis recorded by Lewis and Clark, the "Dotames" or Totoimanas. The translation of Totoimana is "Prairie band," which may reflect their precocious adoption of horse nomadism, compared with the Omisis.

Figure 6 shows how the social structure of the Cheyennes was perceived at various times by European observers. At the bottom of the diagram are the three names for Cheyenne subgroups with their most usual spelling from the early maps, about 1690. We should note that all three names given for the Cheyenne bands are in the Dakota language, "Oudebaton" or Eaters,

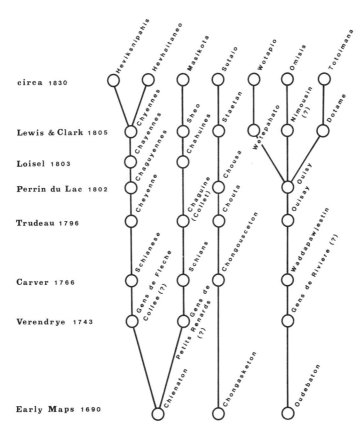

Figure 6.   Historical transformations as perceived by European observers.

"Chongasketon" or Dog People, and "Chienaton" or Red Speakers. All the names are also grammatically parallel, with the same suffix. Compared with other explanations, this starting point for Cheyenne ethnohistory is extremely parsimonious for explaining the names found on the early maps. As we follow the names up the diagram, we will see that these particular group names have considerable explanatory power, because they do not require the usual linguistic gyrations demanded by historical scholars.

For 1743, the names recorded by the Vérendryes are given. However, I regard these identifications as unproved, and so I have followed the French nicknames with question marks. Although these nicknames have some similarity to names applied to Cheyenne groups at other times, I still regard George Hyde's allegations about such names as unproved until more documents or maps come into view.

With Carver's observations of 1766, however, we are on much firmer ground. His names for Cheyenne bands are consistent with what went before and what came afterward. His Waddapawjestin is merely an English literation of the name spelled in French as Oudebaton. Also, his Chongousceton is nearly identical to Chongasketon from the early maps.

Carver, however, was the first to record two groups of "Shians," one resident with the Tetons and another farther west on the Plains. To differentiate these, Carver affixed "-ese" to one, as in Chinese or Burmese. The other he merely called Shians. Since his informants were still Sioux, they used the original Lakota or Dakota names for Cheyenne bands.

In 1796 we find Truteau's description of Cheyenne political structure, which is nearly identical to that of Perrin du Lac, who probably plagiarized Truteau's account. Here we find the first representation of the Eaters' name for themselves, Ouisay, clearly cognate with Omisis by the substitution of the bilabial sound /w/ for /m/. Also we find a Cheyenne rendering of the Sutaios' name for themselves, appearing here as Chouta. Since Truteau was involved in a highly multilingual trading station, it is not clear what the phonetic status of this name might be. But it is certain that a translation into Cheyenne would require the transformation of the ch into an s, since Cheyenne has no ch, and that is exactly what we find on the Lewis and Clark map, with the addition of -hetan as "people of"—Staetan.

In 1796 we find the spelling Chaguiene on Collet's map, similar to the Spanish map's "Chaguiene" and the "Chequiene" in Wheat's atlas. With this background, then, it is less jarring to find the "Chahuines" again on Loisel's list, although as a Lakota group, allied with the Oglalas. Loisel differentiated between this group and the "Chayennes," reflecting the same pattern as Carver before him and Lewis and Clark afterward. In another place, Loisel contrasted the names as "Cheyennes" and "Chaoines."[59]

On Lewis and Clark's chart we find the first listing of the name used by Cheyennes for the band that was resident with the Oglalas. Represented in Lakota, it is Sheo, which means the same thing as the Cheyenne *masi-*. In addition, Lewis and Clark noted the separate existence of the Sutaios and the Cheyennes proper, both differentiated from the Sheos. Also, Lewis and Clark were the first to break down the Eater band into three component subgroups. In addition to the "Nimousins" or Northern Eaters, the other two subgroups are the Wotapios, now become the "Eaters proper" in the same manner as noted in chapter 2 for several other groups, and the Totoimanas, also said by those informants to be an ancient subgroup of the Eaters.

To complete the tribal circle as of 1830, Lewis and Clark's "Chyennes" need only be bifurcated into the Hevhaitaneo and the Heviksnipahis. By this time, however, we are well within the range of reliable historical documents and of firsthand informants' knowledge. Although there are other transformations of the tribal circle and bifurcations that occurred between 1805 and modern times, we will reserve these developments for chapters 6 and 7, after a discussion of the external factors that affected Cheyenne social and political structure in the meantime.

5 /XXX

The Central Plains Environment

Until now, we have mostly considered *what* happened in Cheyenne history, without paying much attention to how and why. For example, we have seen that the Cheyennes migrated generally west and south, without discussing what prompted them to do so. Also, we have seen fission and fusion, once again without fully understanding why these reorganizations were necessary. To understand the *motivations* for these migrations and reorganizations, we must understand some practical but crucial problems of everyday Cheyenne life. For it was in their continual attempts to solve practical problems that the Cheyennes were forced, in the space of two hundred years, to migrate a thousand miles and to modify and reorganize their society several times.

Orthodox Marxism has often been criticized, incorrectly, as advocating economic determinism. But in fact, Marx and his successors have consistently emphasized the role of human intelligence in actively responding to changes in the social and natural world.[1] This is the fundamental idea behind what has been called dialectical or historical materialism. As ecological or economic factors change, human beings adapt to the new conditions. Persons who emerge as leaders to create a new social or political structure can hardly be charged with having a passive role in history. Social innovators, whether tribal culture heroes or modern revolutionaries, must be seen as the agents of an active intelligence. Writers such as Elman Service, who allege that Marxism assigns a passive role to individuals, seem to have taken their ideas not from reading Marx and Engels, but rather from the classics of anticommunism.[2]

For Cheyennes, the practical problems of the late eighteenth and early nineteenth centuries fall under the general headings of economics or ecology, or more technically, "infrastructure." In Cheyenne history the most pressing problems of this kind relate to population size and access to trade, water, wood, and grass. When we have learned something about the form of these problems and how the Cheyennes faced and solved them, we will be better able to interpret the events of the last several chapters. My thesis here is that such great events as wars, rebellions, migrations, and alliances must be understood as the sum and calculus of small events—as simple a problem as finding enough grass for the horses.

The data presented in this chapter represent a surge in American ecological research over the past two decades. Fifty years ago, we could not have examined the logic of Plains ecology with any success, because not enough was known about the historical climate and biology of the area. Although a body of good data now exists, we must still place it within a framework that is appropriate for studying history. That is, though other scientists have paid great attention to grass types, soil patterns, rainfall, and such things, they have not necessarily been interested in the lifeways of the Cheyennes. So we must put their findings within the context of questions we have been developing over the previous chapters—issues of social structure and nation building.

As I began this ecological research, I was not always able to find the answers to my specific questions in the published literature. Therefore, between 1981 and 1983 I embarked on a series of trips across the Plains to visit the aboriginal habitat of the Cheyennes. This not only helped me collect hard-to-find published sources, such as soil surveys and local histories, but also enabled me to talk to local ranchers, farmers, and "old-timers" who had valuable information about how the Plains looked before plows and fences. Especially, I carried with me a map of the favorite or usual camping places of the Cheyennes, as reported by books, articles, and informants, and I tried to visit these sites (see map 5). Several times I ran into field scientists who were also on the track of some important issue in Plains ecology. Their continuing research is reported here.

At different periods in history, ecological factors affected the Cheyennes in different ways. Sometimes water was a determining factor for migration and social structure, sometimes wood. Sometimes the factors that limited Cheyenne society were not those that might have been most apparent to European observers but were more subtle. During their intensive horticultural period, for example, the problem for the Cheyennes was firewood, not garden space. During their nomadic hunting period, the problem was grass for horses, not finding buffaloes. In this chapter I will develop some calculations that support these assertions. For each economic or ecological variable—population, trade, or some natural resource—I will retrace Cheyenne migrations and show how Cheyenne culture changed in each area to reflect an accommodation to a different environment.

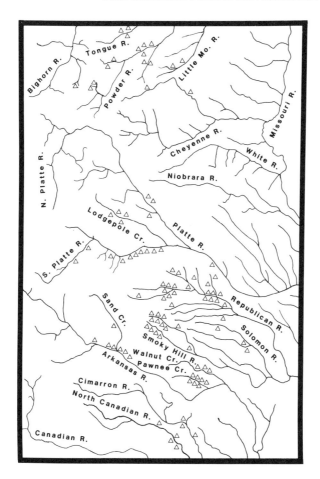

Map 5. Historically known camping places of the Cheyennes. Compiled from Grinnell 1956, George Bent's maps at the University of Colorado, and Ben Clark's manuscript, National Anthropological Archives, Smithsonian Institution. Each triangle represents one incident of camping in the middle nineteenth century.

Population and Politics

Much of the early warfare that affected the Cheyennes was generated by trade competition in the Great Lakes area. When the Cheyennes entered the European documentary record, by means of the maps of the late seventeenth century, the French-Chippewa trade expansion was in full force. The political polarization of this period, between the Chippewas and their Cree and Assiniboine allies on the one side and the Great Sioux Alliance on the other, has already been mentioned in chapter 3. But to understand the particular role of the Cheyennes in these hostilities, we must know something about the gross numbers of participants in this long-term territorial warfare.

In modern times the Chippewas are the most numerous aboriginal people north of Mexico, numbering about 160,000 persons in Canada and the United States. Extrapolating backward from this modern figure, Ritzenthaler estimates that the population of Chippewas at the time of the First European contact was about 100,000. If we add 10,000 Assiniboines and 15,000 Crees, we get a total allied population of 125,000 spread from Wisconsin around the northern rim of the Great Lakes through Ontario.[3] It was from this huge population that the French, and later the British, recruited their trappers to expand the beaver trade westward.

When the French and Chippewas extended their operations to the west and south of Lake Superior, they did it not by means of a gradual expansion, but abruptly, by establishing a beachhead in the form of a large trading post just east of the Chequamegon peninsula on the south shore of the lake. By 1693 this trading post had a population of 1,000, from which satellite Chippewa villages were beginning to extend into Minnesota and Wisconsin. According to the early maps, this extension of Chippewa territory essentially severed the Cheyennes from their closest Algonquian kin, the Kickapoos, Sacs, and Foxes.[4] While these latter three tribes, speaking dialects of the same language, created alliances southward, the Cheyennes were forced northwestward, into the midst of a confrontation between two large populations, the Chippewas and the Sioux.

The best early estimates of Sioux population come from William Clark, of the Lewis and Clark expedition, and from Henry Schoolcraft. In a handwritten report from St. Louis, dated 1816, Clark reported that there were 14,000 Lakota and Dakota Sioux on the Upper Mississippi and Upper Missouri, confronting 6,500 "Chipaways."[5] His count of Chippewas apparently included only those villages in Minnesota and Wisconsin that were actively engaged in warfare against the Sioux—those who later became known as the "Southwestern Chippewas."

Schoolcraft's figures are more comprehensive than Clark's and were published as a semiofficial government report in 1847. Schoolcraft listed 21,070 Sioux as a total for the "Dacota Group," "Sioux of the Mississippi," and "Sioux of the Missouri."[6] He estimated that 18,697 Chippewas were then living in the territory of the United States, comprising the "Algonquin Group" and "Chippewas, west, and Red River, north."

By contrast to these large estimates for the Sioux and Chippewas, estimates for the Cheyennes have always been small. Clark's report estimated their numbers in 1816 as "500 men, 2000 souls." In 1847 Schoolcraft estimated that there were 2,500 Cheyennes, of whom 1,600 were Southern Cheyennes living in the recently acquired territory of New Mexico, including southern Colorado and parts of Texas and Oklahoma.[7] Other estimates, from somewhat earlier, confirm a small population: Pierre Chouteau estimated 400 Cheyenne "hombres" in 1804, and Perrin du Lac gave a total figure of "5000 hunters" for the combined Mandans, Cheyennes, and Hidatsas.[8]

Later in their history, and in contrast to other Indian populations, the Cheyennes continued at about the same population, despite the ravages of war and disease. Alexander Henry even noted that "their numbers have increased surprisingly."[9] In the period of peaceful relations, 1840–60, populations of 770 to 2,536 were reported to the Bureau of Indian Affairs for various combinations of bands, although the agents were never clear about what bands they were counting.[10] The first official and allegedly complete count of Cheyennes was in 1878, after escapes and interreservation travel had settled down, and showed a total Cheyenne population of 3,298.[11] This figure does not include a few families who still lived on reservations at Pine Ridge, Rosebud, and Wind River and at Fort Keogh in Montana. Mooney listed a total Cheyenne population of 3,351 in 1907.[12] From this figure Cheyenne population went steadily downward, reflecting the poverty and poor sanitary conditions that were general among reservation Indians in this period, with a subsequent recovery in total population in the middle of the twentieth century.[13]

We can extrapolate these figures backward toward the time of the early French maps by adjusting the numbers for increase or decrease in birthrate and for deaths from war and disease. That is, by making various assumptions about birthrates and death rates, we can estimate the size of the Cheyenne population in earlier times.[14] But however we adjust such assumptions, we cannot avoid the conclusion that, compared with their neighbors, the Cheyennes were always a very small population. Caught geographically between the Sioux and the Chippewas, they had to make an alliance with someone simply to survive. Under attack by the Chippewas, Crees, and Assiniboines, they allied themselves with the Sioux, with consequences for social structure and band differentiation already noted. The Cheyennes' ultimate solution to their political problem, however, was to slide westward geographically through their Sioux allies and to form a new nation on the Great Plains. While the Dakota Sioux and the Southwestern Chippewas continued to face each other across a military frontier well into the nineteenth century, the Cheyennes, beginning east of the Sioux near

Lake Superior in 1680, actually preceded the Lakotas across the Missouri and into the Black Hills. There were, of course, many political, military, and ecological developments that helped and hampered them during this long process of migration, from 1680 to 1790, but it was a small population that made it necessary.

If the military purpose of the Chippewa Alliance in this period was to deny the Sioux and the Cheyennes clear access to fur-trade networks, it was mostly successful. When traders reported on the Cheyennes, it was always as marginal suppliers of furs, away from the major trade centers.[15] But it was not for lack of trying that the Cheyennes and their allies failed to enter the fur trade. In fact, the first recorded meeting between representatives of the Cheyennes and Europeans consisted of an attempt by a Sioux delegation to persuade La Salle that there were many beavers in their country at the headwaters of the Mississippi, and that the French should begin trading with them: "The *Chaa,* who live on the headwaters of the great river, arrived on the 24th of February and invited us to visit their homeland, where there is a great quantity of beavers, and of pelts."[16] Direct trade with the French did not develop, however, because the Sioux and their Cheyenne allies were soon pushed even farther west by the encroaching Crees, Chippewas, and Assiniboines.

Another motivation for the Cheyenne move westward, in addition to their desire to get away from the Sioux-Chippewa hostilities, was the possibility of getting European goods by another route. Once they had arrived at the Missouri River, they could secure French goods through the Mandans, who, according to the Vérendryes and Carver, had continuous trade relations with the Assiniboines throughout the eighteenth century.[17] Although the Cheyennes could not trade directly with the Assiniboines as long as they themselves were allied with the Sioux, they could trade indirectly from a position west and south, at the village locations noted on map 4. As mentioned in chapter 3, this route of trade from the French to the Mandans was still active at the time of Lewis and Clark.

Having arrived at the Missouri, however, the Cheyennes were still surrounded by sometimes hostile nations that were much more numerous. Just to the north, the Arikaras originally comprised thirty-two villages and 4,000 warriors, according to Truteau.[18] Lewis and Clark estimated the 1794 strength of the Dhegiha Sioux, just to the south, as 2,750 warriors, before the smallpox epidemic of 1802.[19] Applying a five-to-one ratio to reconstruct total population, we get a figure of 20,000 for the Arikaras and 13,750 for the Dhigehas, compared with 3,000 Cheyennes. Farther west, however, the demographic situation for the Cheyennes was more agreeable, since they could muster about the same number of warriors as the other Plains tribes—the Kiowas, Crows, Pawnees, and Arapahos.

Questions concerning the effects of disease on the original populations of Native American tribes are currently being investigated very closely, especially by Henry Dobyns and Russell Thornton. Concerning the Middle Missouri area where the Cheyennes migrated, the dates and extent of the earliest epidemics of European diseases, before Lewis and Clark, are largely unknown. Whether epidemics preceded the period of intensive trade from St. Louis, beginning about 1795 in that region, no one knows for sure. But in any event I have shown in chapter 3 that the Cheyennes were already far west of the river by that date and were nomadic, thereby avoiding the documented and devastating mortalities absorbed in that period by the sedentary riverine groups—the Pawnees, the Arikaras, the Mandans, and the Hidatsas.[20]

The very early population of the Cheyennes, during their movement west, can be estimated by another method—calculating from the sizes of the village sites they left along the way. Having established that there were three proto-Cheyenne divisions—the Chienatons, the Chongasketons, and the Oudebatons, we can make one kind of estimate by trebling population estimates for single village sites. This procedure of course assumes, rightly or wrongly, that the three divisions were of approximately the same size and that there was one division per village.

The best-known village attributed to the Cheyennes is Biesterfeldt, in North Dakota (fig. 7). According to Raymond Wood, there were probably sixty-two coextensive earthen lodges at Biesterfeldt when it was an active village, about 1750–90.[21] If we multiply this number of lodges by the number of persons who usually lived in such lodges in historical times, from twelve to nineteen, we get a population range for Biesterfeldt of 744 to 1,178.[22] Multiplying this by three, for the number of Cheyenne divisions, we get a range of 2,232 to 3,534 for the whole Cheyenne nation, a figure that tallies well with the later estimates of Clark, Schoolcraft, and Truteau. If we use Lehmer and Wood's lower estimate of ten persons per lodge, we still get a total population of 1,860, close to Clark's estimate of 2,000.[23]

If our estimates of Cheyenne population are good, then we can construct the following scenario, a hypothetical one for the present, to describe Cheyenne movements into and out of the Middle Missouri in the eighteenth century. First we see the Cheyenne divisions moving individually or as bands into the Middle Missouri, still maintaining alliances among themselves and with the Sioux, but also becoming neighbors and trading partners of some other Missouri villages, especially the Mandans. At least four

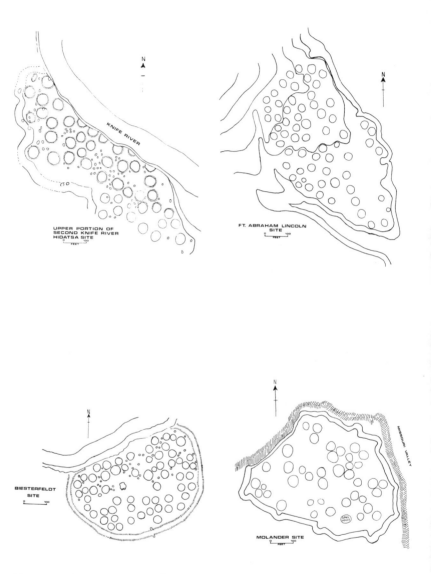

Figure 7.   Four village sites of the Middle Missouri. From Wood 1971, 7; Will 1924, 314, 317, 324. Redrawn on same scale by Rebecca Bateman.

Cheyenne bands developed special political relationships in this period—the "Ree band" with the Arikaras, an unnamed band (probably Omisis) with the Mandans, another unnamed band with the Hidatsas, and the Masikotas with the Tetons.[24] Still denied direct access to French trade and suffering from lack of numbers on the Missouri as they had on the Upper Mississippi, the Cheyennes in the middle part of the eighteenth century decided on yet another move, this time west of the Missouri. First they moved to the Grand River, and then into the Black Hills, as described in the oral history of chapter 4. This time their small population served them well, for they could move their whole group onto a single small river such as the Grand or the Cheyenne, rivers that would not have accommodated the whole populations of Arikaras, for example, or of the Dhegiha Sioux.

From the standpoint of *trade*, these westward moves were very successful, and they testify to the wisdom of Cheyenne leadership in that period. The Cheyennes soon succeeded in establishing themselves as middlemen between the Missouri River villages on the east and the more westerly nomadic nations—the Kiowas, Comanches, Apaches, and Arapahos. Their success as traders is richly documented in Tabeau's narrative, from which the following passages are quoted:

> Now that the Cheyennes have ceased to till the ground, they roam over the prairies west of the Missouri on this side of the Black Hills, from which they come regularly at the beginning of August to visit their old and faithful allies, the Ricaras. The Cheyennes, who have always visited either the whites or the Savages of the St. Peter's River, are, at least, as difficult to trade with as the Ricaras and a man, Guenneville, who came from among them, says nothing good of them. The nation has only a half-knowledge of the value of merchandise and prides itself, none the less, on being ignorant in this respect. This vain-glory has been conducive to my detriment in the slight trade of the Caninanbiches and others who obstinately defer to the Chayennes' judgment. The Ricaras, before this year, carried to the foot of the Black Hills, tobacco and maize. They accompanied the Chayennes and found at the meeting-place, eight other friendly nations—The Caninanbiches, the Squitanes, the Nimoussines, the Padaucas, the Catarkas, the Datamis, the Tchiwak, and the Cayowa. . . . With the exception of the Chayennes, all these nations, although always at peace with the Ricaras, never approached the Missouri; but the warm welcome they received and the inducement of finding a trader there will pledge them probably to an annual visit, as they promised, at the maturity of the corn. According to their statement, the Spaniards whom they see at St. Antonio or Santa Fe make light of their peltries and offer them only some hardware in exchange. In reality, they let

me see only crosses, tears of Job, and Agnus dei. In return, they buy there at a low price as many horses as they wish and rob them at their discretion. The horse is the most important article of their trade with the Ricaras. Most frequently it is given as a present; but, according to their manner, that is to say, is recalled when the tender in exchange does not please. This is an understood restriction. This present is paid ordinarily with a gun, a hundred charges of powder and balls, a knife and other trifles. Deer leather, well-dressed, shirts of antelope-skin, ornamented and worked with different-colored quills of the porcupine, shoes, and especially a quantity of dried meat and of prairie-apple flour are traded for certain commodities, particularly for the tobacco, which the Ricaras sell to them very well, because of this value.[25]

That the Cheyennes controlled trade access to the other Plains tribes is also made explicit in a paragraph from "Truteaux" (Truteau), written in about the same period, 1795–1805.

On the Southwest and to the West, on the branches of a large river (which I name the river of the Cheyennes) which empties into the Missouri about three miles above the second Ricara Village, are situated several nations called the Cayoguas, the Caminanbiches, the Pitapahotos, etc., all of different speech. The Cheyennes wander over the country along the river; a little below those first named. The vast country, not far from here, over which these different nations roam, abounds in beaver and otter, since they have never hunted these animals, not having had any intercourse with white men. It would be easy, by means of the Cheyennes who are their friends, to extend our commerce with those nations and obtain from them fine furs.[26]

Lewis and Clark, we should remember, echoed these same sentiments in their "comments" section on the Cheyennes. Specifically, they noted: "They are well disposed towards the whites, and might easily be induced to settle on the Missouri, if they could be assured of being protected from the Sioux. Their number annually diminishes. Their trade may be made valuable."[27]

After moving west of the Missouri, the main body of Cheyennes occupied three successive areas, each of which was characterized by a different emphasis in economy, different trade patterns, and different patterns of warfare (see map 4). In their first location, just east of the Black Hills, they continued to farm, and they traded between the riverine tribes and the Plains nomads. About 1805 the Cheyennes began to live more often between the forks of the Platte. In that location their major trade goods were beaver and otter skins, which they bartered to Mexican traders or traders from the "civilized Indians" who were beginning to come into the Plains in greater numbers.[28] After 1833 the Cheyennes traded at Bent's Fort on the

Arkansas, although the early trade there still emphasized beavers and otters. After the economic panic of 1837 in the United States, trade emphasis shifted to buffalo robes and horses.[29]

In a classic monograph, Joseph Jablow has written about how the Cheyennes assumed a central role in the trade relations of the Plains. Jablow, however, emphasized the period toward 1840, when the Cheyennes were situated farther south and horses had become their trade specialty.

Patricia Albers has presented a useful model for describing patterns of Plains warfare in the trade period. She says the connections among tribes can best be understood as links in a chain, with each tribe having two contiguous allies in the same chain.[30] For example, in their Black Hills period, the Cheyennes were linked to the Arikaras toward the east and the Kiowas toward the south. Warfare patterns, according to Albers, are not between tribes "linked" on the same chain of trade, but between tribes who represent the same kinds of links on different chains. For that reason Cheyenne warfare in that period was with the Crows, who also traded toward the Missouri.

But as trade patterns changed, patterns of warfare also changed, so that later we find the Cheyennes at war with the Kiowas, as they contested for trade in the central plains. Two recurrent myths concerning Plains warfare should be dealt with. First there is George Grinnell's myth that Plains warfare was not serious, but was conducted only for "coup" and war honors. This is a very myopic and naive view when applied to the Cheyennes, who admit to having exterminated an entire enemy tribe, and who both massacred and were massacred in many episodes of Indian intertribal warfare.[31] The other myth is that Plains tribes fought because they were "traditional enemies." This is no explanation at all, since we find that yesterday's "traditional enemies," such as the Kiowas, are today's "traditional allies." The problem of historical analysis is to discover how these "traditions" started and why.

During their period on the Upper Platte, the Cheyennes joined the Arapahos in warfare against the Crows and Shoshones.[32] The Cheyennes were prompted to leave the Upper Platte, in part, by the creation of the "rendezvous system" of beaver trapping in 1822, which emphasized the role of white trappers over Indians.[33] First the Hevhaitaneo and later the Oivimana band moved south toward the Arkansas, and then the other bands.[34] Horses became an increasingly important item of trade.

Joseph Jablow has described the horse and buffalo robe trade of this later period, from 1828 to 1850. Modern informants say there were basically three methods for obtaining horses in this period: by natural increase of the herd, by theft from other tribes, and by capturing wild horses. Two modern informants, who are the last holders of horse medicine (that is, they are native "horse trainers"), say that natural increase was the preferred source for horses.[35] This way the owner could gentle and doctor a colt from birth rather than "breaking" it, as with captured wild horses. Stolen horses were next in preference, because these presumably had been gentled in a proper manner, although the new owner had to learn a stolen horse's habits and eccentricities by trial and error.

As we shall see when we look at grass resources, the migrations of the Cheyennes in 1800–1850 increasingly placed them in areas where they could keep larger herds of horses through the winter. At more southerly latitudes and at lower elevations, winters were milder and horses could be maintained more successfully. In fact the large herds exhibited by the Cheyennes in 1864 and 1880 could have been kept all together near the Black Hills only at great risk from winter storms.

To enter trade in buffalo robes, the Cheyennes migrated to the region near Bent's Fort in Colorado at the invitation of trader William Bent, who married the daughter of the Cheyenne arrow keeper about 1835.[36] Bent was the first of several traders who entered this area after certain federal restrictions on Indian trade were removed in 1822. During this period, traders such as Bent could more than treble their money on goods brought overland from St. Louis. Bent also enjoyed the benefits of trade with New Mexico, where his brother was the first non-Mexican governor after the Mexican War. While this three-way trade was developing, two literate travelers, Lewis Garrard and George Ruxton, visited Bent's Fort and provided excellent descriptions of how the Cheyennes prepared and traded buffalo robes.[37] Ruxton estimated the total amount of trade at "one hundred thousand buffalo robes . . . annually."[38] In the following year, the Indian agent for the Upper Missouri Agency, comprising the Cheyennes and eight other "tribes," reported that 75,000 buffalo robes had been sold the previous year.[39] The value of these robes he estimated at $225,000 ($3 each) compared with only $35,000 paid that year for "furs, peltries, etc."

The increasing importance of buffalo robes in trade had profound consequences for Cheyenne families. Because the robes embodied a huge amount of women's work, polygynous families grew up that were organized around a group of co-wives who were also co-workers and sisters to one another. My colleague Greg Campbell has collected documents from this period that show how families were reorganized to accommodate the demands of robe making.[40]

It was council chiefs who became the focus of this robe trade, and it was they who were most often polygynous. In fact, the chief's domestic household centered on his role as trader and his wives' roles as producers of robes. We will examine these households in more detail in chapters 8 and 9, but here let me quote trader W. M. Boggs's description of a chief's camp that was mobilized to exploit the trade in buffalo robes.

> The Cheyenne village was located, for the fall and winter of 1844, to surround and kill buffalo and make dress robes for the trade of the Fort at the request of William Bent. The writer of these pages was sent from the Fort in company with "Bill" Gary and goods. Gary was an old trader in the employ of the Company, and was well versed in the Indians' language. He was a Canadian Frenchman but could not write. He could speak the Cheyenne language both by signs and words; he had a Sioux Indian wife, and one little boy, and lived in a lodge near to the large tepee of old Cinemo, the old Cheyenne Chief, who had given one-half of his lodge for the use of Bent's Company to keep their goods in, and received the robes as fast as they were dressed and prepared by the squaws of the village.[41]

W. T. Hamilton also reported that trade was conducted under the sponsorship of a Cheyenne chief. In 1842 he stopped to trade with the Hisiometaneo band, of which White Antelope was the resident council chief. Hamilton reports: "We unpacked and put up a wall tent, which we used for a store. Our stock was put in the chief's care."[42]

Lewis Garrard reported the same pattern when he visited Lean Chief's band in 1846, in company with the trader John Smith. After unpacking at the chief's lodge and presenting him with gifts, they told the chief what goods they had for trade. Lean Chief then summoned a crier, who was sent to address the village approximately as follows: "Blackfoot Smith has come to trade for mules. All who wish, come and trade. He has tobacco, blue blankets, black blankets, white blankets, knives, and beads."[43]

Because of trade, by 1850 the Cheyennes had transformed themselves from a marginal horticultural tribe of the Middle Missouri to a very successful nation of hunters and traders. And it is here that we can ask a significant historical question: How did it happen that the Cheyennes were the only one of the Middle Missouri horticultural tribes that succeeded in making the transition to equestrian nomadism in this period? That is, we should ask not only why the Cheyennes were successful, but also why the Arikaras, Mandans, Hidatsas, and Pawnees remained immobilized on the Missouri, frozen in space, while their cultures and populations were destroyed by war and disease between 1800 and 1860. These are essentially two sides to the same basic question, and we shall see in the following sections that this question can be answered by reference to some ecological and environmental factors that touched the histories of all these tribes. All their populations, large and small, were constrained by the same exacting requirements for wood, grass, and water.

Forests, Gardens, and Firewood

To begin at the beginning, ecologically, we should first consider the size and locations of the three seventeenth-century villages that ultimately became the Cheyenne nation. We should first ask ourselves, Why were they ever separate from each other? Especially during their residences in Minnesota and along the Sheyenne River, it would have been very beneficial, from the standpoint of defense, if the "Chienetons," the "Oudebatons" and the "Chongasketons" had all lived together. They would have been able to muster more warriors quickly, and they would have had the additional benefits of a more flexible economy and a richer social life. But there were ecological factors in Minnesota, in the Dakotas, and subsequently in the central plains that precluded the formation of larger villages.

The Southwestern Chippewas, who followed the Cheyennes as residents of northeastern Minnesota, also were unable to maintain large villages in that area. In the Chippewa case, however, we have a better grasp of ecological factors because there is more information from this later period. Harold Hickerson has researched historical documents and reconstructed Chippewa ecology, and he presented his evidence in a monograph written for the American Anthropological Association in 1962.[44] Essentially, he argued that although the Chippewas were committed to horticulture, they also depended greatly on hunting and gathering. Therefore each village had to have a substantial area where it could forage undisturbed by other tribes or even other Chippewas. It was the availability of wild resources that determined the maximum size of a village. Hickerson also went further and explained the pattern of continuing warfare between the Chippewas and the Dakotas by reference to these same ecological needs.

Although we have no direct historical evidence from the period of Cheyenne residence in Minnesota, we must assume that they were affected by these same ecological limitations when they lived there. The type of horticulture practiced there, "casual" or untended horticulture, was described briefly by Cheyenne informants in chapter 4. In this style of gardening the fields are left untended for part of the growing season, leaving the villagers free to forage. This foraging might last for several weeks or even for months. Schoolcraft reported one such foraging trip for the Chippewas in July 1831: "The lodges were carefully closed, and the grounds and paths around cleanly swept, giving the premises a neat air. The corn was in tassel.

The pumpkins partly grown, the beans fit for boiling. The whole appearance of thrift and industry was pleasing."[45]

American Indian horticulture in general, casual or not, was necessarily confined to forested areas. Indian people, including Chippewas and Cheyennes, were no more successful than European immigrants in finding a means of "busting" the tough sod of the plains and praires. In the eastern woodlands, as well as along the forested banks of the Missouri River as it coursed through the Great Plains, Indian farmers killed or felled trees and then planted their crops in the area previously shaded. Here the soil was rich and full of humus but relatively free of grass and weeds. Perhaps the best description of this type of farming was provided by Buffalo Bird Woman, a Hidatsa who described the whole process of farming to Gilbert Wilson in interviews conducted between 1912 and 1915.[46] Comparisons of different kinds of Indian farming in that area were provided by Will and Hyde (1917) and Preston Holder (1970).

As the Cheyennes moved westward and southward from Minnesota to the Sheyenne, the Missouri, the Grand, and the Black Hills, there was progressively less forest in which to make their gardens. As the Plains opened up to broad expanses of grass in the Dakota uplands, forests were increasingly confined to the floodplains and lowlands adjacent to major rivers. At the Biesterfeldt site in North Dakota, the riverine or "riparian" forest is merely a dark green ribbon curling among the grassy hills.

But what were the ecological consequences for the Cheyennes of moving to an area like this?[47] The basic questions here concern "limiting factors." For example, of the two crucial resources the Cheyennes needed in their village period—firewood and garden space—which would be exhausted first in the various locations they chose? Also, there is the issue of defense in warfare. Although defense, of itself, would encourage people to form the largest possible villages, ecological considerations would dictate smaller villages and a wider dispersal. That is, requirements for defense and for the conservation of resources in this ecological situation were entirely contradictory—one pushed a society toward fusion into large villages, and the other pushed it toward fission and dispersal. We will consider first the issue of defense and then look at requirements for wood and gardens.

Fortifications in this period not only consisted of timber palisades, but usually incorporated a natural precipitous drop-off—the riverbank, the bluff of the floodplain, or a steep terrace. On the Missouri River, some Indian groups maintained two separate fortified villages, one for summer and one for winter.[48] The summer village was typically built on the edge of the first high terrace, away from floods and insects, and the winter village was in the sheltered woods on the floodplain near the river. Although we lack documents to show that the Cheyennes themselves occupied seasonal villages when they lived on the Sheyenne and the Missouri, we do know that the Chippewas maintained such a system in the former Cheyenne homeland, and we know that other contemporary nations did so on the Missouri. We also know from the informants of chapter 4 that this seasonal system was typical of later Cheyenne experience on the Grand and Cheyenne rivers in South Dakota.

The diagrams of figure 7 compare Biesterfeldt with some other Middle Missouri villages of the same period. These diagrams have been redrawn from the originals and put on the same scale as Biesterfeldt.[49] The Molander site was originally thought to be an eighteenth-century Arikara village, but it is now classed as Hidatsa, and Fort Abraham Lincoln is from the same century but is Mandan. The village called Sakakawea (originally "Second Knife River") is reliably known to be Hidatsa. Although the various drawing styles of the original diagrams may have distorted things somewhat, there is still some variability in lodge size. This may help account for the differences in estimates for sizes of households already quoted from Lehmer and Smith. Many other diagrams have been reproduced in the scholarly literature, though only a few such sites have been excavated.[50]

It is interesting that the palisaded villages of this period tended toward a particular size, despite the fact that the riverine nations varied considerably in their total populations. The large nations, such as the Pawnees, Arikaras, and Mandans, were each split into a number of separate villages, although their total populations were in the tens of thousands. As villages were decimated by warfare and disease, the survivors continually combined their fragmented populations into new villages of about the same size as before.[51] This implies, I believe, an optimum size for villages in this period.

Blakeslee and Lehmer and Wood have commented on the social consequences of this geographical interplay among band, village, and tribe.[52] Blakeslee has emphasized the ethnic diversity that was created within Plains tribes by this continuing fragmentation of groups, and Lehmer and Wood have discussed population size and habitat. Bowers has provided an exceptionally detailed sociological study of how the Mandans, Hidatsas, and Arikaras continually juggled their social structure to form new composite villages.[53] Ultimately these three tribes joined together at Fort Berthold in North Dakota, creating fictive clan and ceremonial relationships among themselves to legitimate a new multicultural situation. Clearly, there were compelling natural or ecological forces at work in these years that caused these radical reorganizations, with all the resulting hardship and confusion for the peoples of the Middle Missouri.

It would be helpful, of course, if we had volumes of ecological data from this period regarding garden space and firewood use, but unfortunately the travelers of 1790–1850 were not all good enough ethnographers to go around Indian camps measuring firewood consumption rates or surveying the size of garden plots. Still, there are enough such observations that we can estimate the rates of exhaustion of these two crucial resources, wood and land. We can do this by combining such early observations as exist with an examination of present resources from published reports and scientific papers.

To estimate the garden space required by riverine horticulturists, we can begin with the observations in 1832 of Prince Maximilian of Weid, who gave about the same land use figures as Buffalo Bird Woman in 1912.[54] According to both sources, about five acres (two hectares) was required for the extended family of each lodge. When a village was founded, the small new gardens of different women were dispersed within the area to be used for horticulture, so that as the gardens grew, they would finally be contiguous at their full size of two hectares. At that point the gardens would begin to diminish in productivity, since no fertilizer was applied, and so new gardens had to be cleared nearby, or elsewhere if the village moved.

Although early travelers did not specifically measure firewood use, several noted that it was scarcity of firewood that most often caused villages to move. Griffin and Bowers have collected documents showing this.[55] Buffalo Bird Woman also gave this as a motivation for the move of the Mandans and the Hidatsas to the mouth of the Knife River.[56]

It is easy to confirm these observations on firewood by some rough calculations. In fact, no matter how one calculates firewood use for these riverine villages, the requirements were enormous. Looking at the experiences of army forts during the Plains wars, for example, where rates of use were better documented, we should note that several catastrophic defeats, such as the "Fetterman Fight," were occasioned by the necessity of sending firewood details many miles from the forts.[57] In 1864 a thirty-mile trip was required from Julesburg to get firewood.[58] By 1865 firewood expeditions had to be sent at least seven miles from Fort Larned, Kansas.[59] By 1880 firewood was exhausted within twelve miles of Fort Dodge, Kansas.[60] By estimating riparian timber resources, I calculate that roughly thirty wooded acres were required for every hundred soldiers per year.[61] This figure assumes that the soldiers were clear-cutting the forest, since they had axes and saws.[62] As we shall see, Indian methods were less exhaustive.

Another perspective for calculating firewood uses the modern figures generated by the United Nations and the United States Agency for International Development.[63] One set of figures for three tropical areas, Tanzania,

Gambia, and Thailand, ranges from 1.1 to 1.8 tons per person per year.[64] If we assume for temperate zones, with Graves, that there are ten cords per acre in an average woodland in North America, and that each cord of mixed hardwood weighs about 1.5 tons, then we calculate that a hundred persons would require fifteen acres of clear-cut woodland per year, by tropical standards.[65] This compares with the figure of thirty acres we calculated for the army forts. In part the difference may be that the forts housed mostly adults, who used more firewood per capita than the families with children, who were the basis of calculation for the tropical areas. Also, in tropical areas the winter usage would of course be less than in temperate areas, if the altitude were the same.

Another perspective can be taken from data provided by Robert Heizer.[66] If we use his estimate of 0.83 pounds of wood per family per day for northern California in aboriginal times, we get a yearly per capita figure of 2.3 tons. Using his data from central Mexico, where less wood is needed for winter fuel, we calculate a yearly per capita use of 0.8 tons. Looking at all our figures, then, it is reassuring to note that even beginning with estimates from widely disparate sources, we still calculate a fairly narrow range of per capita usage, from 0.8 tons for central Mexico to 3.6 tons for an army fort in Kansas. The corresponding amount of clear-cut deciduous temperate forest is from 6.7 to 30 acres for a hundred persons in a year.

When we compare the exhaustion of firewood to the exhaustion of garden space on the Middle Missouri by any organized method, we cannot avoid the conclusion that local firewood was used up while garden space was still available. I will not burden the reader here with all the assumptions and subanalyses that were part of my technical article published in 1982, but basically I examined four locations of villages that were alleged to be Cheyenne—Biesterfeldt on the Sheyenne River, Sanger on the Missouri, Grand River as mentioned by Grinnell and some informants in chapter 3, and a site on the Cheyenne River in South Dakota.[67] After examining the contours of the rivers and the density of the adjacent forests, estimating the available firewood and garden resources, and calculating the distance neces-sary for people to travel both to tend their gardens and to get wood for fuel, I concluded in all four cases that firewood was the crucial resource. Figure 8 shows the spatial model I used for my calculations, and table 8 summarizes the results.

The importance of this conclusion is that it explains quantitatively why there were three small proto-Cheyenne villages in the seventeenth century rather than one larger village. It explains why there was no Cheyenne nation before 1740, and why it therefore became necessary to found one. My figures also demonstrate that all of the Cheyennes could in fact have lived

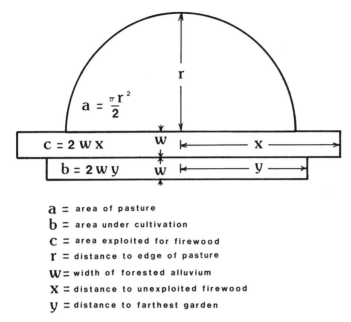

$$a = \frac{\pi r^2}{2}$$

$$c = 2\,w\,x$$

$$b = 2\,w\,y$$

a = area of pasture
b = area under cultivation
c = area exploited for firewood
r = distance to edge of pasture
w = width of forested alluvium
x = distance to unexploited firewood
y = distance to farthest garden

Figure 8.   Spatial model of resource use for riverine villages of the Middle Missouri.

together in the Middle Missouri area if it had been merely a matter of garden space. But this was not the limiting factor—firewood was. And so the Cheyennes, like other people, were split into village-sized units of 800 to 1,000 persons. In the Cheyenne case, there were three villages.

As the crisis of disease and warfare deepened toward the end of the eighteenth century, the Cheyenne villagers found themselves in a rather different position, ecologically, from the other nations of the Middle Missouri. By the time the Cheyennes had arrived at the Black Hills, according to the informants of chapter 4, they had begun to deemphasize farming and had reverted to the kind of horticulture that characterized the Cheyenne homeland in Minnesota. After planting their gardens in the spring and weeding them until the plants were established, the Cheyennes then went elsewhere, hunting and gathering wild plant food. In the words of Michelson's informant Tall Bull, "They came back westwards to hunt buffalo in the spring after they had planted corn. They expected to return when the corn was ripe."[68] This kind of system allowed all the Cheyennes to live together, first on the Grand River, then on the Cheyenne. They did not build a palisaded village in either place, apparently spending less time in

Table 8 Space and Resource Requirements for a Village of Fifty Families

LOCATION AND MAP REFERENCE	W (METERS)	X (METERS) AFTER YEARS				Y (METERS) AFTER YEARS				R_{MAX} (MILES)	A_P (ACRES)	G (ACRES)	P_H	H_{MAX}
		5	10	15	20	5	10	15	20					
Sheyenne River Venlo, N.Dak., 1960	100	6,250	12,500	18,750	25,000	5,000	7,500	8,750	9,375					
Missouri River Sanger N.Dak., 1966	1,200	521	1,041	1,562	2,083					2.3	5,318	72*	6.76	74
Grand River Miscol, S.Dak., 1956	400	1,562	3,125	4,688	6,250	1,250	1,875	2,188	2,344	1.0	1,005	6	2.99	167
Cheyenne River Rattlesnake Lake, SE S.Dak., 1955	200	3,125	6,250	9,375	12,500	2,500	3,750	4,375	4,688	1.2	1,448	5	1.73	290

Note: W = width of forested alluvium; X = distance to unexploited firewood; Y = distance to farthest garden; R_{max} = distance to edge of pasture; A_p = area of pasture; G = acres required per horse per winter; P_h = number of persons per horse; H_{max} = maximum size of horse herd in winter. *Grazing in wooded bottomland, not including browse.

the village and depending instead on their greater population size to protect them.

According to Robert and Lynn Alex, who are now excavating several sites in the Cheyenne River area, this style of village life and horticulture may be very old there.[69] In addition to agricultural opportunities, the Black Hills formerly provided a considerable winter population of buffaloes migrating seasonally from surrounding areas and also sustained populations of elk and deer.[70] It may be these features, and the possibility of horticulture, that earlier had attracted the Kiowas and Plains Apaches from their homelands in the Southwest. Oral traditions and early maps place them in the Black Hills before the Cheyennes. It is documented that the Apaches were occasional farmers, and the linguistic relationships of the Kiowas with the Tanoan pueblos indicates that they too may have previously been horticulturists.[71]

The kind of "casual" planting described by Cheyenne informants for their Black Hills ancestors, although it is an unusual style of horticulture, is not unknown among Plains groups. Some Apaches, even after they became nomadic, continued to practice this kind of casual or untended horticulture occasionally, well into the nineteenth century.[72] The Osages too, also in the middle nineteenth century, continued to plant "squaw patches" before they went westward every summer to hunt for buffaloes.[73] Hyde reports that at certain times the Pawnees did likewise.[74]

Grinnell's assertions that Cheyenne horticulture continued until 1830 are well known, and some modern informants tell me that the Cheyennes never really ceased to practice horticulture, planting in Oklahoma as soon as they arrived on the reservation in 1870.[75] This can be confirmed from government reports for the period 1874–79.[76] The areas on the North Canadian near Fonda (map 24) and farther east near Calumet (maps 21 and 22) were especially suitable, and they soon became the sites of large horticultural Cheyenne camps.[77]

The Cheyennes' struggle to maintain their farming in the face of opposition from the government, from homesteaders, and from local white entrepreneurs has been examined in a doctoral dissertation by Robert Nespor.[78] Contrary to the accepted myth, allotment in severalty was not designed to encourage Cheyenne agriculture, nor did it. Instead, it destroyed a thriving native system of farming and ranching and ensured that the Cheyennes would lose their land and live in poverty. As early as 1876, the agent for the Cheyennes, John Miles, reported the following:

> Seventy-five acres were assigned them from one of the agency-fields, which was subdivided into small patches, containing from one to five acres, for each family, and was generally planted to corn, potatoes, melons, and various

kinds of garden products, the same being furnished by me at Government expense and by Benjamin Coates, a Friend, of Philadelphia, and from their neighbors, the Caddoes. A more earnest effort I never witnessed put forth by any people than was by the Cheyennes, so far as their means and knowledge extended, and as a result they have been quite successful and have already received and are now receiving a fair reward for their industry.

I have seen some of these Cheyennes, who could not secure the use of a plow or hoe, use their axes, sticks of wood, and their hands in preparing the ground, planting and cultivating their garden spots, so anxious were they to make a beginning.[79]

By 1889 the agent reported that 185 family farms were in operation, and in 1892 the projected corn harvest for the Cheyennes was 100,000 bushels.[80] That year, however, the land was given over to white settlers, and so the harvest was aborted and what corn was left on Cheyenne land was soon trampled down by homesteader activity or eaten by their stock.[81] The projected 1892 harvest, however, would have been about 31 bushels per capita, good for those days. Also, the quick success of the Cheyennes in reservation farming confirms, I believe, that they were experienced in horticulture.

To summarize our conclusions so far, we can see that the Cheyenne system of untended horticulture, as it was developed in the Black Hills, had benefits for the people far beyond the annual harvest of produce. First of all, as reported by Tabeau, it left them free during the summer to collect wild fruits and vegetables as a hedge against the failure of their crops.[82] Even after the full shift to nomadism, the Cheyennes continued to trade meat for corn when they could, but the "prairie turnip" soon became a substitute for corn. Second, the system of untended horticulture enabled the Cheyennes to husband their scarce timber resources and to keep a larger population together year-round. Third, the Cheyennes were able to trade at distant places. And last, they now could keep larger herds of horses, for they were no longer bound to their home pastures for the entire growing season. Ultimately, as we shall see, it was this third fringe benefit of untended horticulture—large herds of horses—that made the historical difference, if it did not in fact save them from the annihilation soon visited on the Arikaras, Mandans, and Hidatsas.

Fire, Prairie, and Forests

As the Cheyennes moved west and south, from the Missouri to the Black Hills to the central plains, they were cast adrift on a sea of grass. But their need for firewood still existed: they needed poplar, cottonwood, and other light woods for cooking in the summer, and they needed oak and other hardwoods for heating as well as cooking in the winter.[83] After leaving the Sheyenne River, the Cheyennes became accustomed to finding firewood mostly along Plains rivers, but the patterns of forestation were not the same in the period 1790–1869 as they are now.

Map 6 shows the patterns of riparian and nonriparian forests on the Plains, based on the research of Philip Wells of the University of Kansas.[84] He calls attention not only to the "long stringers of gallery for-

Map 6.   Forests of the central plains. Redrawn from Wells 1965 by Mary Goodman.

est . . . extending westward along the streams" but also to the "local occurrence of woodlands along escarpements or abrupt breaks in topography, remote from fluvial irrigation." He accounts for the distribution of nonriparian forests by noting "the simple fact that abrupt scarps or topographic breaks have acted as natural fire breaks." From early accounts of American settlement on the Plains, it is apparent that these nonriparian forests are not of recent origin. For example, Capt. Eugene Ware described one such forest in far western Nebraska, near Fort Kearney: "Then beautiful valleys were seen, narrow and deep, full of enormous cedar trees, box elders, hackberry, plum trees, and shrubbery. . . . We rode along this plain, over these beautiful valleys, for fully ten miles."[85]

Wells also points out that it is not lack of water that explains the dominance of grasses anywhere on the Great Plains, but rather the periodic destruction of forests by fire. In fact, the evolutionary advantage of grasses over other kinds of plants, since the Oligocene, has been their ability to regenerate quickly after fire.[86] The prevalence and recurrence of fire in North America is discussed at length in Stephan Pyne's recent book, which devotes a section to the intentional firing of the prairie by Indian people.[87] The United States Army also intentionally fired the prairie in periodic attempts to "burn out" the Cheyennes and other hostile tribes. The most ambitious attempt was on 27 January 1865, when troops fired the whole area along the Platte River road, from Kansas to Wyoming. Three days later the same fire is said to have crossed the Arkansas River, two hundred miles to the south, and continued on through the Texas Panhandle.[88]

Modern informants tell me that the Cheyennes often fired the area near a good camping place to promote the growth of new grass. If the camp was moving into the wind, and if it was dry enough, the old grazing area was burned so there would be abundant fresh grass when the campsite was used again. They also say that attempts of the army to burn them out failed because the Cheyennes usually camped in relatively fireproof areas in the riparian forests, and they could set backfires to protect themselves.

Until recently it has been assumed that the distribution of riparian forests on the Plains could be explained by the prevalence of fire. That is, it has been thought that forests could grow along rivers only where the floodplain or bottomlands were protected by the same kind of scarps and steep banks as protected the nonriparian forests elsewhere. In support of this view, modern Plains residents point out that it was not until after World War II, with the improvement of county roads and firebreaks, that forests were able to establish themselves in a continuous band along the Arkansas, Platte, and Niobrara rivers.[89] Before that, it is documented that large prairie fires continually swept over the central plains, even after Indian people had been confined to reservations and the area was characterized by farms and ranches rather than unconfined prairie.[90]

Biologist Joe Tomelleri, however, has provided another explanation for the discontinuity of riverine forests in the aboriginal period. Based on an intensive examination of the Arkansas River in western Kansas, he argues that trees have repopulated the Arkansas riverbed in recent years because of the water control and water conservation of farmers and ranchers in the Arkansas watershed.[91] Aboriginally, he argues, each spring saw huge floods along the river, which destroyed the seedlings of woody plants, except in certain areas of definable height and soil type.

Whether it was fire or recurrent floods that periodically limited the growth of trees along Plains rivers, it seems clear that in the aboriginal period the Plains were characterized by immense expanses of grass, punctuated by smaller areas of forest shade found intermittently along rivers and along the rocky escarpements, as shown in map 6. During the Plains wars, army officers, of course, were very sensitive to the kind of habitat where Indian camps might be found. General George Custer described one such location, in Kansas, as follows: "Like all Indian encampments, the ground chosen was a most romantic spot, and at the same time fulfilled in every respect the requirements of a good camping-ground; wood, water, and grass were abundant."[92] In the fight that followed, Custer remarked that the Indian warriors were "sheltered behind the trunks of the stately forest trees under which their lodges were pitched." Later, at the Battle of the Washita, Custer noted again that the Cheyenne village was situated in "timber," and he fought that battle, likewise, among the trees. Even in one of the driest parts of Texas, the Palo Duro Canyon, army officers noted: "Cedar, cottonwood, and wild china furnished fuel, and the grass was abundant. . . . The recesses of the canyon and of nearby breaks at the edge of the Caprock were favored winter campsites of the Indians because of the protection they provided against the dreaded Plains northers and the easy access to fuel, water, and grass."[93]

A captive of the Cheyennes when they hid in the Palo Duro Canyon in 1874 was Catherine German, who survived to write a narrative of her experiences. Some of her recollections are significant for our ecological study: "There were perhaps three hundred lodges in this village. A general survey of the camping site revealed the lodges surrounding a rainwater pond. . . . This depression was large enough to conceal the lodges if viewed from the distance of a mile or more. This was located on the Staked Plains of Texas where only buffalo grass grew. . . . I saw many squaws coming from a wooded canyon, carrying loads of wood."[94]

From our brief examination of wood resources, we have seen that although the central plains comprise a huge area, only certain portions were desirable from the standpoint of firewood. In addition to Plains forests, sometimes quantities of firewood could be found in immense "drifts"— dead trees killed in some catastrophe—that collected at the bends of rivers or in shallow water where large logs could not float. Whenever possible, according to modern informants, the Cheyennes camped near these drifts. One such camp is documented as the site of the 1840 alliance among the Cheyennes, Arapahos, Kiowas, Comanches, and Apaches. According to historical accounts, the enormous camp, which comprised about 10,000 to 20,000 persons, was "at the mouth of Two Butte Creek, at the south side of the Arkansas River, where the dead timber lies so thick."[95]

Other reservoirs of firewood are preserved in the names of Plains streams, many of which are called Deadwood Creek or Driftwood Creek. One of these streams, in western Nebraska south of Trenton, is still an active producer of driftwood. Situated in an isolated area, the headwaters of the creek are still thickly grown with burr oak and other hardwoods, which are occasionally killed by flood or fire and drop into the creek, causing drifts to build up farther downstream toward the Platte. I visited this area in the summer of 1982, after Cheyenne elders told me it was a refuge area for the Dog Soldiers in the late 1860s, an assertion confirmed by army accounts.[96]

Modern informants say that the Cheyennes, after becoming nomadic, could no longer use the stone mauls of earlier times for breaking firewood. These mauls, like the stone mortars and pestles that were also typical of their more sedentary period, were too heavy to carry great distances, though they were cached around favorite camping places on the Plains where possible.[97] On the Plains a wooden hook was used to collect firewood by pulling dead branches down from standing trees. Forked digging sticks were also used sometimes; the gatherer climbed the tree and pushed branches down to break them. Later, axes became increasingly common among the Cheyennes; forty-nine axes were found in a Cheyenne camp of 111 lodges in 1867.[98] Plate 8 shows the rope rigging Cheyenne women used to carry wood back to camp.

By adopting a nomadic life, then, the Cheyennes solved their firewood problems. No longer foot-bound or confined to the area around a sedentary village, the nomadic Cheyennes could move to new locations to get fresh supplies of firewood, or take their pack horses to bring firewood back to camp. Since wood was no longer a scarce resource, the Cheyennes exploited the forests only superficially, taking only the wood that was easiest to collect. In the next section I will present some calculations showing that, compared with the need for grass, the availability of firewood did not severely limit the movements of Cheyenne bands.

Plate 8.   Rope rigging used by Cheyenne women to carry firewood. Negative no. 13587, Museum of the American Indian, Heye Foundation.

Water and Grass

The term "oasis" did not come into use to describe the well-watered, habitable places within the Great Plains, despite the great contrast between these spots and the rest of what Zebulon Pike had called the "Great American Desert."[99] Anyone nowadays visiting such oases as survive in the Great Plains, even in August, will find them pleasant and habitable islands of water and shade in an area where the late summer sun is still brutal in its effect on people, plants, and animals. One important difference between such areas now and aboriginally, however, is the presence of surface water.

Since the development of the Great Plains for agriculture and ranching, the area has been characterized not only by a radical lowering of the water table, but by an equally radical diminution in the amount of surface runoff.[100] In this area "water conservation" is defined as a combination of practices designed to retain water where it falls as rain and to prevent it from entering surface systems of streams, springs, and lakes. In former times, however, even such dry areas as eastern Colorado were characterized by large lakes and perennial springs, which were usually marked by distinct, isolated stands of poplar, cottonwood, and ash. Custer described Plains watering spots as no more than fifteen miles apart.[101] The springs of the central plains, however, have dried up as the water table has dropped, though some still flow during wet periods. The small stands of aboriginal timber around springs were mostly cut for fence posts and corrals in the early days of American settlement.

Some of the former lakes in eastern Colorado still refill during wet periods. As it happens, one of the years when I did my fieldwork, 1982, was a very wet year, and Lake Sheridan, in the driest part of southwest Colorado, occupied about half its former area but had water plants, ducks, and shorebirds. This is in an area of the Great Plains where present rainfall is about twelve inches per year. Modern informants also say this area formerly maintained large populations of wild horses. This makes sense biologically, since horses require frequent trips to the water hole, perhaps three times a day.[102]

As the Cheyennes entered the central plains from the Black Hills area, it was not enough that they should find surface water; the water had to be fresh and not too saline or alkaline. Map 7 shows the areas of the central plains where water, for at least part of the year, is too full of solutes to be potable for people or horses.[103] Almost always in the spring, however, and sometimes after general rains, even the most saline or alkaline streams are potable for a brief period.[104] So according to early accounts, there was no place on the Plains where water was truly scarce except during the periodic droughts, which affected not only surface water, but also grazing.

Compared with wood and water, grass in general was not so scarce a resource. But *good* grass *was* crucial, and we should now look at the grazing requirements for Indian horses and the availability of various grasses in different areas of the central plains. The consensus among botanists is that water is the most important factor in grass production. More than anything else, rain determines the amount of grass of any variety that will grow in any particular year. Grasses adapted themselves to survive the periodic fires of the prairie and were also adapted to survive drought. In fact, one definitive characteristic of the plains is not only the yearly drought, which occurs in later summer, but also cycles of drought over several years.

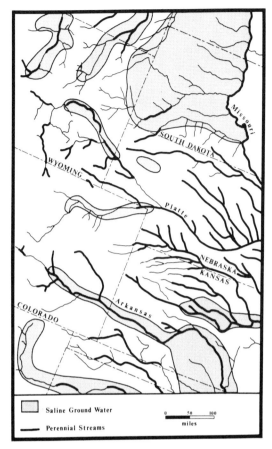

Map 7.   Water resources of the central plains. Redrawn by Mary Goodman from *Water Atlas of the Central Plains* (Geraghty et al. 1973).

Table 9 shows the variability in rainfall over the summer months for eight selected areas of the Great Plains formerly inhabited by the Cheyennes. The pattern of yearly drought in July and August can easily be seen. Cycles of drought over several decades have been discussed by Richard Skaggs. Using western Kansas as an example, he has tried to detect regularities in the cycles.[105] The uncertainty of rainfall meant that, in practical terms, the amount of grass available in any location on the Great Plains was highly variable from year to year.

In my research I have been fortunate to interview some of the last men who were traditional horse trainers, owning medicine bundles originally

Table 9 Monthly Rainfall in Aboriginal Cheyenne Territory in Summer

YEAR	APRIL	MAY	JUNE	JULY	AUGUST	YEAR	APRIL	MAY	JUNE	JULY	AUGUST
	Fort Fetterman, Wyoming						Rapid City, South Dakota				
1869	0.52	0.44	1.26	1.36	0.60	1888	6.41	6.01	4.74	1.69	4.76
1870	1.20	2.26	0.88	0.62	2.46	1889	4.22	2.19	2.97	4.52	0.11
1871	1.44	2.06	1.14	3.20	0.14	1890	1.55	2.46	3.77	0.13	1.83
1872	1.72	4.74	1.51	0.94	1.60	1891	2.72	1.72	3.25	2.09	1.97
1873	1.70	6.04	0.40	0.22	1.02	1892	4.04	4.49	3.80	6.67	2.00
1874	1.96	1.02	2.58	1.75	0.96	1893	1.05	1.73	1.21	1.51	0.63
1875	1.44	1.50	0.93	2.52	0.54	1894	4.24	0.72	4.17	1.31	0.65
1876	0.24	1.00	1.20	2.12	0.30	1895	1.53	2.66	6.22	0.39	0.09
1877	1.10	2.86	0.50	0.78	0.32	1896	1.67	0.60	3.35	1.73	0.13
1878	3.72	2.72	1.23	1.05	0.57	1897	0.69	1.82	2.07	0.71	2.15
	Denver, Colorado						Beaver City, Nebraska				
1872	2.09	3.74	2.07	2.69	1.75	1882	3.43	9.73	5.93	1.79	1.97
1873	2.43	1.75	2.24	2.00	1.41	1883	5.19	3.87	6.94	5.50	4.86
1874	1.70	2.43	1.21	3.35	1.68	1884	4.13	8.73	0.62	6.12	2.62
1875	2.24	1.94	0.43	4.17	1.97	1885	1.87	2.05	8.80	10.24	1.67
1876	1.22	8.57	1.10	1.16	2.03	1886	2.99	4.06	4.44	2.05	4.66
1877	2.77	2.30	1.93	0.33	1.30	1887	5.17	1.68	2.31	2.73	5.54
1878	0.05	2.90	2.78	1.33	2.25	1888	3.44	6.18	2.63	1.74	1.24
1879	2.62	3.36	0.32	0.64	1.38	1889	1.31	2.50	2.62	7.87	1.74
1880	0.31	1.11	1.22	1.38	1.46	1890	2.11	1.56	4.29	1.05	3.69
1881	0.50	2.21	0.09	2.50	2.33	1891	3.28	5.37	8.31	4.34	3.00

Two Buttes, Colorado

Year					
1887	—	—	—	5.00	2.71
1888	3.64	2.36	0.53	2.93	—
1890	6.31	1.03	—	3.19	0.97
1891	0.75	2.56	4.42	4.06	0.97
1892	0.24	4.68	0.37	2.00	1.85
1893	0.21	2.29	0.70	2.92	2.85
1894	1.51	3.22	1.84	0.89	1.23
1895	1.77	1.89	2.98	8.56	1.48
1896	1.67	0.80	1.39	1.75	0.89
1897	1.27	0.89	0.79	4.65	5.19

Amarillo, Texas

Year					
1892	0.21	2.70	1.49	1.85	1.93
1893	0.16	2.19	2.03	2.05	2.67
1894	0.85	1.30	3.59	1.82	3.41
1895	1.31	1.78	6.84	2.88	3.87
1896	1.95	2.20	2.31	7.04	0.63
1897	1.08	4.44	2.32	2.16	2.71
1898	0.98	3.52	4.81	3.88	4.03
1899	0.23	3.12	4.45	6.96	0.51
1900	5.47	4.53	1.84	3.21	0.83
1901	4.90	5.99	0.92	1.56	3.03

Dodge City, Kansas

Year					
1874	—	—	—	—	2.06
1875	0.71	2.26	0.63	3.28	1.03
1876	0.16	1.16	2.53	2.26	4.09
1877	3.38	4.96	3.92	1.79	4.48
1878	1.06	4.63	2.19	1.61	3.75
1879	0.40	0.90	4.40	3.90	5.17
1880	0.11	3.33	1.59	4.00	2.36
1881	2.38	12.82	1.77	5.06	1.07
1882	0.68	3.87	1.51	3.04	5.66
1883	2.40	5.41	4.31	2.61	—

Fort Reno, Oklahoma

Year					
1883	1.00	2.21	9.48	3.59	5.53
1884	3.64	6.79	4.44	2.21	3.22
1885	2.26	9.33	10.33	1.63	2.66
1886	2.80	0.31	2.86	0.82	0.34
1887	0.89	3.99	4.38	1.10	1.90
1888	2.28	4.43	0.28	3.19	2.82
1889	1.22	1.80	6.55	2.54	4.88
1890	6.02	2.87	0.76	1.87	3.21
1891	2.10	3.02	5.02	6.97	1.02
1892	1.12	7.37	2.62	1.80	4.30

Note: Rainfall for first ten years is shown for those locations with the earliest records. Data from U.S. Weather Bureau.

obtained from the Mescalero Apaches. The most desirable grasses for horses, in their opinion, are some particular shortgrasses of the central plains—blue grama and side oats grama, buffalo grass, and little bluestem. In fact, these preferred grasses frequently grow together as discrete plant communities, and their ranges correspond nicely to the area where the Cheyennes lived aboriginally (map 8).[106] It is easy to interpret the Cheyenne pastoral economy as particularly adapted to these grasses.

One characteristic of Plains grass communities that might seem odd at first is the markedly *mosaic* pattern of grass growth. That is, it is quite usual for the growth of grasses to be four times greater on one side of a stream, gully, or ridge than on the other. In some locations this might be because the grass is occasionally subirrigated in one area and not the other, because of proximity to the water table, because of the contours of underlying rock or soil layers, or because south-facing slopes are generally drier. In other locations, however, the difference in grass production is due entirely to difference in soil type. In a recent article Alan Osborn has discussed the variability in Plains environments, although without much discussion of soil, microenvironments, or horse husbandry. These factors are crucial,

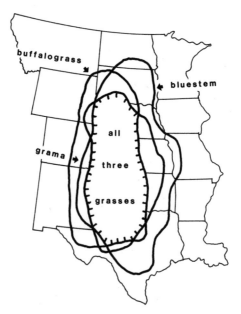

Map 8.   Ranges of three important shortgrasses on the central plains. Redrawn from Archer and Bunch 1953.

however, for as Jesse Leavenworth observed about Indians in 1864, "Wherever the grass fails them they remove to some other point."[107]

Fortunately for our purposes, the soil survey of the Great Plains is now nearly complete, so that maps are readily available from the Soil Conservation Service showing the great contrast in soil types among the microenvironments of the Great Plains. Even the area of the Sand Hills of Nebraska, where one might expect homogeneity, shows tight contrasts in the types of soils found juxtaposed within a distance of a few meters. Map 9 shows the contrasts in soil type and grass production at one particularly relevant site, the Sand Creek Crossing in Kiowa County, Colorado, a favorite camping spot of the Cheyennes and the site of the Sand Creek Massacre in 1864.[108] The modern locations of forest are also shown, as well as the location of a huge aboriginal spring, now mostly dry, and some bluffs along the stream that protected the area from storms.

The half-Cheyenne George Bent, who was present at the massacre, has provided a map of the site from an Indian perspective.[109] Reproduced here as map 10, the diagram confirms that the Cheyennes did indeed pasture their horses in the area of best grass. The present owner of the site, Mr.

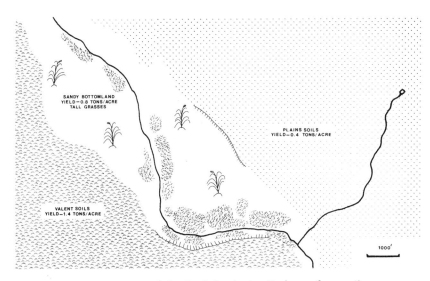

Map 9.   Present contours of the Sand Creek site. Redrawn from soil survey map for Kiowa County, Colorado.

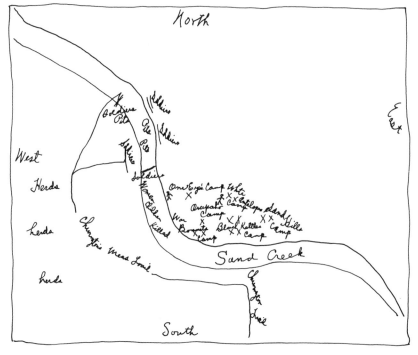

Map 10.   Tracing of George Bent's map of Sand Creek.

Robert Dawson, says that the area still provides better grazing than any of the nearby types of soil.

George Bent also provided a general map of the aboriginal territory of the Cheyenne Indians, preserved in the archives of the University of Colorado at Boulder. Here Bent emphasized the "Big Timbers" areas and other good camping places that I have plotted on map 5. Another map, by cavalry officer Eugene Ware (map 11), shows the area frequented by the Cheyenne Dog Soldiers when they were attacked in the winter of 1865. He also described this "Big Timbers" of the Republican River in terms of the resources of grass, wood, and water found there. This is one of the camping areas noted by George Bent. In Ware's words:

> Up along the stream above the junction was a beautiful level table, with bluffs high and rough but well back. . . . The bluffs were about a mile from the edge of the Republican river. . . . It was stated by the guides that the "Big Timbers" at the Republican practically ceased five miles above this place. The big timbers were enormous cottonwood trees that were along the

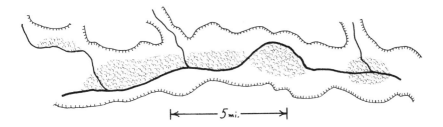

Map 11. Capt. Eugene Ware's map of the Republican "Big Timbers." Redrawn from Ware 1960, 342. This area is between the present towns of Benkelman and Trenton, Nebraska. The bottoms comprise loamy soils of the Bridgeport Association, according to the soil surveys of Dundy and Hitchcock counties, soils that support rich stands of grass.

> Republican in and around here. Above them there were only scattering trees on the river. These trees finally ran out into nothing, towards the west. Nine miles below this place the big timbers almost entirely ceased, so that this camp was in the very midst of the big timbers. These big timbers were therefore about fourteen miles long, and filled most of the bottomlands. There were several springs coming in at this place, and on the edge and through the timbers were dense growths of grass. . . . Above this camp five miles, and ten miles on the north side and ten miles on the south side, streams came in from the hills. These big timbers were all cottonwood trees averaging and exceeding two feet in diameter, and located on an average of about one to every fifty yards square, without a particle of underbrush, but a dense growth of high bottom-grass. Here was where the buffalo used to live, and here we found Indian signs everywhere prevalent.[110]

The best-known "Big Timbers" area was near the present La Junta, Colorado, the site of the "Big Timbers Museum." In fact, many people believe this was the only and original "Big Timbers." Pike originally described the river here as "entirely covered with woods on both sides."[111] In 1847 Abert added, "All along today's and yesterday's march we were passing along the Big Timber, a fine place to locate a fort. The Indians winter here yearly, it has such advantages for wood, grass, water."[112] Visiting the area at about the same time, Ruxton described it as follows: "Our next camping place was the 'Big Timber,' a large grove of cottonwood on the left bank of the river, and a favorite wintering place of the Cheyennes. Their camp was now broken up, and the village had removed to the Platte for their summer hunt. The debris of their fires and lodges were plentifully scattered about, and some stray horses were running about the bottom."[113]

As I visited other historically recorded Cheyenne campsites in summer 1982, the story was everywhere the same—good grass, timber, and fresh water. Even at Summit Springs, Colorado, where there are at present no springs and no trees, local ranchers admired the grass and told me that the area originally had several springs, a marsh, and an enormous canopy of cottonwoods. At Sand Creek some of the cottonwood growth has survived. A grove of cottonwoods from the Big Timbers near La Junta is shown in plate 9.

Another well-preserved former campsite is on the north side of the Cimarron River, near Freedom, Oklahoma. Still another is on the Smoky Hill River, in Kansas, where the river is nearly continuously timbered, with little of the discontinuity owing to fire or flood exhibited by other rivers. This area is also locally known as a "Big Timbers," as on Bent's map and in other early accounts.[114]

It can be shown—by the same techniques used before for wood and garden space—that as the Cheyennes utilized the grazing areas around such campsites in aboriginal times, they exhausted the grass long before they ran out of firewood. We can demonstrate this by making considered estimates of grass and timber resources and then estimating rates of consumption, as we did for riverine villages.

To calculate the utilization of grass by Cheyenne horses, we must first recognize the difference between what agronomists call "increasers" and "decreasers," the latter also colloquially called "ice cream grasses." The ice cream grasses are those horses seem to prefer and seek out in any mixed

Plate 9. Some surviving cottonwoods from the Big Timbers area near La Junta, Colorado. The boy is five feet tall.

pasture. As a consequence of being selectively eaten, these grasses tend to "decrease" in frequency compared with other grasses, while those less preferred tend to increase.

In modern times horses, like other stock, are confined by fences, and so ultimately they must eat the increasers once the decreasers diminish. But in a free-roaming situation, according to modern informants, Indian horses tended to move on to ungrazed areas rather than eat less preferred grasses. Even in the best shortgrass pastures, Cheyenne informants estimate that horses would eat "less than half" of the available grass. Therefore, in Cheyenne horse husbandry, a critical point was reached at each campsite when the herders could no longer keep the horses within sight of camp. At that point the camp had to be moved so that the herds could be more easily watched and guarded.

In winter, however, the horses tended to stay nearer the tipis and the sheltering riparian forests, and they grazed the available grasses to the ground. If local grass was exhausted in winter, the herders could cut cottonwood branches and let the horses chew the bark and twigs. It is only a myth, however, that horses could subsist entirely on tree bark and branches in the wintertime. Any rough estimate of the work required to cut branches for winter feeding of thousands of horses shows the implausibility of the theory. But General Custer nevertheless stated: "In routing the Indians from their winter villages, we invariably discovered them located upon that point of the stream promising the greatest supply of cottonwood bark, while the stream in the vicinity of the village was completely shorn of its supply of timber, and the village itself was strewn with the white branches of the cottonwood entirely stripped of their bark."[115]

According to modern informants, Cheyenne villages were not sited in cottonwood forests primarily to accommodate horses. In agreement with what Ewers reports for the Blackfeet, Cheyennes say that bark was only an emergency food, and that villages were sited with grass, not cottonwoods, as a primary consideration.[116] Optimally, a wintering site would have enough dead hardwood, especially oak, for fires and enough tallgrass so that horses could graze even after a snowfall. Tallgrass in the Plains, however, was usually coarse and lacking in nutrition, according to informants, and so it, like tree bark, was an emergency food.

Finding enough good winter pasture was a crucial consideration in the aboriginal period, and so Cheyennes often broke up into small "wintering groups." In modern ranch practice, however, this is no longer such a problem, because stock can be fed through the winter from barns and haystacks. Therefore it would be difficult to assess the original winter grass capability of the central plains were it not for a remarkable book written in

1871. At that time winter pasture was a problem not only for Indian people, but also for pioneer stockmen.

Hiram Latham's book *Trans-Missouri Stock Raising* was authorized by the Union Pacific Railroad to encourage settlement along their route through the central plains. For that reason, one might expect some exaggeration of the benefits of settlement in that area and some inaccuracies in Latham's data on climate, water, and grass. But much of the book is a compendium of letters from soldiers, traders, and stockmen already in that area, giving data that tally well with what is known at present from more thorough research. One letter, from Gen. L. P. Bradley at Fort Russell, purports to describe the grazing from the Big Horn south to the Smoky Hill: "The air is so fine that the grasses cure on the ground without losing any of their nutriment, and . . . the climate is so mild and genial that stock can range and feed all the winter and keep in excellent condition without artificial shelter or fodder. . . . I believe that there is no place in this section of the country, from latitude 47 degrees down, where cattle and sheep will not winter safely with no feed but what they can pick up, and with only the rudest shelter."[117]

Using the documents in Latham's book as well as some more recent studies of the range potential of various areas in the central plains, augmented by my interviews with ranchers and conservationists in the area, I have calculated the potential for winter pasture of several campsites where the Cheyennes located in aboriginal times.[118] The results are summarized here in figure 9 and table 10, although a fuller presentation of calculations and assumptions can be found in my 1982 article.[119] One basic purpose of these calculations, as with gardens and firewood, is to compare the limitations of grass and firewood as crucial resources. Although there is some leeway in my assumptions and methods of calculation, anyone replicating my work still cannot avoid the conclusion that grass was the crucial factor that dictated, in this case, when it was time to move camp.

Table 10 also tells us something about why Cheyenne bands were a certain size. The larger bands exhausted the grass quickly, and so large gatherings were possible only in early summer, when grass was tall and plentiful. It is significant in this regard that the great ceremonies of the Cheyennes occur just past the peak of spring rainfall, about middle or late June. Data collected for the Kiowas by Levy shows how crucial the rainfall factor was for their ceremonies.[120] Since they were in a drier area farther to the south, there were some years in which the drought and sparseness of grass caused a cancellation of the Kiowa Sun Dance. However, I know of no such report for the Cheyennes.

Some early documents indicate a pattern of transhumance for the

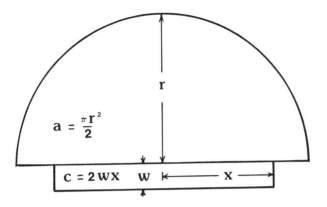

a = area of pasture
c = area exploited for firewood
r = distance to edge of pasture
w = width of forest
x = distance to unexploited firewood

Figure 9.   Spatial model of resource use for nomadic Cheyenne camps.

Cheyennes, as they moved several hundred miles from a wintering area to their summer camps. Ruxton's observation has already been quoted: that the Cheyennes moved one year from their winter camps on the Arkansas Big Timbers to their hunting range on the Upper Platte. Hoistah also reported a pattern of transhumance, this time between the Upper Platte and the Black Hills. She reported that the Black Hills were the wintering area and present-day Wyoming was the summer territory.[121]

So far in this study of Cheyenne ecology, no mention has been made of buffaloes. This is because I believe that chasing buffaloes has been greatly exaggerated as a cause for Plains Indian band movements.[122] First of all, we should note that when the Cheyennes followed the grass, moving to areas where rain had fallen and avoiding the dry areas, they were simultaneously improving pasture for their horses and their prospects of finding buffaloes. There was no contradiction. The buffaloes, like the herdsmen, were looking for grass.

But the wintering behavior of the Cheyennes cannot be explained by reference to buffaloes. The Cheyenne camps broke into smaller units not to facilitate chasing buffaloes, but to find a place where the band could spend the entire cold period without need to break camp and find fresh grass. A

Table 10 Space and Resource Requirements for a Band in Summer and a Camp in Winter

	BAND OF 400 WITH 600 HORSES FOR TWO WEEKS*				CAMP OF 25 WITH 38 HORSES FOR ENTIRE WINTER			
LOCATION AND SOIL SURVEY	W (METERS)	X (METERS)	G$_s$ (ACRES/MONTH)	R (MILES)	LENGTH OF WINTER STAY (DAYS)	X (METERS)	G$_w$ (ACRES/WINTER)	R (MILES)
Cheyenne River Meade County, S. Dak.	200	1,250	.316	.307	150	625	5.0	.434
Upper Platte River Lincoln County, Nebr.	450	556	.273	.285	120	222	3.8	.378
Smoky Hill River Logan County, Kans.	150	1,667	.171	.225	105	583	1.5	.238
Arkansas River Bent County, Colo.	500	500	.600	.423	90	150	1.8	.26c
Wolf Creek Ellis County, Okla.	300	833	.185	.235	75	208	.7	.162

Note: W = width of forest; X = distance to unexploited firewood; R = distance to edge of pasture; G$_s$ = summer grazing factor; G$_w$ = winter grazing factor
*Half a month.

properly selected winter camp, in an area such as the Republican Big Timbers, could be a safe haven for the entire winter, especially if enough jerked buffalo meat had already been prepared.

It was only the advent of war with United States soldiers that interfered with the previous pattern. Using grain-fed horses and operating from storehouses such as Camp Supply, the army raided winter camps and forced the Cheyennes to form larger, more defensible camps, such as at Sand Creek in 1864. George Bent described the typical winter camps before that time as small, with "each small band camped in its own wintering grounds," surrounded with windbreaks like those shown in plate 10.[123] Once the labor was invested in these windbreaks, according to modern informants, the Cheyennes were loath to move.[124] And so each winter they fragmented into groups small enough to spend the entire winter together in one place.

Horse Herds and the Transition to Nomadism

The general southward migration of the Cheyennes after 1800 was of great benefit to their horse herds, if this was not, indeed, a major reason for migrating. In the warmer climate, with milder winters, the Cheyennes could keep larger herds or else maintain themselves in larger camps through the winter. Near the Arkansas in southern Kansas, even the snows left by winter blizzards melt in the sunshine after a few days. On the Upper Platte, by contrast, snow can cover the grass for months on end. Although grass was plentiful on the northern plains, the winters were risky. In general, the central plains of eastern Colorado and western Kansas represent a compromise between rainfall and temperature. It is wet enough for grass to grow in abundance, but not snowy enough to prevent grazing through the winter.

With some understanding of Plains ecology, we can now return to the question why some bands and nations of Indians were successful in becoming equestrian nomads after 1800 while others continued to suffer from warfare, epidemics, and starvation in the palisaded villages of the Middle Missouri. First of all, it is clear that the Cheyennes, with their pattern of casual or untended horticulture in the Black Hills, could maintain larger horse herds than the riverine peoples of the same period, about 1800. After the spring planting, the Cheyennes could move out onto the Plains, allowing the grass near their gardens to recover over the summer. When the cold weather came, they could move back to the Cheyenne River to spend the winter. Even today ranchers along the Cheyenne River reserve the "Cheyenne Breaks," an area about four miles wide along the river, exclusively for winter pasture. District Conservationist Tom Quinn of Rapid City estimates that 20 to 40 percent of the Breaks area is free of snow

Plate 10. Windbreak constructed near Clinton, Oklahoma, in 1911. Photos 177 and 178 from Campbell Collection, Western History Collections, University of Oklahoma Library.

through the winter. Fortunately for ranchers, the periodic windstorms of the winter shift the snow around so that new grass is uncovered as cropped grass is covered up.

Thanks to the work of John Ewers, and thanks also to information from modern Cheyenne informants, we can calculate with some accuracy the number of horses required to reach a "takeoff" point for equestrian nomadism. That is, we can figure the number of horses a family or band must have to become full-time nomads. In his classic monograph on Black-feet horse husbandry, Ewers says that Blackfeet informants in 1941 told him that "ideally" twelve horses per family were required to move the camp.[125] Modern Cheyenne elders, some of whom were born in tipis and rode travois as children, gave figures of three to six horses as a "minimum." This calculation is based on the idea that the lodge cover requires one horse, most of the poles another, and the household head yet another, while the other household goods and family members can be spread among the remaining horses, each of which carries two of the tipi poles as part of a travois. According to them, and in contrast to what Ewers reports for the Blackfeet, all horses were fitted with travois, and no pack saddles were used. This is not contradicted by existing photographs.

In his 1955 monograph, Ewers also collected some comparative data on the number of horses observed among the various Plains tribes by early travelers and explorers. He gave two figures for number of horses per Cheyenne family, 11.1 in 1899 and 13.7 in 1868.[126] Although Ewers cited a total figure for horses captured at Sand Creek, this figure was not broken down by family or individual ownership. However, the list of claims against the government filed by the Cheyennes in 1865 does list the number of horses and mules lost per family head. I present a histogram of these figures in figure 10, which shows not only the total and average number of horses owned by Cheyennes at that time, but also the distribution of horse ownership among the different families. Note, however, that not all the Cheyenne horses at the camp were captured by the soldiers, and there is no accurate count of those that escaped capture.[127] Nevertheless, it seems apparent that horses were rather unevenly distributed, probably requiring the same kind of borrowing of horses to move camp as Ewers noted was normal for the Blackfeet.

Another source for calculating Cheyenne horse wealth is Garrard, who counted 200 horses for a Cheyenne camp of eighteen lodges, which comes to about 11 horses per lodge.[128] Perhaps the best source, however, and the most complete, is the stock census completed for the Cheyennes in 1878, when both the Northern and Southern Cheyennes were in Oklahoma.[129] The count was taken by lodge, giving a mean of 3.81 horses per lodge.

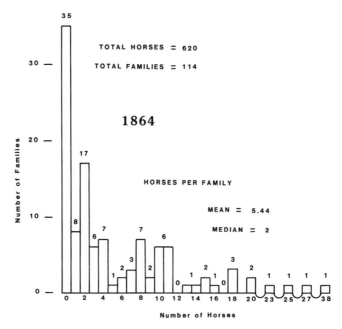

Figure 10.   Horse distribution among Cheyenne families, 1864. Calculated from the claims of the Sand Creek survivors.

Figure 11 shows the distribution of horses among the lodges. In this period, however, horse populations were being manipulated to some extent by the military, and the Cheyennes were suffering considerable theft of horses by white people from Kansas.[130]

Ewers's comparative data on horse ownership points up the relative poverty in horses of the riverine tribes. By most reports, they had only one horse per five persons.[131] From the ecological perspective we have gained in this chapter, we can say *why* the riverine tribes could not keep many horses. Constrained as they were to a palisaded village, from which they dared not wander, the Arikaras, Mandans, and Hidatsas necessarily had very limited grass resources. If they kept too many horses, the herders had to take them far from the village, where they were vulnerable to Tetons and other raiders. Although they had enough horses for occasional warfare or trading expeditions, the riverine peoples never approached the minimum of three to six horses per family that was required to move the whole population. And so, as Preston Holder points out, although the riverine people occasionally might try for a transition to full-time nomadism, they were never suc-

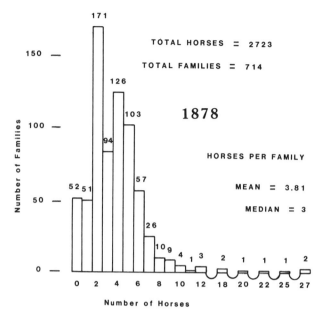

Figure 11.   Horse census for Darlington agency, 1878.

cessful. [132] Success required that they put enough of their population simultaneously on horseback to constitute a viable band.

The Cheyennes, by contrast, made a relatively easy transition to equestrian nomadism. Already adapted by about 1780 to a system of casual horticulture that required them to be nomadic for much of the year, the Cheyennes had only to learn to winter in some place other than their former gardens. In Cheyenne tradition, this last bit of transition is legitimated by the story in which the Rees steal their corn: "They came back westwards to hunt the buffalo in the spring after they had planted corn. They expected to return when the corn was ripe. The Rees came and stole a lot of the corn and went away with it. That is why people think the Rees were the first people to raise corn; but they stole it from the Cheyennes. The Cheyenne went back for their corn. Nearly half of the patches had been taken away." [133]

We can now sketch out some final details of Cheyenne habitat and come to an understanding of precisely where the Cheyennes lived in the broad expanse of prairie, and why they lived there. First of all we see that the Cheyennes, like all human societies, needed springs, streams, and lakes for water. In their free period of history, movements were from stream to river, from lake to spring, from spring to stream. But they did not choose just any area along a stream. They chose those watered areas that also had forests nearby, either the riparian forests watered from surface streams or the nonriparian forests of ridges, scarps, and cliffs. And even within these areas of forested waterways the Cheyennes were selective. They needed good grass, nurtured on good soil.

If we superimpose the map of water resources, map 7, on the map of timber resources, map 6, we can define very closely the Plains habitat that the Cheyennes preferred in the years 1790–1876. Even though the sources used to construct these maps were not specifically oriented toward defining Cheyenne ecology, they have nevertheless done so very nicely. If we further delimit our map by the locations of the dominant shortgrass communities of map 8, we have defined Cheyenne range and ecology even more precisely. Map 12 represents the coincidence of wood, water, and grass resources as defined and discussed in this chapter. I have designated as class I those areas where both wood and water were found in abundance, areas suitable for wintering large groups of people and horses. I have designated as class II those areas where wood was plentiful but water was only seasonal, and I call class III those areas where water was reliable but timber was scarce. By comparing map 12 with map 5, we can see that the map of ecological resources corresponds nicely to the map of actual locations of Cheyenne bands during this historical period, even though I used entirely different methods to construct the two maps.

Of course the truly ideal camping areas were rare, even in the huge expanse of the Great Plains, and Cheyenne bands often had to settle for less. Although they preferred the locations that are well known historically— the three "Big Timbers," Lodgepole Creek, the Sand Creek Crossing, Summit Springs, and the South Platte—in a pinch they could camp almost anywhere. Lacking timber, especially around the lakes of eastern Colorado and western Nebraska, they could burn buffalo chips as fuel. Away from perennial streams, they could find isolated springs or dig in the sand of ostensibly dry creek beds. Everywhere there was grass of some sort, though it was not always the best.

If Cheyenne society was very flexible in the period of equestrian nomadism, it also had peculiar vulnerabilities. The nation was vulnerable in general because it was only rarely that the whole society could camp together, as at the great ceremonies in June. Enriched by horses, the Cheyennes were also handicapped by their enormous horse herds, which constantly had to be moved to fresh grass. Especially in winter, the entire nation had to split into small groups in isolated places, sheltered and

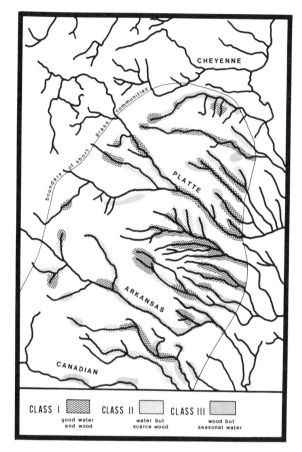

Map 12.   Coincidence of wood and water resources within the ranges of certain shortgrasses on the central plains.

supplied with enough preserved food for people, and enough cured standing grass for their horses, to last through the cold period.

When the United States Army recognized the winter vulnerability of the Cheyennes, they were quick to attack them. Carrying grain for their horses, the army routed the Cheyennes from their winter camps when the Indian horses were weak from hunger and ultimately drove the people to reservations. After the Battle of the Washita in 1868, Custer slaughtered eight hundred Cheyenne horses.[134] After the Sand Creek Massacre of 1864, five hundred horses were driven off by the soldiers.[135]

It was their original and creative ecological system that enabled the

Cheyennes to leave the Black Hills in 1790 and roam the Plains. But it was the vulnerabilities of that ecological system that at last brought them to their knees as a military power.

The Cheyennes: A Pastoral People

Between 1805 and 1856, the Cheyenne nation developed a finely tuned ecological apparatus for extracting subsistence from the shortgrass prairie. The climatic zone to which they were adapted required frequent moves to find the resources they needed, particularly the shortgrasses. In the tallgrass prairies to the east, where such nations as the Pawnees and the Osages lived, such frequent moves were not so necessary. Neither was it necessary for those nations toward the north, in the moister regions of the Plains, to move frequently—the Crows, Blackfeet, and Assiniboines. In their ecological adaptation, the Cheyennes were most like the groups to their south— the Kiowas, Comances, and Plains Apaches—whose societies were also predicated on frequent moves and the ability to split into small groups.

It is misleading to call the Cheyennes a hunting people. This implies that the determining factor for their organization and movements was the availability of game. I have presented data in this chapter that prove it was a scarcity of other resources—grass, wood, and water—that determined their movements and the size of their residence groups. The size of Cheyenne groups indicates a trade-off between the advantages of larger units, for protection, social life, and trade, and the advantages offered by a smaller size—the slower exhaustion of crucial resources, especially wood and grass. When circumstances permitted, especially for the major ceremonies after spring rains, large groups could be formed. At that time all the manhao groups could come together and exhibit their membership in a unified nation. At other times during the year, "bunches" and "camps" of Cheyennes could cluster at some place that had grass, wood, and water. These bunches could grow larger or diminish depending on circumstances, either climatic or political.

It is ironic that the creation of the Cheyenne nation also saw the creation of a small living unit—the family camp—that was unprecedented in Cheyenne experience. That is, although the Cheyennes combined to form a nation of three thousand people in the late eighteenth century, they could physically demonstrate this nationhood only briefly each year. Except for the annual ceremonies, the Cheyennes were forced to split into smaller groups capable of exploiting the scarce and dispersed resources of the central plains. But there was a positive side, militarily, to this dispersion. It meant, first of all, that a relatively small number of people were able to control a vast territory. They did this by having good intelligence of enemies invading or crossing their territory and by their ability to mobilize the whole nation to defend any part of their vast domain. These were the two contradictory sides of the new Cheyenne nation from the beginning. The Cheyennes created for themselves a nation that was strong and integrated politically but dispersed over hundreds of miles of open prairie for most of the year.

To review a moment, in chapter 2 we learned the names of the Cheyenne bands and the complex relationships that existed among them in the late free period, just before reservation life began. But we had no idea then of why the bands were of a particular size or why their relationships were so complex. In chapter 3 we learned how these various bands had been connected historically and saw that they had migrated nearly a thousand miles in the course of two hundred years. But we had little idea why they had migrated or what consequences this migration had for their social and economic life. In chapter 4 we took a different perspective on this same period of history, the perspective of the Cheyennes themselves, and in the course of hearing origin stories for the major bands, we collected some clues about historical motivations and about reorganizations necessitated by their migrations. And now at last, in this chapter, we have put some of our central historical questions inside a solid scientific framework. We now have a good idea of the role ecology played in setting limits to the sizes of Cheyenne groups and of how these limits varied from north to south and east to west. We have learned how each successive move by Cheyenne groups put them under the control of new limiting factors for the number of people and horses that could live together in various seasons of the year. But we still do not know how these various Cheyenne "groups" differed from each other. Were they different only quantitatively—that is, in numbers of people and horses—or were there *qualitative* differences as well? Were they seen as being different kinds of things—a band, a bunch, a camp, a sacred band?[136] Once again we will find that the best answers to these questions come not from anthropologists or historians, but from the Cheyennes themselves, for the definition and identification of legitimate "groups" of various kinds was the central task facing native Cheyenne sociology in the early eighteenth century.

6 /XXX

The Structure of Cheyenne Society

In this chapter I will define and describe the four kinds of "bands" that have been important in Cheyenne history, using the ecological background developed in the last chapter. We will see that each kind of band had different functions, economically and politically. Although they have mostly coexisted in Cheyenne history, they were sometimes antagonistic to one another. These four kinds of bands, from smallest to largest, are the *vestoz* or "camp," the *manhastoz* or "bunch," the *notxestoz* or military society, and the *manhao* or "sacred band."

Before looking at the meanings of these words in the native language, we should be aware that Cheyennes ordinarily translate these terms using English words that can be confusing to outsiders. For example, modern Cheyennes use the word "clan" in reference to their military or soldier societies. In anthropological language, such groups are called "voluntary associations" or, even more technically, "sodalities." But Cheyennes say "clan," and they know what they mean. For example, during the course of our most intensive fieldwork, I and the Cheyennes involved most directly in collecting data were casually referred to as the "Research clan" by several elders. This usage communicated very well to other Cheyennes the kind of group we had put together—a group of people, not necessarily related, who were pursuing a common interest.

In talking to modern Cheyennes in English, the word "band" does not work very well either. When Cheyennes want to describe a group of people who are resident together—what an anthropologist would call a band—they say "bunch," as in "the Seiling bunch," or "that Scabby bunch." Just as the Navahos have taken the English word "outfit" to describe a unit of their social structure, the Cheyennes have taken the English word "bunch," which is a literal translation of the Cheyenne expression *manhastoz*.[1]

One of the most comic, and tragic, episodes in Cheyenne ethnology must bc the interview recorded in western Oklahoma in 1967 with Mrs. Birdie Burns, a knowledgeable bilingual Cheyenne. After a few minutes of hearing Mrs. Burns talk about "bunches" and "clans," the researcher decided to straighten out her sociology. "You don't mean clan, you mean society," corrected the interviewer, "and you don't mean bunch, you mean band." After that, Mrs. Burns didn't have much to say.[2]

The English word "family" is also used differently by Cheyennes. Generally it includes any kind of blood relative, no matter how distant. Among modern Cheyennes, it is the notion of "family" that regulates marriage. People of the same "family" are not allowed to marry. In practice this means that marriages are permitted only between people with no known relationship. It is the business of authorized "camp criers" to keep track of family genealogies.

A family, then, is not a band. Some members of a family will live together, having the same residence, while others live elsewhere. That is, "families" crosscut residence units and are not the same thing.

The smallest residence unit of the Cheyennes was the tipi or *ve*, a word that provides the root for *vestoz*, which literally means "that which has tipis," the camp. In aboriginal times a tipi, comprising a nuclear family, did not camp apart from the other tipis, but it could and did change its group affiliation from time to time. Our best source for discovering the number of people in a tipi is probably the 1880 census, taken when all the Cheyennes still lived in these portable lodges and before they had been affected very much by agents and missionaries. Only 262 of the 378 household schedules survive from this census, but they are enough to give us some general idea of the number and kind of people in a lodge.[3]

Figure 12 is a histogram showing the number of people per tipi in 1880, for which the mean is 5.56 persons. A further statistical analysis gives more detail about the composition of a lodge, showing that ninety-five lodges, or 36 percent, were of the form husband-wife or husband-wife-child. Twenty-five other lodges contained a husband, a sibling of the husband, and the wives and children of the husband. Twenty-four lodges consisted of female family heads (who might be wives of men in other lodges) and their children. Nineteen lodges were of the form husband-wife-child, but with the addition of a sibling of the wife. Seven lodges had a female head with at least one child and one grandchild, and seven more had a male family head with at least one parent and one sibling. There were five or fewer examples of the other kinds of households, a total of eighty-five of these "miscellaneous" households. (See table 17 on p. 298.)

The 1880 census also gives us an opportunity to measure the extent of Cheyenne polygyny. The census was taken in the years before multiple

1880 U.S. Census

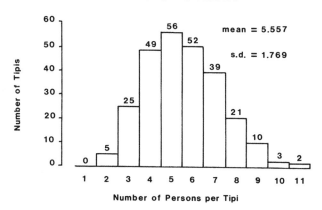

Figure 12.   Size of Cheyenne households, 1880

marriage had become a sensitive issue, and before agents and missionaries had set out to destroy the practice. Therefore, in 1880 nineteen families reported that there were two wives living in the same tipi, while two families reported three wives. This was not the total extent of polygyny, however, because second and third wives were frequently given their own tipis.[4] Working with modern informants and genealogies, I have identified a total of thirty-six men with two wives in 1880 and five with three wives. The total of forty-one polygynous families is generally consistent with the ideal number of council chiefs among the Cheyennes and with the total number of manhastoz units as calculated from other sources.

Camps and Bunches

The most subtle differentiation in Cheyenne society, and perhaps the most important, is between vestoz and manhastoz. (Hereafter I will use the word "camp" for vestoz and "bunch" for manhastoz.) Part of the subtlety is because a bunch is sometimes referred to as a camp and at other times can be called a manhao, or "sacred band," depending on the context. Manhao also means "island" in Cheyenne, perhaps implying autonomy and self-sufficiency. The word bunch is used in a context like "Little Robe's bunch," by reference to the leader of the group or, in modern times by reference to the location of the group, "the Hammon bunch." But the physical location of the tents and tipis of a bunch is called a camp. At the annual ceremonies, people refer to the location of the Oivimana band, for example, as a "camp," even though the term comprises, in this context, several hundred people.

When elders refer to aboriginal times, they reserve the term bunch for polygynous groups led by a council chief. The descendants of these chief-led groups regard themselves as an elite or, as one informant put it, "kind of like Cheyenne royalty . . . the descendants of chiefs shouldn't marry commoners, or if they did, people would make fun of them." Instead of living in bunches, commoners are said to have lived in camps. The modern descendants of chiefs regard it as pretentious for "commoners" to use the word "bunch" in referring to their ancestral group. Of course this whole pattern of usage is disputed by people who have little or no ancestry among the aboriginal council chiefs.

The difference between camp and bunch shows up clearly in some of the early reservation records. As part of his plan to spread the Cheyennes across the reservation and make the bands more self-sufficient, Capt. Jesse Lee allowed viable groups to organize themselves "according to custom."[5] Although many Cheyennes continued to gather around the agency, 1,126 people organized themselves into nomadic residence units and dispersed, returning to the agency only for beef rations. The sizes of these units show the existence of two distinct kinds of groups—large groups or "bunches," and small groups or "camps."

On figure 13 are plotted the sizes of the "beef bands," as they were called, as they existed for the second quarter of 1880. In this figure the number of persons in each band is plotted against the age of its leader. The result is two clusters of points, through which I have drawn regression lines. Including the ages of the leaders on the figure emphasizes even further that there were two types of "customary bands" among the Cheyennes in these years. The core of a bunch was a *veho* or polygynous chief and his family, while a camp was led by a *manawa,* or "family head."[6] The plot of band size against frequency, without the ages of leaders, merely shows a bimodal distribution of band size, without showing what I believe to be the developmental sequences of figure 13. That is, I believe the data show that both kinds of bands got larger as the leaders got older, but there was always a normal difference in size for camps and bunches at the same stage of development. This difference is shown by the vertical distance between the two lines that are plotted. From this data the mean size of a bunch is calculated as 39.3 persons, and the mean size of a camp is 25.1 persons. I am indebted to Dori Penny, of our research group, for discovering this clustering for the two types of bands.

It is surprising that, despite the wealth of material on the Cheyennes, little has been published about the physical structure and orientation of the

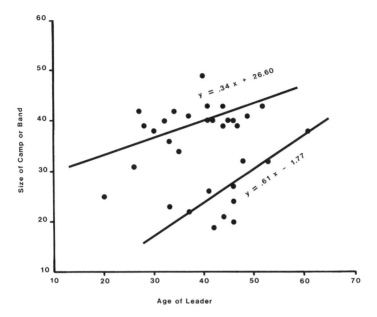

Figure 13.   Age of leader related to size of group for some beef bands of 1880.

individual camps, the clusters of tipis. In 1847 Ruxton described a linear structure: "The lodges, about fifty in number, were all regularly planted in rows of ten; the chief's lodge being in the centre, and the skins of it being dyed a conspicuous red."[7] These painted lodges, we should note, were typical of council chiefs in this period and were described in detail by Mooney.[8] Two such are pictured in plate 11.

Although Ruxton described "rows" of lodges, it is more likely that they were in irregular clusters and only appeared to be rows from a distance. For example, plate 12 shows what are apparently two lines of lodges, but on closer inspection these are seen to be two clusters of tipis viewed from a distance. Two photographs by Churchill, in the collection of the Museum of the American Indian, give us an unusual opportunity to see the actual arrangement of tipis in a camp. Since Churchill made two photographs of the same camp in 1901, the two-dimensional arrangement of the tipis on the ground can be determined by triangulation. Figure 14 shows the actual arrangement of the tipis, while plate 13 is one of the photographs. A ledger-book drawing by Howling Wolf (plate 14) shows essentially the same kind of arrangement, which seems to have been typical of both camps and bunches.[9]

Plate 11. Two painted tipis near Fort Reno, Oklahoma Territory, in 1890.
Photo no. 21 in the Shuck Collection, Western History Collections, University
of Oklahoma Library.

Plate 12. Cheyenne camps near Fort Reno, Oklahoma Territory, about 1890.
Photo no. 20 in the Shuck Collection, Western History Collections, University
of Oklahoma Library.

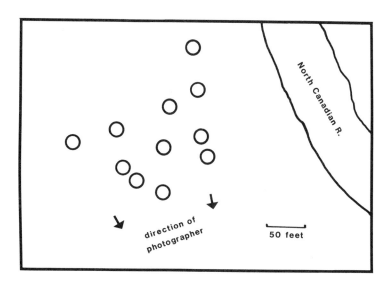

Figure 14. Location of tipis within a Cheyenne camp.

Plate 13. Photograph of Cheyenne camp by Churchill. Negative no. 27321, Museum of the American Indian, Heye Foundation.

Plate 14.   Drawing of Indian camps by Howling Wolf. Photo by Candace Green, from Field Museum drawing FMNH 83,999, Chicago, Illinois.

The relations between camps and bunches in early reservation times were sometimes very turbulent. The chiefs, leaders of the bunches, regarded camps as subordinate to their bunches and continually demanded that all rations be given to them for redistribution to the camps. The camps, for their part, considered themselves independent political units and wanted a direct distribution of annuities. In response to such demands, Captain Lee tried to arrange the combination of small camps into groups approximating forty persons, the optimum size to receive a whole beef. A beef band list from 1886 shows the results of this kind of manipulation, with each band containing thirty-nine, forty, or forty-one persons. [10] This contrasts strongly with the data of figure 13.

It is difficult to say how long the bunches and camps had coexisted in Cheyenne society, or in what proportions, but is clear that they had different economic emphases. The bunches were organized for trade, whereas the camps were better suited for hunting and for gathering natural resources. Fortunately, some of the hunting behavior of the camps is preserved in reservation records, because the early agents allowed the Cheyennes to travel west to hunt as long as there were still buffaloes. On 15 November 1876 George Bent wrote a report from his "Camp on Wolf River," where he had gone to accompany the hunters: "Sir, I have the honor to report again so as to let you know that the Cheyennes have scattered in small camps. You know it is best to let them camp in small camps. They can kill more buffalos by doing so." [11]

If we want to reconstruct the relationships between bunches and related camps for the middle nineteenth century, we might use the statistics from 1880. Suppose, for the moment, that there was a full complement of 44 chiefs, each with a bunch of 40 persons. From a total population of 2,500 people, using Schoolcraft's estimate, this would mean that 1,760 Cheyennes would live in bunches and the remainder, 740, would live in camps. Dividing by 25, this would mean about 30 camps. This is close to the ratio of bunches to camps in figure 13. We should file for future reference the fact that there are more bunches than there are sacred bands, meaning that some sacred bands must comprise two or more bunches, and perhaps several camps as well.

The early reports of traders Ruxton and Boggs indicate a patterned relationship between camps and bunches. The bunch apparently functioned as a kind of base camp, dominated by a council chief, with a constant coming and going of smaller groups. From those reports, however, we cannot say for sure whether the smaller groups were merely subdivisions of the bunch or whether these were satellite camps that had come to trade under the sponsorship of a council chief. But it is clear in either event that it was the chief who was the agent of trade, as described in chapter 5, and had the monopoly for that camp. This monopoly was recognized by the traders, who gave the chief presents upon their arrival, to establish their relationship for the trading season. George Ruxton reported the complaint of one Cheyenne chief, Yellow Wolf, in about 1846: "Now O-cun-no-whurst, the Yellow Wolf, grand chief of the Shian, complains of certain grave offences against the dignity of his nation! A trader from the 'big lodge' (the fort) has been in his village, and before the trade was opened, in a laying of the customary chief's gift 'on the prairie' has not 'opened his hand,' but 'squeezed out his present between his fingers' grudgingly and with too sparing measure. This was hard to bear, but the Yellow Wolf would say no more!"[12]

In sum, I interpret the bunches as chief-led groups and the council chiefs primarily as traders. This interpretation of bunches explains, among other things, why the chiefs are not emphasized in the origin stories, why they became more important in the first half of the nineteenth century, and why they were less important after trade faltered in 1845–50. The origin stories of the Cheyennes, we should remember, emphasize the military societies over the chiefs, and some origin stories do not mention the chiefs at all. Some elders have given an entirely different origin for the chiefs' council, as a group organized at the suggestion of a captive woman. If the chiefs did not become important until the period of intensive trading began, about 1820, then we can understand better why their origins are not so shrouded in legends and sacred traditions.

In their role as traders, the chiefs could not have been so important in the period when the Cheyenne bands were between the forks of the Platte, where trade routes were few and goods were scarce before 1822. In those years the Cheyennes traded with contiguous nations, and also probably with the eastern tribes—Shawnees, Delawares, and Kickapoos—who increasingly sent representatives to the Plains in those years. Unfortunately, however, no diaries or travel accounts have come to light from literate Indian traders of that period.

Hispanic trade in that time also is relatively undocumented, in part because by the laws of New Mexico it was often illegal for Mexican citizens to trade north of the Arkansas River. Also, for political reasons, the United States wanted to deny the prior occupancy by Spain and Mexico of the territories north of the river, and so the Hispanic presence there is minimized in early English accounts. For example, the Mexican trading station just west of the Black Hills appears on Chittenden's map as "Portuguese Houses."[13] Despite all this, there is some evidence for Cheyenne-Hispanic trade in this period. Several names of Spanish traders are preserved in Cheyenne personal names to modern times. Flacco is a modern surname preserving the nickname of a Mexican trader, "Skinny," while "McGill" is an English corruption of "Miguel," the name of another early trader who married into the Cheyenne nation. "Naranho" is yet another Spanish-Cheyenne surname. Other less personal residues of Hispanic influence are preserved in the family names "Mexican" and "Beard." "Bearded Ones" is the Cheyenne term for Mexicans.

Cheyenne trade at the Spanish town and Indian pueblo at Taos has gone on at least since 1795. A map of that date refers to the "Chaguaguanas."[14] The trade there in aboriginal items—tipi poles, herbs, paints, buffalo skulls, and white-tanned deerskin—goes on uninterrupted, according to modern informants. I myself have served as an occasional agent of such trade over the past ten years.

Intermarriage with traders has always been a key method for creating trade relations between a council chief and outsiders. It was common practice for a council chief to offer his own daughter for a "marriage of convenience." The most celebrated marriage of this kind was between William Bent and two daughters of the arrow keeper, Gray Thunder.[15] This sealed an important trading bond for Bent's Fort over the next several decades. The other most prominent trader on the Arkansas in that period, John Prowers, was also married to the daughter of a council chief, in this case One Eye, who along with Black Kettle was the most important council chief of the 1850s.[16]

On the Upper Platte River, the other nexus of Cheyenne trade in the middle 1800s, Lancaster Lupton, the founder of Fort Lupton, married a chief's daughter named Thomass. In response, the other major trader of the South Platte, Marcellus St. Vrain, married another Cheyenne daughter, Spotted Fawn, to secure his own trading privileges. [17]

For council chiefs, it was important to control women for the production of buffalo robes as well as for maintaining intimate relationships with traders. Women, then, were doubly important to the structure I have called "uterine" in its general makeup. Most important, chiefs were usually polygynous, marrying groups of sisters when they could. We will examine this practice at greater length in subsequent chapters. The work role of Plains women has been admirably addressed in the ongoing work of Patricia Albers and Alan Klein and is part of the research efforts of feminist scholars such as Eleanor Leacock. [18]

Council chiefs, then, presided over a social structure that had as its economic base both subsistence and production for trade. Ecologically, the system depended on the ability of the manhastoz to be self-sufficient when necessary, but to have the flexibility to combine with other bunches and camps and form larger groups when advisable. The early documents indicate what I have called a "base camp" structure, under the sponsorship of a council chief, where other camps and bunches brought their robes to trade. The council chief's status, then, depended on the quality of his trade relations with Anglo traders and his ability to keep peace among the bunches and camps who traded under his sponsorship.

From this perspective, the chief's role as peacemaker makes eminent good sense. If a council chief wanted trade to proceed smoothly, he had to assume the classic role of pipecarrier and go-between. The many episodes of adjudication recorded in Llewellyn and Hoebel's book are sensible in light of the role of the chief in mobilizing economic resources and trading this production for goods from the outside.

From the perspective of the bunch as trading unit and the chief as trader, we can also understand a chief's role in foreign affairs. As a trader whose status depended on the success of production and trade, the council chief often deplored warfare, as when Gray Thunder denied the Bowstrings permission to go to war in 1837. On the other hand, when warfare had the consequence of enhancing trade, either by extending territory into areas where buffaloes or horses could be more easily found or by denying other tribes access to traders, then the self-interest of the council chiefs demanded that they go to war. Horse raiding enhanced Cheyenne trade, and so we find council chiefs prominent among horse raiders, but taking a backseat to the organized soldier societies in the large-scale warfare of the spring season. [19]

In the early part of the nineteenth century, we see council chiefs dominating a structure that emphasized the versatility of the vestoz-manhastoz system as an ecological adaptation. They are also projecting their own roles as peacemakers in their bands and masters of foreign policy as a corporate unit, the Council of Forty-four. But from the beginning, it is clear that the power of the council and the role of the chief were very limited. The council could not make war without the consent of the soldier societies. They could only opt for peace.[20] The chiefs' authority centered on three functions: trading, peacekeeping, and deciding on the seasonal movements of the bunch.[21] Of these three roles, I believe that the chief's role as trader both conditioned and determined the other two.

In support of this thesis, we should remember that it was council chiefs, Yellow Wolf and High-Backed Wolf, who first arranged with William Bent that they would trade at his new fort on the Arkansas and who continued to bring in their bands to negotiate prevailing terms of trade for the entire existence of the fort. Also, we should recall Ruxton's, Boggs's, and Hamilton's descriptions of how the chiefs always negotiated and approved the terms of trade between the traders and the other members of the band.

The bands also may have had trade specializations. From the beginning, Yellow Wolf is noted as the premier horse raider and horse capturer for his Hevhaitaneo band, not for his abilities as a warrior.[22] The name of the Oivimana band, "Scabbies," implies a joke about the condition of the buffalo robes they traded. With these two bands on the Arkansas and the Heviksnipahis still on the Platte in 1830, we can postulate a division of labor among these three Cheyenne bands. The Hevhaitaneos were oriented toward the horse trade, the Oivimanas toward the production of robes, while the Heviksnipahis remained in the beaver trade.[23] Their three nicknames indicate lassos, robes, and beavers, respectively. Other bands might also have had productive specialties, but it is difficult to determine this from existing documents.

The orientation of certain of the Cheyenne bands toward particular neighbors as trading partners also had positive benefits for the entire nation. We have already noted the special relationship between the Wotapios and the Kiowas. According to modern informants, the Oivimanas and Hevhaitaneos had special relationships of marriage and trade with the Arapahos, while several bands had special friends among the Lakotas. Turkey Legs's band traveled with, traded with, and intermarried with the Brulé Sioux, and Little Chief's band was so involved with the Oglalas that it remained with them at Pine Ridge from 1876 to 1884, and some are still there.[24] The Omisis band fought side by side with the Lakotas at the Little Big Horn, while the Masikota and Dog Soldier bands, as we shall see in the next chapter, were by 1870 almost indistinguishable from their Lakota allies. The "Mandan bunch" of Cheyennes, and the "Ree band" have already been mentioned in the context of their special economic relationships.

It is misleading, I think, to claim that the strength of the Cheyenne nation lay in its tight political integration, its homogeneity, and its maintenance of ethnic boundaries. I believe it is much more accurate to say that the political and military strength of the Cheyennes lay in their dispersal across broad reaches of the central plains, their economic and productive specializations, and their special trade relationships and intermarriages with neighboring groups.

Ethnically the Cheyennes were a very mixed bag, with many intermarriages with allied groups such as the Arapahos and Sioux, and with many women and children captured and adopted from enemy tribes such as the Crows and Pawnees. Map 13 shows the geographical distribution of women with foreign names on the 1892 allotment map. In late aboriginal times all kinds of Americans and eastern Indians, white, black, and red, were likewise adopted into the Cheyenne nation. The early census roles of the Cheyennes show this very clearly. "Kiowa Dutch" was a German from Texas who opted to live as a Cheyenne and survived to take his allotment near Gotebo (see plate 15). "Black White Man" was an American Negro who

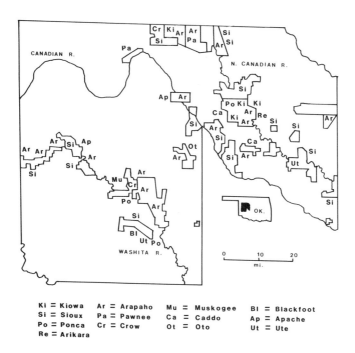

Ki = Kiowa   Ar = Arapaho   Mu = Muskogee   Bl = Blackfoot
Si = Sioux   Pa = Pawnee   Ca = Caddo   Ap = Apache
Po = Ponca   Cr = Crow   Ot = Oto   Ut = Ute
Re = Arikara

Map 13. Southern Cheyenne women with foreign names from the 1892 allotment map.

Plate 15.   Kiowa Dutch, a German from East Texas adopted into the Cheyenne
nation. Photo no. 29, Phillips Collection, Western History Collections,
University of Oklahoma Library.

found his freedom with the Cheyennes and became a leading man.[25] According to Grinnell and Bent, about twenty young Blackfeet men were adopted in the early 1800s.[26] Grinnell has listed twenty-eight foreign nations from which the Cheyenne "melting pot" absorbed its citizens.[27] Hundreds of Cheyennes were originally Lakotas, Seminoles, or Delawares, all recruited and integrated into the daily life of the Cheyenne nation that, as we have seen, already consisted of three somewhat distinct ethnic groups—the Chianetons, the Chongasketons, and the Oudebatons.

All this amalgamation, however, in no way undermined the strength and significance of the Cheyenne nation. Adoptees and captives of all stripes, after a period of residence, became citizens of the nation. They had a camping place in the ceremonial circle, they had ritual and military obligations, and it was a crime to kill or injure them.[28] According to modern elders, there was no onus of "mixed blood" in those years. Although captives and adoptees were sometimes denied certain ritual roles because of their inability to speak Cheyenne, their Cheyenne-speaking children were full citizens. The basis of citizenship was not "racial" or biological but was established by birth in a Cheyenne band. In aboriginal times there was no adoption ceremony, and a captive or adoptee was accepted merely by consensus of the camp.

It is only in reservation times that certain non-Cheyennes have been honored by receiving a name and "giving away," but this is not adoption. Also, in early reservation times the Bureau of Indian Affairs developed the notion of "blood quantum," which is quite contrary to Cheyenne law. Traditionally, either you are a Cheyenne or you are not; there is no middle ground. But in the days just after land allotment, the government, bankers, and land speculators found it useful to machinate in terms of blood quantum and the partition of heirship, and oil and gas lessees continue to do so today.

One anecdote about adoption, widely told among Northern Cheyennes, concerns the nominally Cheyenne author Hyemeyosts Storm. Knowing very little about traditional ways or the Cheyenne language, Storm allegedly brought a "hippy" friend to a respected chief "to be adopted." Perplexed but not wanting to be rude, the chief took Storm and his friend into the front yard, stood in front of them, and turned his eyes upward. In Cheyenne, he appealed to the heavens as follows: "Almighty, we ask your forgiveness for this poor man, born a Cheyenne, who has lost his language and knows so little about our religion. He has brought his friend here to be adopted, but I can do nothing for them. Please excuse me speaking in this strange way, but I don't know what else to do." The chief then shook their hands, and both of them left satisfied.

The Beginnings of Polarization

In view of the orientation of the council chiefs toward trade and peace, we can easily understand why, when war with the United States threatened, they became a strong voice for compromise. Perhaps the first document expressing this desire was Yellow Wolf's statement to Lt. J. W. Abert in 1848. This was when the trade for buffalo robes was beginning to deteriorate, and the council chiefs were looking for new options. According to Abert:

> To day a number of Cheyennes visited the fort, amongst them were Old Bark, his son "Ah-mah-nah-co," and Yellow Wolf, "O-cum-who wast." The latter is a man of considerable influence, of enlarged views, and gifted with more foresight than any other man in his tribe. He frequently talks of the diminishing numbers of his people, and the decrease of the once abundant buffalo. He says that in a few years they will become extinct; and unless the Indians wish to pass away also, they will have to adopt the habits of the white people, using such measures to produce subsistence as will render them independent of the precarious reliance afforded by the game.
>
> He has proposed to the interpreter at Bent's fort, to give him a number of mules, in the proportion of one from every man in the tribe, if he would build them a structure similar to Bent's fort, and instruct them to cultivate the ground, and to raise cattle. He says that for some time his people would not be content to relinquish to delights of the chase, and then the old men and squaws might remain at home cultivating the grounds, and be safely secured in their fort from the depredations of hostile tribes.[29]

The next year, 1849, another council chief, Red Wolf, made the same kind of statement, according to a frontier newspaper of the period: "Mr. Fisher says, that in some of his conversations with Red Wolf, the chief of the Chayennes, the chief told him he was very anxious for Mr. Fitzpatrick to return, as he promised; that he and the old men of the tribe wanted to live with him; that the young men were desirous of fighting with the whites. He also said to those at the Fort to keep the gates closed against many of the Arrapahoes, as they would do them injury."[30]

Even before the Sand Creek Massacre, the polarization of the Cheyenne nation between a peace faction and a war faction was far advanced, to the point of armed conflict. Fearing war, the council chiefs invited Major Edward Wynkoop to a council on the Smoky Hill River in 1864. At the council, they returned some white prisoners and expressed their alarm at the preparations for war being made in Denver. Speaking at the council, One Eye (the father-in-law of trader Prowers) even offered to help the Americans against the Dog Soldeirs. Evidence for the deteriorating relations between chiefs and Dog Soldiers was presented by Wynkoop and Governor John Evans at the Sand Creek inquiry.

> Question to Wynkoop. Did One-Eye at any time while on this expedition state to the Indians that you and your command should be protected from all harm from the Indians, and that he had pledged himself to protect you and

your command, and that if the Indians harmed you or your command he would go with the whites and fight against the Indians?

Answer. His remarks as interpreted to me by the United States Indian interpreter were to the effect that if they (the Indians) still determined to fight against the whites he would assist the whites.[31]

Alarmed by their meeting with Wynkoop, the council chiefs traveled to Denver for a conference with Governor Evans. According to Evans, the council chiefs by that time were afraid for their lives: "The chiefs who signed that treaty told Gerry that they were obliged to repudiate the signing of that treaty of Fort Wise, or the Dog soldiers would kill them."

The best way to look at the events of the 1860s, I believe, is in terms of political economy. Until that time the Cheyennes had been part of a huge trading system that supplied skins and furs to eastern cities. By 1860, however, the Cheyennes were being encircled, along the Platte and the Arkansas, by people with other interests—farming, ranching, and mining. All these new interests were interconnected by banks and the currency system and had their political representation in the territorial government of Colorado. And it was from Denver that brutal attacks were mounted against the Cheyennes in these years, despite the protests of traders such as Bent and Prowers, who were allies of the Cheyennes in the old trading system.

Attacked and massacred at Sand Creek in November 1864, the peace faction was diminished to eighty lodges and signed another treaty the next year.[32] Brutalized again at the Battle of the Washita in 1868, the peace faction gathered about the Indian agencies at Fort Supply and Fort Sill, and lived on rations. But by that time their following had steadily diminished, as had their reputation among other Cheyennes. But throughout this period the numbers and locations of Cheyenne groups were carefully noted by Americans, allowing us to gain a deeper understanding of Cheyenne political structure.

The Sacred Bands

In certain contexts, chiefs' bunches have been referred to as manhao, or sacred bands, implying their central position in the organization of the larger units. But they are not the same thing, as some simple arithmetic will teach us. For example, there is the Sand Creek Massacre. Although George Bent and other witnesses have claimed that six of the eight major manhao were present at the massacre, the total number of lodges present was 120, according to testimony at the subsequent investigation. Using the figures of 5.56 persons per lodge, already developed, we can figure that this number of lodges represents only about 660 persons, or perhaps ten groups the size of a chiefs' manhastoz of 1880. Not even a third of the nation was actually present.

The figures for Sand Creek casualties also imply that the entire memberships of the manhao were not present. Although a total of 120 persons were killed at Sand Creek, George Bent nevertheless gave the following estimates of the fractions of the "bands" killed there:

> Of these clans, Black Kettle's (the Wutapiu Clan) was the heaviest loser. Very few men of this clan escaped. Chief Sand Hill's band (the Heviqsnipahis Clan) had few killed; this band was camped farther down the creek than any of the others and most of the people escaped before the soldiers could reach their camp. Yellow Wolf's band (Hevhaitaniu Clan) lost half its people in killed, including the old chief, Yellow Wolf, who was then eighty-five years old, and his brother Big Man. War Bonnet's band (Oivimana Clan) lost half its people. The Ridge Men, Chief White Antelope (Hisiometanio or Ridge Men Clan) lost very heavily also. Chief One Eye was killed together with many of his band, and the Suhtai Clan lost a few people, but not very many. The Masikota Clan and the Dog Soldiers, together with some other small Cheyenne bands, were not present."[33]

These proportions of casualties, then, were only of certain *core groups* or manhastoz, not of the complete manhao units, since the total mortalities were 120. An entire original manhao, before the separation of the "Dog Soldiers," would comprise nearly a hundred lodges and several hundred people. If the same proportion of mortalities listed by Bent were applied to these larger units, and not just to the central cores, the total mortality would have been nearer one thousand than one hundred. But Bent said that "other small Cheyenne bands, were not present," although he does not say how many there were. Also, he does not mention in this quotation that the Omisis and Totoimana bands, the groups later known as the "Northern Cheyennes," also were not present.

Figure 15 represents an attempt to reconstruct the size of the major Cheyenne bands, or manhao, in the nineteenth century. Beginning with the population figures of 1891–92, I have apportioned the population of reservation bands in accordance with their histories. That is, if a reservation band was descended from two prereservation bands, I assigned half the population to each of those aboriginal bands. The particular band histories used in the apportionment are discussed in the next chapter.

For the reconstruction, I have also replaced the number of people killed in the various massacres and epidemics suffered by the Cheyennes, the most

Population Reconstruction

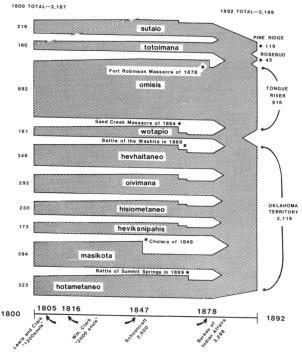

Figure 15.   Reconstruction of Cheyenne population by band, 1800 to 1892.

important of which are noted on the diagram. Rather than trying to account for the impact of recurring endemic disease or trying to estimate fertility in the previous century, I have simply assumed an overall increase in population of 10 percent from 1800 to 1849, the year of the cholera epidemic. This assumption does not violate too far the population estimates of contemporary observers, shown on a scale at the bottom of the figure.

The figures at the left show my estimates for the sizes of the various bands at the beginning of the century. The Sutaio band turned out to be much smaller than I had supposed, and the Omisis band much larger. But the tribal circles and band lists of chapter 2 are in agreement with my results. Many subgroups of the Omisis were listed by informants, for example, but none for the Sutaios. The range in size for the bands is from 161 (Wotapios) to 892 (Omisis), which means that even the smallest manhao must have had more than one component manhastoz, or chief's bunch.

There emerges from these calculations a model for understanding

Cheyenne social and political structure in 1845–65 and for understanding the ease with which Cheyenne bands were transformed from a nation that emphasized trade and the pastoral life to one mobilized for war. The transformation was accomplished largely by a switch of allegiance on the part of the marginal bands. That is, to accomplish the transformation, the vestoz units not present at Sand Creek and not part of the political cores of the manhao merely transferred their political affiliation to a soldier society and perhaps moved their camps to the proximity of the Dog Soldiers. Instead of being satellites to council chiefs, they were now satellites to the headsmen of the military societies. As George Bent put it, "a large number of ambitious young men were attracted to the new camp and the Dog Soldier band became stronger as the other bands weakened." The cores of the traditional manhao units, however, now consisting mostly of the council chiefs and their immediate families (80 lodges or 440 persons), refused to join the raids by which the Cheyennes retaliated for Sand Creek. According to Jay Black, a descendant of Black Kettle born about 1878, there were only "twenty-eight camps" left in the peace faction after the Sand Creek Massacre.[34] I interpret this to mean that there were twenty-eight vestoz or manhastoz units after 1864 that were not allied with the Dog Soldier faction.

If the polarization of Cheyenne society were merely a switch in allegiance of marginal bands from a trading to a raiding way of life, the event would be merely interesting to social scientists. As it is, the event is absolutely compelling—because, in the process of reorganizing Cheyenne politics, the Dog Soldiers reversed one of the most fundamental rules of human social life. To repeat George Bent's words, "The Dog Soldier men dropped the old custom by which a man, when he married, went to live in the camp of his wife's band. They brought their wives home to their own." That is, the Dog Soldiers reversed the traditional rule of residence.[35]

The rise of the Dog Soldiers, as I have already implied, is intimately related to the emergence of a new Colorado economy and the destruction of resources needed by the old trading economy. The westward emigrations along the Santa Fe and Oregon trails drove the Cheyennes away from their best camping places along the Platte and the Arkansas. Trade along these rivers then became reoriented toward the emigrant traffic as "ranches" and other forms of hostels sprang up every few miles along the trails. The livestock of the emigrants and of the ranch owners denuded the pastures along the rivers, and the riparian forests were cut for construction and firewood.

The Dog Soldiers emerged from this new situation and represented a reorganization of Cheyenne society, a geographical movement, and most especially a strong position on a political question. Unlike the council chiefs, the Dog Soldiers were unwilling to accommodate to white expansion. Instead, they resolved to live by their military tradition. Denied access to trade, not only by the monopolies exercised by the council chiefs but also by the deteriorating situation along the rivers, the Dog Soldiers decided to live by raiding.

The Military Imperative

By the 1860s then, there was a new kind of residence band in the Cheyenne nation, one consisting of members of the same soldier society—notxestoz. And these bands were not led by council chiefs concerned with trade and with maintaining peace relationships, but by headsmen or "soldier chiefs" who were interested in raiding and plunder. After Sand Creek, they attacked Julesburg and emptied the company warehouse, but they left the building standing so that the company could refill it.[36] In 1865 Cheyenne camps were described as "filled with plunder taken from the captured wagon-trains; warriors were strutting about with ladies' silk cloaks and bonnets on and the Indian women were making shirts for the young men out of the finest silk."[37] Throughout the 1860s, the soldier bands conducted hundreds of raids in Kansas, Nebraska, and Colorado, as recorded in the official War Department records.[38] By 1867 they were derailing trains in central Kansas, bringing strings of pack animals to carry off goods from the railroad cars.[39]

This trend toward maintaining soldier societies as permanent residence bands rather than as seasonal war units began as early as 1836, with the expulsion of Porcupine Bear, a Dog Soldier headsman, from the Cheyenne nation. As was so often the case, this fissioning of a new group was occasioned by a dispute, in this case a murder.[40] After expulsion Porcupine Bear, instead of following the main camps for a few years and then slinking back to rejoin the nation, as was usual, set up his own separate camp and was quickly joined by his friends and relatives. When the great attack was made on the Kiowas in 1838, this group of Dog Soldiers distinguished themselves by striking the first coup and by aggressively punishing the Kiowas throughout the battle.[41]

At first the withdrawal of some Dog Soldiers to form a band of a new type may have seemed unimportant to ordinary Cheyenne citizens. The best reporter for these events is probably George Bent, who was raised as a Cheyenne in these years. Concerning the original expulsion, Bent relates the circumstances of the murder committed by Porcupine Bear, then the headsman of the Dog Soldiers: "For this deed Porcupine Bear and all his relations were outlawed by the tribe, and the Dog Soldier Society, of which Porcupine Bear was the first chief, was also disgraced."[42] But Porcupine Bear's little group of exiles soon became a permanent band. As Bent put it: "After he had killed Little Creek and been outlawed by the tribe, Porcupine Bear had formed a camp of his own, made up mainly of his relations; and all these people were treated as outcasts and were not permitted to camp or move with the rest of the tribe."[43] Later on, Bent says, "the Dog Soldiers lived on the Republican and Smoky Hill rivers most of the time and were great friends of the Oglala and Brule Sioux, who hunted and camped in that region. The Dog Soldiers and Sioux intermarried a great deal. Tall Bull's mother was a Sioux woman, and a great many of the Dog Soldiers were half Sioux. The young men of this band were very wild and reckless, great raiders, and being hard to control were always in mischief. In this way, they get the rest of the tribe into trouble. These young men would make a raid and get out of the way, and the troops would come and stumble across some other band of Cheyennes and punish them for what the Dog Soldiers had done."[44]

As the Dog Soldiers gained strength, they carved out a new territory for themselves east of the other Cheyenne bands, on the Republican and Smoky Hill headwaters between the Platte and the Arkansas. Grass was better in this area, enabling larger camps to stay together. Captain Ware's descriptions of the remarkable campsites on the Republican River were included in the previous chapter. This move to the east was made possible by the removal of Pawnee influence from that area. The Pawnees were motivated to move because the combined Sioux and Cheyennes drove them south, because the Pawnees were increasingly employed by the army as scouts, and because they had been assigned new reservation lands to the south and east of Dog Soldier territory.[45] It was in this period, between 1838 and 1856, that the Dog Soldiers increasingly relied on raiding for subsistence and began to treat traders in a high-handed manner. Also in this period, they were increasingly thrown into conflict with the council chiefs because their raiding caused counterattacks on the chiefs' bunches, as mentioned by George Bent, which disrupted the trading and subsistence activities so essential for the peace faction.

In this period "Dog Soldiers" became a generic name for all the "hostiles" who lived in that area, whether they were Cheyennes or Sioux.[46] By the 1860s Sioux and Cheyenne "Dog Soldiers" formed large camps together, and were greatly intermarried. Tall Bull, headsman of the Cheyenne Dog Soldiers, had a Lakota mother. According to Hayden, most of these Cheyennes were bilingual in this period, using Lakota as a trade language, since it was better known to Platte River traders than Cheyenne.[47]

From the time of Porcupine Bear's expulsion in 1838 until the final defeat of the Dog Soldiers at Summit Springs in 1869, there was a steady increase in their numbers. Originally, the Dog Soldier group consisted of Porcupine Bear, his "cousins," and their families, probably about 10 to 20 lodges.[48] In 1867 General Winfield Hancock captured the main Dog Soldier camp, which consisted of 111 Cheyenne lodges and 140 Sioux lodges.[49] After the Battle of Summit Springs in 1869, 84 Cheyenne lodges were burned by the victorious United States soldiers and Pawnee scouts.[50] After that disastrous defeat, however, many Cheyennes who had sought refuge with the Dog Soldiers began to rejoin their original bands on the Oklahoma reservation. By 1873 John Miles reported that there were only 14 lodges in the Dog Soldier camp, on Beaver Creek some fifty miles from the main body of Cheyennes (map 14).[51] During these same years the "peace faction" reached its low point in numbers at the Battle of the Washita, where there were only 47 lodges with Black Kettle.[52] By 1877, however, the main body of the Cheyennes, gathered around the council chiefs, had rebounded to 262 lodges (map 15).[53]

Our best non-Indian informant for this period of flux, when Dog Soldiers were trying to dominate Cheyenne politics, is John Prowers, whose trading ambitions on the Arkansas were thwarted by the intransigence and mili-

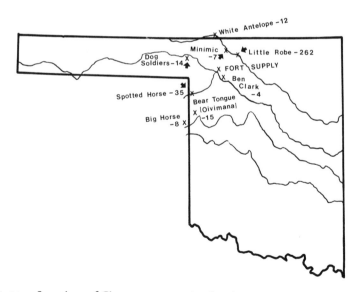

Map 14.   Locations of Cheyenne reservation bands in 1873.

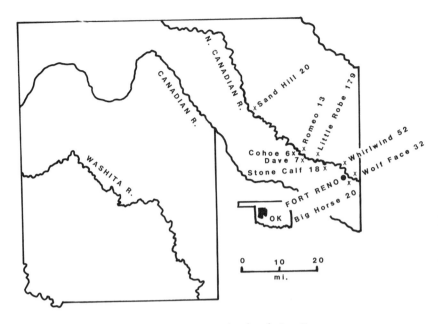

Map 15. Locations of Cheyenne reservation bands in 1877.

tance of the Dog Soldier grouping. Testifying at the Sand Creek hearing in 1865, Prowers noted the following facts about the Dog Soldiers:

> They came here in 1856, and drew their presents from Major Robert Miller, Indian agent, and have not been back here since. They live most of the time on the Smoky Hill and Republican, and have done their trading altogether on the Platte, sometimes on the North and sometimes on the South Platte. They have done no trading on this river, nor with any one from here, to my knowledge, since 1856. They have been sent for often, but would never come into this place, for some reason of difficulty between themselves and other bands of Cheyennes. They have drawn off from Black Kettle's band, and refused to have anything to do with him, and have appointed their own trading man. They do not claim any connection to Black Kettle's band whatever. They have often tried to persuade Black Kettle's band to go north of the Platte to their old lands between the Platte and the Missouri river. Black Kettle always refused and never would go. The Dog Soldiers have always been very mean to white traders, always wanting to make the traders trade as the Dog Soldiers pleased. They have often thrown the traders' goods into the fire.[54]

Since the Dog Soldiers were reputedly throwing traders' goods on the fire, one must assume that already in 1856 they had a good idea where they could get the pots, steel tools, guns, ammunition, and even wagons they had come to depend on. But before the Sand Creek Massacre in 1864, Dog Soldier raids were limited in scale—supply wagons on the Platte Road and the Santa Fe Trail, and raids on white farms and ranches between the Platte and the Arkansas. After 1864, however, the vulnerable farms and ranches strung out along the Platte and the Arkansas were viciously and continually attacked. In addition, the Dog Soldiers attacked the Kansas settlements west from central Kansas on the Smoky Hill, and they closed the "Smoky Hill Road." Looting and theft of stock were always the results. From August until October 1868, 958 cattle were reported to the Department of the Missouri as stolen by Indians.[55]

Although the militant faction of the Cheyennes was continually called "Dog Soldiers" in these years, it seems clear from the Cheyenne side that the political structure of the "war faction" was more complicated than that. Not only were many of the "Dog Soldiers" actually Sioux warriors, but some of the Cheyennes were not Dog Soldiers at all, in the strict sense, since they belonged to other military societies. Roman Nose, for example, was actually a Crooked Lance, while Little Hawk was an Elk Soldier. Dull Knife, also reputedly a Dog Soldier headsman, was actually a council chief of the Omisis band.[56]

In these years other military societies followed the Dog Soldier example and organized themselves as a new type of band. The Elk Soldiers, the Fox Soldiers, and several subgroups of Dog Soldiers are also reported as constituting separate, autonomous bands in this period. By the time of the Julesburg attack each society, with families in tow, marched separately on the trail.[57] So here we see a massive shift in Cheyenne social relations, accomplished within a very short time. But to what extent was this shift a physical realignment of bands and camps and to what extent was it a matter of *perspective?*

Many North American Indian nations were known to maintain a peace/war "dual organization" of some type in their period of contact with whites. Frederick Gearing has described the "red" and "white" structure of the Cherokees—red for war and white for peace.[58] In the Cherokee case there was an official transfer of political power from peace chiefs to war chiefs when war was declared, and an official transfer back to the peace chiefs when the war was finished. The Creeks and Seminoles had a similar political structure originally, until the intransigent war leaders, the "Red Sticks," joined the Seminoles in Florida and continued their warfare full time.[59] That is, Muskogee society was polarized in a manner reminiscent of the polarization of the Cheyennes.

The Cheyenne dual system, however, which we saw in chapter 2, was from the beginning somewhat different from the Cherokee or Creek system. First of all, there was no official transfer of power. Instead there was a seasonal pattern of warfare beginning in early summer, when the headsmen of the military societies led their warriors against enemy nations, with the council chiefs gradually assuming power in late summer as the bands went their separate ways for grazing, hunting, and trade. Remember from chapter 2 that the dual nature of Cheyenne society is reflected in many ways, especially in the organization of the ceremonial camp circle on successive days. The military societies take the four corners of the circle for their initiations in the early days of the ceremonies, and the "sacred bands" occupy their positions after the societies have finished.

The relative ease with which Cheyenne society was transformed onto a war footing in the 1860s, then, can be partly understood in terms of this preexisting dual structure. One way of looking at it is that the so-called Dog Soldiers were merely making permanent an organizational form that was previously only seasonal. Another difference was that they now had their families in camp with them instead of leaving them in some safe area. Less than a year after Sand Creek, according to George Bent, Cheyenne bands had completely reorganized themselves into military units. They traveled together and stayed together the whole winter in the Big Timbers areas of the Republican and Smoky Hill rivers which were among the few places remaining in their hands that could support such large groups of people and horses.

One might argue, for the period 1864–69, that the militant faction was taking the first steps toward the formation of a new "Dog Soldier nation," amalgamated from the militant factions of the Cheyennes and the Lakota Sioux. One bit of evidence for this is the seizure of the sacred arrows by the militants after the Sand Creek Massacre and their appointment of the Fox Soldiers as special protectors of the arrow bundle.[60] According to modern informants, it was at this juncture that the Foxes acquired their nickname Moiseo or "Flint People," the name previously applied to the Tsistsistas band. The change in names implied a change in guardianship of the sacred arrows with their flint points. The militants then sponsored their own Sun Dance on Medicine Lodge Creek in Kansas.[61] Insofar as a Sun Dance implies political unity and autonomy from other nations, then there was a Dog Soldier nation in the 1860s. The birth of this nation, however, was aborted by the military disaster at Summit Springs in 1869, when Dog Soldier families were massacred, their belongings burned, and the survivors dispersed across the southern plains.

After they had been collected onto the Oklahoma reservation, the Dog

Soldiers managed to continually reassert their militant resistance to American domination and in fact were capable of vetoing or sabotoging plans made by the Indian agents. Recognizing their power, Captain Lee enrolled the Dog Soldiers as reservation police, working through Mower, whom Lee recognized as leader of all the Cheyennes and through whom he tried to initiate a system of indirect rule in 1885.[62] After Lee's departure, however, the Dog Soldiers quickly became an independent force once again.[63]

In sum, we must recognize that the main reason Cheyenne society could be transformed so quickly between 1850 and 1864 relates to the fluid nature of the trading-subsistence structure typical of the earlier period, 1805–56, and the preexistence of a dual organization. In the dual structure there were certain bands—the manhastoz or chiefs' bunches—that were central, composing a core for each manhao, while the small units—camps or vestoz—were marginal to the trading structure. In chapters 8 and 9 we will look more closely at the internal structures of these groups, but for the present we need only understand that each core group consisted of one or more polygynous chiefs and their "bunches." The other bunches and camps

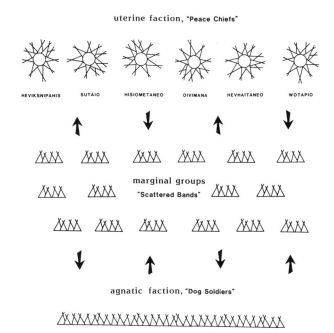

Figure 16.   Polarization of Cheyenne society in the 1860s.

of the manhao consisted of people who were more distantly related to the core groups and who might also have kin relations with other sacred bands. That is, some camps and bunches in each manhao were strongly and definitely members of that band, while others were less strongly related to the central core. These marginal units could, with some legitimacy, be considered members of some other manhao as well, by tracing other lines of ancestry. The reorganization of Cheyenne society in 1838–69, then, was accomplished merely by the desertion of the marginal units to the "Dog Soldiers," leaving only the core units as components of each manhao. These core units were the groups attacked at Sand Creek.

Figure 16 is a diagram of the form polarization took for Cheyenne society in the middle of the nineteenth century. The symbols at the top, borrowed from maps drawn by Cheyennes in the 1880s, represent the core bunches of the various sacred bands.[64] The symbols in the center represent the vestoz or marginal camps in this period, both the original camps that traded under the sponsorship of some council chief and the camps formed by the disintegration of some of the bunches after Sand Creek. The line of tipis at the bottom represents the notxestoz or soldier bands, which attracted camps as the peace faction suffered in numbers. In the next chapter we will look at the histories of these different kinds of bands and see how they have interacted in the period from the founding of the Cheyenne nation to the present.

7 ⩙⩙

Histories of Cheyenne Bands

In this chapter we will trace the histories of particular "bands" prominent in historical documents and oral histories of the Cheyennes. We have already traced the origins of the earliest groups and followed them in their migrations from Minnesota to the Black Hills. From there the movements of the bands become more complicated, but we can still trace them because of the richness of historical documents.

In addition to examining documents, there is another way to determine the general movements of the nation, based on the twelfth census of the United States, taken in 1900. In it all American respondents, including Indians, were asked their state or territory of birth and that of their parents. Fortunately for our purposes, most Cheyenne people responded as best they could, on individual schedules now kept in the National Archives.

The historical depth of these responses is much greater than we might at first suppose. The parents of people who themselves were elderly in 1900 were born in the late 1700s, before Lewis and Clark. And so the 1900 census can give us a complete historical profile of Cheyenne migrations in the nineteenth century if we know how to approach the data. State and territorial boundaries were different then, of course, and we also have the problem of matching children with parents, part of what demographers call "linkage."

Rough Data

The 1900 census contains a column entitled "Nativity" in which the respondents were supposed to enter their own place of birth and that of their parents. [1] Since the parents are not identified by name, we must make some assumptions in order to use this information. One method of estimating the birth year of a parent, since their ages are not given, is to calculate the difference in age between an "average" child and a parent and subtract that figure from the birth year of the child. From the 1880 United States census,[2] we learn that the average age of fathers at the birth of their children was 29.9 years, while the average age of mothers was 25.6 years. That is, these are the average or "mean" differences in age between parents and children. These average figures allow us to estimate the birth dates of the parents of people listed on the 1900 census simply by subtracting that number of years from the birth dates given for the respondents. For example, we can estimate that a woman born in 1850 will have a father born 29.9 years earlier and a mother born 25.6 years earlier. For convenience, we can round these off to 30 and 26 years and estimate parental birth dates of 1820 and 1824 in this case.

When we estimate birth dates in this manner for Cheyennes who were living in Oklahoma Territory at the time of the 1900 census, we discover that seventy-one of their parents were born before 1810. Table 11 shows the percentage of these parents born in the several Plains states, with the states arranged more or less from north to south. As we look at the names of the states and territories, we should remember that the political boundaries of Nebraska, Wyoming, and Montana changed significantly in the nineteenth century, and it is not always clear which boundaries the Cheyenne respondents were referring to. Nevertheless, the general position of the nation in this period can be seen from the fact that roughly a third of the Cheyennes in that generation were born in the Dakotas, which includes not only the Black Hills but also the headwaters of the Bad River and some tributaries of the Niobrara. Also, "Dakota" included Pine Ridge, present

Table 11   Percentage of Southern
Cheyennes Born in Various States and
Territories

STATE	BORN BEFORE 1810	BORN 1811–30
Minnesota	3	0
Dakota	34	33
Montana	37	21
Wyoming	3	20
Nebraska	7	8
Colorado	17	15
Kansas	0	2
Oklahoma	0	1

Source: U.S. census, 1900.

home of the Oglala Sioux, which is the historic range of some of the Cheyenne bands we shall discuss in this chapter.

When we look at the birthplaces of Cheyennes born in the period 1811–30, roughly the next generation, we get a somewhat different picture. First of all, we see a significant movement into the territory of the Upper Platte, which has its major tributaries in present Wyoming and Colorado. In the right-hand column of table 11 the number of persons born in Wyoming jumps from 3 percent to 20 percent. Also, we see a movement out of Montana, perhaps reflecting the effects of warfare with the Crows, who inflicted severe defeats on the Cheyennes in this period. Also, we see that while two of the very oldest Cheyennes had been born in Minnesota before 1810, none of the Cheyennes in the later period gave Minnesota as their birthplace. But seven of the Cheyennes recorded for 1811–30 gave Kansas and Oklahoma as their birthplaces, the areas into which the Cheyennes were expanding.

Table 12 tabulates data on the actual respondents to the 1900 census, rather than their parents. The format and calculations were done by J. J. Chen-Chou. The states or territories of birth are listed down the left column, and the decades of birth across the top. Looking at the entry for people born in the Indian Territory in the 1880s, for example, we discover that there were thirty-six. Looking at the percentages just underneath, we discover that 36 people constitutes 2.50 percent of the total interviewed, 48.65 percent of all the people who gave Indian Teritory as their place of birth (the horizontal row), and 8.39 percent of all people born in that decade (the vertical column).

By studying this table, we get another perspective on the general movements of the Southern Cheyennes in the nineteenth century. In each horizontal row, for example, there is a peak figure that represents the period of maximum occupancy of that state. For Nebraska, to use one example, the maximum number of Cheyenne births was twenty-two in the 1850s, when the Dog Soldiers were beginning to occupy the Republican River valley. All in all, the table confirms what I have proposed so far about Cheyenne history, but we will learn more when we can sort out these people by band and look at the states of birth for individual band members.

By contrast the Northern Cheyennes, on the same census, do not show a strong pattern of migration. Except for a band of Southern Cheyennes who had moved to Montana in 1884 and whose parents were born in the south, the Northern Cheyenne census indicates locations in the area of the Black Hills and westward. In a project now continuing, Greg Campbell is developing techniques for tracing Northern Cheyenne band movements more specifically in this early period, before 1830.

Table 12   Birthplaces of Southern Cheyennes in the Nineteenth Century

BIRTHPLACE	1800s	1810s	1820s	1830s	1840s	1850s	1860s	1870s	1880s	1890s	TOTAL
Indian Territory	—	—	—	—	—	2[a]	8	25	36	3	74
						0.14[b]	0.56	1.74	2.50	0.21	5.14
						2.70[c]	10.81	33.78	48.65	4.05	
						1.23[d]	4.21	12.82	8.39	0.99	
Oklahoma				2		6	44	121	382	297	852
				0.14		0.42	3.06	8.40	26.53	20.63	59.17
				0.23		0.70	5.16	14.20	44.84	34.86	
				3.64		3.70	23.16	62.05	89.04	98.02	
Colorado			5	4	15	54	50	11	—	1	140
			0.35	0.28	1.04	3.75	3.47	0.76		0.07	9.72
			3.57	2.86	10.71	38.57	35.71	7.86		0.71	
			21.74	7.27	20.00	33.33	26.32	5.64		0.33	
Kansas				2	6	7	41	18	5	—	79
				0.14	0.42	0.49	2.85	1.25	0.35		5.49
				2.53	7.59	8.86	51.90	22.78	6.33		
				3.64	8.00	4.32	21.58	9.23	1.17		
Nebraska			4	—	3	22	15	2	1	—	47
			0.28		0.21	1.53	1.04	0.14	0.07		3.26
			11.43		6.38	46.81	31.91	5.71	2.13		
			17.39		4.00	13.58	7.89	1.03	0.23		

	1	2	3	4	5	6	7	8	9	10	Total
Wyoming [a]	—	1	4	6	9	9	3	2	1	—	35
[b]	—	0.07	0.28	0.42	0.63	0.63	0.21	0.14	0.07	—	2.43
[c]	—	2.86	11.43	17.14	25.71	25.71	8.57	5.26	2.86	—	
[d]	—	14.29	17.39	10.91	12.00	5.56	1.58	1.03	0.23	—	
Dakota [a]	—	4	5	27	23	46	16	8	1	1	131
[b]	—	0.28	0.35	1.88	1.60	3.19	1.11	0.56	0.07	0.07	9.10
[c]	—	3.05	3.82	20.61	17.56	35.11	12.21	6.11	0.76	0.76	
[d]	—	57.14	21.74	49.09	30.67	28.40	8.42	4.10	0.23	0.33	
Montana [a]	—	1	3	7	11	9	4	2	1	—	38
[b]	—	0.07	0.21	0.49	0.76	0.63	0.28	0.14	0.07	—	2.64
[c]	—	2.63	7.89	18.42	28.95	23.68	10.53	5.26	2.63	—	
[d]	—	14.29	13.04	12.73	14.67	5.56	2.11	1.03	0.23	—	
Other [a]	1	1	2	7	8	7	9	6	2	1	44
[b]	0.07	0.07	0.14	0.49	0.56	0.49	0.63	0.42	0.14	0.07	3.06
[c]	2.27	2.27	4.55	15.91	18.18	15.91	20.45	13.64	4.55	2.27	
[d]	100.00	14.29	8.70	12.73	10.67	4.32	4.74	3.08	0.47	0.33	
Total [a]	1	7	23	55	75	162	190	195	429	303	1,440
[b]	0.07	0.49	1.60	3.82	5.21	11.25	13.19	13.54	29.79	21.04	100.00

[a] Number born in state or territory.
[b] Percentage of total interviewed.
[c] Percentage of those giving state or territory as place of birth.
[d] Percentage of those born in decade.

After 1830 all the Cheyenne bands became more discrete and more dispersed, and we must use some ingenuity in reconstructing their movements. One incredible stroke of luck, which in fact helped inspire this research from the very beginning, was that the different Southern Cheyenne bands were given discrete blocks of allotments on their Oklahoma reservation in 1892. That is, instead of being crowded all together into a mass in which bands, bunches, and camps were indistinguishable, the band allotments were spread out over an area of approximately 10,000 square miles, giving them adequate space to express their social preferences and social structure.[3]

This dispersal of allotents was made possible by the policies of Capt. Jesse Lee, Indian agent in 1885–86, who sent his charges to different habitable places on the reservation because rations were short.[4] He thought that if the bands were dispersed in some normal manner, they could find or raise much of their own food and also find adequate grazing for their horses. To disperse the Cheyenne bands, Lee had to fight tooth and nail with politicians and bureaucrats, who had already decided to give each Indian a small individual allotment and to open the rest of the reservation to white settlement. This was finally accomplished with the Dawes Act of 1887.[5]

Two statements from modern informants help document that the pattern of allotments did indeed represent aboriginal social structure. The first statement is from Ed Burns, Sr., of Clinton: "When the Indians were allotted this land, they'd get all their relatives of one man to be allotted together. One man moved to Hammon. He moved his people to Hammon, his relatives. And this man, Big Jake, moved his over here to Clinton. Another man, Old Crow, he moved his people over here to Thomas. And another man moved his bunch down to Colony."[6]

Another such statement is from Jasper Reynolds, of Weatherford:

> This is about back home again. About when the Indians still was in bunches you might say. And there wasn't a reservation, but they was allotted 160 acres apiece. And seems like the Indians that picked their land out, they was all in groups. They picked on east side of some creeks, and on the east side of the river. I noticed today, when I was young, there was quite a few families from down at—I say, "Up the creek." Where the creek is flowing toward, we used to call it "up the creek." And on each side of the creek the Indians chose land. There was neighbors all the way up—maybe 20 to 30 miles on each side of the creek. That way they used to visit each other, when they wasn't doing anything.
>
> And they had districts from then on, after they got their allotments. And today we have seven districts, I think, among the Cheyennes. And each one

of the districts, Cheyennes have names for them districts, for something that happened, or the way they was living or the way what somebody done. They went by the names; they had names for them Indians.[7]

The situation of the Southern Cheyennes was unusual, because they had a large reservation and because they were dispersed on it instead of being crowded around a fort or agency. For that reason, among others, they stoutly resisted allotment, which, according to law, required ratification by three-fourths of Cheyenne males over eighteen. Soon after the Dawes Act was passed in 1887, however, it was obvious that the Cheyennes would never consent. So officials of the United States government, the notorious Jerome Commission, embarked on a policy of outright fraud in 1890 to gain the appearance of approval from the Cheyennes.

First of all, the Southern Cheyennes and the Southern Arapahos were alleged to constitute the same "tribe," over the objections of both. And then certain mixed-blood agents were sent among the Arapahos to give them bribes and jobs in the classic "divide and conquer" strategy. Still lacking enough votes to approve allotment, the number of adult males was "certified" at a low figure—618—from which 464 was taken to constitute the required three-fourths approval. However, official reports in 1888 and 1891, before and after the Jerome Commission, stated that the number of males over eighteen was 827 and 833, respectively. This would have required at least 620 signatures, not 464.

Having collected only about a hundred signatures by all means at hand, including threats and bribery, the Jerome Commission began entering the names of women, children, and even "made-up" names like Oscar Wild, Chester A. Arthur, and Jay Gould. There were multiple signatures, with one man signing three times, as "Contestor," "Mr. Contestor," and "Ned Contestor." Still lacking enough signatures, they resorted to phony "powers of attorney" under the following rationale: "In the execution of the contract the fact that some of the male adults, entitled to sign, were absent from the reservation attending school at Carlisle Penn. and Lawrence, Kansas, and others were distant from the agency and unable without great inconvenience to come there, and the further fact that it was deemed both unwise and impracticable for the Commission to visit them, we have resorted to the use of powers of attorney, which are attached to the contract enclosed."[8]

Of course one of the reasons it was "unwise" for the commission to visit Cheyenne communities was that the Indians were fighting mad. But the Cheyennes were powerless to stop the fraud, and the commission soon forwarded its signatures to the president saying it had "the honor and very great satisfaction to report to you that we have concluded a contract with the

Cheyenne and Arapahoe Tribes of Indians in this Territory." Further, it said that "the dullest Indian was made to understand the terms of the contract, and its effect." Of the signatures sent to the president, only 146 can be verified from the official 1888 census.[9]

Outraged at being defauded of their land, some of the Cheyennes refused to select allotments and refused to accept the stacks of silver dollars being offered by the government. Faced with a potential rebellion, the Bureau of Indian Affairs then convened a council of friendly elders and chiefs to select allotments for the hostile bands, blocks of allotments that represented the land where the bands were already camped.[10] The idea was that the land could be allotted with less chance of bloodshed if care was taken in the selection. It is for this reason, then, that the blocks of allotments appearing on map 16 bear such a close resemblance to the actual location and social structure of the Cheyenne Indians in 1892, even for those bands that opposed allotment.

They Cheyennes then placed their hopes in various lawsuits being brought by themselves and other Indian nations that had been similarly

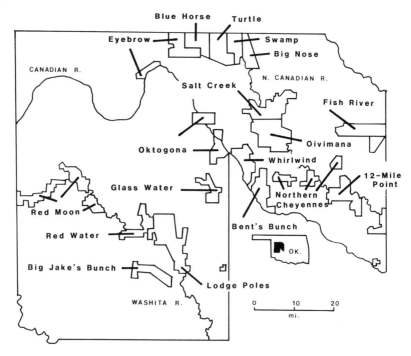

Map 16. Southern Cheyenne bands at allotment in 1892.

defrauded. All such suits came to an end with the infamous Lone Wolf decision, which said that if a fraud against Indians was ratified by Congress, no matter how outrageous it was, it thereby became lawful and irreversible.[11] It was this same allotment in severalty that destroyed Cheyenne farming, we should remember, and it was a sorry chapter in American history, even though it resulted in the remarkable allotment map we can analyze for so many useful purposes.

The allotment map I will use here, the "base map" labeled map 16, is considerably improved over the one published in *Science* in 1980. Still, it is not perfect. No doubt other information will surface over the next several years that will resolve some ambiguities and perhaps even change the identities of some of the bands on the map.

Map 17 shows the antecedent aboriginal bands for the groups identifed from the allotment map. The abbreviations shown are the same used in chapter 2. Identifying the continuity between aboriginal and reservation bands has been one of the central purposes of this research and has consumed

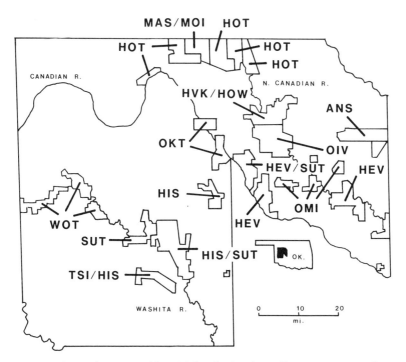

Map 17.   Antecedent "sacred bands" for the Southern Cheyenne groups of 1892.

the most time. The results are based on interviews, field notes, and various computer analyses of census names, all of which are discussed here. We will see in the next chapter what is meant by "continuity" from an aboriginal band to a reservation band and thence to a modern Cheyenne community.

The allotment blocks on the map are separated either by spaces between groups of allotments or by discontinuities in the allotment list. The spaces between Cheyenne allotments are either unallotted lands or lands taken by Arapahos, especially around Geary and Canton. Discontinuities in the list are represented by lines drawn across the allotment blocks—for example, the horizontal line separating the Heviksnipahis from the Oivimana band.

The sizes of some allotment blocks are misleading. Although most of the blocks represent solid areas of allotment, some have spaces within them or a fringe that is less dense. For graphic clarity, I have simplified the edges of some blocks and ignored the interior vacant spaces of unallotted land, which comprise land reserved for public schools and land retained by the federal government.

Some of the smaller blocks of allotments do not represent separate bands at all but were taken by certain members of a nearby band. These small blocks represent areas of special interest—lakes, timber, and salt deposits, for example—that certain bands reserved for themselves although they did not live there.

At the time of allotment, some bands were known by two or three names simultaneously. I have entered on the map only the best-known name for each, although I will discuss the other names in the text. Some bands were also undergoing fission or fusion at the time of allotment; I will also discuss these situations, as I know of them.

Map 18 represents a rough test of the extent of polarization of the Cheyennes in the 1860s. The triangles on the map are the locations of the allotments of Dog Soldiers identified from the "capture lists" made after the Battle of Summit Springs in 1869. The circles are the survivors of the Sand Creek Massacre who lived until allotment. We can see that the oral traditions about location of the factions are correct. The agnatic faction did in fact tend to take allotments in the northern strip from Seiling to Longdale, while people from the uterine faction, led by council chiefs, located elsewhere. Although there were some Dog Soldiers spread over the rest of the reservation, among the uterine faction, no Sand Creek survivors took allotments in the northern tier.

If we wish to get additional information about the discrete bands (maps 16 and 17), we must do some preliminary work. First, we must link the people on the allotment map with the 1900 census, and then we can see where the band members and their parents are born. If the parents of band

LOCATIONS OF AGNATIC AND UTERINE FACTIONS AT ALLOTMENT

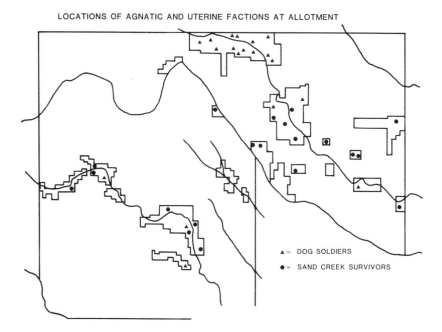

Map 18. Locations of agnatic and uterine factions at allotment. Lists are from Indian Archives Division, Oklahoma Historical Society.

members show different states and territories of birth than their children, in some structured way, then we can describe the movements of the band in the late eighteenth and early nineteenth centuries, just as we traced the general movements of the nation earlier in this chapter.

When I first attempted this technique, in the summer of 1981, I tried out one band I knew to have northern origins, the Kingfisher band, which split off from the Northern Cheyennes in very early reservation days, perhaps about 1885. I was able to find twenty-five people on the 1900 census who had taken their allotments at Kingfisher in 1892. Of these, all but one said their parents were born in Montana, and that one, Fred Bushy, said his parents were born in Nebraska. The other bands, as we shall see, also gave responses consistent with what is known about their history, but the great bonanza from this technique was learning the histories of bands for which historical accounts did not exist—Hisiometaneos, Masikotas, and Oktogonas, for example.

Map 19 shows the locations of the discrete Cheyenne bands about 1845. To generate these results, I first linked as many people as I could from the

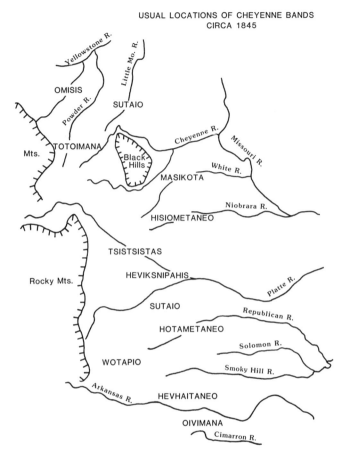

USUAL LOCATIONS OF CHEYENNE BANDS
CIRCA 1845

Map 19. Usual locations of Cheyenne bands about 1845.

1892 allotment map to the 1900 census. Then I examined each band, as a group, to see if the states of birth of self and parents indicated a "home range" for the band. Of course the range varied through time, but map 19 shows the situation in 1845. Nearly all bands, however, showed some variability in birth locations, probably because of the transhumant patterns of some bands. In the case of the Hisiometaneo band, for example, I do not know whether the Niobrara River area represented the summer or winter range, though I suspect the latter. But the band showed a minority of births in Wyoming and Colorado in this period, the area of the Upper Platte. In addition to the 1900 census, I have used some other information to place the bands on this map, information to be discussed in the rest of this chapter.

In the following pages we will learn something about the history of nation building among the Cheyennes and about the general character of nomadic nations composed of bands that are widely dispersed. We will also gain some understanding of how and why bands change their names and character through time. Apparently the most important process, along with fission, was hybridization. Modern informants report that the second generation of reservation bands, for example, was hybridized from the first generation, with parts of two bands combining by marriage to form a new band or continue an old one. We will see that this process is also typical of the prereservation period, when hybridization occurred not only among the bands, but between Cheyenne bands and foreign nations.

In these band histories I will not identify the informants for different bits of information, except where there is some difference of opinion or some other good reason to do so. In the history of each band or community, I have regarded as most reliable the opinions of elders raised in that community. Most of this information comes from Ed and Minnie Red Hat (plate 16),

Plate 16.   Edward and Minnie Red Hat of Longdale, Oklahoma. Photo by David T. Hughes.

Roy and Kathryn Bull Coming (plate 17), John and Susie Black Owl (plate 18), Lucy Cometsevah, Ed and Birdie Burns, Ed Whitethunder, Katie Osage (plate 19), John Greany, Walter Hamilton (plate 20), Roy Night-walker (plate 21), Clarence Stoneroad, Harry Whitehorse, and Vinnie Hoffman. Information on Northern Cheyenne bands was collected by Henry Tall Bull and Greg Campbell.

The Eaters

The Eaters was one of the original bands of the Cheyennes. In chapter 3 we traced its history from Minnesota to the Black Hills, where we found it split into one band with the Dakota name "Wotapio" and another with the original Cheyenne name, "Omisis." On the Lewis and Clark map, we found

Plate 17. Roy Bull Coming of Seiling, Oklahoma. Photo by Dan Purcell.

Plate 18.   John Black Owl of El Reno, Oklahoma. Photo by Dan Purcell.

Plate 19.   Katie Osage of Canton, Oklahoma. Photo no. 28–28a in the John Moore Collection, Western History Collections, University of Oklahoma Library.

the Wotapios camped with the Kiowas on the North Platte, and we find this special relationship with the Kiowas characteristic of the Wotapios throughout their history. We will look first at the Wotapio band of "Eaters" and then at the Omisis proper and the band's other subgroups.

After Lewis and Clark, there are two accounts of Cheyenne bands resident with Kiowas. Unfortunately the names of the bands were not recorded, either by Edwin James or by Jacob Fowler, nor do we have the names of the

Plate 20. Walter R. Hamilton of Geary, Oklahoma. Photo by Dan Purcell.

Plate 21. Roy Nightwalker of Fonda, Oklahoma. Photo by Dan Purcell.

chiefs. But the special relationship with the Kiowas tends to identify these Cheyennes as Wotapios, at least until better information surfaces.

Edwin James was the botanist and geologist for the Stephen Long expedition up the Arkansas River in 1819 and 1820. He recorded for 27 September 1820, from a camp on the Arkansas in Colorado, that a delegation of chiefs had been sent from four bands "of the same number of different nations here associated together, and consisting of Kiawas, Kaskaias, or Bad-hearts, Shiennes (sometimes written Chayenne) and Arrapahoes."[12] James noted further that the overall or "grand chief" of the assemblage was an Arapaho named Bear Tooth, and he added: "The Shiennes or Shawhays, who have united their destiny with these wanderers, are a band of seceders from their own nation, and some time since on the occurrence of a serious dispute with their kindred on Shienne river of the Missouri, flew their country, and placed themselves under the protection of the Bear-tooth."

What the nature of this dispute might have been is lost to history, but we should note, from modern times, that disputes and murder are *always* given as the reasons for the formation of new bands. Modern Cheyennes usually mention some homicide, manslaughter, or serious interfamily dispute as the reason for maintaining boundaries among modern bands or as the historical reasons why early reservation bands were different in the first place.

Although such events are traumatic in themselves, they are also the mechanism for the fission of bands into new and viable groups. Among small bands and communities such traumatic events do not result in the fission of the group, but among larger groups they do.[13] Small groups smoke and smooth over the differences; large groups stop talking to each other and move apart physically. One way of looking at the situation is that when stress already exists in a band, and where there is already some good reason for a split, a traumatic event such as homicide or adultery is seized upon as a rationale for creating a new band. And so it is not surprising that the band leader James interviewed gave a "serious dispute" as the reason for separation from a parent group. This is consistently the reason given for the formation of a new band, whenever reasons are given.

In 1821 trader Jacob Fowler visited the same area along the Arkansas where Long had traveled, and in fact he met with the same people. Fowler's account, in which I preserve the original spelling and grammar, is as follows: "The Princeple Cheefs Informed us that When mager longe Was there He told them that the Presedent Wold Send them plenty of goods and that the goods We Head Ware Sent to Him and that We Head no Wright to traid them but When He discovered that His demands Wold not be Complyed With Chainged His disposetion and Seems very frendly."[14] Concerning the number of Cheyennes in the camp, Fowler estimated that there were two hundred Cheyenne lodges, from a total of seven hundred for the entire camp.

Unfortunately we cannot use the 1900 census to trace the Wotapio band in this period, because the Hammon people, the descendants of this band, refused to cooperate with Anglo census takers for the twelfth United States census. Only a few people interviewed would even give their ages, and only five would give their places of birth. None gave the state or territories in which their parents were born.

Despite their special friendship with the Kiowas, the Wotapios apparently participated in the great battle against them in 1838. After the Hevhaitaneo and Oivimana bands moved south about 1828, there had been increasing friction between the Cheyennes and the Kiowas. Also, the Kiowas traded with the Crows and were friendly with them, and this trade was interrupted by the warfare between the Cheyennes and the Crows. In any event, Grinnell's informants said that all the bands were present when the sacred arrows were moved against the Kiowas in 1838.[15] The moving of the arrows was the ultimate military strategy of the Cheyennes and in fact demonstrated the strength of the nation, as a nation. The Cheyennes' ability to mobilize all their dispersed bands for warfare was what allowed them to be so successful in Plains warfare. Other nations that were more loosely organized, such as the Comanches and Shoshones, could not bring their full numbers to bear against an enemy as the Cheyennes could.

In this same period the "Kiowas" were also organizing themselves into a nation and adopting the Sun Dance, and I suggest that one of the component bands of the Kiowa nation may have been a hybrid Cheyenne-Kiowa band of the same name as the Cheyenne "Wotapios." We should remember that Lewis and Clark put the winter camp of the "Wetapahatoes" and the "Kiawas" together on the North Platte, indicating a close relationship. And although Fowler estimated that there were 200 lodges in the Cheyenne band he observed in 1821, the Wotapio band that remained with the Cheyennes can be reconstructed at only about 161 people and 30 lodges. I believe the rest of the Wetepahatos joined the Kiowas and were absorbed culturally and linguistically, if indeed much adjustment was necessary in a band that was already predominately Kiowa. This amalgamation of a hybrid Cheyenne band into the Kiowa nation, I further believe, resulted in the use of the term "Wetapahatos" as the Cheyenne designation for the Kiowa nation.

This absorption of a hybrid band by the Kiowas, I suggest, is the same process by which the Cheyenne nation absorbed the Masikotas, a band hybridized between the Cheyennes and Lakotas. In both cases the hybrid bands might have gone either way in their choice of national identity or might have split, like the Wotapios, with fragments going to two nations. The general pressures for nation building, I argue, were caused by the adoption of horses and the availability of trade. So from the congeries of multilingual and multicultural bands extant on the Plains in the late eighteenth century, discrete nations were slowly being carved out. The Sun Dance was the idiom of national identity, and the Kiowa Sun Dance circle, no less than the Cheyenne circle, organized a new nation from among some highly dissimilar bands. [16]

To trace further the movements of the Wotapio band in this early period, we can work backward from information supplied by Grinnell's informants. They identified Old Bark or Bear with Feathers (a literal translation is "Bear with Wings") as the chief of the Wotapio band, a man who was succeeded by the famous Black Kettle in 1850. This Old Bark was the same man who befriended Lt. J. W. Abert in his two explorations along the Arkansas, in 1845 and 1846. During this time, and apparently for some while afterward, the Wotapio band was divided into at least two bunches, one of which was named "Log People." Grinnell represented the name Log People as "Hoohktsitan," which is merely an alternative version of the name of the chief of the bunch—Old Bark, Old Bark of Tree, Old Log, and such. [17]

Some additional details about the Wotapio band were supplied by George Bent, who married a woman from that band in about 1866. In fact, this is the most explicit account of the history of any band in this early period:

> This was a small division of the Cheyennes, and is called the Cheyenne-Sioux band by the old people. This band was made up of Moiseyu and Cheyenne people, and the old Cheyennes say the Moiseyu were Sioux. The Moiseyu left the Cheyennes about 1815 and moved north of the Missouri. I know some old women still living whose mothers were Moiseyu, and these women still speak Sioux. When Black Kettle married into the Wotapio he went to live with his wife's people, as was the old custom. The chief of this band at that time was Bear with Feathers, and when he died in 1850 Black Kettle was elected chief. The Wotapio were famed for the number of fine horses they owned, also for their fine large lodges. Everything they had was clean and of the best quality, and by the other Cheyenne bands they were called "Stingies," because they did not like to give away their things as presents like the others. [18]

Petter also collected the name "Stingies" or "penurious ones" from his informants, but as the name of another Wotapio bunch, not the whole band. He spelled the name in Cheyenne as Hovxnova, thereby allowing us to divide the Wotapios into at least two bunches in the late aboriginal period, the Logmen and the Stingies. [19]

Before reservation times, the Wotapios suffered a severe diminution in their numbers, not only from losing people to the Kiowa nation, but also as the result of two massacres and several epidemics. Like other bands that emphasized trade, the Wotapios became members of the peace faction, where Black Kettle became a prominent leader. In the Sand Creek Massacre, according to George Bent, the Wotapio band "was the heaviest loser."

Four years later, at the Battle of the Washita, Black Kettle himself was killed in an attack led by General Custer. This time the Cheyenne peace faction was on the way to Fort Cobb, having been alerted by an army officer that Custer was in the field and intended to attack all Indian camps, friendly or not. This attack further diminished the numbers of the Wotapios, and the escaping survivors either joined their Kiowa relatives at Fort Cobb or joined the camps of the militant Dog Soldier grouping north of the Arkansas.

The first epidemic suffered by the Wotapios and other bands, of which there is record, was documented by Lieutenant Abert in 1846. He mentioned that "the Cheyennes" had diminished from four hundred to two hundred lodges over the past seventeen years, as a result of "the measles and the hooping cough." [20] This information apparently came from Yellow Wolf, a leader of the Hevhaitaneo band, though it is not clear from the context whether he was talking about his own band, or the Southern Cheyennes in general, or the whole nation. The number of lodges mentioned seems to indicate that he is referring to the Hevhaitaneos in general, the Southern Cheyennes. Another epidemic of this period was the cholera of 1849, though the Wotapios are not mentioned specifically as suffering mortalities.

Red Moon's association with the Wotapio band is recorded as early as 1865, after the epidemics and after Sand Creek, but before the Battle of the Washita. In that year the Wotapios again wintered with the Kiowas, maintaining their long-standing friendship. According to George Bent, Red Moon, who would succeed Black Kettle, was the son of Yellow Wolf, the Hevhaitaneo leader mentioned above. [21] Red Moon married into the Wotapio band sometime before 1865. After the Battle of the Washita and the dispersion of the Wotapios, it is not clear what happened to Red Moon, but he emerged in early reservation days as an acknowledged tribal leader. Although his band broke out with the others in 1874, Red Moon was not one of the militant war leaders. He apparently tried to take his band away from the fighting, south toward the Kiowas.

In April of 1875 Red Moon showed up at the Darlington agency in

Oklahoma Territory as the leader of a band of thirty-one men, forty-one women, and twenty-nine children.[22] The composition of the band in itself indicates that it was not a warrior group. The warrior bands who surrendered after the outbreak were smaller and consisted mostly of men. The group led by Wolf on a Hill, for example, included eight men and four women. Bob-tailed Wolf had four men with him and two women. Neither group had any children with them, so they seem to have been groups organized for raiding, not for subsistence.

Eleven family heads from Red Moon's 1875 band can be reliably located on the allotment list of 1892. Five of them, including Red Moon, took their allotments at Hammon, in the group that became known successively as Red Moon's band, White Shield's band, West Camp, and the Hammon bunch. Throughout the early reservation period, the Red Moon band remained aloof from other Cheyennes, preferring to keep company with the Kiowas, whose reservation was just to the south. In fact the allotment blocks of the Red Moon band were closer to the traditionalist Kiowas, around Gotebo, Oklahoma, than to the Cheyenne agency at Darlington. The record of "passes and permits" issued by the army and the Bureau of Indian Affairs in the early reservation period shows a continual pattern of visitation between Hammon and the Kiowas, which continues to this day. The Red Moon band attended the major Cheyenne ceremonies only sporadically in this period, missing the Sun Dance recorded by Mooney and George Dorsey in 1901, though they are represented on Dorsey's 1903 diagram as "Outlaw band."

The winter count of Chunky Fingernails, who was himself a member of the Red Moon band, also confirms a sporadic participation in the Cheyenne ceremonies in this period.[23] According to modern ceremonial leaders, the Hammon people did not attend the ceremonies *as a band* between World War II and the late 1960s, although individuals did attend. For the 1936 ceremonies, Ed Red Hat noted the attendance of nine families from Hammon (fig. 1), while Katie Osage said they were absent from the 1914 ceremonies.

Two landmarks of social history for the Wotapio band were the reorganization accomplished by White Shield (plate 22) and their affiliation with the Mennonites in 1898. According to modern informants, at the death of Red Moon about 1900, White Shield explicitly told the Hammon band that they were different from other Cheyennes and that though other bands might not marry among themselves, the Hammon people could do so. This would allow them to continue to live all together. Whereas Red Moon had made an attempt to recharter the band as the Wotapios and had also referred to the band he led as the Rainbow People, White Shield called

Plate 22. White Shield, a leader of the Red Moon band. Negative no. 322, National Anthropological Archives, Smithsonian Institution.

it the Red Moon band, a name that was maintained during his lifetime. Since his death some of his descendants have referred to the band as the White Shield band.

The affiliation with the Mennonites began in 1898 and continued through the construction of a mission building in 1899 and the baptism of the first members in 1906.[24] Hammon autonomy was encouraged by the distribution of rations there beginning in 1893 and the building of a separate school for the Hammon Cheyennes in 1900.[25]

Strong Hammon feelings of autonomy and separateness from other Cheyennes continue to the present. The Hammon band has been sensitive to accusation of improper or even incestuous marriages, since they have continued to allow marriage among themselves. Their fierce militance was exhibited most recently in 1975, when they established their own Freedom School, with little assistance from the tribal government, and they have steadfastly asserted their political equality in a community where racist epithets are an everyday occurrence and some public facilities endure a de facto segregation by race. Their special relationship with the Kiowas has lasted since the days of Lewis and Clark, and Kiowa expressions are spliced into their everyday language in a manner unusual for Cheyennes. The Hammon people realize that they are different though not all of them are aware of the historical reasons for the difference.

The Hammon Cheyennes may have been the last of the tipi Indians. Many of them lived in wall tents and tipis at West Camp, north of Hammon, until 1968, at which time a per capita payment from the federal government allowed the last of the Wotapios to move into permanent houses in Hammon. Many of the Hammon people were in fact born in tents and tipis, which is a source of great pride to them, symbolizing their resistance to acculturation.

The only other *organized* group from the Omisis or Eaters to take allotments in Oklahoma was the Kingfisher group. Once again, the rationale given for the separation was a dispute, but in this case we know its exact nature. In 1872 the group had been given responsibility for taking care of the sacred buffalo hat of the Sutaio band. From this we can infer that at least some of the bunch, including the keeper, Broken Dish, were of Sutaio ancestry, since that is a legal requirement to be keeper. In any event, there was a dispute over the care of the bundle and then a shooting, which caused Turkey Leg's bunch, of which Broken Dish was a member, to be ostracized by other members of the Omisis band. Although they stayed near Dull Knife's bunch and traveled with the other Northern Cheyennes to Indian Territory in 1877, they decided to stay in Indian Territory thereafter rather than moving back north in 1884, where they might experience continued ostracism from other Omisis people.[26]

One participant in all these movements, a woman named Standing Out, was interviewed for the Oklahoma Indian-Pioneer Project in 1938. She said there were originally thirty families who came from Montana, but some left the group after a few years.[27]

The original name of the bunch was Anskowinis, translated as "people with eyes close together" or "people with narrow nose bridges." The main body of this group, which took their allotments near Kingfisher in 1892, became known as the Noimeohas, or "Fish River People," which is what the Cheyennes called Kingfisher Creek before allotment. Beginning about 1881, and owing to the efforts of David Pendleton, a returned captive from Fort Marion, some of the Kingfisher people became Episcopalians. These people took their allotments toward the western part of the Kingfisher allotment block and became known as the Nonaestos, the "Crippled Bunch." The eastern half of the Kingfisher group soon thereafter took the name Maiyehutenah or "Tassel Bunch," to differentiate themselves from the Episcopalians.

I should mention here that the kinds of nicknames given to Cheyenne bands and bunches are particularly hard to translate, because they are supposed to be humorous, to have vague double or triple meanings. The difficulties might be appreciated by someone trying to explain, in simple terms, the meanings of such English nicknames as "Four Eyes" "Gimpy," or "Scooter." These are the kinds of teasing names Cheyennes give to residence bands and also, very affectionately, to their most respected chiefs and priests. For example, some of the leading Cheyenne men of my acquaintance are known in English as Boomer, Sparky, Gunsmoke, Superchief, and Big Boy. These gentle nicknames help take the edge off the tremendous responsibilities these men bear, but the names themselves, like the nicknames given in Cheyenne to the bunches and family groups, are notoriously hard to explain or translate.

One other group of Northern Cheyennes who took allotments in Oklahoma was organized only after allotment. In 1883 the government was preparing a Montana reservation for the Northern Cheyennes, who had been a source of continual problems for the government, especially including the breakout and long march of Dull Knife and Little Wolf in 1878, an event recounted in the semidocumentary novel *Cheyenne Autumn*. By July of that year the bands of Little Wolf and Little Chief were already in the north, and the Darlington agency attempted to send a final group to join them. Agent John Miles's annual report to the Bureau of Indian Affairs for that year includes the following passage:

> On the 18th of July 391 Cheyennes and 14 Arapahoes, with rations of beef, flour, sugar, coffee, &c., for sixty days, were transferred to the military to be

escorted to Pine Ridge Agency, Dakota. They left the agency on the morning of the 19th. On reaching Fort Supply, Indian Territory, it was found that 48 persons had left the party and were returning to the agency. They have since reached the agency, have expressed the desire and intention of remaining, and have been re-enrolled. They assign as their reason for returning that they are intermarried with the Southern Cheyennes, and have families here that they do not wish to be separated from, and that they had no desire or intention of going North, but were compelled by their chiefs to enroll and start, and they made use of the first opportunity to return.

According to modern informants, these Northern Cheyenne men took their allotments in a scattered fashion around the Darlington agency rather than among the larger blocks of allotments that we can identify as discrete Southern Cheyenne bands. These intermarried Northern Cheyennes constituted the "White Wolf band" of early reservation times. This "band" was mostly organized for ceremonial purposes, however, and camped in the tribal circle alongside the other Omisis groups. About half of the White Wolf band lived around some permanent lakes near El Reno, where they were later known as the Downstream People. Their leader White Wolf, however, lived near Canton. As the original "White Wolf band" died out in the early twentieth century, their descendants discontinued the practice of camping together at ceremonies.

Omisis

The major portion of the Eaters, or the Omisis proper, never moved south of the Platte in any numbers. Always, however, there was visiting back and forth and intermarriage. For example, 48.6 percent of persons listed as Southern Cheyennes in 1900 had at least one parent from the north—Montana, South Dakota, or Wyoming. For their part, 42.8 percent of the Montana Cheyennes in 1900 listed southern origins for at least one parent.

Although the name Oudebaton appears on the early maps for the Eater band, both the Sioux version, Wotapio, and the Cheyenne version, Omisis, had emerged by the time of Lewis and Clark. Even after the Wotapio band had hived off, the Omisis were still the largest band of Cheyennes. They also apparently spent more time together as an entity, which they were able to do because of differences in climate between north and south. In the land of the Omisis, in the area between the Black Hills and the Powder River, grass and rainfall were sufficient to keep the whole manhao together most of the time.

It was only after the Battle of the Little Bighorn that the Omisis band had to split drastically to escape the pursuit of the United States Army. They were mostly reunited again at Camp Robinson in 1877 and were removed as a body to Oklahoma. At that time, however, one major subgroup, the Totoimanas or "Plains people," remained separate, ultimately coming to rest at Pine Ridge with the Oglala Sioux. Some other small groups of Omisis also remained free or took refuge with other tribes in this period.

Although Peter Powell has written a long narrative of events for the Omisis band from 1869 to 1884, he does so mostly by reference to the subgroups as chief-led units, rather than using their sacred band names or nicknames. Therefore it is not clear which of the groups, led variously by Little Wolf, Dull Knife, Little Chief, and others, are cognate with which named bands. But the major schism among the Northern Cheyennes in these years was between the band that escaped from the Oklahoma reservation in 1878 and the remainder who stayed behind. The escaped group itself later split into two bands, one led by Little Wolf and the other by Dull Knife. Dull Knife's group was soon massacred in custody in a particularly brutal manner at Fort Robinson. Seventy-four men, women, and children were shot or stabbed or froze to death on 9 January 1879, after eight days of starvation in an unheated army barracks.[28] Modern Northern Cheyennes say that their Montana reservation was not "given" to them. In the words of my friend the late Henry Tall Bull, "This reservation was bought with the blood of the men, women, and little children who died that night so that the rest of their people could come home again."

When the Omisis band arrived back in Montana in 1884, they initially sorted themselves into five communities (map 20). I do not know how or if these communities reflect the chief-led groups mentioned by Powell, but these were the Ree band, the White River people, Little Wolf's band, the Black Lodges, and the Scalpers. The Ree band was a small group having ancestry among the Arikaras, which settled on the middle reaches of Rosebud Creek. The White River people, a larger group named after their previous residence in Dakota, settled on the headwaters of Rosebud Creek. The combined groups were sometimes known as the Rosebud people. Little Wolf's band, which is the only group I can reliably connect with one of Powell's chief-led groups, settled on Muddy Creek, just to the east, while the main body of the Omisis band, the Black Lodges, settled near the agency on Lame Deer Creek.

The Cheyenne group that settled near present Birney, on the Tongue River, was in some ways the mirror immage of the "White Wolf band" that settled in Oklahoma. Both groups consisted of intermarried Omisis, Sutaio, and Southern Cheyenne people. The Birney group was predominantly Oivimana and Sutaio, and in fact that community is said to be the only place where the Sutaio dialect is still spoken.[29] The 1900 census

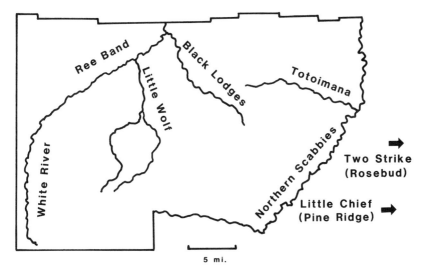

Map 20.   Locations of early reservation bands on the Tongue River
Reservation, Montana, about 1900.

confirms modern informants' statements that this group was strongly intermarried with Southern Cheyennes of the Oivimana or Scabby band, causing
the Birney people to be nicknamed "Northern Scabbies." The other and
earlier nickname for the Birney people, Scalpers, is said to reflect a Lakota
nickname.

The nucleus of the Ashland group was a subgroup of the Totoimana
band, named on the Lewis and Clark map as "Dotame." When the Tongue
River reservation was established, Cheyennes living with the Oglala Sioux
at Pine Ridge were given the option of moving to Montana. Those who
chose to do so became known as the "Strangers" and later simply as the
Ashland people. One subgroup of this band was the Crazy Hats, according
to the oral tradition maintained by Harry Littlebird. The half of the band
who remained behind at Pine Ridge took the name of their leader and
became known as the Littlechief band. Daniel Littlechief, an informant for
A. S. Gatschet, was of this band, the son of the original Little Chief.[30]

Gatschet asked Daniel Littlechief about bands and recorded, under a
heading "the Gentile System," a list of "bunches" and "families" he knew
about. Some are familiar, such as Hisiometaneos and Sutaios, but some are
exceptional, such as "Boat Rowers." In asking about these names among
modern Cheyennes, I was told that they were old names no longer used, and
no one knew much about them.

At about the same time I was puzzling over these exceptional names, Cheyennes had been telling me that there was a band of Cheyennes who lived at the Rosebud Reservation among the Brulé Sioux. Previously I had seen the name "Rosebud band" on some lists, but I had assumed this was a reference to the Rosebud Creek bands in Montana. Through a mutual friend, Patricia Albers, I met a descendant of the Rosebud Reservation band in Rapid City, South Dakota, in November 1983. Sam De Cory told me that this bunch of Cheyennes had married into the Brulé Sioux and had been nicknamed "Two Strike band" from their location on the Rosebud Reservation. He said family tradition maintained that the group was descended from the Omisis chief Dull Knife, whose name has been preserved as a family name in the Two Strike band.

By another stroke of luck, I ran into Cal Fast Wolf later the same year at the Newberry Library in Chicago, where he had been puzzling over Lakota band names from early censuses. As we talked shop, it occurred to Cal that some of the names he had though strange or foreign were in fact Cheyenne names rather than Lakota names. And sure enough, in looking at the censuses together, we discovered the Two Strike band of Cheyennes, entered as "Northern band" on the Brulé census. However, I am unable to match this name with any of Daniel Littlechief's "clans."

The Sutaios

The very early history of the Sutaio band was related in chapter 3, under the names Chongasketon, and so on, from the early French maps. According to Michelson's informant Coyote, born in 1859, there were originally four bunches of Sutaios, "named after the four leaders."[31] Another of Michelson's informants, White Bull, said that one of the Sutaio chiefs was named White Buffalo Tail. White Bull said further that the Sutaios had crossed the Missouri in two groups, one meeting the Cheyennes at the mouth of the Yellowstone in present Montana, and the other meeting the Cheyennes at the mouth of the Cheyenne River in South Dakota, just east of the Black Hills.[32]

Although it is difficult to trace the movements of the Sutaio bunches in the early nineteenth century, it is clear that by reservation times there were two Sutaio groups, the larger one at Birney, Montana, associated with the "Northern Scabbies" and the smaller at Clinton, Oklahoma, associated with the Hisiometaneo band of Southern Cheyennes.[33] They appear on map 16 among the "Red Water People." This southern band of Sutaios also appears in accounts of the Sand Creek Massacre as "Black Shin's band of Sutaios."[34] Powell lists some other Sutaio leaders in his recent volumes of

Cheyenne history, though he does not discriminate between chiefs who were born as Sutaio but led non-Sutaio bands and chiefs who led bands that were predominantly Sutaio in membership. For example, Black Kettle, Grey Beard, and Heap of Birds were all born Sutaio, although they became leaders of other bands.[35]

Because the Sutaio bunches had originally been independent and had frequently married among themselves, they maintained that option after they were incorporated into the Cheyenne nation. Other Cheyennes, however, considered it improper to marry within one's own manhao or band, though they admitted that the Sutaios had a traditional right to do so. We will discuss this problem of "marrying-in" versus "marrying-out" further in the next chapter.

Sometime during their residence with the Cheyennes, the Southern Sutaios, known for part of the time as "Black Shin's bunch," began an association with the Hisiometaneos, or "Ridge People," In fact, it may even be that it was this association or hybridization with the Sutaios that originally caused the Hisiometaneos to split off from the other bands of the Hevhaitaneos, or "Hair Rope People." We should remember, at this point, that Hevhaitaneo is also the generic term Northern Cheyennes use for Southern Cheyennes. In any event, both Mooney and Petter noted that the Southern Sutaios and the Hisiometaneos were heavily intermarried, while Mooney and Hewitt noted that the two intermarried groups had taken their allotments together near present Clinton, Oklahoma.[36]

Because the Southern Sutaios and the Hisiometaneos took their allotments among each other and because they were intermarried, their census entries cannot be easily separated for analysis. Modern Cheyennes say, however, that older Sutaio people tended to have distinctive kinds of names, often taken from the birds and animals of streams, lakes, and marshes. The allotment list from the Clinton area, however, does not seem to support this idea. I have discussed elsewhere the kinds of names taken by Cheyennes.[37]

If we use the 1900 census to track the origins of the intermarried Sutaio-Hisiometaneo grouping, we can learn something about their original territory and their migrations in the early nineteenth century. The census can in fact solve one thorny problem, the meaning of the nickname "Ridge Men," a translation of Hisiometaneo. According to Mooney, the ridge in question was perhaps in the Staked Plains of Texas or on the headwaters of the Smoky Hill River.[38] According to the informants of the 1900 census, however, the range of the band between 1800 and 1850 was Dakota and Nebraska, pointing to the well-known Pine Ridge as the feature that gave the band its name. This is not surprising in view of the Lewis and Clark map, which showed the Sutaio band as the one nearest that area. For those unfamiliar with the area, I should note that Pine Ridge is a large expanse of pine forest that parallels the Niobrara River for scores of miles along the border of Nebraska and South Dakota. It is the feature for which the Pine Ridge Sioux Reservation in South Dakota was named, where most of the Oglala Sioux live at present.

The population reconstruction of figure 15 indicates that the Sutaio people were never very numerous, although they were always interesting to Cheyenne elders and to ethnographers because of their unique history. By reservation times, however, there seem to have been only two Sutaio groups large enough to deserve mention—the one with the Hisiometaneos at Clinton, Oklahoma, and the one with the Northern Scalpers at Birney, Montana.

The Cheyennes Proper

At the time of Lewis and Clark, the main body of Cheyennes had apparently not yet divided into discrete bands with separate histories. It was only the accumulation of horses, the opportunity for trade, and the adoption of a new ecology that finally forced this multiple fission. As far as we know this main body called "Cheyennes" then comprised most of the ancestors of the manhao groups named Tsistsistas, Heviksnipahis, Hevhaitaneo, Oivimana, and Hisiometaneo, plus their derivative groups. At that same time, in 1804, the various Eater groups were already separate from the "Cheyennes," and the Masikota band was still with the Lakotas. The Wotapios and the Sutaios, as mentioned before, had already located south of the main body, along the Platte, and the Wotapios moved to the Arkansas before anyone else.

The main body of Cheyennes seems to have migrated to the Upper Platte all together, although the movement may have been over as much as two decades. As we know from our ecological study, a flexible range in geography and a seasonal transhumance were normal for assuming a nomadic pastoral existence, since rainfall variability would dictate somewhat different pastures and somewhat different seasonal patterns of movements from year to year. But the general direction of migration, as shown from the data of tables 11 and 12, was toward the forks of the Upper Platte, in the present area of Wyoming and northeastern Colorado.

These years were characterized by intensive warfare with the Crows, who had moved to the Yellowstone area about 1775 and who were seeking to extend their trade relations southward. The Cheyennes, for their part, were attempting to break the direct trade relations between the Kiowas and Crows, thereby increasing the importance of their own "middleman" role in the horse trade.[39] So the move of the "Cheyennes proper" to the Upper Platte not only ensured better access to buffaloes, which were then plentiful in that area, but also was strategic, politically and economically.

Another major military problem in the years 1800–1830 was the Pawnees, who were accustomed to hunt and camp in the forks of the Platte, even though they had no permanent villages there. The Cheyenne solution to this problem was to create and maintain smooth relationships with the Tetons, who were attacking the Pawnees incessantly from the north. Although there are some records of early hostilities between the Cheyennes and the Tetons in the late eighteenth century, these were apparently smoothed over by the early nineteenth century, as the Cheyennes allowed the Tetons joint occupancy, with themselves, of the Black Hills area and cooperated with them in attacks on the Pawnees and Crows.[40]

After several decades between the forks of the Platte, the number of buffaloes reportedly began to diminish. Perhaps this was from hunting, or perhaps the buffaloes were merely disturbed in this area, causing them to move out toward the central plains. One major disturbance in this period was the reorganization of beaver trapping by new fur companies, which caused large numbers of free trappers to enter this area beginning about 1822.[41] The "rendezvous system" required the non-Indian trappers to stay in the field year-round, along with their wives and helpers. These hundreds of camps no doubt contributed to the increasing scarcity of buffaloes in the area.

In any event, by 1828 one important section of the main body of Cheyennes began to negotiate with trader William Bent, who offered to build a fort on the Arkansas if the Cheyennes would move south and trade with him. The first group to agree to do so was the Hevhaitaneo band or Hair Rope People, who moved south in 1828 under the leadership of their chief Yellow Wolf.[42] The name Hevhaitaneo was inaugurated at that time to designate the groups who had moved with Yellow Wolf; there is no record of the name before that.[43] According to all accounts, the name implied a group of people who specialized in horse trade and horse raiding. Soon after, the Oivimana or Scabby band also hived off from the main body of Cheyennes and joined the Hevhaitaneos at Bent's Fort, which was built in 1834. We should remember that the Wotapios were already in this area of the Arkansas, having separated from the other Eaters somewhat earlier as an "outlaw" band.

The bands left behind on the Platte, then, were the associated Tsistsistas and Heviksnipahis, and the associated Hisiometanios and Southern Sutaios. According to the 1900 census, the intermarried Sutaios and Hisiometaneos soon moved out east of the Upper Platte, to Pine Ridge, if they had in fact ever left there. The last band to move south was the Heviksnipahis, which is not recorded on the Arkansas until the Sand Creek Massacre of 1864.

This late migration of the Heviksnipahis can be verified from the 1900 census. According to modern informants, most of the Heviksnipahis people took their allotments north of Watonga, Oklahoma, at what is now Roman Nose State Park, a remarkable camping spot with canyons, springs, timber, and a supply of natural salt. When we find these people on the 1900 census, we see that a disproportionate number of those aged fifty and over were born in Wyoming. Compared with the other Watonga people, who were mainly the descendants of the Oivimana band, the census shows that the Heviksnipahis people continued to live on the Upper Platte in 1830–50, after the Hevhaitaneos and Oivimanas had moved to the Arkansas.

Clarence Stoneroad, one of the few Cheyenne elders who continues his identification with the Heviksnipahis band, says that his band was always coresident with the Tsistsistas band, which carried the sacred arrows in these early years of the nineteenth century. This indicates that the arrows, symbols of national existence, were kept in the area of the Upper Platte between 1800 and 1850, which would make sense geographically, since that was a central location for all the bands of the nation and convenient for the performance of the annual ceremonies.

The beaver tabu of the Heviksnipahis also makes sense if we consider that they remained on the Upper Platte trapping beavers after other bands had gone south to engage in trade for buffalo robes. Following is the version of the story as told by Clarence Stoneroad:

> A man and his wife—a family—now this man didn't believe anything, like this "Indian Lore" or tradition. He found a den of little beavers. Well, he uncovered it all up and took all these little beavers; he was going to give them to his children as pets. Now it happened that this mother beaver had been used in a ceremony, and if these beavers were treated good they would bring blessings to the people, and if they were treated mean, they would curse the people.
>
> This man took these little beavers. That night he had a dream that this mother beaver came to the camp. She said, "If you bring back my little children, I will give you a blessing that will last forever. If you don't I will put a curse on you that will last forever." So next morning he told his wife, "A giant beaver came and talked to me and wants her little children back. And if I don't take them back, she will curse us."
>
> So his wife said, "Go ahead and take them back; we would like to have the blessings this beaver has offered." The man said, "I don't believe these

things. We will eat these beavers. They are tender and nice and good to eat." They did just that. He killed the little beavers and ate them, and the children played with them for pets.

A few nights later, the mother beaver came again. She said, "Since you didn't bring my little ones back, the curse is on you and your future generations." Now he didn't know what the curse was, and he didn't believe it.

But later, when the man went down to the river, he got sick, he got so very sick. They tried to doctor him, but it was no good—three days, four days, five days, six. He was ready to die. But finally he started to get better. The same way with his family; his family would get sick. His wife knew what it meant. She didn't get sick, because she had tried to get him to take the beavers back.

The mother beaver appeared to the woman and said, "Your husband and his children will continue to get sick but you, I'll give you the blessing, because you tried to save my children. Your husband and all his descendants will always get sick any time they go to the river or the creek, where there is beavers up the creek. The odor will flow down through the water and make them sick. They can't eat fish or anything that comes from the water. They will always get sick."

In its historical context, I believe this story supplied a rationale for the Heviksnipahis band to finally give up beaver trapping and join the other Southern Cheyennes, about 1850 or 1860. According to Mr. Stoneroad, the Heviksnipahis are not properly included in the generic term "Hevhaitaneo" to designate all the Southern Cheyennes, and his opinion is supported by the informants who gave the diagrams of camp circles discussed in chapter 2. Historically, the Heviksnipahis band were not Southern Cheyennes, but rather were the remnants of the main body of Cheyennes or "Chianatons," left behind after the Hevhaitaneos and Oivimanas left for Bent's Fort and the buffalo trade about 1828.

Although the Tsistsistas proper, or Arrow People, were associated with the Heviksnipahis until about 1855, their special role as custodians of the arrows was terminated in 1864, after the Sand Creek Massacre. At that time the Fox Soldiers, fearing that something might happen to the arrows if they remained with the "peace faction," became the custodians of the arrows and also adopted the name Moiseo or "Flint People." That is, after 1864, the arrows could be moved only by the Kit Foxes and could not be moved without them. Although some members of other societies have objected to this special role taken by the Kit Foxes, in practice this special privilege has usually been recognized.

Masikotas and Kit Foxes

The bands discussed so far have clearly been manhao or "sacred bands" of a traditional type. I have defined these as being centered on a core group, or perhaps several core groups, consisting of polygynous council chiefs. The bands to be discussed now, however, are the "bands of a new type" that began to appear in the nineteenth century. Structurally, they are centered on the membership of a soldier or military society rather than on a matrilocal, polygynous extended family. But the histories of these new kinds of bands contain periods in which they were transitional, dual, or ambiguous in their social character.

Perhaps no band exhibits this ambiguity more profoundly than the Masikotas. This group shows how a band can be simultaneously a soldier society and a manhao, depending on perspective and circumstances. This multiplicity of roles and complexity of behavior has already been shown, I believe, in their appearance as "Petits Renards" to the Vérendryes, in their role as "Sheos" to the Lakotas (and their role as instructors for the Lakota Kit Fox Society), and their appearance after 1838 as the Masikotas, a manhao of the Cheyenne nation.[44] The rest of the story, however, and the continuation of Masikota and Kit Fox identity to the present, can be told from information supplied by modern informants.

Grinnell and Bent have already noted that the Masikota band suffered terribly from cholera in 1849 and took refuge with the Dog Soldiers, increasing the numbers of that faction vis-à-vis the peace group gathering around Black Kettle.[45] It is not reported, however, that this event also saw the creation of a special relationship between the Dog Soldiers and the Kit Foxes that still continues. In about 1850 they created a special bond of "friendship" between the two societies, and from that time they have shared laws, customs, rituals, and initiation procedures. Since these matters are private to the men of those societies, I will not describe them here but will only report that they are the same.

Although the Kit Foxes were submerged into the Dog Soldiers after about 1850, in the eyes of many historical documents, they nonetheless maintained a separate identity and a special relationship with their Kit Fox comrades among the Brulé Sioux to the north. This dyadic friendship was one basis of the broad alliance between the Cheyennes and the Teton Sioux that prevailed from 1840 until 1876, and that continues in different form to the present.

So it is not entirely accurate to say that the Masikotas joined the Dog Soldiers and were absorbed by them, or that the Dog Soldiers assumed the place of the Masikotas in the tribal circle. It is more correct to note that after

1849 the people of the Masikota band ceased to use the Masikota identity socially and began to use the term "Flint Men," a nickname that was more orthodox as the designation of a manhao. As noted in the diagrams of chapter 2, it was these Flint Men who maintained the continuity of their position in the tribal circle, and it was the Dog Soldiers, their special comrades, who joined them there. This is the story as told in modern times by the Kit Foxes and concurred in by the Dog Soldiers.

At least two major bands were spawned by the Masikotas from the time they entered the Cheyenne nation. The older and better known was the Oktogona band, which had its origin sometime before 1849. In that year, according to George Bent, this band, like the Masikotas proper, suffered from cholera and diminished sharply in numbers.[46] According to modern informants, the remnants of the Oktogonas reorganized and took allotments north of Thomas in 1892. The other Masikota subgroup, the Hownowas or "Poor People," intermarried with the Heviksnipahis north of Watonga, becoming the Salt Creek people.

At allotment, many of the descendants of the Masikota band took their land around Fonda, Oklahoma, and settled there. This grouping then became known as the Veenotas, "bushy eyebrows" or "owl eyebrows," named from a prominent man who did not pluck his eyebrows in proper Cheyenne manner. Although the group at first was predominantly Masikota/Kit Fox in its membership, many later members have been Dog Soldiers and have considered the Veenotas a subgroup of the Hotamhetaneos. But modern elders remember the origins of the band and its original members.

Reservation Bands

After being gathered onto the Oklahoma reservation in 1869–76, the Cheyenne nation went through a substantial reorganization. This was occasioned by several circumstances of warfare and confinement. First of all, epidemic diseases and the massacres of the peace faction had mostly destroyed the traditional manhao core groups, which then were further diminished when young families, the "scattered bands" of figure 16, joined the Dog Soldier faction toward the end of the Indian wars. Second, the United States Army and the Indian agents at first required that the Cheyennes stay near the agencies, first Camp Supply and later Fort Reno, so that they could receive rations and be controlled in their movements. The army, quite rightly as it turned out, feared armed outbreaks among the Cheyennes. The major outbreaks were in 1874, when most of the Cheyennes escaped and raided for several months, and in 1878, when three hundred Northern Cheyennes escaped for the Dakotas.

Map 14 shows the locations of Cheyenne camps collected around Camp Supply in January and February 1873. Although there were separate camps of Dog Soldiers and Northern Cheyennes (Spotted Horse), the great majority of the nation was gathered all together on a tributary of the Cimarron.

Map 15 shows the May 1877 locations of Cheyenne bands, somewhat reorganized, after the agency had been created at Darlington and after the outbreak of 1874. The huge majority of Cheyennes were still in the camp of Little Robe (plate 23), this time numbering 179 lodges. From this map we can pick up several of the bands that later took allotments together and reestablished independent existence. Little Robe's band, although diminished by the subtraction of several bands, ultimately settled along the North Canadian, from present Seiling to Longdale, Oklahoma, the group-

Plate 23.   Little Robe, a major chief of the 1870s. Negative no. 312, National Anthropological Archives, Smithsonian Institution.

ing I have called the "agnatic faction" comprising most of the Dog Soldiers and Fox Soldiers. Whirlwind (plate 24) became the leader of a different band, situated west of Watonga on the North Canadian, consisting mostly of Hevhaitaneos, with the addition of some Sutaios.

The birth and rebirth of some reservation bands was enabled by Captain Lee's dispersion policy toward Cheyenne bands. We have noted that some groups took advantage of this situation to re-form or recharter some traditional bands along the major rivers. The Wotapios, given new life under

Plate 24. Whirlwind, leader of the Peneteka faction of the Hevhaitaneo band. Photo no. 107, Campbell Collection, Western History Collections, University of Oklahoma Library.

Red Moon and White Shield, gathered at Hammon, or West Camp, though they took three separate clumps of allotments along the forested part of the Washita. The Arrow People and part of the Hisiometaneos formed a camp south of Clinton called "Big Jake's Crossing." Other Hisiometaneos and the Sutaios with whom they were intermarried settled just northeast of Clinton at the mouth of Beaver Creek. This area (map 21) is characterized by the spring-fed tributary, Beaver Creek, and by a wide expanse of riparian forest. The Heviksnipahis, as mentioned, were in the springs and forests of what is now Roman Nose State Park. The Oktogonas were north of Thomas, but near their parent Masikota band, by then known as the Veenotas and living near Fonda.

If we began with a bare map of the Cheyenne reservation in 1870, we could easily predict where the Cheyenne bands would locate themselves, based on what we know about their use of natural resources in that period. Consistently, the Cheyennes chose areas of forest near fresh water. Salt Creek Canyon, now incorporated into Roman Nose State Park, and the Crow Neck camp north of Clinton are only two examples. The most remarkable

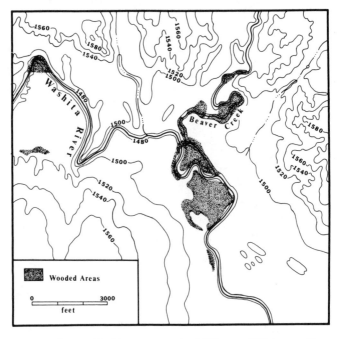

Map 21.   Site of Crow Neck's camp north of Clinton, Oklahoma. Drawn by Mary Goodman. Numbers are elevations in feet.

area was the site called "Twelve Mile Point" in the early reservation documents because it was twelve miles up the North Canadian River from the agency at Darlington. Even now the area has a nearly legendary reputation among older informants.

A tour of the area as it now exists is remarkable enough. The most prominent features are some deep spring-fed ponds that were once bends of the river (map 22), many cottonwoods along the ponds, and a nearby escarpment where hardwoods, especially oak, are plentiful. But if one looks at the original 1870 survey map of the area, the extraordinary quality of the place is apparent (map 23).[47] In the words of one informant, "It is a place where the Almighty formed a camping circle for the Cheyennes. Each band

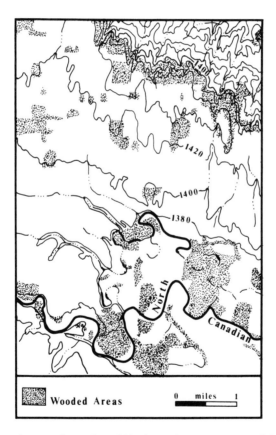

Map 22.   Modern configuration of Twelve Mile Point, north of Calumet, Oklahoma. Drawn by Mary Goodman. Numbers are elevations in feet.

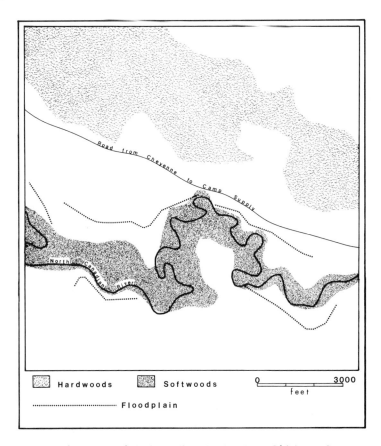

Map 23. Configuration of Twelve Mile Point in 1870. Oklahoma State Archives, Manuscript Group 31, series 1 and 2, U.S. Bureau of Land Management. Redrawn by Regina Steuben.

had its regular place. We could camp there for a long time. Later on, they herded horses in the middle at night, so they could keep an eye on them."

The North Canadian was also rich in resources along the nothern tier of allotments, where the agnatic faction came to rest. Map 24 shows the juxtaposition of grass, hardwoods, softwood, and water in the restricted area along the river, according to the 1870 survey. Historically this area has been called by Cheyennes "Where the Forest Meets the Plains." Map 24 also shows the location of an especially sacred place, Meat's Ranch, where the annual ceremonies were held in early reservation times. All the allotment areas were sanctified in early times, however, because of the burials that

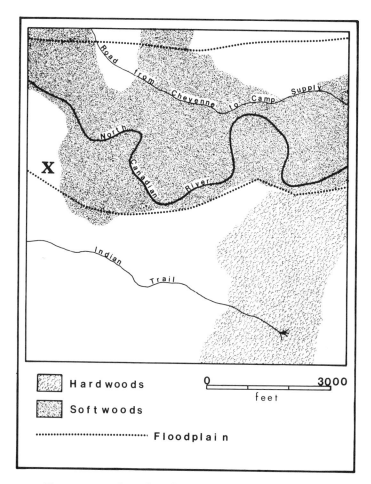

Map 24. The area around Fonda, Oklahoma, in 1870. Meat's Ranch (R14, T19, section 9, SW) is marked with an X. Redrawn by Regina Steuben.

were made along the rivers, both tree and ground burials. These burial places were marked off by buffalo skulls in early times, though these have since disappeared.

Returning to the question of band names, we should note that some bands of the early reservation period bear names that do not appear in prereservation documents and oral histories. The implication is that they were newly formed during this period of reorganization, 1869–92, although we cannot be sure of this. It may also be that the "new" bands that appeared about 1892 were previously family groups, such as those listed by Daniel Littlechief, now grown large enough by births and alliances to form larger units of proper size for a manhastoz or manhao.

So although it may be that the "new" bands appearing in early reservation times merely carry old family names, these names were not collected by ethnographers until 1890–1910. The process of allotment in itself had the effect of "freezing" the naming process, forming blocks of allotments that had clear reference to a group of people. For that reason, modern elders tend to give very consistent responses concerning the names of the bands that existed just after allotment.

The largest group of new band names came from the huge group led by Little Robe, which set itself in clusters along the North Canadian. Although the allotments taken by these people formed a physically continuous block, the actual camps of the new bands were discrete, mostly in areas now covered by Canton Lake. The camps were separated for reasons of grazing discussed in previous chapters. According to modern elders, there were five main bands, known from west to east as the Veenotas or Owl Eyebrows, the Blue Horse band, the Turtle People, the Swamp People, and the Big Noses. The Swamp People name is derived from their location, near a marshy area east of Canton, Oklahoma, now submerged in Canton Lake, and the term Big Nose is a nickname from the first leader of this group.

Whirlwind's band was given a new name before allotment, because of his role as government collaborator during the outbreak of 1874. Because of that role, Whirlwind's band was dubbed "Peneteka" by the other Cheyennes, the name of a Comanche band that was employed by the government to hunt down and kill other Comanches. Regarded as traitors by other Cheyennes of that period, Whirlwind and his band took their allotments near the allotments of the band led by George Bent, who also had problems of acceptance among the militant Cheyennes. As soon as the opportunity presented itself, Whirlwind allied himself with some Episcopalian missionaries, who built a church and school for his band at what was called "Whirlwind Mission." There followed a struggle for administrative control between the church and the Bureau of Indian Affairs, which has been recounted in Robert Nespor's doctoral dissertation.

The band that took its allotments at Deer Creek, between Weatherford and Thomas, was split off from the Hisiometaneo band and called itself Glass Water or Crystal Water People. Other Cheyennes were less flattering with their choice of nicknames, however, and called them Hobahetans, or Bragging People. After allotment, the Oktogona people from north of Thomas amalgamated with this group and were also known as Hobahetans. At that time, about 1910, the group preferred to translate their nickname as Dusty band or Puffball band. The Cheyenne expression for bragging is literally "like the dust from a puffball." Sharp Mountain people, from a local landmark, was an alternative name. After Mennonite missionaries entered the Thomas area in 1928 and served as a focal point, the group became simply the Deer Creek people or Thomas people.

Several other band names came and went before Cheyennes had decided upon certain town names to designate their communities. For a brief period between 1890 and 1910, the people at Clinton, from both camps, were called Lodge Pole people, since the Washita River was called the Lodge Pole River. The river was named after an event of prereservation times when the Cheyennes had found a camp hurriedly deserted, in which the lodge poles had been left, though the covers had been taken. The name Crossroads People was also sometimes used for the Clinton people, because two early railroads crossed at that spot.

Between 1930 and 1950, people living in Watonga have been collectively known as the People in the Center and Black People. The former name comes from their location vis-à-vis the other bands allotted in Oklahoma, and the latter name was the nickname for a particular family group of Oivimanas. Of all the original names of Cheyenne sacred bands, only the name Oivimana or Scabby band is preserved among younger Cheyennes in Oklahoma. Even young people monolingual in English still recognize the designation Oivimana or Scabby for the Watonga people, and many use it instead. The origin of the town name Watonga is disputed between the Cheyennes and Arapahos. The Cheyennes claim it is derived from the expression "one feather," meaning a chief in Cheyenne. The Arapahos claim that the name is from the Arapaho expression for "red water," meaning the North Canadian, which flows just west of Watonga. Many Arapahos have intermarried with Cheyennes both before and after allotment. This has been especially true around Watonga, Geary, and Calumet. The Arapaho marriages of the Red Moon band (map 13) were mostly prereservation. The predominant pattern is for Cheyenne men to marry Arapaho women (hypergamy) rather than the other way around.

One major goal of this research has been to identify the modern descendants of the people who suffered the Sand Creek Massacre. All evidence indicates that the descendants, as of 1892, were the bands identified on map 17 as Wotapio, Sutaio, Tsistsistas, Hisiometaneo, Heviksnipahis, Hevhaitaneo, and Oivimana. By the time of allotment, two subgroups of the Masikotas, the Hownowas and the Oktogonas, had already intermarried with Sand Creek descendants. In addition, parts of two Southern Cheyenne bands had intermarried with the Northern Cheyennes and moved to Montana. The Northern Scabbies constitute the first fifty-seven families on the

1900 United States census, and a fragment of the Heviksnipahis constitutes families numbered 145–47 (Red Wolf's bunch). Other small groups and individuals who are Sand Creek descendants can be found among the Northern Cheyennes and within the northern tier of agnatic groups in Oklahoma, but their descent and qualifications for any claim against the government must be determined genealogically, rather than by band membership. But we can be sure that everyone descended from the specified bands on the map had at least one ancestor who was a Sand Creek victim or survivor.[48]

I fear that there are many loose ends left in my research on Cheyenne community names in Oklahoma. Most of the remaining issues represent differences of opinion among elders or foggy memory. But by and large we can see that the process of naming and renaming discrete Cheyenne groups did not stop at their confinement to a reservation or at allotment. By extrapolation I believe that the processes we can document for reservation times are structurally similar to the processes that went on aboriginally. Bands are hybridized and undergo fission. New band names are invented and old ones are carried on. And always there is variability and dispute concerning what each band is properly called, depending on the perspective of the informant. I have tried to summarize my findings on band histories in figure 17.

This figure attempts to show the intermingled histories of the individual bands from 1680 to the present. The major difficulty is that we have better and more detailed information from the reservation period than from aboriginal times. No doubt the earlier bands had just as many subgroups and as many reorganizations as later times, but they are lost to history. But I have tried to account for all the major bands of the aboriginal period as best I could. In general, the figure shows all the major fissions and fusions of these times, as recounted by Cheyenne informants. Each fission or fusion shown is supposed to represent a *major* social event, not just the marriage of a few people into another band. But here lies another problem.

As is so often the case in empirical science, and fortunately so, we discover that having examined and mostly solved one set of problems concerning band identities, we are left with another set that is even more formidable, and potentially more important. In our case, having investigated the individual histories of the bands and camps very closely, and having already postulated on ecological grounds why the groups were the size they were, not smaller or larger, and having seen the bands transformed from one size to another and from one kind of named group to another, we now discover that we do not at all understand what a band actually is, in terms of membership. In the case of the Wotapio band, for example, we have on map

DAKOTA
TERMS   CIRCA 1845   CIRCA 1890   MODERN

Figure 17.   Historical relationships among Cheyenne bands, 1680–1985.

16 the locations of people "allied" or "associated" with Red Moon as he reorganized the Wotapio band in 1892.

But what sense is there in marking any continuity at all to this group from the major Oudebaton group on the French maps of 1680? Many generations of Eater people were born and died between 1680 and 1892. Many people have married in and married out of the Wotapio band in three hundred years. So when we say that the Hammon bunch constitutes the descendants of the Oudebatons, what does this mean in terms of personnel or membership? Are these the sons of the sons of the sons of the Oudebatons? Are they the daughters of the daughters of the daughters? Is there in fact any biological connection at all from the Oudebaton band to the Wotapio people known to Black Kettle, and to a modern youth from Hammon? Or is the connection only fictive, made up for sociological convenience or to flatter the historical sensitivities of the band?

When we ask such questions about the continuity of these older bands, we are also asking reciprocal questions about the creation and disappearance of other, short-lived bands, such as the Ononeos, the Nakoimanas, and the score of other bands listed by Petter and Daniel Littlechief. We must ask what this process is by which bands can appear, diminish, disappear, and reappear with such regularity in Cheyenne history. Is there some structure to this dynamic cycle, or is it random and capricious? In the remaining three chapters I will argue that it has structure and order and that we can describe its structure by reference to the census data available on the Cheyennes, augmented as usual by the knowledge of learned elders. For when these elders speak among themselves about their history and structure, they speak in terms of *manhestanov*, "the renewal of generations." And it is in this expression that we will find our key for understanding the dynamic cycles of growth that constitute the history of the Cheyenne nation.

8 /XXX

Patterns of Marriage

We should now increase our expectations from these historical and sociological investigations and try to understand the inner workings of Cheyenne bands in more specific terms. To do this, we should try to use the vocabulary ethnologists have developed over the years—technical terms with precise meanings. We must know whether Cheyenne bands were *endogamous*—whether the members married among themselves—or *exogamous,* required by custom to find a spouse from some other band. If marriage was exogamous, we need to discover the rule of residence— whether the rule was matrilocal and the man went to live in his wife's band, or whether the rule was patrilocal and she went to his band. George Bent recognized such questions as fundamental to Cheyenne society a long time ago, even though he was not an ethnologist. In fact, throughout the writings of George Bent and the narrations of Cheyenne informants who spoke to Mooney and Michelson, we find them struggling to express these important concepts, but without a precise technical vocabulary.

From the responses of informants, ethnographers have had a singular lack of success in deciding whether the Cheyenne bands were endogamous or exogamous and whether they were matrilocal or patrilocal. The most forceful advocate of the idea that the Cheyenne bands, or manhao, were the same as the "clans" described for other nations in the world was George Grinnell: "The most aged men of the Cheyennes from about the year 1890 on for twenty-odd years have declared to me that in old times the different groups were supposed to be bodies of kindred, descendents of a common ancestor, but this was not thought to be true of the Suhtai. . . . In the effort to learn something definite about exogamy among the Cheyenne groups, I made—about 1902—detailed inquiry concerning more than fifty marriages of old people, with the result that in all cases, except where the Suhtai were concerned, the man and the woman had belonged to different groups."[1]

In response to Grinnell's assertions, James Mooney argued the contrary, although politely refraining from mentioning Grinnell by name, as was customary among scholars in those gentler days. Mooney alluded to George Bent, one of Grinnell's primary informants, as an "educated half-breed," as follows:

> It has been stated by a distinguished writer on the Plains tribes that these are true exogamic clans, in which, until a very recent period a man was forbidden to marry a woman of the same division, and in which the children were always of the clan of the mother. This statement appears to rest chiefly on the testimony of an educated half-breed of the tribe, who, while exceptionally well versed in the language and recent history of the Cheyenne, is not in touch with their traditional, religious, or ceremonial life. It is directly contradicted by the testimony of all the recognized priestly authorities and leaders of societies with whom the author has consulted.[2]

If we look back at the original field notes and other documents of Mooney and Grinnell, we find that neither of them is playing fair with the reader. Grinnell apparently did not take a sample of marriages from his informants and then figure whether they were exogamous or endogamous; rather, he *directed* George Bent to go out and find some exogamous marriages. He wanted to hear only about the marriages that conformed to his theories, not the others. At least that was George Bent's understanding of his task, according to a letter he sent to George Hyde.[3] This request was made not in 1902, as Grinnell said, but in 1912. Perhaps Grinnell misrepresented the date because he had already, in 1902, published an article strongly alleging that Cheyennes had clans "descended from a common ancestor." But Bent said in his 1912 letter:

> I got a letter from Grinnell when he was here last June he wanted me to get up List Old Custom Marriages of Cheyennes, those that married in Other Clans. Clans of Cheyennes were supposed to be related to one another, and there were 9 Clans of Cheyennes. If young man and woman got married both of same Clan it was disgrace, and they were talked about for Marry. These were a ran away Matches. If young Man was going to buy his Wife from her folks, belonging to Same Clan, of course this would be objected on grounds being related to one another. He told Me (Grinnell) that if I got up 25 Old Marriages in good shape he would give me $25.00 so that 5 months ago I send him 40 names of these marriages. He said in his letter he would be down again some time to have talk with some old folks. Next time I am not

going to bother myself in getten these Old people for him as he Will not pay them anything. Last time Porcupine Bull and His Wife were here 2 weeks telling him Old time tales. What do you think he paid them, 50 cents apiece.

In addition to the fact that Grinnell may not have paid his informants very well, another unpleasant aspect of his scholarly work is shown in his unpublished papers at the Southwest Museum in Los Angeles. According to the letters to and from George Hyde, it was Hyde, not Grinnell, who researched the ethnohistorical portions of Grinnell's published work. But Grinnell apparently had the idea that if you paid someone for research and writing you did not have to acknowledge him, so in his introduction to *The Cheyenne Indians,* Grinnell said only that Hyde "helped me with the index." In fact it is clear from the original documents that most of the information published on early history by Grinnell, Hyde, and Bent had but one origin—George Bent's inquiries among contemporary elders, supplemented by Hyde's careful library work and published by Hyde and Grinnell in different forms.

The other large body of original information from this same period was the product of James Mooney's fieldwork, from 1891 to 1918. Since Mooney was the other antagonist in the debate about Cheyenne exogamy, one might expect his field notes to substantiate his position--but they do not. In fact, some of Mooney's informants who said that endogamy was proper had themselves made exogamous marriages, and some others had said explicitly that exogamy was quite proper, in disagreement with Mooney but in accordance with Grinnell's position. Also, Mooney's informants had a variety of views about the exogamy of soldier societies, saying both that one could and that one could not properly marry a woman whose father was in one's own soldier society. But despite this plethora of contradictory views, Mooney took the opposite side from Grinnell, maintaining that his own opinion was backed by "the testimony of all the recognized priestly authorities and leaders of societies with whom the author has consulted." But where does the truth lie?

If you ask a silly question, you get a silly answer; or as we say nowadays with computers, "Garbage in, garbage out." This is nowhere so apparent as in the questions concerning exogamy directed at Cheyenne informants in early reservation days, and in the responses they made to Grinnell, Bent, and Mooney. One basic problem is that if you ask a question in terms of what one *ought* to do or what kind of marriage is *proper,* one necessarily gets responses that describe *ideal* rather than *actual* practice. Asking modern Americans whether divorce is proper is not the same as asking them whether they are divorced. But in the Cheyenne case there was another basic problem. Respondents gave not one ideal answer, but two, depending on whether the informant was agnatic or uterine in his perspective.

The variability in answers concerning band exogamy, given not only to early fieldworkers but also to Fred Eggan, myself, and anyone else who has ever worked with the Cheyennes, merely reflects the same duality or polarity of political organization that we have already seen exhibited several times in earlier chapters. From the standpoint of the uterine or "peace" faction, led by council chiefs and organized for trade and production, band exogamy was necessary, useful, and in a word "proper." Marriages within the band did not create alliances or trading relationships between bands and might very well lead to destructive jealousies and political competition among brothers. It is documented that Black Kettle, Bear Above, Red Moon, Whirlwind, Little Chief, Heap of Birds, High-Backed Wolf, and Wolf on a Hill were all the sons of council chiefs, married off into other bands.[4] These kinds of chiefs were the nucleus of the peace faction.

From the standpoint of the agnatic or "Dog Soldier" faction, however, there was no great advantage to exogamy. Since they cared little for trade, they did not need far-flung alliances. Anyway, they were committed to keeping large militant camps, summer and winter, both for defense and to facilitate raiding against white settlements, supply trains, and the railroads.

Therefore Mooney was told in 1906 that the warrior chiefs "try hard to have men marry in their own band to retain warriors."[5] Since the emphasis was on men and on warfare in the agnatic groups, the status of women suffered considerably, and they were sometimes subjected to organized brutality. My debate with other scholars on the matter of gang rape has appeared in *Plains Anthropologist*.[6] In any event, lacking any commitment to trade, peace, or the productive role of women in making buffalo robes, members of the agnatic faction did not necessarily see exogamy as *proper*. Table 13 shows the informants used by Mooney, Michelson, and Gatschet and gives their opinions concerning the propriety of exogamy. Clearly, those who identified themselves as Dog Soldiers or Fox Soldiers, or who lived in that area, were of one opinion, while the uterine faction, Sutaios, and people in other areas held a different opinion. One especially interesting response is from White Eagle (plate 25), a Dog Soldier who married into the Red Moon band (fig. 20), where White Shield had defined endogamy as acceptable. Following his brother's lead, White Eagle also says that "clans" were endogamous.

But whatever our responses concerning the "correctness" of band exogamy, there remains the question of actual practice among the Cheyennes

Table 13   Informants' Opinions about Marriage and Residence

INFORMANT	BAND	REFERENCE	OPINION
Uterine faction			
Wolf Face	Oiv	Gatschet 61	Only chiefs were polygynous
American Horse	Hvk	Michelson 2822	Bands exogamous, except Sutaio; societies mostly exogamous
Left Hand Shield	Hev	Mooney B	Bands exogamous
She Bear	His	Michelson 2811	Bands exogamous, societies not
Agnatic faction			
White Eagle	Hot	Michelson 2822	"Clans" endogamous, societies exogamous
Good Bear	Masi	Mooney B	Bands patrilocal, except "mixed-bloods"; endogamy permitted
Lone Wolf	Hot	Mooney 2213	Exogamy permitted
Sutaio and Omisis			
Daniel Littlechief	Tot	Gatschet 54	Bands patrilineal, no rules of exogamy
White Bull	Omi	Michelson 2822	"Clans" endogamous, societies exogamous
Buffalo Thigh	Sut	Mooney 2213	Endogamy permitted

in the middle and late nineteenth century. It is one thing to note what people *said* was their ideal practice and quite another to see what they actually did, and why.

There are two data bases available for determining the actual practice of Cheyennes in choice of spouse in the period just before confinement to the Oklahoma reservation. The first data base was collected by Mooney, not for the examination of band exogamy, but because of his interest in Cheyenne shields and warfare. Fortunately, Mooney collected the band affiliations of his informants, all of whom were men, their parents' affiliations, and the affiliations of their first wives. (Several stated they were polygynous.)

The second data base for examining exogamy in marriage choices is the 1900 census, which we have already used in determining the histories of the

Plate 25. White Eagle, a Dog Soldier who married into the Red Moon band. Negative no. 340-A, -B, National Anthropological Archives, Smithsonian Institution.

various bands. But this time, by determining whether a person's parents were born in different states or in the same state, we can get some notion of exogamy. We then can compare rates of exogamy in different bands and at different times. This data base, like that collected by Mooney, has certain advantages and certain weaknesses. With Mooney's data, we have the various bands identified as such, explicitly, but with the inaccuracies I have already noted concerning the nesting of names and variabilities owing to different perspectives. We do not know, for example, when Mooney's informants gave "Hevhaitaneo" as the affiliation of a parent, whether they were using the name to mean the manhao of that name or the Southern Cheyennes in general. The names Omisis and Tsistsistas have the same problem enbedded in them, for the same reason. But we can be sure, with Mooney's data, that a Hisiometaneo married to an Oktogona is an exogamous marriage, for these are names that are not nested.

With the data from the 1900 census, we cannot be sure that spouses born in the same state or territory, according to their children, were necessarily members of the same band. At some times in their history, two or more manhao camped together, especially in their wintering areas in the Big Timbers of the Arkansas. Also, since the bands moved seasonally and in response to drought, it may be that a pair of spouses were born in the same band, although in different states. But even with these disadvantages, the state-of-birth data can tell us something *comparatively* about exogamy, especially if we analyze each group separately, with some prior knowledge of its history. For example, we are not surprised to find that the Clinton people mostly had parents born in the Dakotas, since we know that the two Clinton bands, the Hisiometaneos and Black Shin's Sutaio band, traveled together and intermarried. So despite the fact that two parents were born in the same territory—Dakota—we know from oral history that they were most likely from different bands.

Similarly, we are not surprised that a couple from the Kingfisher or Anskowinis band should comprise two spouses born in Montana. From a Southern Cheyenne standpoint these people were both Omisis, but from a Northern Cheyenne perspective one may have been Totoimana or Sutaio while the other was from another Omisis subgroup. That is, the marriages may have been exogamous from the standpoint of a person familiar with the different Northern Cheyenne bands but endogamous from the standpoint of a Southern Cheyenne who called all northerners "Omisis."

Table 14 shows the marriage patterns that result from an analysis of Mooney's data. To the information supplied by Mooney for thirty-six marriages, I have added some similar data from Michelson for fifteen other marriages, a total of fifty-one.

Many of the marriage patterns exhibited in table 14 are just what we would expect, though the sample is small. First of all, we note that most endogamous marriages are among people identified as Sutaio, Hevhaitaneo, and Omisis. The Sutaio endogamy is expected, because informants have said all along that the Sutaio were exempt from the rule of exogamy, since they were an incorporated tribe. We should also expect endogamy for people identified as Hevhaitaneo and Omisis because these are generic

Table 14   Marriage Choices of Mooney's and Michelson's Informants

	FEMALE												
MALE	HVK	TSI	SUT	HEV	OIV	HIS	WOT	MAS	HOT	OKT	OMI	FOREIGNERS	TOTAL
HVK	1				1		1			1		1	5
TSI		1										1	2
SUT			3	1				1				1	6
HEV	1	1		3		1			2		3	3	14
OIV				1									1
HIS	1		1								1		3
WOT			1		1							1	3
MAS	1		1			1		2			1	1	7
HOT	1								1				2
OKT											1		1
OMI	1		1								3	1	6
Foreigners						1							1
Total	6	2	7	5	2	3	1	3	3	1	9	9	51

Source: Mooney 2531, NAA; Michelson 3320, 2822, 2811, NAA.

names for Southern and Northern Cheyennes, respectively, in addition to being the names of particular manhao groups. The single endogamous entry for the Tsistsistas may also be the result of using the band term to mean the larger group, in this case the whole nation.

If we disregard these generic terms for the moment, we can test whether the agnatic faction was any more endogamous than the uterine faction. From the table, we see that of sixteen individuals in the three agnatic groups, the Hotamhetaneos, Masikotas, and Oktogonas, six were involved in endogamous marriages, or 38.5 percent. Of the decidedly uterine groups—Heviksnipahis, Oivimanas, and Hisiometaneos—only one couple, or two persons out of twenty-five, was involved in an endogamous marriage, 8 percent. Although these samples are small, they at least, I think, show a trend, and we should be glad at this late date to have any data at all to examine for endogamy. (In this chapter we will discuss both rates of exogamy and rates of endogamy. Mathematically the two rates are complementary, their sum being equal to one.)

The data from the United States census must be approached in a somewhat different manner. First of all, we do not have band affiliations, but only states of birth for individuals interviewed and the states of birth of their two parents, although the parents' names are not listed.

If we want to look for evidence of exogamy here, we should focus on the period of Cheyenne history when the "clan" system was most active, after the bands were dispersed across the central plains but before the devastating epidemic of 1849. We know from the band histories that this epidemic took a great toll on the Masikota and Oktogona bands, and perhaps other bands as well.[7] In general, the diminution of band size and the reorganization into new bands had the consequence of putting together people who were not closely related. Therefore a marriageable man or woman had more opportunity to marry exogamously within his or her reorganized, composite band, since the band now included more young adults with no known relationship—possible mates.

In Cheyenne history the period when exogamy was most likely is from about 1835, when bands were fully dispersed and the trade in buffalo hides was in full swing, to 1849, the year of the cholera epidemic. Table 15 estimates the number of marriages in this period, from the Southern Cheyenne census, arranged by state of birth of the spouses. The marriage dates were estimated from the ages of their adult descendants at the time of the 1900 census. That is, the marriages on the table represent parents of people on the census, born between 1835 and 1849, whose ages were listed in 1900 as fifty-one to sixty-five.

Surprisingly, the table does not show a great deal of intermarriage among

Table 15 Exogamy as Measured by State of Birth, for Parents of Respondents on the 1900 Census, Born between 1835 and 1865

	TEX	INT[a]	COL	KAN	NEB	WYO	DAK	MON	MIN	OTHER
TEX										
INT[a]		3								
COL			21		2	1	2			
KAN			1	1			1			
NEB					3	2	2		1	1
WYO			1			9			1	1
DAK		1			1	2	35			
MON							1	11		
MIN						1			2	
Other										4

[a]INT = Indian Territory.

parents born in different states. While data from Mooney's and Michelson's informants gave us a calculated percentage of endogamy of 38.5 and 8 for the agnatic and uterine groups, respectively, the endogamy calculated from the census is 80.9 percent, much higher. To put it another way, Mooney's and Michelson's informants seem much more exogamous than the general population, though we have calculated the rates from data sets that are somewhat different in character. So we have the problem of deciding whether the difference is due to the actual practice of the people or to the way we have taken our sample.

To take another perspective on the problem of exogamy, we can lump the bands listed by Mooney's and Michelson's informants in a manner that approximates the factions of 1840–70. Since we have a good picture of band locations from chapter 7, we can lump the bands living together and then calculate new rates of endogamy. Table 16 shows the agnatic and uterine factions lumped together, with the Omisis and foreigners considered separately. Uterine endogamy is somewhat higher, 46.3 instead of 38.5 percent, and agnatic endogamy is now 26.7 percent instead of 8 percent. Even with lumping, however, the data base still shows that the informants had a much higher rate of exogamy than the general population as shown by the 1900 census.

One possible explanation for this difference is that the informants represent a different period of Cheyenne history than the people on table 14. But we can tell from the birth dates supplied by Mooney and Michelson, cross checked from censuses, that the periods in question are roughly the same. The ages of the informants imply that they were married in the same period

Table 16   Marriage Patterns for Groups of Bands

Marriages within uterine group	19
(HVK, TSI, HEV, OIV, HIS, WOT, SUT)	
Marriages within agnatic group	4
(MAS, HOT, OKT)	
Uterine-agnatic marriages	9
Omisis-Omisis marriages	3
Omisis-uterine marriages	5
Omisis-agnatic marriages	1
Uterine-foreigner marriages	8
Agnatic-foreigner marriages	1
Omisis-foreigner marriages	1
Total	51

Note: Data reorganized from table 14.

examined from the standpoint of the 1900 census, 1835 to 1849. Another possible explanation, and one that is more plausible, emerges from our discussion of the differences between camp, bunch, and band.

If the council chiefs were indeed primarily and fundamentally involved in trading, we can see why they might be inclined toward exogamy, to improve their relations with other trading chiefs. But fifteen of the informants interviewed by Mooney and Michelson indicated by their affiliations that they were from the agnatic rather than the uterine faction. We have already seen, from table 16, that their rate of endogamy was lower than that of the uterine group. With the aid of the 1900 census, we can ask this same question about the whole population rather than just Mooney's and Michelson's informants. Were there, in fact, any discernible differences in the rates of exogamy between the agnatic faction, who took their allotments on the North Canadian, and the uterine faction, who took their allotments in the central and western parts of the Oklahoma reservation?

Several of the uterine groups are difficult to examine statistically. The Hammon people, as we noted, refused to answer questions in 1900 and so are not represented in the sample. The Clinton people had a special relationship between their component Sutaio, Hisiometaneo, and Tsistsistas subgroups and so do not appear to be exogamous from the census, though we know they were from other data. Therefore it is safest to try to contrast the Oivimana or Watonga band, which responded to the census takers, with the agnatic group from Cantonment, which also responded. That is, if the agnatic and uterine factions had different rates of endogamy, we would expect it to show as a contrast between these two emphatically different and discrete reservation groups. But I can find no contrast between them. In fact, the calculated rates of endogamy by state are nearly the same, eighteen of twenty-three, or 78.3 percent, for Watonga and twenty-two of twenty-nine, or 75.9 percent, for Cantonment.

We still have not explained why the informants of Mooney and Michelson were apparently so much more exogamous than the general population of Cheyennes. The only remaining explanation, and the one we are left with as a hypothesis, is that exogamy was a matter of *rank*, not of band or faction. That is, all the people who talked to the ethnographers were tribal leaders—chiefs, headsmen, or prominent warriors. The field notes of the ethnographers clearly indicate that they talked only to powerful, prominent people, and it was these men, I hypothesize, who were more likely to be exogamous by band. Lower-ranking men, we should remember, were more likely to be members of a vestoz than a manhastoz and therefore more likely to find a spouse within their manhao unit.

The reason for the exogamy of the council chiefs has already been discussed. Marriages in other bands and other nations promoted trade. For example, eight of the nine marriages with foreign women were made by uterine chiefs (table 16). But the data base indicates that soldier headsmen also made exogamous marriages, although the pattern was somewhat different. In this case the headsmen apparently made strategic marriages among the vestoz groups who took refuge with the agnatic faction as the influence of the uterine leaders dwindled. Marriage data, to be presented later in this chapter, show that the society headsmen, like the chiefs, were polygynous and made not one, but several strategic marriages to consolidate their personal power and prestige. The data we have examined so far, which list only band identities of married couples, make it appear that the marriages of headsmen were the same as the marriages of chiefs; but we will see in the following sections that the form of the marriage was very different. As George Bent said, while the chiefs went to live with their wives, the headsmen brought their wives to their own camps. The contrast was in residence, not in the extent of exogamy.

Residence

That husbands, in the uterine bands, went to live with their wives' families at marriage can be confirmed by looking for Sand Creek survivors on the allotment map. The Sand Creek Descendants Association has on file genealogical information from 3,099 people descended from the core groups ("bunches" or manhastoz) who were present at Sand Creek. We can use that data for our analysis.

The two rules of residence we wish to contrast here resulted in two different ideal social patterns. If a husband moved to his wife's family, the wife could live with her parents for the remainder of her parents' lives, but if the wife moved to her husband's family, the husband could live with his parents for the rest of his parents' lives. The first or matrilocal pattern allows the bond between a woman and her parents to remain unbroken, while the second or patrilocal pattern preserves the bond between parents and sons.

We can test the residence patterns of the Sand Creek descendants, the core of the uterine group, by examining the pattern of allotments taken by parents and their children from the 1892 allotment map. If married women can be found taking allotments near their parents, then we can call the residence pattern matrilocal; but if married sons are found to be living near their own parents instead of with their wives' parents, we can call the choice patrilocal. We know from George Bent that the ideal residence pattern for the uterine faction was supposed to be matrilocal.

In a previous article, I measured the distances between center points of the allotments of mothers and children from the Sand Creek genealogies.[8] Mothers were used instead of fathers for two reasons: first, because women tended to live longer than men, increasing the sample size, and second, because name changes were more frequent for men than women, making it easier to link women from one list to another. The conclusion offered is that though not all of the Sand Creek descendants married matrilocally, most did. Of the marriage cases analyzed, twenty-five of thirty-seven, or 67.6 percent, were matrilocal.

Matrilocality can also be confirmed from the Northern Cheyenne census of 1900 by looking at the Northern Scabby band. This band consisted, we should recall, of intermarried Northern and Southern Cheyennes, the southerners being Oivimanas or "Scabbies." By seeing whether the husband or the wife of a Northern Scabby couple was the southerner, we can see whether the marriage was matrilocal, with the couple living near her parents, also northerners. Using the state-of-birth data, we find that in thirteen of the twenty cases of exogamous marriages in the Northern Scabby band, 65 percent, the marriage was matrilocal. These results, along with the Sand Creek genealogies, help confirm George Bent's assertion about the matrilocal trend among the uterine people.

It is much more difficult to confirm the other side of Bent's allegation— that the agnatic faction required new brides to move to their husbands' camps and away from their own families. The reasons for this are partly historical and partly "technical." Even if we cannot fully confirm Bent's assertion from the Dog Soldier side, I should mention the reasons why not. Until now I have presented only the results of *successful* social analyses. So let me here indulge myself and explain the frustrations of *not* being able to confirm patrilocality from the agnatic side.

First of all, we do not have good genealogies from the Dog Soldier side. Although both factions were brutally attacked in the period of warfare— the uterine faction at Sand Creek and the agnatic faction at Summit Springs—no promise of indemnities was ever made to the Dog Soldier descendants. And so, while Sand Creek descendants have remembered the treaty promise of 1865 and mostly kept track of their ancestry, there has been no such incentive for the Dog Soldiers. Also, male mortality was high at Summit Springs, and so the link between father and son, the one we need to confirm patrilocality, has been largely broken. That is, although many men of the Dog Soldier faction settled in the Cantonment area and took allotments there, they never had the opportunity to live near their fathers, since many fathers had been killed at Summit Springs.

Also, the early documents that identify who was in the Dog Soldier faction, the "capture lists" of 1868–74, list only the names of men. Since a young man's mother was not listed on the capture lists, we cannot tell from later lists whether a man was living near his mother. These links cannot be made from the allotment list either, since the list showed only kinship relations among living people. The parents of adults are not indicated. So while we can find the parents and siblings of adults in the uterine faction from the Sand Creek genealogies, we have no way of getting the same information for the agnatic faction.

Patrilocality of the Dog Soldier faction might also be confirmed if we could find an older unmarried son on an earlier census and then see if he was married and living near his parents at allotment in 1892. And in fact, if we look at the United States census of 1880 and the Bureau of Indian Affairs census of 1888, we can find twenty-four members of the Dog Soldier faction with thirty-nine sons approaching a marriageable age. One might hope, then, to find allotments of these same sons and then measure how close they were to the allotments of their fathers and brothers, using the same method as for the Sand Creek descendants. But when we work with men's names rather than women's, we must deal with the name changes at puberty. Of thirty-nine sons identified from earlier lists, none can be reliably identified on the 1892 allotment list. To be *reliably* identified, in my opinion, requires having a name that is at least an alternative translation of the same Cheyenne name and being within five years of the same age. An even more stringent requirement, which I have imposed on myself, is to exclude from the sample all names carried by more than one person, since I could not be sure which of several possibilities was the man in question. And so, of the thirty-nine men identified as being the sons of Dog Soldiers, none can be found under the same names. And we cannot indulge in circular reasoning by assuming that if they are near the older generation they are therefore sons and then concluding, if you can call it that, that the agnatic faction was patrilocal.

For the present, pending the development of more data or the invention of some clever technique, we must be content with George Bent's normative statement about the marriage practices of the Dog Soldiers. However, we can add a few remarks from the people who served as informants for Mooney and Michelson. Although for the most part they were discussing the recent reservation period, they did have some things to say about whether they lived with their own or their wives' families.

Of the uterine faction, Packer told Mooney that he had gone to live with his Masikota wife, and he also said that he had thereby become a Masikota;[9] Mad Wolf, an arrow man, said he had gone to live with his wife's Oktogona band;[10] Hill, whose band is not given, said he had made matrilocal resience with his Omisis wife;[11] Wolf Tongue, who gave his band as Heviksnipahis, said he lived with the Oivimanas;[12] and Wolf Road, a Masikota, lived with his Oivimana wife.[13] Two generalizations made by other leaders of the uterine faction also support Bent's statement. Crow Chief told Mooney that "young men on marrying generally go live with wife's people,"[14] and Sun Dancer indicated that the child's band was determined by the residence of the mother.[15]

Of the agnatic faction, some of whom are reported on table 13, White Eagle told Michelson that bands were endogamous but societies were exogamous.[16] Good Bear told Mooney that bands were patrilocal, except for mixed-bloods, who could live with their wives.[17] Lone Wolf told Mooney that band endogamy was "permitted."[18] Grasshopper and White Bull, who I am told were Dog Soldiers, told Michelson there was no particular rule about residence.[19]

It is interesting that the polarization of opinion was not between those informants who said that matrilocality was proper and those who argued for patrilocality, but between those of matrilocal persuasion and those who said it did not matter. By and large, it was the chiefs of the uterine faction who made the former assertion and the people of agnatic affiliation who said it did not matter. Even in George Bent's day it may have been that the agnatic faction insisted on their right to break the matrilocal rule, but did not necessarily want to impose a new rule on the whole society. After they were physically separated from Black Kettle's peace faction, it was sufficient to legitimate their own marriage practices without criticizing traditional matrilocal practice.

The Band Cycle

So far we have established three major points in regard to Cheyenne marriage practices in the prereservation period. First, we have established that the leaders of the uterine faction, the council chiefs, were generally exogamous and matrilocal, although the rest of the people in uterine bands may not have been. Next we have established that the agnatic or Dog Soldier leaders were also exogamous by band and like the uterine chiefs tried to build up a large "bunch" of immediate kin. And last, we have contrasted at least the *rules* of residence for the uterine and agnatic factions. While the uterine leaders tended to say that matrilocal residence was the only proper pattern, the agnatic leaders said there was no special rule. But even knowing all this with some assurance, we have no specific idea of how camps and bands changed and re-formed and how they were related to the larger units of society.

Until 1978 I tended to inquire into these matters as an interviewer, with fragmented results. Although elders could answer specific questions very clearly, there still did not emerge a clear pattern of social organization. That is, the pieces of information I picked up did not make a whole. I felt as if I had been given some pieces of jigsaw puzzle but could not get them to fit together and did not even know how many different puzzles were represented among the pieces. So about 1978 I decided to take a much more passive role in learning about kinship. Also, my ability to understand spoken Cheyenne had improved so that informants were more confident I could understand what they were trying to say. Although other fieldworkers have collected Cheyenne kinship terms in the native language, as far as I know I am the only one who has tried to understand Cheyenne sociology in native terms. My particular informants for this section were John and Susie Black Owl, Roy and Kathryn Bull Coming, Ed and Minnie Red Hat, Walter R. Hamilton, Vinnie Hoffman, and Joe Antelope, the former arrow keeper (plate 26).

According to these elders, the way Cheyenne society maintains itself in time and space is called *manhestanov*, a word that is very abstract and difficult to translate. John Black Owl explained this as "the way that things are made over, like we make over these arrows. In old times these bands and families were made over same way." Other informants emphasized the analogy between human life and the life of a band with a cycle proceeding through birth, youth, maturity, and death. Etymologically, informants related the word both to manhao, "band," and to manhastoz, "bunch." One informant said the word had something to do with a thing that was being continually opened and closed, or being inside and being outside. Rodolphe Petter's definition, I believe, comes more from the usage of the word than from its etymology. He defined manhestanov as "the succession of generations." In any event, it is clear that the expression is intended to convey a dynamic notion of the regeneration of society.

In Cheyenne the word used most often to describe social dynamics, and perhaps the most important word in Cheyenne sociology, is *nisson,* a word that varies in meaning depending on whether the speaker is male or female. When a woman says nisson, she usually translates this as "my bunch of sisters," but she includes not only her own biological sisters, but also the daughters of her mother's sister (her female matrilateral first cousins) and perhaps other women of her generation as well, all connected through female links. An ethnologist would say these women are all connected as matrilateral uterine kin. As it happens, a photograph exists for one such group, the women of the Goose family (plate 27).

When a man says nisson, he means his biological brothers and also other men of his generation to whom he is connected through the male line—his

Plate 26.   Joe Antelope, former keeper of the sacred arrows. Photo no. 16A–17 in the John Moore Collection, Western History Collections, University of Oklahoma Library.

patrilateral agnatic kin. So these are the basic building blocks for the continuation of Cheyenne society, bunches of "brothers" and bunches of "sisters," both called nisson. Figures 18 and 19 are diagrams of these two kinds of sibling "bunches."

These nisson units help structure marriages in Cheyenne society. Worldwide, it is not unusual to find societies in which a man marries a group of sisters. Murdock noted twenty-one such societies in his 1949 survey of 250 societies scattered around the world. It is more unusual, however, to find a

Plate 27. Women of the Goose family, the core of a traditional band. *Standing, from left:* White Buffalo Woman, Susie Standingbird, Elizabeth Curioushorn, and Esther Goose, with daughter Charlotte. *Sitting in chairs, from left:* Sage Woman, Cora Curioushorn, and Measure Woman. *Sitting on ground:* Verna and Wilbur Standingbird. Photo no. 247 in the Campbell Collection, Western History Collections, University of Oklahoma Library.

society in which brothers share marriage with a group of sisters. Murdock did not count them in his survey. But the Cheyenne nisson unit included more people than simply biological brothers and sisters, the basis of Murdock's analysis.

One might wonder at the outset why it was necessary for Cheyennes to go beyond siblings to create and name these nisson units in their society. The answer I propose is that biological realities did not conform to sociological necessities. That is, large groups of brothers or sisters did not occur biologically often enough to serve their social utility. The social function of a nisson unit might require, for example, six brothers of a certain age range, but these were not born as often as was necessary. Therefore other kinds of relatives—same-sex cousins—were recruited to fill out a nisson of the proper size.

To support these assertions about why cousins were recruited to the nisson, I developed, with the assistance of Dan Swan and J. J. Chen-Chou, a

Plate 28.   Everett Yellowman, a Sun Dance priest of Watonga, Oklahoma.
Photo no. 27–28 in the John Moore Collection, Western History Collections,
University of Oklahoma Library.

computer simulation of the numbers of brothers and sisters produced by
Cheyenne mothers in the aboriginal period. Without stating all the assumptions of the simulation method, which is called SIBSIM, I will note
only that it uses real rates of fertility and mortality to show how often one
might expect to find different mixes of sons and daughters in the offspring of
a Cheyenne mother. On average, only 15 percent of Cheyenne mothers
could expect to have as many as four children of the same sex. Therefore the
production of large same-sex groups of siblings was too unusual to be relied
upon for implementing the institution of manhestanov, and so cousins were
recruited into the nisson groups.

Plate 29. Willie Fletcher, a Sun Dance priest of Geary, Oklahoma. Photo no. 3A–6A in the John Moore Collection, Western History Collections, University of Oklahoma Library.

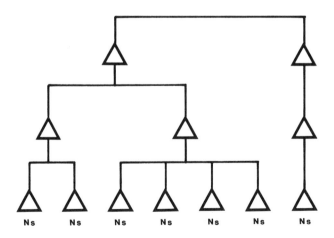

Figure 18. Members of a male nisson unit.

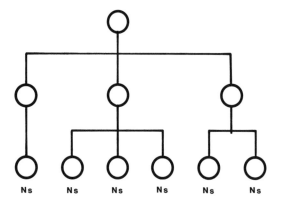

Figure 19.   Members of a female nisson unit.

In narrations of band history the female nisson, or "bunch of sisters," is referred to most often in two contexts—polygynous marriage and the founding of bands. For example, High-Backed Wolf, the leader and probably the founder of the Hevhaitaneo band, was married to a bunch of six sisters and reputedly had thirty children. Brown Lodge, an informant for James Mooney, said that High-Backed Wolf had been born a Masikota but had made exogamous marriages to form the Hevhaitaneos.[20] Old Whirlwind, chief of the Hevhaitaneos, was married to three sisters, two of whom are pictured in plate 24, and Black Kettle was married to four sisters.[21] White Buffalo Woman told Michelson that the four wives of Black Kettle were all "cousins" to one another and had seventeen children among them.[22] Nearly all of them were killed either at Sand Creek in 1864 or at the Battle of the Washita in 1868. Round Stone, another council chief, had three wives who were "classificatory sisters."[23]

Groups of "sisters" are also mentioned as the founders of bands, both in aboriginal times and in the early reservation period. The sisters married by High-Backed Wolf, as mentioned, formed the core group of the Hevhaitaneo band. Four sisters from the Black Lodges were the founding nisson for the Two Strike band, according to their modern descendants. Groups of sisters are mentioned in the founding of four other reservation bands, but this time paired off with bunches of "brothers."

The Red Moon band, which had some claim to being a continuation of the Wotapio band, was organized between two founding groups who, according to Mrs. Vinnie Hoffman, "were all brothers and sisters to one another" (fig. 20). The political independence and unusual marriage relations that developed in this band were mentioned in the previous chapter.

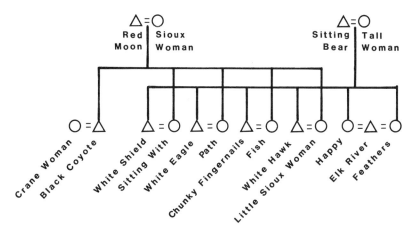

Figure 20.   Founding cohorts of the Red Moon band.

The Glass Water People were also said to be founded by five brothers who married "sisters." Two other bands were either founded or refounded by the exchange of nisson groups, in these cases between the descendants of the Fox Soldiers and the descendants of the Dog Soldiers. The Blue Horse band, according to modern descendants, was formed from Fox Soldier daughters and Dog Soldier sons, and the Owl Eyebrow band was formed from Dog Soldier daughters and Fox Soldier sons (see fig. 17). The important thing to note in these examples is that the marriage of the nisson groups was the point at which the band was refounded, in these cases taking a new name in the process.

According to Roy Bull Coming, male nisson units were often marked off by sharing the same war medicines, especially shields. The ideal number of men bearing the same shield or sharing the same medicine was four. Little Chief's drawing (plate 2) shows no more than four shields of the same kind, and we can find two nisson units explicitly listed in Mooney's field notes on shields.[24] The famous warrior Medicine Water was one of four brothers—Slender Calf, Iron Shirt, Man on Cloud, and Medicine Water. Big Head was the shield instructor for four warriors of the Heviksnipahis band who were sons or nephews to Big Head (brothers or cousins to each other). These were Bear Tail, Red Coyote, Gray Hail, and Two Lances.

Among modern traditionalists, men frequently say they are one of four brothers, or that they have four sons. Often, however, cousins, half-brothers and nephews are included as "sons" or "brothers" to make a total of four. From SIBSIM we calculate that on average only 34.4 percent of Cheyenne women had as many as three sisters, and only 35.4 percent of Cheyenne men had as many as three biological brothers. To approach the ideal of four brothers, obviously, some persons had to juggle biological facts in favor of sociological facts.

So here we have, I believe, the essential meaning of the term man-hestanov, the "succession of generations." It is nothing less than a periodic renewing of an old band, or the chartering and founding of a new band, by the marriage of same-sex cohorts of spouses. The renewal, however, according to present informants, was gradual and not abrupt. That is, there was no huge ceremony and mass marriage. Instead, a man might marry the eldest "sister" of a female nisson. If he were successful and honorable for a few years, he might then marry another sister, and perhaps get his brother to do the same. After a certain number of these marriages, ideally four, people might start referring to the band by a new name. If the marriages, however, had been matrilocal, with men moving into one of the traditional band cores or manhastoz, the band might retain the high-status manhao name—Heviksnipahis or Oivimana. Otherwise, if fission of a large band was the result or if the new band moved to a different territory, then a new band name could be inaugurated, of the sort we have seen many times in our recitation of Cheyenne ethnohistory. But here is the social mechanism for this fissioning, rechartering, renaming, and founding of bands—man-hestanov, the renewal of generations.

The agnatic groups apparently, as they got started in the previous century, had a great deal of trouble in getting women and their families to consent to any kind of arrangement other than the traditional matrilocality. The widely discussed institution of "putting women on the prairie," submitting them to the gang rape of a soldier society, I interpret as part of this forced reorganization of Cheyenne society.[25] Little Robe, for example, the chief of the Dog Soldiers, who already had two sisters for wives in 1864, raped another half-sister to force her to marry him.[26] Buffalo Hump, along with "his gang of cousins," also resorted to rape to force marriage on an unwilling younger sister.[27] Other such cases are reported in the case histories collected by Grinnell, Llewellyn, and Hoebel.[28] By contrast the council chiefs seem to have encouraged marriages in a more positive way, by offering status and political power to young men of other bands, especially the sons of other chiefs, who would be willing to make a matrilocal marriage. And so we see that council chiefs were usually succeeded by the sons of chiefs from other bands. Wolf-on-a-Hill married into the Southern Sutaio band and fathered Black Kettle.[29] Black Kettle, in turn, married into the Wotapio band, along with his two "brothers," Black Hairy Dog and Gentle Horse, where Black Kettle became band chief.[30] He in turn was succeeded by Red Moon, the son of Yellow Coyote, the chief and founder of the Hevhaitaneos.[31] Red Moon, in turn, was succeeded as band chief by White Shield, who married into the Red Moon band along with his "bunch of brothers," White Eagle, Chunky Fingernails, and White Hawk—four men comprising an ideal traditional nisson.

Figure 20 represents the central core of the Red Moon band, as best I can reconstruct it from letters, reports, and modern informants.[32] A few of the documents contradict this structure, so this diagram represents only the "best guess" of actual biological relationships. However, since four-person nisson units are ideal, we should remain skeptical that these were the actual blood ties. That is, the diagram probably represents social realities better than biological facts.

Teaching about Marriage

Since manhestanov was such an important part of traditional philosophy and sociology, it is not surprising to find a prominent teaching story addressed to this topic. Like all children, young Cheyennes learned about proper marriage and family life by literary means. Just as American children might watch "Leave It to Beaver" or "The Waltons" to discover ideal family arrangements, Cheyenne children listened to traditional stories, and they do so today. These teaching stories are different from the sacred stories and are not necessarily told for the truth, but carry a moral lesson. Children in all cultures seem to learn more willingly from stories than when they are preached to or threatened. And so we have the story of "The Woman's Camp."

Although the story is still told among Cheyenne people, here I will repeat the version recorded by George Grinnell about 1910 and published in 1961.[33] I do this for two reasons—first, because this version is more likely to be contemporaneous with the time when manhestanov was a living institution, and second, because the story is such a clear confirmation of the importance of nisson marriage, that I do not want anyone to think I made it up to suit the theory. Although I do not want to be too much of a structuralist in my interpretation of the story, it seems clear that it constitutes an exaggeration of recommended social practice, from a uterine perspective. I maintain that the single-sex camps of the story symbolically represent the male and female nisson groups described above. The character featured in the story as a comic figure, Wihio, is the same "Trickster" character who appears in many such stories among North American nations.

> Wihio was traveling up the river when he came to a big camp. All the people were outside, and when he walked up to them he saw they were all women; there was not one man among them. When they saw him, they all ran toward

him and began calling out, "Come with me; come to my lodge," and some caught hold of him, but he said, "No; I own another [I see another woman that I like better]," for behind him he saw a very handsome woman. Wihio said to the others, "Keep quiet now; this one first picked me out for her husband." The others let him go, so he walked up to this one and she took him to her lodge; there was only one trail by which to reach it, for the timber was growing close all around it. There were many big plum bushes there. The lodge was painted with stripes all around it and when he went in he saw on each side a nice bed, with white buffalo skins hanging over the head and backrests. The lodge lining was decorated with porcupine quills. He married this woman.

One day he told his wife he was going on a trip up the river. When he had gone a long distance, he came to another camp, but here, instead of women, all the people were men. Wihio said to them: "Come here, my friends; come around me. I have something to tell you." The men all crowded around him and he said, "Farther down the river I have found a camp in which there are only women; that will be a very good thing for all of us." The men said to one another, "That is good; take us there." Others said, "Let us go with him." They got around him and said, "Wait; you may go off and leave us, for you are a swift runner."

The news was so good they were afraid he would get away before he had showed them the village. So they tied rocks to his feet and put a robe on him and filled it with stones. After they had loaded him with stones, they said, "Where is the camp?" And when he told them, they all started to run there. Wihio's burden of stones was so heavy that he could hardly walk, so he followed behind slowly. He called to them, asking them to come back and wait for him, and when they did not stop he told them to look out for his lodge and said it was painted in stripes and that his wife was a handsome woman; they must not go there. They all answered, "Oh, no, we will not go there."

The Indians all ran to the camp and picked out the best-looking women for their wives; and one of them chose Wihio's wife for his wife. When Wihio arrived he walked up to his lodge, saying to himself, "I think everything is right, in here," but he found a man in the lodge sitting beside his wife. This man said, "I have taken your wife; you will have to go out and get another; be quick now before they are all gone." So Wihio had to go out and stand in the middle of the camp with the rocks still tied all around him. He hunted all over and finally found a little old lodge off to one side. He went in and found a very old woman sitting there. She said, "Come in, my son-in-law." Wihio said, "I am not your son-in-law," but she still said he was, though he said again that he was not. He walked up to her and sat down beside her and said,

"I want to marry you; I want you for my wife." So she agreed and he married her. She was the oldest woman in the camp.

Other Cheyenne teaching stories describe the problems created by exogamy, and especially by rules of residence. In one such story, the daughter of a chief wants to marry for love instead of staying in her band and making the marriage arranged by her father.[34] So she runs away with a young man from another band who says his name is Red Eye. After arriving at the band of her lover (thereby taking up patrilocal residence), she soon suspects that she has married not a human being, but something else. Meanwhile her father has organized her old suitors to look for her, and the story ends as follows:

> At the girl's home there was great trouble. The chief's daughter had disappeared, and no one knew what had become of her. Her father and mother were crying because their daughter was lost. All the young men were out searching for her. They could not find her, nor any trace of her. When they could not find her, her father felt still worse, and said to the young men who were searching for her, "The young man who finds my daughter shall marry her."
>
> When the girl awoke in the morning, she found that she was in a big hollow tree, and all about the tree were sitting mountain rats. The buffalo robes on which they had been lying were grass nests.
>
> A young Cheyenne man was out looking for this girl, and as he passed a great hollow tree the girl came crawling out from it.
>
> "Girl," he said, "where have you been? Everyone in camp is in great sorrow because you are lost. We have been searching for you everywhere."
>
> "Friend," said the girl, "the rats stole me away, and brought me here to this tree." Then the young man took her back to her father's lodge, and afterward he married her.

One of the most popular of all teaching stories, however, and the one that best expresses the dilemma between matrilocality and patrilocality, is called "The Buffalo Wife." In the paragraphs below I have edited and spliced two versions, the beginning of one version and the end of another, to omit irrelevant material.[35] One version was collected by Grinnell and the other by Randolph. The story is about a man who marries two women from distant or "foreign" bands. In this story the foreignness is exaggerated by making the women were-animals. The drama of the story is the torn loyalties of the husband, married to two women who are not sisters to each other but are from distant bands.

Once the tribe was scattered out, camping in small parties in different places. In one of the camps there was a very handsome young man. His father loved him dearly, and used to put up for him a lodge in which he lived by himself. Several girls had wanted to marry him, but he refused them.

One day a girl came to his village—a very beautiful girl with yellow hair. He liked her and took her to his lodge and married her. Afterward another girl came in. She too was very handsome. Her hair was dark. He married her too. The first girl was an elk, and the second a young buffalo cow; but the young man did not know this, for they were human in shape. The young man lived with these two wives. After a time each had a child, and these boys grew up until they were big enough to run about and play together. One day they began to dispute about something, and soon they were fighting. From this time on the two women began to dispute, each one taking the part of her child. One day they quarreled, and the elk girl became angry and went away from the camp, taking her boy with her. The buffalo girl declared that she would not stay there, and she too went away.

The young man followed the buffalo girl. Her tracks led to a bare hilltop where no grass grew. From there he saw buffalo tracks in place of his wife's footprints. He followed the hoof marks for a long time. At last he gave up the pursuit and resolved to find the elk girl.

Returning to the camp, he took up the trail of the yellow-haired wife and her child. When he had followed their tracks for a great distance, they disappeared. In their place were the footprints of an elk and her young.

The young man again returned to his tepee. The more he though about his wives, the more curious he became as to where they had gone. At last he set out again to find the buffalo girl.

Taking up her trail where he had left it, the young man followed the buffalo tracks for two days. More and more hoof prints were to be seen as he went along. The sun was setting behind the western hills on the evening of the second day when he came upon a great herd of buffalo grazing in a valley. The chief of these animals came to meet him.

"What do you want here?" demanded the old buffalo.

"I am looking for my wife. I believe she is with your people."

"So you are the Indian who took my daughter," bellowed the buffalo chief. "She has returned to her own people because she did not like the way you treated her. She and her son are here in this herd. They will not return to your camp. I will not let her leave her home again."

The young man was sorry to hear these unkind words from the old buffalo. He pleaded with the chief, telling him how much he needed the woman in his camp and how he missed the little boy.

At last the old buffalo promised to return his daughter to the young man on one condition.

"I don't believe you would know your wife if you saw her," he said. "Tomorrow all the buffalo in this herd will stand in a line. If you can tell which one is your wife, you may take her home with you."

Next morning, the young man walked about among the buffalo, looking for his wife. All of them looked alike to him.

When the time for the test came, the chief cried to the buffalo to form a line so the man could look for his wife. As they were running past him, one of them stopped beside the young man.

"Your wife wants to return to your camp," he said. "She was angry when she left but she has wished many times to return. Her father, the chief, will not let her leave the herd. She says that when the buffalo are in line she will move her ears so you may know her. Watch the ears and when you see a pair that moves, you will know that it is she."

The buffalo formed a long line, and the young man looked from one to another, watching closely the heads of each animal. At last he saw one moving its ears.

"That is my wife," he cried.

"You are right," said the chief. "You have picked her out, and she may go with you."

The chief saw that he was beaten but he was determined not to permit his daughter to go back to the young man's camp.

"Now you have found your wife," he said. "Your son is still with us. I will have all the calves stand in a line. If you can tell which one is your boy, he too may return with you."

The young man was dismayed to hear this. He thought the boy would return with his mother. The calves all looked alike to him. As the buffalo were leading their young about to form a line, one of the older animals ran to the young man.

"Watch the calves' legs," he whispered. "When you see one moving its front legs, you will know it is your son."

The calves formed a line, and the young man found his son by doing as the old buffalo had told him.

The son was glad to be with his father again. The three set out for their home camp. The young man strode along in front of the mother and child. Evening came, and the young man stopped to make camp for the night. When he looked around to see if the buffalo were still following him, he saw, instead of the ugly beasts, his own beautiful wife and his little boy.

The happy family lived in their tepee for several days. They were glad to be together once more. The young man came to think more and more of his other wife who had left him. He did not like to carry water for the camp. The dark-haired girl had all she could do to prepare the food.

"I am going to try to find my other wife," he said early one morning. "It would be nice if we could all be together again."

So he set out to follow her tracks. He traveled several days. At last he came to the home of a band of elk. He soon learned that his wife was the daughter of the chief of this band.

"I must have my wife," he told the elk chief. "I need her to carry water. I miss my little boy."

The elk chief was not moved by this speech but he wanted the young man to think him very wise.

"You can have your wife," he said. "But first you must pick her out from the members of my band."

The young man walked about the camp, trying to think of some means by which he would know his wife. There were many elk but none of them looked like any human being he had ever seen. At last he sat down in a clump of bushes to make some plans.

As he sat there an elk came to him.

"O my husband!" she cried. "I would return to your camp, but my father will not permit me to leave him. I was angry when I left you but have wished many times that I was in human form again. Our son cries every day to see his father. Tell the chief to have all the elk stand in line so you can choose me from the herd. I will nod my head when you look at me."

The young man went to the elk chief.

"Have your people stand in a line where I can see them," he said. "Then I will pick out my wife."

The chief agreed to do this. Soon the elk were standing in a long line. The young man picked out his wife when she nodded her head. The ruler of the band did not try to keep his grandson from going with his mother.

The young man, the elk mother and her young set out for home. Before they reached it, the mother and son resumed their human form. And so, the beautiful, fair-haired woman and the boy lived again in the camp of the young man.

Confirming Marriage Practices

Before leaving the subjects of marriage and residence, we should try to confirm what we can from census records and other documents that are available. Especially we should try to get some measure of the cohesion of these sets of siblings, or nisson groups, within the context of the whole nation. And we might even try to confirm a more exotic aspect of Cheyenne social structure, the building of nisson groups by the actual exchange of children.

Modern informants say that the exchange of young children among aunts, uncles, and grandparents is an ordinary thing even now. Any social worker in western Oklahoma can tell you the same thing. In fact, the coparenting of Cheyenne society is institutionalized in the use of the term *nako,* or mother, for all members of the mother's nisson—all her uterine cousins of the same generation. Similarly, a child says *niscehem,* "my father," to all his father's agnatic kin—his father's brothers and cousins. During the course of his or her childhood, a Cheyenne usually lives with a wide assortment of different mothers and fathers, getting to know them and their children. As he or she develops an attachment to same-sex cousins, his residence with that coparent and those children might be made permanent.

What is missing from modern practice, but is still retained in the memory of elders, is the practice of building up large cohorts of boys or girls in particular bands to facilitate marriage. From the standpoint of children, this was also desirable because the child would then have a larger number of playmates of the same sex and about the same age. In aboriginal and early reservation times, the exchange of children was more necessary than it is now, because the bands were more isolated. The migration to towns, which began in mid-1930s, has created neighborhoods of Indian people with large play groups of kin-related children, so that the exchange of children is much less institutionalized and less necessary than it was before. Also, automobiles have made visiting easier. But still, the nisson groups are active and functional. Cheyenne teenagers, for example, like Anglo teenagers, hang out in same-sex groups. But the Cheyenne group—a carload of boys, a group of girls at a high-school dance or powwow—is most likely a "bunch of cousins" who grew up together rather than a group of unrelated "friends" as in Anglo society.

Looking back at the early reservation censuses, we might expect that the exchange of children among bands would be partly obscured because some of the bands took allotments that were closely intermingled with allotments of a neighboring band. Also, we cannot know, in the larger groups, whether two groups might have exchanged children evenly, so that the balance of ages and sexes was unaffected, or whether they did not exchange children at all. The Clinton group, for example, consisted of at least three bands—Sutaio, Hisiometaneo, and Tsistsistas—and the censuses show a good balance between the sexes of children, as shown in figure 21.

If the large-scale exchange of children existed in early times, it might be

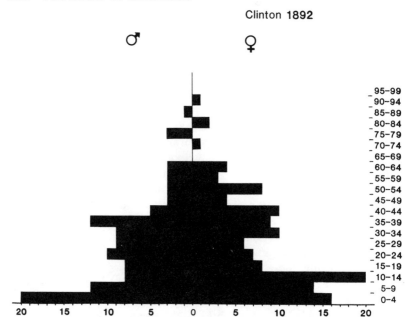

Figure 21.   Population pyramid of Cheyennes near Clinton, Oklahoma, 1892.

exhibited more clearly in the population profiles of the smaller, more isolated groups. That is, if parents were in fact exchanging small children and building up nisson groups in the early reservation period, this should be exhibited in a disproportion of younger people of one sex or the other in the smaller groups. We find an almost amazing confirmation of this practice in the Bessie and Thomas groups. The population pyramids shown in figures 22 and 23 demonstrate a huge disproportion of boys in Bessie and of girls in Thomas.

Having interpreted these pyramids as confirmation of the practice of child exchange and the building of nisson groups, let me leave the door open for other interpretations. First of all, there is a slim chance that the disproportion occurred entirely by accident, and not by design. But as I calculate it, the odds that the disproportion by sex in Bessie occurred by chance alone are slightly more than one in one thousand (0.0013), while the Thomas situation is even less likely. It may also be that recruitment to reservation schools for boys and girls has caused the disproportion. For example, girls of a certain age from Bessie may have been moved to boarding schools, while boys from Thomas moved to another boarding school. But I can find no documentary evidence that this happened, and anyway it seems that these persons would have been allotted with their families in any

Bessie **1892**

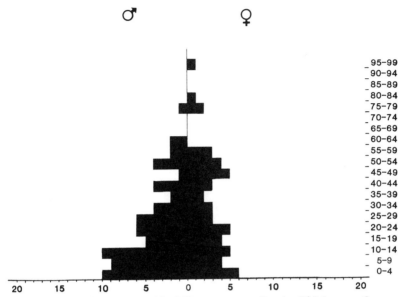

Figure 22. Population pyramid of Cheyennes near Bessie, Oklahoma, 1892.

Thomas **1892**

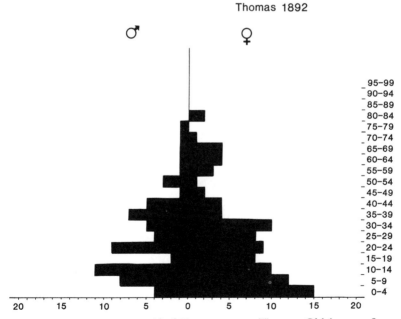

Figure 23. Population pyramid of Cheyennes near Thomas, Oklahoma, 1892.

event. So my present opinion is that the band pyramids confirm the social practices that modern informants say were normal in that period, practices that are further confirmed, symbolically, in the story of the woman's camp.

Earlier in this chapter I discussed the problems of tracing young men from census to census, noting that it was nearly impossible because of name changes. With women the problem is different: although women did not customarily change their names at adulthood, many women shared the same name and could not be distinguished. For example, there are thirty-five persons named Little Woman on the 1880 census, twenty named Fan Woman, and fourteen named Big Belly Woman, many of the same age. Nevertheless, I was interested in whether any groups of sisters took their allotments in the same band in 1892, thereby confirming their marriage to the same man, to brothers, or to members of the same male nisson.

Looking first at the 1880 census, I confined my analysis to people explicitly identified as sisters, living in the same lodge, and old enough to be married by the time of allotment, 1892. To be on the safe side, I used only sisters who had unequivocally unique names. I could find only three sets of

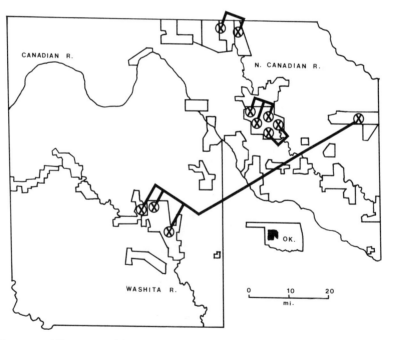

Map 25.   Allotments of four sister cohorts in 1892.

such sisters on the 1880 census, which I supplemented by another set from the Sand Creek genealogies. When I plotted their 1892 allotments, I discovered that in all four cases the sisters seem to have stayed together, except for one woman who lived near Kingfisher although her three sisters were allotted near Clinton (map 25). We cannot perform the same operation on "bunches of brothers," however, because of name changing at adulthood.

So in this chapter we have uncovered the mechanism by which Cheyenne society replicated itself in aboriginal times; we have found the "social engine" of Cheyenne band life. In all human societies, of course, generations are merely fictive conveniences; new babies are born every year, not in batches. But in the Cheyenne case, we have seen an attempt to make the biological world correspond to the social world. This was accomplished by the exchange of children and the building of nisson groups of the same sex and similar ages. If the pyramids from Thomas and Bessie are correct, there was an astonishing amount of such exchange.

The model of social practice described here represents the "ideal" for Cheyenne society. Of course a council chief, with several wives and many children, could come closer to establishing a nisson with his children than could a monogamous man with no brothers. Therefore, it seems likely that the marriage of nisson cohorts, as well as band exogamy, was more typical for a chief-led manhastoz than for a smaller vestoz. Still, the goal of building a nisson among one's children and thereby increasing one's own status and prestige, must have been general throughout Cheyenne society. At least we know that the agnatic headsman, even though they reorganized Cheyenne society, still tried to marry polygynously as a way of increasing their power. What the poor and fragmented families of Cheyennes did, though, and what they thought about the institution of manhestanov, is difficult to say. They were not interviewed by anthropologists.

9 /xxx

Cheyenne Kinship

The study of kinship separates the wheat from the chaff among those who are interested in tribal societies. It separates the work of amateur Indian buffs, such as Thomas Mails and Peter Powell, from that of serious scholars such as Lewis Henry Morgan and Fred Eggan. Kinship studies must be phrased in the native language, and they allow us to see family structure from the inside, just as our study of band structure in previous chapters, with attention paid to native terms, enabled us to see band and tribal structure from the inside. But kinship studies, as they are at present conducted by ethnologists and social anthropologists, are far from perfect. They have built-in assumptions and prejudices that often are not readily apparent.

Kinship studies use diagrams such as figure 24. The graphic symbols used in these diagrams, the lines and the geometric shapes, have two separate historical sources. The practice of using lines to show descent and the relationships among siblings is derived from diagrams showing the succession of titles among European nobility in the Middle Ages. In king lists of the period, however, names appeared at the ends of the lines, not the triangles and circles shown in figure 24. These symbols have a different history and derivation.

As far as I know, it was the British social anthropologist W. H. R. Rivers who first used triangles to denote males and circles for females. After borrowing the biological symbols for Mars and Venus from Linnaeus for his monograph of 1906, he encouraged British anthropologists to use the simpler notation in various editions of the handbook *Notes and Queries on Anthropology*.[1] Before this the "father" of kinship studies, Lewis Henry Morgan (plate 30), used circles for both sexes in his monumental *Systems of Consanguinity,* adding written notes on whether the people were male or female.[2]

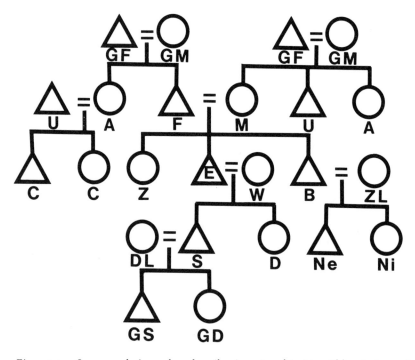

Figure 24. Some symbols used to describe American kinship. Abbreviations of actual kin terms are used, except that Z is used for sister to avoid confusion with S for son.

Kinship diagrams are different from genealogies in that the symbols represent not real people, but categories of kin. As far as I know it was Morgan, in the book mentioned above, who brought the idea of "ego" into the study of kinship. This idea is absolutely essential in kinship studies, for it pins down or freezes all the kinship terms on a diagram such as figure 24 by giving them all a person of reference, an individual (marked E) speaking the terms. That is, any person can have a large number of kin terms applied to himself or herself. A man is simultaneously someone's father and someone else's brother or husband or son. The use of an ego freezes the terms, so that we look at them from the standpoint of one particular person.

Since the turn of the century, then, anthropologists have proceeded in kinship studies by sitting down with an informant and asking him what he calls his mother, his mother's brother, his mother's sister, and so forth, and filling in blank spaces on a kinship schedule such as figure 24. The anthropologist then "interprets" the schedule and compares it with kinship

Plate 30. Lewis Henry Morgan, the founder of kinship studies. Lewis Henry Morgan Papers, University of Rochester Library.

schedules collected for other tribes. An elaborate taxonomy of "types" of kinship then can be prepared. Lewis Henry Morgan had the idea that by collecting enough schedules, one could uncover deep historical relationships among tribes, deeper than could be detected from studying linguistic affinities.[3]

The problem with kinship studies done in this way, however, is that they assume the high importance of *individuals* and of individual relationships with other people rather than recognizing the importance of *groups*. And there are always gaps and loose ends when kinship is done using ego-centered diagrams. For example, in the previous chapter we saw that the term nisson was used by men to refer to their brothers and patrilateral male cousins. There is no separate term for cousin apart from the term that also includes brothers. For that reason, Cheyenne informants have always been puzzled when they were asked to give the term on the kinship schedule for cousin. Sometimes anthropologists have reported that their Cheyenne informants "couldn't remember" the terms, or that they did not have one. But the problem the informant faced was having to give a foolish answer to a foolish question.

When anthropologists leave Indian people free to describe their own kinship systems, they most often do it by reference to groups, not individuals. One of the best examples of this appears in an interview between William Gilbert and a Cherokee man, published by Gilbert in 1937. Following are excerpts from that interview as the man undertook to explain to Gilbert the correct use of kinship terms in Cherokee society.

> My father I call *gidada*. I also say *gidada* when speaking to my father's brothers, and to any member of my father's clan who is a male. When I speak to my father's sister, or to any female belonging to his clan, I say *giloki*. My father and his clan must be respected by me, and I can never joke with them or be on familiar terms with them. . . . My sister I call *ungida*. She calls me *ungida* too, I call any woman of my own clan *ungida*, except those whom I call *gidzi* ("mother") and *gilisi* ("grandmother"). My older brother I call *unkinili*, and my younger brother I call *unkinutsi*. For protection, my sister looks to me, and I look to my older brother. My sister calls her sister *ungilu'i* and does not distinguish older from younger. All the male members of my clan who are older then I am, I call *unkinili*, except those whom I call *gidudji*, and those who are younger than myself I call *unkinutsi*. I am on terms of familiarity with all of them and can play all sorts of tricks on them. In speaking of ourselves my brothers, sisters, and myself call ourselves *otsalinudji*, "we brothers and sisters."

The Cherokee narrative goes on like this for several pages, and it is the complexity of such systems that has discouraged amateur scholars. This ignorance of kinship, however, has seriously flawed the analyses and historical accounts of writers such as Powell and Mails. They report people as "brothers" or father-son or mother-daughter, with blissful ignorance that Native American kin terms are any different from English. But in Cheyenne distant cousins are siblings, uncles are fathers, cousins do not exist, and parents-in-law are grandparents. It is very superficial and misleading to discuss any aspect of Cheyenne family or band life without first noting these profound differences in their kinship system.

In the Cheyenne case, studying kinship has a historical payoff. By an enormous stroke of luck, one of the tribes studied personally by Lewis Henry Morgan was the Cheyennes. One of the first kinship schedules collected anywhere was a Cheyenne schedule. Thus we have the opportunity of studying the changes of Cheyenne kinship through time, through the historical periods in which the tribe was polarized between agnatic and uterine factions, defeated in war, and put on the reservation. And because of the reservation fieldwork of Grinnell and Fred Eggan, we can see changes in kinship right through to modern times.

Changes in Cheyenne kinship in the nineteenth century are directly related to the reorganization of bands and families accomplished by the soldier societies, and so the investment of time to understand the kinship system is certainly worthwhile. In addition. we will discover some exotic and unexpected aspects of Cheyenne kinship in that period, which become understandable in view of their situation. To the general reader, I promise that I will not make the following sections any more complex than necessary to explain the structure of the family and the changes in family structure that occurred as Cheyenne society shifted from uterine to agnatic forms. But before we examine the structure of Cheyenne families, we should look at the history of Cheyenne kinship studies.

History of Cheyenne Kinship Studies

Morgan's trip to Cheyenne country in 1860 was part of his effort to collect large numbers of kinship schedules from around the world.[4] He also mailed out inquiries to missionaries and American embassies throughout the Old World. By comparing collected kinship schedules, Morgan hoped to reconstruct historical and prehistoric relationships between Asia and the Americas, among other things. Unfortunately however, most of Morgan's correspondents and collaborators in the Old World did not understand what they were supposed to do or were confused by the blank schedules they received in the mail. So most of the schedules that were finally published in *Systems of Consanguinity* were from North America. Many of these were collected by Morgan himself in several long trips he made overland and by riverboat, from 1859 to 1862.[5]

The compendium of his results, with the ungainly full title *Systems of Consanguinity and Affinity of the Human Family,* was almost refused publication. No one but Morgan truly understood the significance of his work, and other scholars puzzled over his manuscript for several years before the Smithsonian Institution finally agreed to publish it in 1871.

The form of Morgan's book was one barrier to its publication. He spread the kinship terms used by each tribe over many pages of one-line entries. The Cheyenne terms, for example, appear as line fifty-three on eighty-seven consecutive tabulated pages. Like most modern kinship workers, Morgan proceeded from an ego to all his other categories of kin, 268 categories in all. That is, Morgan apparently sat down with Indian informants and asked them 268 questions, such as, What do you call your father's father's father's sister's daughter's daughter's daughter's daughter? (column 215). One can only imagine the persistence of such a fieldworker and the patience of his informants.

Morgan's informant for Cheyenne kinship was a trader named Tesson and his Cheyenne family.[6] A person of mixed French and Cheyenne ancestry (presumably with a Cheyenne mother), Tesson was raised as a Cheyenne and took a Cheyenne wife. He traded around Bent's Fort and was associated with the council chiefs, or uterine faction. After twenty years as a trader, he took his family to a farm at Rulo, Nebraska, near the Missouri River. It was there that Morgan sought him out as he made a steamboat trip up the Missouri in 1860.

Tesson was probably not the most patient of Morgan's informants. Seventy of the 268 columns are empty for the Cheyennes, indicating, I think, either Tesson's unwillingness to follow Morgan's complex questions or his inability to explain in English what he wanted to say. For example, we have seen in the previous chapter that women use the same term for their female matrilateral cousins as men use for their male patrilateral cousins. Perhaps Tesson despaired of explaining this to Morgan, so the female kin categories were left blank.

The fundamental characteristics of Cheyenne kinship, however, emerge clearly from the schedule produced by Morgan and the Tesson family. Although Morgan did not collect the term *nisis,* the existence of the nisson group is apparent because all of ego's male agnates, male speaking, are called brother. Also, we see that a man calls his brother's children son and daughter, but not his sister's children. A woman calls her sister's children son and daughter, but not her brother's children. That is, Morgan's schedule implies that the members of a nisson group were co-parenting, sharing motherhood or fatherhood with the other members. Morgan and Tesson also showed that the kinship structure was different in some fundamental ways depending on whether a man or a woman was speaking.

In the same year that Morgan was working, 1860, F. V. Hayden was also interviewing Cheyennes to collect information published in 1863 by the

American Philosophical Society.[7] Among the bits of information he collected were some kinship terms, although Hayden did not try to be systematic in this effort. His kinship terms simply appear as entries in his short dictionary. Nevertheless, Hayden's work confirms the accuracy of Morgan's, although Hayden used a different spelling for Cheyenne words. For example, Hayden wrote *nanimshim* for grandfather instead of Morgan's *namashim*.

While Morgan did not manage to collect the term nisis from Tesson, Hayden did record the term, spelling it *nisis*. Rib, the Cheyenne man who was Hayden's major informant, defined the term as "your male cousin." Apparently Hayden did not learn that women also used the term, perhaps because Rib was not himself married to a Cheyenne.

Before Rodolphe Petter began his thorough and serious study of the Cheyenne language about 1891, there were several small attempts to collect word lists, some of which are important for the study of Cheyenne kinship.[8] Perhaps the earliest list was collected by John Smith, a trader; it was never published in its entirety, although it was sent to the Smithsonian.[9] In it Smith gave terms for the nuclear family that are the same as those in later lists.

All the early Cheyenne kin lists vary in their spelling. Perhaps part of the variance was due to the existence of three different dialects of Cheyenne— Northern, Southern, and Sutaio. Additionally, many of the early writers of lists were uneducated men, like John Smith, who did not spell very well but simply did their best to record something like the sounds of the different words. Recognizing cognates among these lists is important for our study of Cheyenne kinship, since we are interested in changes in the use of these terms, their redefinition to suit new social purposes. For example, Morgan listed *Na-vish'-kim* as grandmother and *Na-ri-skim* as mother-in-law, two separate terms. Although I have followed Morgan's use in the following diagrams, I still suspect that these were the same word in 1860, as they were in Petter's day. In a later article I will discuss problems of cognates in Morgan's work in more detail.

The next serious attempt to collect Cheyenne kin terms was made by Albert Gatschet, who first worked with the Cheyennes in 1879. Unfortunately, Gatschet was not familiar with Morgan's published writing and apparently did not have the foggiest notion that the Cheyennes counted kin any differently than he did. He recorded the terms used in the nuclear family and then combined them for all the other terms he collected. Although he had been equipped with an elaborate printed kinship schedule by the Bureau of American Ethnology, he filled it out merely by translating the terms from English to Cheyenne. For example, for "daughter's son's son"

Gatschet wrote *na'htuna heiha heiha,* a literal translation of the question. [10] So Gatschet never learned how the Cheyennes sorted their kin and never understood his task. He made the same mistake in asking questions about birds, and he somehow persuaded his informants to translate into Cheyenne the English names of birds they surely had never seen, including the Carolina parakeet. In kinship, Gatschet collected what anthropologists call "descriptive" kin terms instead of "classificatory" ones.

Lt. Heber Creel, though not a trained ethnographer, did a competent job of collecting information on Cheyenne history, customs, and kinship—including an explanation of the nisis term. He translated his term *ne-sis* as a "general name for brothers and near cousins . . . can be used for both." Creel was a bit less clear on the use of the term by females, however, since he defined *ne-sis, gus-e-a* as "female relative," *ne-sis-ha-eh* as "cousin woman," and *ne-ho-a-he-ah-ki-a-im* as the "general name for sisters and female cousins." Like Gatschet, Creel became confused between descriptive and classificatory terms, and he did not understand that usage was different depending on whether a man or a woman was speaking. [11]

J. N. B. Hewitt, a trained linguist, constructed another small dictionary in 1901 and made some special inquiries into kinship. [12] The terms he collected did not deviate much from previous efforts, and he, like Hayden, was aware that something unique was going on in the use of the term nisis. In one place in his field notes Hewitt apparently thought the term meant cousin, but a later entry says: "nississ—my brother, cousin (gen. term), male or female." Hewitt provided a further clue when he collected the plural for *nississ, nisson,* which he defined as brothers or sisters. male or female speaking. One last bit of information Hewitt did not get: that it was brothers, male speaking, or sisters, female speaking. Two other terms referring to the same-sex cohort, or nisson group, were also collected by Hewitt. He defined *nawohestoto* as "my kindred" and *natowamo* as "my kindred by our children's marriage." We will see in the next section how these terms, and these groups, fit into the complete picture.

More than anyone else, Rodolphe Petter understood the intricacies of Cheyenne kin terms and how they were used. After several decades of speaking Cheyenne every day, Petter probably understood Cheyenne usage at the turn of the century as well as any native speaker. But still he reported some variability in the use of kinship terms, reflecting some previous changes in the system and some additional changes that were going on in reservation times.

We will look at the terms Petter collected in the next section, but I should note here that most of what we know about Cheyenne kinship in late aboriginal and early reservation times comes from Petter. Grinnell, Dorsey, and Mooney collected almost nothing of this sort. Even though he was not a trained ethnographer and in fact had a great deal of contempt for much of Cheyenne culture, especially "heathen" ceremonies, which he regarded as "devil worship," Petter still was a careful linguist. He was especially careful about kinship terms because he knew how important they were for a tribal society such as the Cheyennes, and he wanted the missionaries he trained to be polite and formal in their speech. He was therefore careful to note who was or was not included in various categories of kin. Most of this information is printed in his massive dictionary, and some is in the *Cheyenne Grammar,* passed around as a manuscript among missionaries but not published until after Petter's death. [13]

In 1932 and 1933 two further efforts were made to collect Cheyenne kin terms, one thorough and knowledgeable effort and another on a par with previous limited efforts. The limited effort was by Truman Michelson, who was more interested in other things, and the thorough job was done by Fred Eggan, who single-mindedly set out to get Cheyenne kinship straight and into print. Whereas Michelson mostly confirmed terms previously collected for the nuclear family, Eggan was limited only by his own energy, which was boundless, and by the built-in strictures of his method, which were serious.

Eggan was trained at the University of Chicago by A. R. Radcliffe-Brown, the father of structural functionalism. [14] In this school of thought, kinship terms were explained by the behavior that accompanied their use. That is, practitioners of structural functionalism were urged first to make an elaborate kinship schedule and then to explain what kinds of behavior accompanied the "roles" implied by using the terms. [15] The assumption was made, quite correctly I think, that if you used the same kin term for several people, then your behavior toward them was also very similar, as was their reciprocal behavior to you.

Eggan's field notebooks, which he has been kind enough to lend me, show him as one of the very best practitioners of the method of structural functionalism. But the difficulty in the method is the one mentioned early in this chapter—the informant does not have the opportunity to answer any sort of question at all, only those put by the interviewer. These questions have built-in assumptions about an ego-based system and tend to ignore the importance of groups.

One classic loose end of structural-functionalist kinship schedules is that all of mother's sisters frequently end up being married to "fathers," although the schedule gives no notion of where these "fathers" came from, or to whom they are related. That is, we have people of unknown ancestry in our chart married to mother's sisters, but whom the informants nonetheless clearly identify as "father." In the Cheyenne case, and perhaps in others as well, we know why these people are fathers—it is because they are members of father's nisson, married to mother's nisson. A more efficient picture of the situation is of two groups of people, one male sibling set called "father" married to another called "mother." But structural-functionalist theory makes it difficult to see these relationships because we are forced to look at people as individuals, not as groups.

Another problem of structural functionalism, often mentioned, is that the method forces us to ignore historical developments and contradictions in the kinship system.[16] In fact it is the fieldworker's business, in this method, to resolve such contradictions or lack of fit and to create an internally consistent system. Confronted with a difference of opinion among informants, the fieldworker is supposed to decide who is "correct" and report that case. In orthodox structural-functionalist manner then, Eggan reported "correct" Cheyenne kinship and kin terms in his classic 1937 article. Missing is any notion of conflict or contradiction in Cheyenne society. And missing is the nisis term, and in fact any native term at all for social groupings.

We have already seen the wide range of opinion among Cheyenne informants concerning matters of structure and sociology. Who camped where and what was the nature of the Cheyenne bands were subjects hotly disputed among Cheyenne informants. But in looking at Eggan's kinship schedule, for all its intrinsic worth and good intentions, we get no inkling of conflict or the growth of new ideas about Cheyenne society. I do not mean to fault Eggan personally for his Cheyenne ethnography. In fact, he executed the structural-functionalist method as well as it could be done. The fault is in the method; its results only confirm its assumptions. If you ask no questions that allow an informant to discuss conflict and change, then surely you must ultimately, in your report, describe a social structure with no conflict and no change.

The Dynamics of Cheyenne Bands

In the following paragraphs I will try to describe Cheyenne kinship, as it relates to bands and families, as clearly as I can by reference to three bodies of data. First I rely on modern informants whom I allowed to talk, instead of asking them questions. I particularly wish to acknowledge, once again, my adoptive father Ed Red Hat, his wife Minnie Red Hat, Vinnie Hoffman, Katie Osage, Roy and Kathryn Bull Coming, Clarence Stone Road, Henry Mann, my grandfather John Black Owl, his wife Susie Black Owl, John Greany, Joe Antelope, and Walter R. Hamilton. Some of these were the last

Cheyenne generation born in tipis, and I am glad they paid attention to their elders.

The second body of data I will use here is the kinship schedules collected by the ethnologists mentioned in the previous section. Unlike a structural functionalist, I am not trying to reconcile the differences in the schedules and terms collected over the past 150 years. Instead I am interested in systematic differences, and in why things changed through time. Third, I will analyze census records statistically, trying to confirm various theories, just as I have done in previous chapters.

According to modern informants, residence was much more important than lineage in determining what kin terms were used. In the words of one elder:

> It all depended on whether you were acquainted with them, that is, if they lived in the same bunch with you. If your father had a brother and he was married into the same family, then you called him "father" too. But if he had another brother who married another way, then you called him "uncle" or something else. He wasn't entitled to be called father unless he took care of you. Even if he wasn't related to your father but he was married in, then you still might call him father. The way Cheyennes say it, "If you didn't water the tree, you can't camp in the shade. . . ." If you don't take care of your children, they won't take care of you. It worked the same way on the women's side. If a woman was married in and worked along with your mother, then you called her mother, same way like with the men. [17]

But the kin terms ego uses for other people can change through time, depending on circumstance and the age of ego. In 1983 I heard a man of about fifty-five refer to another man as brother, uncle, and grandfather in the course of the same formal speech. By "brother," he meant that he and the other man had been raised in the same community and had parents who were classified as siblings. By "uncle," he meant that he and the man had married two women related to each other, but of different generations. By using the term "grandfather," he alluded to the man's age and status in the community of traditionalists. [18]

The flexibility of Cheyenne kin terms and family structure, described by modern informants, is confirmed by early censuses. Despite the massacres and epidemics of the nineteenth century, Cheyenne families had been restructured into remarkable conformity by 1880, only four years after the cessation of the wars on the Plains. Despite all the mortalities of the period, adoption and remarriage had formed the nation by 1880 into the configuration shown in table 17. These data were mentioned in chapter 6.

The number of adoptions in the 1880 households can be judged by

Table 17 Frequencies of Family Types in 1880

FREQUENCY	KIN COMPONENTS OF FAMILY
95	Husband-wife-child
25	Husband-wife-sibling-child
24	Wife-child
19	Husband-wife-wife's sibling-child
7	Mother-child-grandchild
7	Man-sibling-parent
5	Man-wife-nephew/niece-child
5	Woman-sibling-child
4	Husband-wife-child-grandchild
4	Husband-wife-sibling-wife's sibling-child
4	Woman-sibling-nephew/niece
15	Husband-wife-child-miscellaneous others
7	Woman-child-miscellaneous others
12	Structure other than parent-child
23	Man-parent-miscellaneous others
6	Woman-parent-miscellaneous others

looking at the relative ages of the categories of kin (table 18). While mothers were listed as being, on average, 25.8 years older than the family head, daughters were listed as being, on average, 30.4 years younger than the family head. Since the ages of older people are customarily exaggerated on censuses, the difference was probably even greater than five years (30.4 − 25.8 = 4.6). In any event, the discrepancy indicates the adoption of young girls by their older aunts and grandmothers. The purpose of such adoptions was to keep some children in every home, and the practice is still maintained by Cheyennes.

Other characteristics of the 1880 census also, I believe, indicate that biological ties were being radically manipulated to suit social needs. The standard deviations and especially the ranges of the stated kin terms indicate a large number of biological impossibilities, even when we translate the terms into Cheyenne usage. Sons, for example, were listed as being as much as sixty-one years younger than ego, and one son was listed as a year older than his father. Daughters ranged from fifty-eight to six years younger than ego. We should bear these anomalies in mind as we look at the ideal models of Cheyenne family structure that follow.

In looking at Cheyenne family structure, then, we should constantly remind ourselves that we are dealing with social categories, not biological

Table 18   Age Differences (Years) between Head of Household and Some Stated Categories of Kin on the 1880 Census

KIN TERM	NUMBER	MEAN	SD	RANGE
Aunt	8	25.6	19.5	1 to 51
Brother	74	−11.4	8.3	−31 to 18
Brother-in-law	24	−17.8	10.7	−38 to 8
Cousin	13	−11.3	7.1	−24 to 2
Daughter	314	−30.4	9.5	−58 to −6
Granddaughter	16	−50.9	14.1	−78 to −37
Grandson	17	−48.4	8.8	−67 to −37
Nephew	16	−20.4	8.5	−36 to −5
Niece	12	−33.5	22.2	−83 to −8
Mother	25	25.8	11.6	6 to 47
Son	361	−29.7	9.1	−61 to 1
Sister	55	−8.2	11.6	−31 to 20
Sister-in-law	24	−14.3	12.5	−33 to 13

ones. The basic nisson units were ad hoc groupings of male agnates or female uterine kin, with a lot of gerrymandering of relationships to arrange marriages and to place orphans, surplus children, widows, and widowers in some kind of standard family structure. This is what we have learned by our analysis of the early censuses.

Ideal Kinship Patterns

To present this analysis properly, I will deviate from the usual kind of ego-centered kin schedule (fig. 24) that I have criticized. I do this not casually, but with the recognition that I am departing significantly from orthodoxy. Still, I feel it is important to break the theoretical bonds imposed by kin schedules, so I will use a notation that emphasizes groups of kin rather than individuals.[19] I will use block diagrams, with lines to separate sexes and generations. Male ego is represented by a triangle within the block, in his proper generation. Female ego is a circle, also in the proper generation. Each space in the block contains the kin term used by ego for that category of kin. Each pigeonhole in each block represents not a particular person, but all persons of that kin category in that band. In the Cheyenne case each category is a nisson, a group of all men or all women who call each other brother, sister, or "nisis."

I hope readers are not misled by my use of English terms for categories of kin. Although the initial U is used for uncle, for example, the reader should understand that a Cheyenne uncle is nothing like an American uncle. But I know from teaching kinship that it is difficult to remember and follow kin terms in an unfamiliar language, so I am using abbreviations from English. I will mention the important terms in Cheyenne; the others can be read in Eggan's article, along with his commentary on behavior.

Figure 25 represents the family band, manhastoz or vestoz, of an ego of either sex as a child. This set of terms is identical with the one derived from Tesson by Morgan in 1860 and is consistent with most of the kin schedules collected later. It represents, I believe, the original terms used by bands of uterine persuasion and is associated with the ordinary cycle of bands described by John Black Owl and other informants. In this kind of band membership ideally continued through the female line, while males were recruited from other bands. In the classic case of the chief's bunch, or manhastoz, the grandfathers of the band were the sons of a chief, and all were born in another band. After they married into the band and became fathers, they recruited the sons of another chief to become their sons-in-law and live in this band. All three generations of older men, then, had been recruited to this band by their fathers-in-law in the same manner. In previous chapters, several historical examples of this kind of succession in a chief's band were given.

Figures 25–27 show the ordinary cycle of events in the life of a band, from the standpoint of a woman. Figure 25 represents the view of a man as well, since the terms used within the band would be the same for both. Boys and girls used the terms OB (*naniha*) for older brothers and OZ (*namhan*) for

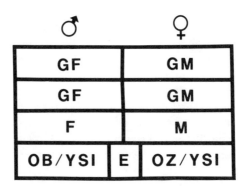

Figure 25.   Terms used by ego of either sex within the natal band. *YSI* is younger sibling.

older sisters, while the term for younger siblings is represented by YSI (*nasima*), and was applied regardless of the sex of the younger child.

Ego called all his or her co-mothers M (*nako*), whether or not they were biological mothers. In the same way, ego called the group of men who married into the band F (*nihoe*), a group comprising his or her biological father and whatever brothers and cousins were part of that same nisson. The previous generation of two intermarried nisson units were called grand-father, GF (*namcem*), and grandmother, GM (*niscehem*), and the same terms were used for the older generations also if they were still living. All the women down the right column, then, were ideally mothers and daughters to each other, though our analysis of the ages of people on the 1880 census shows that cousins and older nieces were often recruited to make a viable nisson unit.

As female ego grew up and prepared to marry in this system, there was opportunity for adjustment of the nisson units represented by her and by her brothers. Perhaps half-sisters, cousins, or nieces would be recruited to make a nisson of the proper size. Three to eight persons would be proper in bands of forty to sixty persons. It was also at this stage in the life of the band that something could go wrong. The band might become too large or too small. Suppose, for example, that band members planned erroneously when they borrowed, exchanged, or sent off children of a particular sex in the manner evidenced by the Bessie and Thomas groups (figs. 22 and 23). Or suppose a chief such as High-Backed Wolf, One Eye, or Black Kettle was very successful in trade and a large body of kinsmen formed around him. Or suppose a large cohort of sisters refused attempts to split them apart and resolved to stay together in the same band. As their own children grew up, the band would become too large to be ecologically viable and should split—fission. Or suppose conversely that many nisson members were killed by war or disease or were simply lacking in fertility. In these latter cases, the group would have to join some other band—fusion.

Problems of relative ages and sexual mixture of children, and of the gross number of children, have caused the fissions, fusions, and reformations we have seen throughout Cheyenne history. If a chief's bunch, manhastoz, did not have enough marriageable girls and the chief could not recruit his wife's nieces, then the band would falter and fail. Or perhaps a young and viable group, of low status or fragmented background, could join a faltering band and prevent its disintegration, as in the case of the Red Moon band. Here the name of the chief's bunch might be carried on, but the biological composition might largely be new people, not of the chief's descent.

Fertility, then, seems to be one of the crucial issues for the formation and reformation of bands. High fertility also helps explain how a chief's bunch, a manhastoz, can be transformed into a manhao, a group of related man-hastoz units, all deriving from a common ancestor or an original nisson unit. If a person, particularly a chief, had a large number of descendants in a relatively short time, he could father an entire manhao, sociologically. That is, he could become the classificatory grandfather of a large number of people. In addition to being "father" to all the children of his classificatory "brothers," he was probably polygynous as well. And though the fertility of women is lower in polygynous marriages than in monogamous ones, the fertility of the polygynous man is greater—he has more children than a man with only one wife.

A look at the Sand Creek genealogies shows the enormous fertility of some of the aboriginal Cheyenne men, especially council chiefs. We should remember, however, that table 19, emphasizes *social* fertility, not neces-sarily biological fertility. [20] Often we do not know the biological parentage of people who claim descent from these apical ancestors, but from the standpoint of tribal law and the tracing of social and political events, biology is irrelevant.

Table 19 Numbers of Descendants Living in 1967, for Certain Sand Creek Victims and Survivors

NAME	BORN	NUMBER OF DESCENDANTS
Dirt Nose	1838	91
Andrew Haag	1861	69
Black Kettle	1801	84
Elk Woman	1842	104
Spanish Woman	1835	55
Tall Woman	1836	57
White Antelope	1789	78
Red Woman	1854	64
Sioux Woman	1807	71
Big Bear	1852	54
Cut Nose	1807	71
Sand Hill	1842	104
Yellow Shirt	1856	67
Lame Bear	1821	70
Sitting Bear	1826	77
Creek Woman	1854	91
Standing Moving	1828	84
Big Owl	1831	65

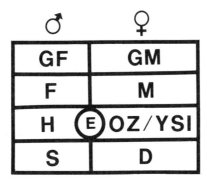

Figure 26. Kin terms used by female ego as mother in her own band.

Returning now to the question of kinship terms used within a band, figure 26 shows the situation after husbands have been recruited for ego and her sisters. Her brothers have all gone to another band to take wives, while ego calls all members of her husband's nisson husband, H (*nahyam*). Her children, and all her sisters' children, she calls son, S (*naa*), or daughter, D (*natona*). Her sisters and all their husbands do the same.

In figure 27, ego is a grandmother in her band. She has lived to see her sons marry out into some other band and her daughters take husbands from outside. She uses a special sexless term for her sons-in-law that I translate as "child-in-law," CL (*nixa*). She uses the same term, CL, for her sons' wives, who live in another band, and men use this CL term in the same way. All her

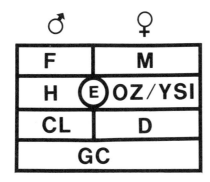

Figure 27. Kin terms used by female ego as grandmother in her own band. *CL* is "child-in-law."

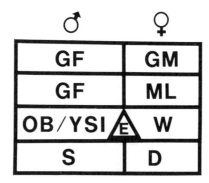

Figure 28.   Terms used by male ego in his band of marriage.

grandsons and granddaughters are referred to by another sexless term, which we translate as grandchild, GC (*nahka*).

From the standpoint of the ideal male ego, the picture of kinship is a little different. Born into his mother's band, he uses the same terms as female ego until he marries. At that point he moves to another band, along with other members of his nisson, whom he calls older brother, younger sibling, or "nisis." In his band of marriage (fig. 28) he calls his wife and the members of her nisson a term we translate as wife, W (*nasim*). He calls his father-in-law the same as his own grandfather, implying an intimate though respectful relationship, but he has a special term for his mother-in-law, instead of calling her grandmother. Because he must especially respect and avoid this woman and her sisters, he calls them a special term that we translate as mother-in-law, ML (*nariskim*). His wife's grandparents he calls GF and GM, and he uses the terms S, D, and GC the same way as his wife does.

The more complicated kin terms are used by ego to refer to people in the band he was born in and moved away from, his natal band. These people are also his wife's in-laws, so she too has kin terms to apply to them. Let us first consider the simplest case, when two bands are successful in exchanging nisson groups, so that the sons of one band are exchanged for the sons of the other band, like the Hotamhetaneos and Moiseyos in chapter 7. In that case, from the standpoint of a child, all your uncles are married to your aunts, simplifying things considerably.

Figure 29 shows the results of this ideal kind of nisson exchange from the standpoint of a man. The terms are the same he used as a child, except that his brothers-in-law, BL (*nitov*), have replaced him and his brothers in the

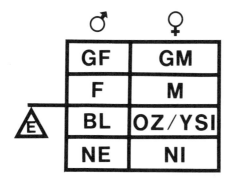

Figure 29. Terms used by absent male ego for his natal band.

band. The children of these marriages are people whom ego calls nephew, NE (*nazenota*), and niece, NI (*neshemis*).

Women, however, had several unique kinship usages for people in their husbands' bands (fig. 30). As might be predicted, they continued to call their departed brothers OB and YSI, as before. But a woman did not use the mother-in-law term for their husband's mother. Instead, she used the term we translate as grandmother. The reason for this is obvious—since a woman did not live in the same band as her mother-in-law, it was not necessary to practice avoidance with either mother-in-law or father-in-law. So this less intense relationship was symbolized by the use of grandparent terms, instead of the special term the husband used for the ML whom he had to avoid and respect daily.

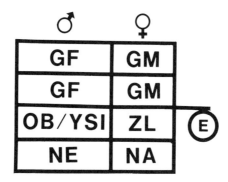

Figure 30. Terms used by female ego for her husband's natal band.

Another special relationship existed between a woman and her brothers' daughters. Instead of calling them nieces, in a manner parallel with men, a woman used a term we translate as namesake, NA (*naun*). For her namesakes a Cheyenne woman beaded a diamond-shaped umbilical charm. This was a reciprocal term, and the older woman was called in turn NA by her brothers' daughters. This is a very unusual feature for any kinship system, but it was collected both by Morgan and by Hayden and is confirmed by modern informants. The term is still used in this way in the context of naming.

I will forgo here an analysis of other kinds of kin terms used for people in other bands. I have not described, for example, the terms used in the band where nephews marry or looked at the children of nieces. But the terms outlined above will give us a solid basis for examining the changes that took place in Cheyenne kinship in the nineteenth century. The reader should remember that the system above is the ideal uterine system, used by those bands that were matrilocal, that maintained themselves by recruiting husbands for their daughters, and that were oriented toward hunting, robe production, and trade. But we will see that many of these features changed dramatically with the rise of the Dog Soldiers during the central portion of the century. By changing the rules of recruitment for spouses, and by disrupting the orderly exchange of children and the formation of nisson groups, the agnatic faction radically transformed the way most Cheyennes counted their kin.

Spouses and Siblings

The basic difference between the agnatic bands and the uterine bands was that while the uterine bands maintained the fiction that each nisson was "all brothers" or "all sisters," the agnatic groups made no such claim. The men of an agnatic band may or may not have been brothers or agnatic cousins biologically, but they were certainly "brothers" in an institutionalized military sense and "friends" in another institutionalized sense. As fellow initiates of a soldier society, men could call each other younger brother, *nisima,* whatever their biological relationship. And if they wanted to formalize a "friendship," there were ceremonies and gift exchanges that institutionalized their nonkin relationship.

The women in an agnatic band were thrown together more by chance than by lineage. They were simply the wives of those men who had joined the militant faction. The force sometimes used against such women to extract them from their natal bands has already been discussed. As a consequence, the women in a band might be relatives or might not—there was no assurance of close relationship, as in the uterine bands. Most of the changes we observe in Cheyenne kinship in the nineteenth century, re-corded by Petter, are traceable to this essential difference—that co-wives are no longer necessarily "sisters" to each other, members of the same nisson.

The most predictable change in kinship in this period was the dropping of the nisis term itself, as a definition of the members of a cohort, and the inauguration of a new term, *naveo,* to mean "co-wife" (fig. 31). In Morgan's day, naveo meant half- or step-sister. In traditional uterine groups it was not necessary for a woman to have a special term for co-wife, since all her co-wives were members of her nisson and called nisis or sister (OZ or YSI). But with the coming of agnatic groups, the term "co-wife" was inaugurated for women and the term nisis was redefined to designate especially first cousins and step- and half-siblings. The previous extension of the term to mean more distant second or third cousins was abandoned, as was the difference in meaning depending on whether male or female was speaking.

Part of this difference may have arisen because the agnatic bands were usually larger than the older uterine bands. Defense required a larger group camped together, as we have seen in previous chapters, and the increased reliance on captured goods made large camps easier to maintain. Within such a camp a woman called her co-wives naveo, and for women with whom she shared one parent or a grandparent, she used the old term nisis.

Kin terms for a woman's in-laws also changed. Now she sometimes used the ML term, since in the new situation a woman might very well be living in the same camp as her mother-in-law. The same held true for her use of a father-in-law term. If he were in the same camp, he was FL (*nanimshim*); if he lived elsewhere, he was GF.

The new situation also required a kin term for sister's husband. In the old

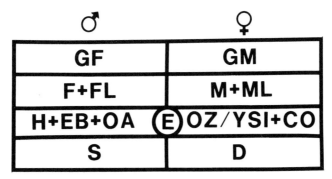

Figure 31. Terms used by female ego in an agnatic band.

uterine scheme, a woman called her sister's husband H, since all her husbands and all her sisters' husbands were the same people. But in the new situation, a sister's husbands were not necessarily the same as her own, and they were not necessarily people her husband called brother. Therefore a new term was brought over from more obscure usage, a term we can translate "opposite-sex affine," OA (*netum*). This term had previously been used by both men and women to mean the spouses of their cousins, as well as half-siblings who lived elsewhere. But now the term also meant "my co-wife's husband," a person who lived in ego's camp but was not her husband.

Two other new terms were necessary to show a woman's relationships to her husband's siblings. Previously, husband's brothers were all husbands, and husband's sisters were all sisters-in-law (married to her brothers), but now some new terms were required. For husband's brother, a term was borrowed that had formerly been used only by men to indicate their brothers-in-law, *nitov*, for which we have already used the abbreviation BL. An entirely new term was inaugurated for husband's sister, which was spelled *naaxaeheme* by Petter and *naaxaehem* by Gatschet and Hewitt.[21] The word is difficult to translate literally, but it means something like "the woman my husband calls sister." We will see in a moment that this term reflects new usage by men also.

Another casualty of the agnatic reorganization was the namesake term, NA. In the agnatic groups, this term was dropped as used by father's sister for brother's daughter and was used only upward in generation, for father's sister. In the new situation an aunt might very well live in the same camp as her brother's daughter and be a functional "mother" to her, thereby undercutting the formality of the previous type of relationship. Paralleling this dropping of the namesake relationship is the redefinition of "older brother" by women. The old term used by women was the same as that used by men, *naniha*, but women in the agnatic bands inaugurated a new term, *natatanem*, which has implications of avoidance. In the uterine system, a woman did not have to avoid her older brother as an adult, since he was in a different camp, but in the agnatic situation, an older brother might very well be living in a nearby lodge and had to be avoided by a respectful sister. This new term I represent in figure 31 as EB rather than OB. Use of this term by sisters also engendered the use of the new reciprocal, *naaxaeheme/naxaehem/naaxaehem*, translated in this case as older sister, male speaking. This is the same term used by a wife referring to her husband's sister.

There are other modifications and changes in the kin system other than these in the nineteenth century, but I am sure the average reader has had enough for one sitting. Generally speaking, the kinship schedules collected by the various fieldworkers describe either the uterine system or the agnatic system, with only Petter understanding that these two sets of terms represented a regular variability between two distinct systems. Without his careful and thorough research, it would be difficult to discern what was going on in Cheyenne kinship in the previous century.

Among modern informants, the uterine system is remembered but not practiced. The agnatic system is regarded by some informants as "wrong" and the product of an unfortunate upbringing. Modern informants also tend to think that the agnatic system is of recent vintage, but Petter's dictionary, together with the fragments from earlier schedules, allows us to put it in a correct historical position. Informants from the Longdale and Seiling areas, however, regard the agnatic system as correct and the uterine system as "Arapaho." However, the early schedules of Morgan and Hayden show that this is an early Cheyenne system, whatever the realities of present tribal politics. It should be clear to the reader by now that "correctness" in kinship, along with correctness in remembering tribal stories and ceremonies, is just another method by which different families, communities, and factions criticize one another and maintain a social distance. While there is frequently difference of opinion among Cheyennes about matters of kinship, it is often hard for an objective observer to discern that any group is more "correct" or more "traditional" than another.

Against this background of conflict and change, then, we can better appreciate the kinship situation faced by Eggan (and Michelson) in the 1930s. By that time there had been an attempt by educated middle-aged persons to simplify the system and bring it more into line with English-language kinship. Michelson's primary informant, Mack Haag, and Eggan's primary informant, Kish Hawkins (plate 31), both represented the educated, intelligent, bilingual group of Cheyennes produced by the boarding-school system at the turn of the century. My own elderly informants, we should note, are one generation younger and of different communities—by which I mean both geographical communities and communities of interest. That is, while I have no doubt that many Cheyenne people behaved in accordance with the kinship schedule collected by Eggan with the assistance of Hawkins in 1933, my informants tell me there were other Indian communities that even then had some very different ideas about proper kin relations.

The schedule collected by Eggan represents fairly closely the kin system used today by most middle-aged Cheyennes. Much has been simplified from the original uterine system, and many terms symbolizing obsolete practices have been lost. Mainly, differences between male and female speaking have been simplified, so that among younger people both sexes use the same terms. Most of the other changes have been caused by the different

Plate 31. Kish Hawkins, Fred Eggan's primary informant for kinship. Photo no. 132 in the Shuck Collection, Western History Collections, University of Oklahoma Library.

manner of marriage recruitment used by Cheyenne extended families in modern times.

Nowadays a person might live with almost any combination of parents, siblings of parents, and grandparents. Reflecting this, a modern Cheyenne child calls all his parents' siblings who are familiar to the household "mother" and "father." As always, it is residence, not lineage that determines the use of these terms, but a child's co-parents might equally be matrilateral or partrilateral in modern times. Extended families currently are organized bilaterally, and the component nuclear families show a great deal of mobility from one extended family to another.

Modern Cheyenne children call brother and sister all those siblings, half-siblings, and cousins of all descriptions who are resident in the extended family household or neighborhood. Cousins, siblings, and half-siblings who live elsewhere are called nisis in Cheyenne and cousin in English.

One remaining question about Cheyenne kinship needs to be answered before we conclude this chapter. I will ask it by reference to Eggan's field notes, but it could just as easily be asked by someone reading my own field notes or listening to the tape recordings I have made with informants. In Eggan's notes there is continual contradiction among informants about kin usage and the correctness of kin terms, and there are fragmented attempts by informants to explain "something big" about kinship, something transcendent and more profound than the simple kin terms Eggan was recording. On one page, in response to some pleading by Kish Hawkins, Eggan wrote "nisis" and underlined it twice, followed by "covers all relatives way way back." On nearby pages, he recorded "nisis" for Kish Hawkins's sisters, and "nisis" again for some brothers and parallel cousins. Two sisters are also noted as naxa'em. But in his published study of Cheyenne kinship the word nisis never appeared, either in the plural form "nisson" as the name for a group, or as an individual kin term. Neither did the term naxa'em appear, the agnatic term used by a brother for the sister he must avoid, and used by the agnatic wife for her husband's sister. Eggan also reported no terms for groups of people, although modern informants report that, in the uterine system, a man used nawohestoto for his natal band, and both men and women used natovamo for the band into which their sons married.

Despite the fact that Eggan talked to only five informants, his notebooks show continual disagreement, contradiction, and variation in the kin terms given him. But in the best structural-functionalist fashion, Eggan settled on a "normal" kin schedule from this body of conflicting data and reported "normal" reciprocal behavior between various categories of kin. But the fault in Eggan's work, if it can be called that, is not poor scholarship or lack of thoroughness. On the contrary, Eggan presented the first logical, scientific treatment of Cheyenne kinship—still the definitive study. The fault lies in the theoretical assumptions of structural functionalism and in the functionalist methodology. After assuming that social structures are in harmony, the structural functionalist cannot see disharmony, contradiction, and the workings of history. Equipped with a kinship schedule and an interview technique, the structural functionalist cannot see groups, the redefinitions of groups, and radical transformations through time. Like other structural functionalists, Eggan was a creature of his assumptions, his values, and his period in the history of American anthropology. But so am I. And so are we all creatures of our historical period.

10

Conclusion

In this concluding chapter I wish to summarize and elaborate on three issues that have been raised repeatedly in the previous chapters. First, I shall describe the evolution of Cheyenne society as elegantly as I can, emphasizing the origins of the Cheyenne nation. Second, I shall discuss the issues of "nation" and "tribe" raised in chapter 1 in light of what we have now learned from the Cheyenne illustration. And last, I shall emphasize the continuity of the Cheyenne nation into modern times by reference to some new data on the tribal circle that I will introduce here.

We must understand that, like every nation in the world, the Cheyennes have cosmopolitan origins. Beginning as three nation-villages kept apart by ecological forces, they had separate histories in their migrations from the Great Lakes and Upper Mississippi, across the Middle Missouri, until they came to rest in the Black Hills. Along the way, each of the proto-Cheyenne bands had its own experiences, both with other nations and with some contrasting geographical situations.

The Cheyennes proper, the Tsistsistas or Chienaton band, split about 1700 into two groups as a consequence of their relations with the Teton Sioux. The group that became known as the Sheos and later the Masikotas was hybridized both biologically and culturally with the Oglalas. The hybridization left its mark on the Masikotas and on the Oglalas as well. Ultimately, part of this hybrid Cheyenne-Sioux group rejoined the Cheyennes proper as a band, after a dispute with the Oglalas.

Meanwhile the Cheyennes proper had come to rest in the Black Hills, after occupying a series of palisaded horticultural villages from Minnesota to South Dakota. In the Black Hills they began to collect large herds of horses and also adopted or readopted a pattern of casual horticulture, abandoning their home villages in the summer and returning in the fall to harvest their gardens and to winter in the Black Hills. As Cheyenne horse herds and pasture requirements became larger, wintering in the northern plains became an increasing problem.

From oral history and from archeology, it is not clear when the Omisis band was horticultural. The original locations of the "Oudebaton" villages in the Great Lakes area imply farming. and perhaps some of the archeological sites between Minnesota and South Dakota were Omisis sites. But by the time of Lewis and Clark the various "Eater" bands had adopted a pattern of dispersing for the winter in areas west of the Black Hills where horticulture could not have been practiced.

The Sutaio band, the last of the original proto-Cheyenne villages to arrive from the Great Lakes, was evidently always a smaller group. Whereas the Omisis and Cheyenne bands had acquired sizable herds of horses by about 1740, the Sutaios were horse poor. With the arrival of the Sutaios, the stage was set for the founding of the Cheyenne nation. By the mid-eighteenth century there were, in the vicinity of the Black Hills, four proto-Cheyenne bands speaking dialects of the same language. All of them had problems, the most important being lack of numbers, limited access to trade, and poverty in horses compared with the southern tribes.

The prophet called Sweet Medicine brought the charter for solving all these problems. He was a real person and a political genius. He created a multidimensional charter for the Cheyenne nation by initiating or legitimating the central institutions of the new nation. He forbade warfare among the bands by defining interband killing as murder and requiring exile for Cheyenne murderers and the ritual cleansing of the sacred arrows. He defined the relations of the military societies to the national collectivity, defined the residence bands as "sacred," placed the manhao in the tribal circle, and created a new kind of political and judicial institution, the Council of Forty-four. He made a rule that war chiefs had to resign from their military societies to be peace chiefs.

Sweet Medicine also brought a charter for military expansion in the form of the "man arrows" that would kill their enemies if and only if all the bands united behind the arrow keeper when the arrows were "moved" against an enemy. He set Cheyennes on a nomadic style of life by giving them two "buffalo arrows" and declaring that buffaloes were intended for the exclusive use of the Cheyenne people.

In the first years of its existence, the Cheyenne nation lived between the forks of the Platte and fought against surrounding tribes in alliance with the Arapahos, whom they allowed to place a pipe among their sacred arrows.[1] After the intrusion of white trappers and prospectors on the Platte about 1828–38, and with the founding of Bent's Fort on the Arkansas, the Southern Cheyenne bands gradually moved south, the Heviksnipahis being the last to abandon beaver trapping and migrate, under the impetus of a "beaver taboo." The Omisis and Totoimana bands remained north of the Platte and increasingly allied themselves with the Teton Sioux.

In this period the power of the council chiefs steadily increased, as they took a central role as agents of trade between the bands and the white traders. Intense warfare against the southern tribes—the Kiowas, Comanches, and Apaches—also was typical of this period as all the Cheyenne bands joined in a movement of the arrows against the Kiowas in 1838. The war ended indecisively in 1840, as the five tribes of the central and southern plains united against a new invading nation, the United States of America.

Cheyenne society became polarized after 1840 when the militant "Dog Soldiers" formed separate bands and invaded eastward into the land left vacant by the emigrating Pawnees, Delawares, Shawnees, and Osages. With the Arkansas River trade preempted by the council chiefs, the Dog Soldiers sought to trade on the Platte. Soon they confronted the encroaching Kansas frontier and allied themselves with the Oglalas, whose ranks also included important groups of militants.

While the traditional uterine bands continued to trade and hunt between the upper Platte and the Arkansas, the Dog Soldiers increasingly relied on raiding after 1855. Retaliation for the raids fell on the peace faction, at Sand Creek and at the Battle of the Washita. Ultimately the Dog Soldiers began to regard themselves as a separate nation, sponsoring their own ceremonies and heaping derision on the council chiefs. For their part the uterine faction at last became so exasperated that they offered to join the United States Army in attacks against the Dog Soldiers. This tendency toward national fission was arrested by the defeat on the Dog Soldiers in 1869 and their assignment to the same Oklahoma reservation as the peace faction.

The northern bands maintained their free existence longer than the southern bands. Together with the combined Teton Sioux, the Northern Cheyennes defeated Custer at the Little Big Horn. Defeated, dispersed, and finally moved to Oklahoma in 1877, some escaped and were brutally massacred at Fort Robinson. Outraged at reports of the massacre, the American public pressed for the creation of a separate reservation in Montana for the Northern Cheyennes, thereby formally setting apart the northern bands as a separate nation. The Cheyennes themselves did not consider the split legal until a council was held in 1895. But many southern Cheyennes joined the northerners in Montana in 1884, intermarriage has always been substantial, and the northerners still do not hold their own ceremonies until the Arrow Renewal has been completed in Oklahoma, implying the continued existence of a single Cheyenne nation.

The Cheyennes were never a homogeneous body. Of the original four bands, the Tsistsistas and the Omisis always spoke distinct dialects of Cheyenne, and they still do. There is still not enough intermarriage in modern times to extinguish the differences. The Sutaio dialect, which was allegedly more different than the other two, now seems to be extinct. The Masikota and Dog Soldier groups, which contained a large number of Sioux speakers, converged with standard Cheyenne speakers in reservation times and have gradually become Anglicized along with the rest of the Southern Cheyennes.

Although the council chiefs became increasingly influential in the early nineteenth century, the military headsmen of course never disappeared. At the peak of their influence, the council chiefs proliferated into new bands that gathered around Bent's Fort. But when trade faltered, white emigrants invaded the river valleys, and genocidal warfare threatened, the military headsmen again rose to prominence.

Polarizing the nation around political issues, the "Dog Soldiers" also created a constellation of new and contrastive cultural and social features. Eschewing trade, they embraced raiding; caring little for the productive role of women in the robe trade, they redefined families, bands, and kinship, with the consequences we have seen in chapters 8 and 9.

Throughout this book I have painted a picture of the emergence of the Cheyenne nation from three original villages and four original bands. I have shown the forces that held the nation together—trade, warfare, the ceremonies, the chiefs, the sacred traditions—while other forces tore it apart—the autonomy of bands, the necessity for seasonal dispersal, the militancy of the agnatic faction, and changes in trade patterns. But the question remains whether the Cheyennes were typical of Plains Indian nations in the eighteen and nineteenth centuries or whether they were exceptional. This is a very old issue in Plains ethnology, but it has never been answered satisfactorily.[2] Superficially, there seem to be important differences, say, in the general political structure of the Comanches as compared with the Cheyennes. But many of the contrasts described for Plains societies have been based on the most superficial of analyses, usually from secondary sources.

To make proper comparisons among Plains tribes, I maintain that field workers must make the same kind of inquiries about other tribes as I have made about the Cheyennes. And I would not recommend the job to anyone with less than a decade to devote to it. We need ecological data from other areas of the Plains, the parts inhabited by the Comanches, Assiniboines, and Blackfeet. We need thorough examinations of early maps and travelers' reports by researchers familiar with languages spoken in the area. And last, we need field researchers who will examine the veracity of oral history by reference to early documents. In raising these issues here, I am challenging both the extent of specialization and the superficiality that have characterized much recent Plains scholarship. In history, for example, we have people so specialized they can do nothing but examine Spanish maps from a particular period or locale. In archeology we have specialists in some state, river basin, or even county who know little about other areas. We have ethnologists who have spent years in the company of Indians but who seldom walk in the library or talk to other ethnologists. But with the increasing availability of maps, documents, and archival deposits on microfilm, there is less and less excuse for any scholar to fail to read broadly or study written materials from early times. In fact, we can look forward to a great fruition in Indian studies, for this very reason.

I must admit, however, that I do not understand at all the failure of some anthropologists and historians to do fieldwork. I am constantly amazed to see people at scholarly meetings who are willing to discuss the mind-set of some Native American group at great length but who have seldom or never talked to an Indian. I even know famous scholars who pale and run from the opportunity of meeting Indian people who might enlighten them about some point of ethnology. Perhaps it is fear of the cross-cultural experience or of making some faux pas. Perhaps it is fear that they might be wrong about something, or fear that articles they have published might be considered insulting by Indian people. If that is the case, I would suspect the research was on the wrong track from the beginning. But if it is merely a matter of embarrassment, I must subscribe to a statement by my friend David Maybury-Lewis: "Anyone afraid of humiliation simply cannot be a good fieldworker." And I must make a final point here—that any historian or ethnohistorian who raises issues that are within the experience of modern informants simply *cannot* be excused from the necessity of doing fieldwork.

I am glad to report that there is much good research going on at present by people who are interested in the feedback among fieldwork, published sources, and archival manuscripts. These are people who are truly in the holistic tradition of such anthropologists as Mooney, Grinnell, and Michelson. At the University of Oklahoma, where informants are only an hour away from the library, there are Greg Campbell, Dan Swan, and Richard Sattler, investigating the Northern Cheyennes, the Osages, and the Seminoles, respectively. They are interested in the fit between published ethnography, modern practice, and early documents. At the Newberry Library, Fred Hoxie is interested in the Crows and David Miller in the Assiniboines. Though Fred Hoxie is a historian, not an ethnologist, he recognizes the value of narratives collected from modern informants. And at the University of New Mexico, Tom Kavanagh is presently capping off ten years of research with the Comanches in which he addresses many of the same questions I have raised in this book.

I believe that any kind of comparative questions we might like to ask about the politics, band structure, or ecology of Plains societies are best left for the completion of the research mentioned above. I think there will be some real surprises when the data are in and careful comparisons are made. Melburn Thurman is already comparing band structures from early reservation times and believes there is a certain normal band size, about forty-five people, that might characterize the entire Plains from Mexico to the Arctic. If this theory is correct, then many of the radical cultural differences that have been alleged to exist among the Plains tribes will assume a rather minor significance. I would not be surprised to see the idea of "culture area" criticized and abandoned for the Plains and prairies. Also, I doubt that our "standard brands" of "tribes" will continue to have the same significance much longer. "Bands" rather than "tribes" might become the central focus. But to explain what I mean by this, let me return to some of the theoretical issues raised in the first chapter.

Bands and Nations

Concerning the idea of "tribal nation" that I advocated in chapter 1, we have now seen what one such nation, the Cheyennes, looks like from the inside. In this case the tribal nation was a political alliance among bands, reinforced by the highest religious principles and beliefs. The bands within the tribal nation showed their status as member bands by their adherence to tribal institutions and their attendance at the national ceremonies. Each member band was assigned a place in the tribal circle. I must continue to emphasize the importance of the Sun Dance as emblematic of national identity. Not only the Cheyennes, but all the tribal nations of the Plains symbolized the physical extent of their nations by assigning bands particular places in the tribal circle. But what are these "bands" that continue to hold our attention in the history and politics of the Plains?

I agree with Helen Tanner that it was bands, not tribes, that were the most significant units of social and political structure on the Plains, and perhaps in the Great Lakes area as well.[3] The bands were the functioning economic and domestic units; these were people who knew each other personally, were related to one another, and shared each other's good fortune and hardship. But what was a band on the Plains? Was it a subtribe, an ethnic unit, or something else?

In the first place, bands were emphatically multiethnic and multilingual. In addition to traders' and travelers' observations about this, the United States census of 1900 shows thousands of "interethnic" marriages among Indians in the early nineteenth century. From our examination of Cheyenne bands, we know why there was so much intermarriage. In the first place, any young person was usually related to all or most of the eligible spouses in the home band, because they were all children of intermarried nisson groups. Avoidance of incest therefore dictated marriage in another band. But why marry into a "foreign" band, rather than into a band that was ethnically similar?

From the Cheyenne case, we know that increased access to trade and beneficial military alliances were acquired by marrying into a foreign band. The Cheyennes did this not only with the Kiowas, the Sioux, the Mandans, the Arikaras, and perhaps the Comanches, but continually with Anglo and Mexican traders into the nineteenth century. It is this constant mixing or hybridization of bands that makes Plains ethnohistory so confusing and so interesting. We can understand the general ideal pattern of hybridization by reference to figure 32.

It may or may not be that other Plains societies arranged marriages by nisson groups as the Cheyennes did. It has been difficult enough for me to find evidence for the Cheyenne example. But in any event let us assume for the moment that when marriages were arranged between two bands of different language or ethnicity there was not one marriage, but several. Let us assume that a group of spouses went from each band to the other. What are the consequences of these marriages for the bands and for the nations of which they are members?

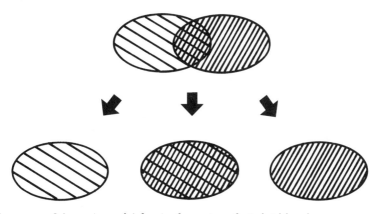

Figure 32. Schematic model for the formation of a hybrid band.

For the first several years there would be few significant consequences, but as time went on there would be an increasing number of bilingual children. If the pattern of exchanging spouses continued for several generations, as it did for the Masikotas and Dog Soldiers, the band or bands would be truly hybrid and equally capable of assuming a place in either of the parent nations. This binational characteristic of bands helps account for the bewildering multiplicity of band names appearing on the maps examined by such scholars as Tanner. It also accounts for divergent early figures for "total population," especially in the years before the Sioux began sorting themselves into discrete nations of the Great Sioux Alliance.

This then is the political consequence of the large-scale marriage of sibling cohorts between nations. The band becomes truly chameleonlike, capable of joining more than one political entity. In the case of the "Kiowa Apaches," for example, an Apache band joined the Kiowa nation that was completely unlike the other bands in its language and "ethnicity." But it was political, military, and trade benefits that held the Kiowas and Apaches together, not their shared language, ethnicity, or culture—for indeed they had little.

As long as the tribal nation is in existence, however, there are strong forces toward cultural integration. A national language and a national religion have compelling attraction for member bands. Proximity and happenstance make for more marriages within the nation than outside it, provided the nation is large enough. Associations such as the Cheyenne military societies also become national in scope, although we have seen an international society of Fox Soldiers among the Cheyennes and Brulé Sioux, and comrades to the Cheyenne Dog Soldiers among the Oglalas.

In the nineteenth century, bands within the Cheyenne nation were often multiethnic, torn between the loyalties of nationhood and the beneficial consequences of alliances with foreigners. The Wotapios, for example, longtime allies and trading partners of the Kiowas, were nevertheless forced by their tribal nation to attack the Kiowas in 1838. One can only imagine the sentiments of the Wotapio chief Black Kettle as he joined the camp of the Cheyenne nation to make war against his old friends. Not to mention the feelings of One Eye, also torn by conflicting loyalties as he promised Governor Evans that his bands too would join in the fight against their relatives the Dog Soldiers. But if people wish to enjoy the benefits of national citizenship, they must pay the price. In experiencing conflicts of loyalty, tribal nations are no different from any other kind of multiethnic nation-state that seeks to make war as a collectivity.

Having looked at the evidence for the founding of the Cheyenne nation, we can now examine Fried's questions about national origins with more clarity. We should remember that Fried—following Steward and along with Service, Sahlins, and others—has said that the proximity of a civilization, a stratified state-led society, is the necessary element for the creation of "tribes"—what I have called "tribal nations." Already we can suspect, however, that this theory is too vague to be tested, and if we can test it at all by reference to the Cheyennes, it is proved false.

At the time it was founded, in about 1740 in the Black Hills, the Cheyenne nation was five hundred miles from the nearest French or British military post, Fort Mackinaw, and three hundred miles from the Mexican border. When the nation was chartered the Cheyennes had never seen a soldier from any European country, and this happened not at the high point in the fur trade, but during a great hiatus. In what sense, then, can one say it was the proximity of nation-states that caused this tribal nation to be founded?

Certainly it is true that the European fur trade caused the massive movements west around the Great Lakes that we examined in chapter 3. But were such mass movements not also typical of the prehistoric period? If not, how did the various linguistic groups of North America get so widely dispersed? Siouan-speaking peoples were spread from the Carolinas (the Catawbas) to the Great Lakes prehistorically, and the Athabaskans and Algonquian speakers were dispersed over equally large portions of the continent. Do these huge displacements not imply prehistoric mass movements that at least equaled if not surpassed the displacements caused by the Europeans?

Nor was transcontinental trade invented by the Europeans. Yellowstone obsidian, bow wood from the Ozarks, mica from the Appalachians, and native copper from the Great Lakes were traded for hundreds of years all across North America. My point, of course, is that the conditions faced by the Cheyennes—displacement from a homeland and the necessity for trade—were neither unprecedented in North America nor unique to the eighteenth century. They were merely part of a periodic historical situation in North America, as everywhere, in which people make radical responses to ecological changes, new technological opportunities, or the unwelcome rise to prominence of a neighboring and aggressive tribal nation.

The Cheyennes' response was also typical for North America and completely unrelated to the presence of Europeans. They might just as well have been responding to the incursions of the Iroquois or the Muskogees, and the trading opportunity might just as well have been wild rice or native copper as horses and beaver skins. The response was that the Cheyennes chartered a new nation from among four local bands that had some common history and that shared linguistic and cultural traits. The nation was chartered for particular purposes—military, political, and religious—and proceeded to act on its charter over the next three hundred years. As nations go, the Cheyenne nation has lasted a very long time. It is older than the United States of America, which is one of the more venerable of the world's nation-states.

So the challenge I present to Fried's theory is the case history of a tribal nation whose genesis is well documented and clear to see. It shows a group of Native Americans who rationally and intelligently, and without any guidance from a "superior" society, constructed among themselves the entire fabric of a nation. They defined citizenship, a national religion, and a national language, forbade warfare among the member bands, and made war against national enemies as a disciplined, collective entity. They had a body of law to bind their citizens. Whatever its later problems, the Cheyenne nation clearly crystallized in history long before its members were buffeted by a nation-state.

Fried might salvage his theory, I suppose, by stating that the founding of the Cheyenne nation was the result of an indirect "ripple effect" that stretched to the Cheyennes from the Dakota Alliance, from the Chippewas and Iroquois and all the way back from the East Coast of North America. But that is not much of a theory. In its extreme form it suggests that as soon as any nation-state appears anywhere in the world, tribes might form anywhere else where there was indirect contact. Even before the coming of the Europeans, one might argue that the tribal nations of North America were the results of "rippling" from the Aztec empire, a thousand miles away.

Also, what form does this "influence" take as it allegedly causes a tribal nation to form? Is it in the form of direct trade for commodities manufactured by some civilized nation? Or is this influence only in the form of invasion by a "civilized" nation-state? In the absence of confrontation and trade, then, shall we find no tribes? If we want to test this theory, where shall we find an example of a society not linked even indirectly to any civilized nation or using commodities produced in such a nation? Once again, Fried is in the position of the little boy who wants to know about the refrigerator light. The theory is perfectly safe because it cannot be tested by finding any society pristine enough to test it. The theory then has no more status than the other just-so stories invented by all varieties of evolutionary theorists since John Lubbock.[4]

The actual case of the Cheyennes, however, does teach us something, at a theoretical level, about the consequences of nation building. First of all, we see that the component bands, having created a nation, are themselves transformed in the process. Bands do not merely create a representation of themselves at a higher level; instead, they create a social species of a different order entirely. A tribal nation is not merely a group of bands, nor is a band merely a subdivision of a tribal nation. Bands and nation exist at two entirely different levels of reality. As Bernhard Stern put it, "Every level of organization . . . has its own regularities and principles not reducible to those appropriate to lower levels." Julian Steward added that lower levels "gradually become modified as specialized, dependent parts of new kinds of total configurations."[5]

Cheyenne bands were domestic, productive units comprising people related to one another by blood or marriage. Their size was determined by their ecology and by the necessity for cooperative labor among themselves. The Cheyenne band was flexible, allowing for seasonal variations in size, so that animals could be hunted and plants gathered with greatest efficiency. Horses and pasture also determined the size of the bands in different locations and at different seasons.

By contrast, the Cheyenne nation was predicated on political, not ecological, arrangements. Ecologically it was awkward. It was not a productive or domestic unit but had extranational purposes in its structure and behavior. This was the unit that made war, made peace, and ensured that interband hostilities did not get out of control. To perform its international functions, the nation maintained ceremonies, laws, and customs that bound the people together. Since there was no bond of biological kinship, more explicitly ideological means had to be used.

The founding of a nation also has consequences for the member bands. That is, the bands of a nation are different from bands that are autonomous. For one thing, the bands are relieved of the necessity of maintaining ceremonies and sacred symbols, such as the Cheyenne rainbow tipi or buffalo hat. In a nation these symbols are a national responsibility, and the band is secularized. Also, the band gains by receiving the counsel of other bands in determining their relative seasonal movements. Cheyenne history is full of episodes in which bands inform one another of their locations and their success in finding game.

I also argue that membership in a nation gives the bands more ecological flexibility. Defended militarily at the national level, the bands are free to split seasonally into smaller units, with the option of linking up with other bands as necessity dictates. Although an autonomous band might fear to split into fragments lest they be unable to find one another later, the bands of a dispersed nation, living in a shared national territory, can split with more certainty about their safety.

So it is not accurate to speak of a "tribal" level of social integration in which all the attributes of bandhood are abandoned for the advantages of a qualitatively new "nationhood." Nor is it accurate to see nationhood as a level of organization simply tacked on to the activities of bands, while they continue as before. It is more correct to see nationhood as adding certain dimensions to the inventory of social and political behavior while modifying band life in the process.

The Modern Cheyenne Nation

From late aboriginal times to the present, the population of Cheyennes has more than tripled. Like other Native Americans placed on reservations, the Cheyennes at first diminished in numbers because of poor diet and lack of medical care, but the population rebounded after 1930.[6] In 1877, the year of the first thorough census, there were 3,298 Cheyennes in Indian Territory, a figure that does not include the Cheyennes at Pine Ridge and Rosebud (see fig. 15). In 1892, after the establishment of the Northern Cheyenne reservation in Montana, there were 2,119 Southern Cheyennes and 916 Northern Cheyennes, a proportion of 30/70 between these two groups. In the same year, 1,091 Southern Arapahos were being administered with the Southern Cheyennes, a proportion of 34/66 between the Southern Cheyennes and Southern Arapahos.

After 1924 it was legally possible for Cheyennes to live elsewhere, beyond the administrative control of the Bureau of Indian Affairs, and so it becomes more difficult to count total numbers. Only when there has been some unusual benefit to be derived have out-of-state Cheyennes bothered to enroll themselves and their children. For example, in 1968 money was distributed from a claim settled by the Indian Claims Commission, and so the total number of enrolled Southern Cheyennes and Arapahos (no longer counted separately) rose to 6,674. In 1985, in preparation for another distribution of money, the total tribal enrollment for Southern Cheyennes and Arapahos stood at 8,681. The 1985 total for Northern Cheyennes was 5,042. Dividing the 1985 total of Southern Cheyenne and Southern Arapaho population by the same proportion as in early reservation days, 34/66, we get a total Southern Cheyenne population of 5,729, to make a grand total of 10,771 for Northern and Southern Cheyennes in 1985.

Figure 33 shows trends among Cheyenne and Arapaho populations since reservation life began, based on official government figures. These figures, however, have serious distortions. The first distortion is exhibited in the inflated figures of the mid-1880s. There are two versions of why the figures are inflated. The Indian agent's version was that Indian people were borrowing children among families to increase family rations, so that some children were counted more than once. The Indian version, carried on through

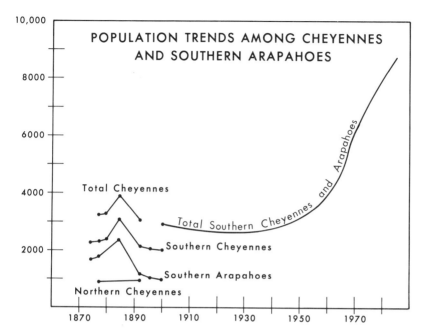

Figure 33. Total population figures for Cheyennes and Southern Arapahos in the historical period.

oral history, is that Agent John Miles built up his own herd by taking cattle intended for nonexistent Indians.[7]

The curve representing total Southern Cheyennes and Arapahos has several sources of distortion. As already mentioned, migration out of the original reservation area to major cities after 1924 caused an undercounting for enrollment, and both before and after 1924 there has been migration to other reservations. Some Southern Arapahos, for example, joined the Northern Arapahos at the Wind River Reservation in Montana in 1891 rather than submit to allotment in severalty in Oklahoma. For this reason the Arapaho population curve dips rather dramatically in the 1890s, more than that for the Cheyennes. Since allotment, however, there has been less opportunity to move, both for Cheyennes and for Arapahos, although marriage between northern and southern individuals has allowed their children to select either group for their place of enrollment.

The greatest puzzle about Cheyenne population is why we currently calculate approximately the same number of Northern as Southern Cheyennes, although the ratio of their populations in 1892 was 30/70. There are at least three possible solutions: either the Northern Cheyennes have been more fertile in the intervening period, there has been migration from south to north, or many more southerners than northerners have left the reservation area so that their descendants are perhaps enrolled with some other tribe or not enrolled at all. A great deal more work with tribal and United States censuses is required to solve this puzzle.

Map 26 shows the geographical distribution of those Southern Cheyennes and Arapahos now living in the original area of their reservation. For a base map, I have used one devised for the mobilization and assignment of Community Health Representatives in 1968. I have adjusted this map for population movements since that time, using samples (not the whole population) taken from the 1975 and 1985 improvements of total enrollment. The number of Cheyennes and Arapahos now residing in the eight-county area, according to 1985 zip codes, is roughly half the total enrollment, about 4,200 people. Of the communities listed, the Arapaho population is largely in Geary, Watonga, and Canton and in the rural (shaded) areas between. The other communities are predominantly Cheyenne—some ex-

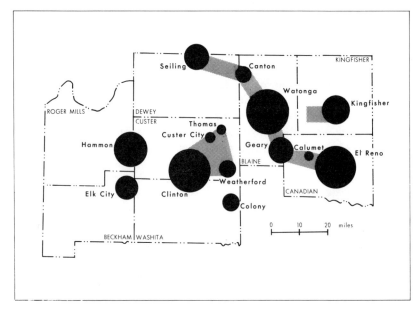

Map 26. Approximate distribution of Cheyenne and Arapaho population in recent years.

clusively so. The populations of the communities are indicated by the size of the circles.

Since coming to their Oklahoma reservation, many Cheyennes have married Arapahos or members of other Oklahoma tribes. Also, there has been a steady acculturation of Cheyennes into the ideas and mores of the dominant society, as well as a steady drain of population into urban centers, especially Oklahoma City, Dallas, and Los Angeles. Ironically however, there are probably as many core traditionalists now as there have ever been, because of the increased total population. For just as every generation sees the absorption of certain individuals and families into a non-Cheyenne way of life, every new generation of the traditionalist community is larger than the previous one. That is, the fertility of the remaining traditionalist families helps compensate for the attrition of the marginal groups, so that the total number of core traditionalists remains about the same.

Traditionalists still maintain extended families as residence groups, either in rural hamlets or in contiguous houses in the small towns of western Oklahoma. In the towns, an extended family will occupy two or more houses in the same block, facing each other across the street or back to back facing different streets. Federally subsidized housing has given Cheyennes some choice over where they live, and one of the eternal struggles with the housing office is trying to get federal regulations to conform to the actual configuration of the extended family. The regulations do not explicitly allow related families to choose adjoining houses, and there is much trading around and rescheduling of grants so that a traditionalist extended family can live in the same block.

In rural areas, extended families tend to locate on a parcel of original trust land. Typically the houses, some of them built under "self-help" and similar federal programs, face each other around an open area that is crisscrossed with pathways and driveways from one house to another. I estimate that there are about forty such hamlets still in existence, among the original allotments of the agnatic group, in the northern tier of map 16, and twenty more scattered about in other places in Southern Cheyenne country. These groups are usually referred to in English as families or bunches. Only very elderly people would use the terms vestoz and manhastoz in Cheyenne to refer to these groups.

Map 27 shows an extended family hamlet in Blaine County, Oklahoma. In summer 1984, thirty-six people lived in this hamlet. The superimposed genealogy on the map shows the kin relationships among the people living in the various houses. This particular hamlet has existed continuously since 1892, although some houses have been abandoned as they fell into disrepair. In addition to the unoccupied house shown on the map, two other

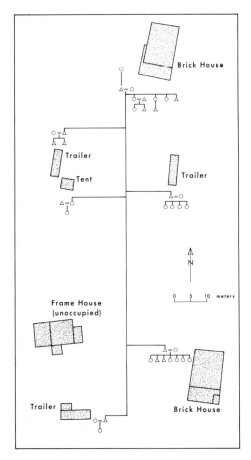

Map 27. Hamlet of a modern Cheyenne extended family.

even older unoccupied houses are situated to the east of the houses shown, off the map. I am indebted to Reza Ahmadi-Siahpoosh and Pat Gilman for collecting this information.

The core activity for traditional families, for over a hundred years, has been the encampment for annual ceremonies, usually in June. The senior members of each extended family nowadays set up a camp of tents and tipis within the tribal circle, where they are visited by other members of the family for several days at a time. The senior people usually stay the entire two weeks of the encampment. Traditionalists call the families who maintain an annual camp the "strong families." There are perhaps eighty to one hundred strong Southern Cheyenne families, comprising perhaps three or four thousand people. The traditionalists like to think that during these two weeks every summer, things are as they used to be in aboriginal times. Prestige is based on speaking the language, respecting the religion, and honoring ancient laws of etiquette regarding food, visiting, conversation, and general camp behavior.

In my own fieldwork, I have felt obliged to collect certain data concerning the annual tribal encampments, the same kind of data gathered by my predecessors. Diagrams of the tribal circles previously collected already span 150 years from the founding of the nation to the early ceremonies observed by Mooney and Dorsey in 1901. Therefore I have sought to gather data from 1901 to the present, in the hope of creating a continuous record of Cheyenne tribal structure, for the benefit of future generations of Cheyenne ethnographers.

Mooney's field diagram of 1902 has never been published, and so I have traced and relettered it, and I present it here as figure 34. My most elderly

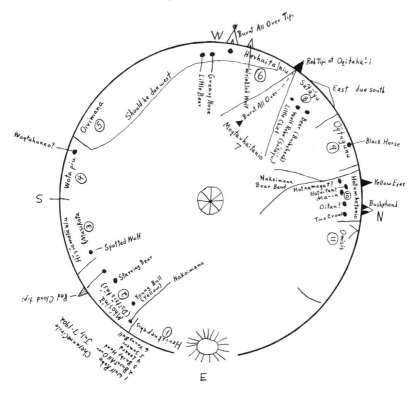

Figure 34.   Mooney's 1901 field diagram of the Cheyenne Sun Dance. Traced and relettered by the author.

informant, Katie Osage, was present at that Sun Dance, although she was only a child of nine. By 1914, however, Katie Osage was a young woman, and fully cognizant of the importance of the ceremonies she was witnessing. At my request, she made a diagram of the locations of the bands at the 1914 camp, and she wrote a list of all the heads of families she could remember who were active in the traditional ceremonies at that time. I reproduce her diagram as figure 35. Her list of participants, in my field notes, overlaps Mooney's.

By coincidence, the ceremonies of the year just previous, 1913, were photographed by Walter S. Campbell. One photograph is reproduced here as plate 32. Remember that 1914 was the last year, according to Katie Osage, that the bands tried to camp as bands, rather than as communities. We are fortunate to have a photograph from this time and to have Katie Osage's list. I should add that I have taken no photographs at all of the ceremonies or ceremonial circle in my own fieldwork, out of respect for Cheyenne sensitivities. Especially since the publication of Father Powell's photographs of private matters in 1968, and the scandals that followed, I have tried to be very cautious about describing such things.

For the tribal circle of 1936, Wayne Red Hat convened a group of elders, including his mother and his father, the arrow keeper, to prepare the

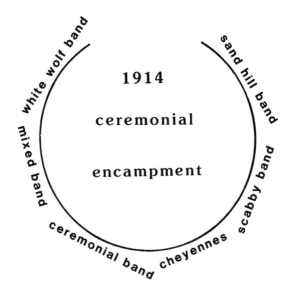

Figure 35.   Katie Osage's diagram of the 1914 Cheyenne encampment.

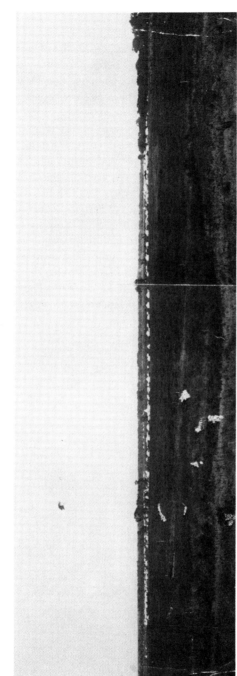

Plate 32.   Panorama of the 1913 Cheyenne ceremonial encampment. Photo no. 430, Campbell Collection, Western History Collections, University of Oklahoma Library.

diagram of figure 1. Along with a comprehensive list of participants in my files, it represents the active ceremonial people of 1936, twenty-two years after Katie Osage's list and diagram. For the 1950 Sun Dance, Wayne Red Hat prepared figure 36, comprising the major ceremonial leaders of that year.

The diagrams of recent Sun Dances were prepared by my friend Terry Wilson, a modernday Sun Dance priest. I identify the family heads only by number here, not by name, for privacy and to protect certain matters of ritual priority. Although Terry Wilson has been diligent enough to prepare diagrams of eight nearly consecutive years, 1974–83, I present here only two of the most complete, for 1977 and 1978 (figs. 38 and 39). The value of the diagrams is to show the yearly variability in camping arrangements. I have identified family heads with the same number over both years, to show how some of the camps move around among themselves and how discontinuous yearly attendance can be. I should also note that the circle is squared off in this location partly because of lack of space. The right-hand, or southern, camps are backed against a fencerow. However, Little Chief's

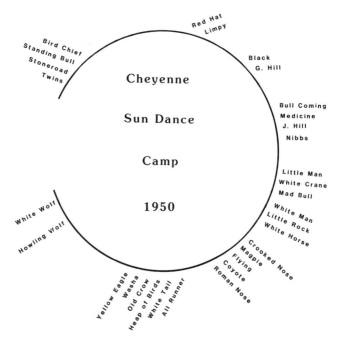

Figure 36.   Ceremonial leaders of the 1950 Sun Dance.

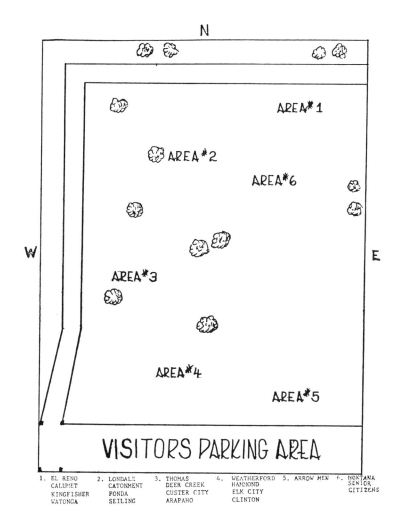

N

W

E

AREA*1

AREA*2

AREA*6

AREA*3

AREA*4

AREA*5

VISITORS PARKING AREA

1. EL RENO	2. LONDALE	3. THOMAS	4. WEATHERFORD	5. ARROW MEN	6. MONTANA
CALUMET	CATONMENT	DEER CREEK	HAMMOND		SENIOR
KINGFISHER	FONDA	CUSTER CITY	ELK CITY		CITIZENS
WATONGA	SEILING	ARAPAHO	CLINTON		

Figure 37.   Camping instructions distributed at the 1978 ceremonies.

drawing of an aboriginal circle is also squared off, reflecting the dual structure discussed in chapter 2 (plate 2). Figure 37 is the actual diagram distributed to Cheyennes and visitors as they arrived at the Walking Woman allotment in 1978.

Remember from chapter 5 that Mooney's and Michelson's informants

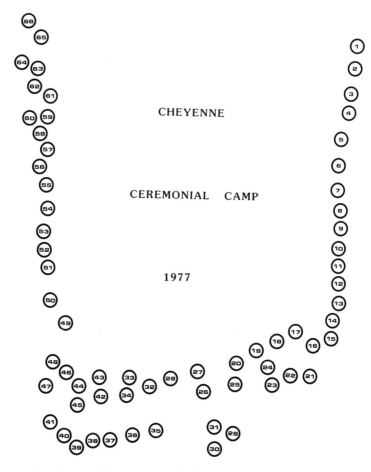

Figure 38.   Ceremonial camp at the Walking Woman allotment, 1977.

said they sometimes camped with their own natal band and sometimes with their wives' bands. Variability in camping place is not so apparent in modern times, although seventeen families from 1977 did not reappear in 1978, while twenty new families did appear. Factors creating variability are the timing of the arrival at the campsite, current friendships, and current hard feelings among families. The diagrams show only the modern Cheyennes who camp at the ceremonies for the duration. The actual number of people in attendance at some time in the two-week period is probably close to six thousand, Cheyennes and their guests.

The current vitality of the tribal circle and the attendance at ceremonies reflects the continuing strength of traditional organizations, especially the

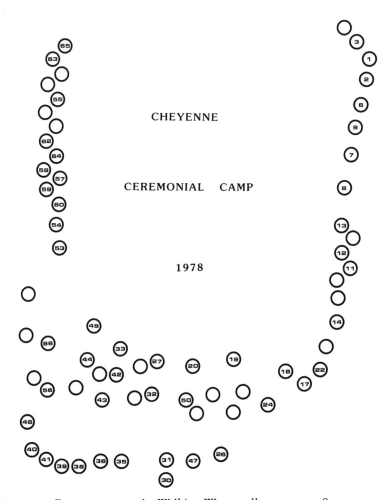

Figure 39. Encampment at the Walking Woman allotment, 1978.

military societies, the organized priesthood, and the council of chiefs. Despite the best efforts of the Bureau of Indian Affairs and Christian missionaries, the traditional Cheyenne nation still thrives.

Denied access to a tribal government that is increasingly dominated by acculturated Arapahos and Cheyennes, the traditionalist nation simply ignores the officially sanctioned "business committee." The impossibility of imposing a phony "tribal government" on an unwilling nation is demonstrated daily in the life of the Cheyennes. While the "official" government cannot govern even itself, the chiefs, priests, and headsmen yearly mobilize thousands of Cheyennes for powwows, benefits, meetings, and ceremonies. While the tribal government is wracked by monthly shouting matches and periodic fistfights, impeachments, and criminal prosecutions, the council of chiefs has the same stable membership of respected men from year to year, and elections are held only when the membership is diminished by death. While the tribal bureaucracy, every week, enacts scenarios straight from Gilbert and Sullivan, the real government of the Cheyenne nation, the chiefs and headsmen, goes soberly and solidly forward, motivated and enriched by their great ceremonies.

But everything is not eternally calm among the traditionalists. The hostilities of the late aboriginal period still occasionally crowd into the consciousness and ceremonial life of the Cheyenne people. An anecdote from recent years shows that there are still forces that hold the nation together and others that threaten to split it apart. These events began about 1981.

Until 1981, the annual ceremonies were held on the Walking Woman allotment near Watonga, Oklahoma. In 1981 our research project ("the Research clan") donated $1,000 to help with the ceremonies. This was to compensate the hundreds of Cheyenne people who had assisted with the research but had not received pay as informants. As an indirect method of "paying" everyone, we donated money for portable restrooms and a water wagon to be brought to the ceremonial grounds. Since the Bowstring Society had put up the 1981 ceremonies, we gave a check for $1,000 to the treasurer of that society.

But in 1982, as the ceremonies approached again, it rained constantly and flooded the Walking Woman allotment. The date of the ceremonies was postponed several times by the Bowstrings, again the sponsors of the ceremony, until finally the Dog Soldiers and Fox Soldiers became impatient and physically moved the arrows and the arrow keeper to the old Seiling ceremonial ground, thereby beginning the cycle of ceremonies. By that time the second payment of $1,000, representing the second year of our research, had already been paid to the Bowstrings. During the course of the dispute, some disparaging comments had already been made about the Research clan and about the money.

Within a week, the traditional Cheyennes were polarized along familiar lines and had decided to conduct two sets of ceremonies, one sponsored by the agnatic group in Seiling (Dog Soldiers and Foxes) and the other by the Bowstrings and chiefs in Concho. I was distraught, thinking the gift of money had precipitated the dispute. Trying to make amends, I bought meat and groceries, loaded them in my van, and went to the Seiling campground. After a long and painful discussion with the Seiling people, I was told that it was really not my fault—that I had been victimized by the other faction. Whereupon there began a two-hour recitation of all the faults of the other faction, going all the way back to, and especially including, the whipping of the arrow keeper by certain Bowstrings—in 1837.

Although stunned by the agnatic group's grasp of history, I was really not convinced I was blameless, since I had made two consecutive donations to the same military society—the Bowstrings. Also, my best friends and closest co-workers had usually been Bowstrings, and I felt guilty of favoritism in my social as well as economic arrangements. Although everyone, Bowstring and Dog Soldier alike, made attempts to console me, I was depressed and despondent for two weeks as both factions performed their ceremonies. And then I ran across the following account by the artist Frederic Remington, concerning events among Oklahoma Cheyennes in 1889: "At the time of our visit to this camp, the people were at loggerheads regarding the locality where the great annual Sun Dance, or more literally, "The Big Medicine," should be held. The men of the camp that I visited {uterine faction} wanted it at one place, and those of the "upper camp" [agnatic faction] wanted it at another. The chief could not arrange the matter, and so the solution of the difficulty was placed in the hands of the agent."[8]

The moral of this story, for me, is that no matter how clearly one might recognize that conflict and change occur regularly and are the most important of all historical events, episodes of conflict are nonetheless very painful. Decent people are led to radical action not so much by their love of conflict as by their adherence to important new principles. The "Cheyennes" in 1740 and the Dog Soldiers in 1845 embraced revolutionary social designs not because they wanted to see their world turned topsy-turvy, but because they thought these new designs were appropriate for a new historical situation. But each new design implies new principles and therefore conflicts with old principles and their advocates.

This historical process is unending. Each social or political innovation creates unprecedented demands on the national citizenry and puts pressure on neighboring nations. These demands and pressures, in turn, create new problems both within a tribal nation and between the nation and its neighbors. Sometimes these conflicts are serious enough to cause the forming of a new tribal nation. The process I have described for the Cheyennes is exactly parallel to the situation of the Nuer nation of Africa, carving out a new territory from the Dinka.[9]

In closing this book I would like to formulate, as clearly as I can, a theory of history as it pertains to tribal nations. This theory embodies the basic principles of orthodox Marxism as I understand them. In this theory, the nation is the social species. Tribal nations, however, are different from nation-states in having no classes and no state bureaucracy. Nevertheless, they manifest some fundamental characteristics typical of all nations. First of all, tribal nations are called into being by problems that are unsolvable within the old structure. Therefore a new nation is formed from the fragments of old nations under a novel charter explicitly designed to solve existing problems.

The new tribal nation frequently cuts across preexisting tribal, linguistic, ethnic, and geographic boundaries. Once formed, the nation exhibits strongly homogeneous tendencies, tending to obliterate cultural differences. At the same time, dissident factions within the nation rally around these variable traits and use them symbolically and concretely to mark their differences from the dominant national trends.

As history progresses, the natural and political environment always changes. Resources are lost, technology is invented, population characteristics change, and tribal nations migrate—a whole host of new problems are created that are unsolvable within the existing structure, and so the whole process is repeated. That is, the "tribe" does not evolve slowly through time but bounces through history in a series of national identities, periodically forming and re-forming. [10] While individuals might see only one re-formation in their lifetimes, we ethnohistorians have a broader view and can see structure and order in the repetitions of the process.

It has often been noted that linguistic, biological, and cultural boundaries do not coincide anywhere in the world. In the Cheyenne case, we have seen specifically why this is true. I believe that this process, expressed theoretically as above, is universal in its significance. It is as applicable to the early historical tribal nations of Europe—Celts, Germans, and Huns—as to the Indians of North America. The basic contradiction, which has confused many ethnologists, is that although nations extol uniformity and homogeneity, the actual and unavoidable consequences of nation building are heterogeneity and, ultimately, the fissioning of old nations and their recombination into new nations. The dialectics of history, among tribal nations, are played out between the tendencies toward nationhood, on the one hand, and inexorable structural tensions within the nation, on the other, which seize upon the variability that was never eliminated and never can be, galvanizing this variability into the formation of new and unprecedented cultural features.

Linguistic Appendix

In tracing Indian band names from document to document and from place to place across the Plains and Great Lakes area, the fundamental problem is that the names are most often presented divorced from a proper etymological or semantic context, and with only an approximate phonetic representation. Ideally one would like to have an accurate phonetic transcription, either an etymology of the name or definitions of the lexemic roots, and the tribal and linguistic affiliations of the person supplying the name. But most often what we find is simply an approximate spelling, perhaps idiosyncratic to the recorder, from an anonymous speaker.

All too often there is no clear modern referent, properly transcribed and interpreted between modern linguists and Indian informants, for the paleographic entries. For example, the entries under *W-T-P* in table 20 might be attempts to transcribe the Sioux words *wótapi*, "eaters," *witapaha*, "Kiowa," or *witapáhätu*, "island butte people." If all the entries could be reduced to one of these possibilities, excluding the others, with a proper etymology, we would be in marvelous shape for doing ethnohistory. But since they cannot, I prefer to take a graphic perspective on the entries, grouping them by the way they were written, while trying to account for the graphic differences among the salient European and Indian languages. That is, I believe the first task in making sense of these band names is to account systematically for the European spelling biases. Even if we cannot tell what these words mean, we can at least judge whether they represent the same spoken utterance and group them on that basis.

Table 21 shows some of the possible transcriptions, in English and French, of sounds from three of the languages we are interested in. To represent the sounds of Lakota, Cheyenne, and Dakota, I have used the phonetic systems devised by scholars who studied these languages in the nineteenth century. To determine how Europeans might have written these

Table 20 Various Transcriptions of Early Names of Towns and Nations of the Great Lakes Area

SH-NG-SK-T	S-S-T-N
Chongasketon	Cissitons
Chongaskabe	Saussetons
Chongaskabion	Seeseetoan
Chongaskethon	Seeseetwaun
Chongonsceton	Sesetons
Chougousceton	Sessatons
Chonkasketowan	Shahsweentowahs
Chongaskaby	Sinsitwans
Chougaskabees	Sisatoons
Chougasketon	Sisetonwans
Cnongasgaba	Sissetongs
Conkasketonwah	Sistasoona
Sankaskitons	Sistons
Songasketons	
Songaskicons	
Songatskitons	W-T-P
Songeskitons	
Songeskitoux	Wetepahato
Sougaskicons	Watahpahata
	Wetepanatoes
	Watepaneto
	Wetahato
W-P-T	Wetopahata
Wahpetons	Wettaphato
Wabipetons	Witapaha
Wahkpatoan	Witapahat
Wahpaytoan	Witapahatu
Wahpaytoanwan	Witapatu
Wahpeeton	Witapata
Wahpetongs	Witupatu
Wahpetongwant	Vitapatui
Wakpayton	
Wapatone	Oetbatons
Wapintowaher	Oudbatons
Wappitong	Houetbatons
Warkpeytwawn	Ouadebathons
Warpetwans	Ouadebatons
Washpelong	Oudebaetons

Note: A complete listing is given in Hodge 1907, 2:892–93, 1:701.

Lakota (Buechel)

English

b	c	g	h	ng	j	k	m	n	p	s	t	w	y	z
b	j	g	h	ng	j	g	m	l	b	s	t	y	y	z
	ch	ch		nk	sh	k		n	p	sh	d	w		
		k						d						

French

b	g	k	h	gn	g	g	m	n	b	s	t	w	j	g
	z	g			j	k		l	p	z	d	ou	h	z
	ch	h				c		d		c		8	y	
	j							agn				ui		
	h													

Cheyenne (Petter)

English

b	d	g	h	k	m	n	p	q	t	v	x	y	w	z
b	d	g	h	k	m	n	b	k	t	v	k	y	w	y
p	t	k		g			p	q		w	ch			z
b	d	g	j	k			b	k		v		j		j
p	t	k	h	q			p	q		w	k	y		
				c				c		ou	q	h		
										8				
										ui				

French

b	c	d	g	h	k	l	m	n	ng	p	s	t	w	z
b	ch	d	g	g	q	l	m	n	n	p	x	t	w	s
			k	h	k	r			ng		s			z
				k							sh			j

Dakota (Riggs, Williamson)

English

French

b	g	d	k	j	c	l	m	n	n	p	t	v	y	g
	s	g	g	h	k	r			gn		s	w	j	z
	ch				q						ch	ou	h	
											c	ui		
												8		

Source: Compiled from Fouche 1961 and Dobson 1968.

sounds, I have used some paleographic dictionaries that give the sound structure of English and French in the seventeenth through nineteenth centuries.[1] Under each of the consonants in the three native languages are the most likely letters that could legitimately have been used by contemporary Europeans to represent the sounds. Part of the variability in the literation arises because the native sound had an articulation intermediate between two phonemic sounds of the European language. Other variability is due to spelling peculiarities of the European languages.

I have not tried to include any native vowels in table 21, because they appear to be more variable and can be literated by a multitude of European letters, depending on the preceding and following consonants. The variations in consonants written on the table, I should point out, have not been derived from the actual variability observed in transcriptions such as table 20, but are rather some of the consonants that are theoretically possible based on sound structure and spelling.

To create the categories of table 20, I have utilized some graphic rules, derived from the phonetic data of table 21. Explicitly, the rules are as follows:

1. First priority is assigned to the order of consonants in the band names.

2. Consonants articulated in a similar manner are considered equivalent for present purposes. For example, /b/ and /p/ can easily be confused in transcribing a word, because the sounds are articulated in a similar manner, but it would be more difficult for a European listener to confuse /b/ with /k/ or /n/, depending of course on the languages of the speaker and listener.

Table 20 shows some of the huge variety of names created by English and French travelers who tried to listen to Indian speech and write down what they heard. But even professional linguists often supply disparate spellings for the same word. For example, the Mandan word for the Cheyennes reported by Will and Spinden is "Tamahonruckape," while Hollow's more recent dictionary represents it as "Tawahhurruskap," substituting *w* for *m* and dropping *n* and *e*. Among Cheyenne scholars, at least four major and seven minor alphabets have been used to represent Cheyenne words. Alford and Leman have helped develop two different alphabets, only one of which uses English letters exclusively. To compare spellings for just one word, Petter represented the Cheyennes' name for themselves as "Zezestasso," while Alford and Leman spell it "Tsetséhésestaestse." Mooney spelled the word "Dzitsistas," while Grinnell spelled it "Tsistsistas," as I have done in this book.[2]

Within the categories I have created for table 20, it can be seen that the remaining variation is mostly between sounds that have a similar articulation. Just as *z, dz,* and *ts* varied in transcriptions of the Cheyennes' name for themselves, *g, k,* and *q* were freely substituted in different versions of "Songaskiton." Generally speaking, I insist only that my own interpretations of spellings in the text of this book do fall within the range of variable spellings exhibited in tables 20 and 21.

Concerning the identification between Dotame and Totoimana, the Cheyenne language does not distinguish between what English or French speakers would call *d* and *t* (both apicoalveolar stops), and so the range of articulation for this letter in Cheyenne is greater than for the English *t.* Especially in the initial position, the sound can be heard as *d* by European listeners as, for example, when Mooney wrote "Dzitsistas." Whereas Alford and Leman have used the letter *T* to represent the sound, Petter used a *D,* explaining that it "sounds like a faulty pronunciation of t."[3] The order of consonants in Totoimana is the same as Dotame, *T/D-T-M,* except that Totoimana has an additional syllable beginning with *N.* This can be any one of several suffixes in Cheyenne, depending on the sentence in which it was spoken.

Looking at the band name "Ouisy," we must understand the relationship in spelling and pronunciation between Ouisy and Omisis. To begin with, a French letter used in the eighteenth century to represent both *oo* and *wa* was often 8. The use of the same symbol for both indicates the similarity in articulation. Both sounds are articulated between the lips (bilabials). The sound *oo* is made as the lips are pursed, whereas *wa* is made as the lips are unpursed. Most often, however, the sound was written *ou* in standard French. For example, the French versions of "west" and "wake," according to Fouche, were spelled *ouest* and *ouake.*[4]

The sound of *M* is also articulated bilabially; remember that while Will and Spinden used an *M* to spell the Mandan word Ta*m*ahonruckape, Hollow represented the sound as *W,* which he wrote Ta*w*ahhurruskap. So I argue from the original French orthography that the sounds represented as Ouisy can legitimately be rewritten Omisy, for the Omisis band, with the notation *W/M-S.*

To interpret the band name "Chouta," we should also refer to the French language. Note that *ch* has only a soft fricative sound in standard French, as in *cherchez* or "Cheyenne," rather than a hard sound as in the English "chitchat" or "change." The sound is more properly represented in English as *sh* rather than *ch.* Therefore various transcriptions of the name Chongasketon in table 20 have several variants beginning with *s* instead of *ch,* such as Songasketons and Sankaskitons. By the same principle, Chouta and Sutaio are merely variations of the same word, represented *SH/S-T.*

Regarding Carver's name Waddapawjestin, we should note that both *D* and *T* are apicoalveolar stops articulated in Cheyenne, as Petter said, "like a faulty pronunciation of t." The suffix *-jestin* is defined in Carver's short dictionary as meaning "little."[5] Williamson's dictionary, however, lists this only as a prefix, not a suffix. Another alternative is the translation "named," which is more likely as a suffix.[6]

A possible tribal identification for the Chongasketons, the most orthodox, is with the Sisseton Sioux. But this is one of the identifications, in my opinion, that seem to be carved in stone for no good reason. I argue here, by reference to the tables, that the early names listed for the Sissetons fall easily into two distinct phonetic groups, one for the Sissetons and the other for an early progenitor of the Sutaios.

Using as a sample the list from the *Handbook of American Indians*, I have divided the names into two columns on table 20, one labeled *S-S-T-N* and the other *SH-NG-SK-T*. It is interesting that the names in the second column were collected in the early years of European contact, before the Cheyennes migrated onto the Plains. At least one reporter listed a name from each column simultaneously, indicating that they were two different groups. Carver lists Shahsweentowah for Sisseton and Chongousceton for the other group, which I make to be the proto-Sutaios.[7]

On the earliest French maps, literation of the name Oudebaton uses the symbol *8* as the first syllable.[8] From table 21, we can see that the sound represented by Riggs and Williamson as *w* can legitimately be literated either by the English letter *W* or by any of several French letters, including *OU* and *8*.

In addition to being mentioned by La Salle, the Oudebatons are also mentioned by Lahontan, who says that they, like the Chongasketons, are Algonquian speakers.[9] Apparently La Chesnaye did not consider them to be Siouan either, since in his 1697 memoir he said that the Issaquy, identified as "Cioux," live on the opposite side of the lake from the Oetbatons, who are not so identified.[10] Other documents of the same period also mention the Oudebatons (Houetbatons, etc.) as separate from the "Nadoussioux." One persuasive piece of evidence that the Oudebatons are not the same as the Wahpetons comes from Le Sueur in 1697, who placed both the "Ouadebatons," with a *b*, and the "Ouaepetons," with a *p*, on the same list of tribes.[11] He listed the former with the eastern Sioux and the latter with the western Sioux. Obviously he did not consider them the same people. And we should note from table 21 that /*b*/ and /*p*/ are distinct in Dakota, as they are in French and English.

When the name is presented as "Ou de baton," it has the appearance of being a French nickname. However, the expression is nonsense in French, having the literal translation "or of stick." The French spelling also obscures the fact that phonetically the word is the same as the English name Wotapio or, as Carver rendered it, "Waddapaw-." These variants are merely attempts to represent the same native word in French and in English, as we can see from tables 20 and 21. The French spelling of the name, however, has tended to prevent its identification with the English version.

Succinctly put, the diachronic theory I espouse in this book is that there were originally three proto-Cheyenne bands, known by different names, that migrated across the northern plains from the Great Lakes, ultimately forming the Cheyenne nation in the Black Hills, and that the linguistic data support this theory. The orthodox theory, which I claim is inferior because it explains less, is that the identity of tribal nations has been the same since 1680. Let me summarize below the points from chapter 3, supplemented by the Linguistic Appendix, clarified by this diachronic theory and that are left unexplained by orthodox theory. The diachronic theory explains:

1. Why a certain cluster of Lewis and Clark's bands were closely affiliated in their trade relations and military arrangements about 1805.

2. Why the "Chyanne nation" in their documents is so unaccountably small.

3. What happened to the Sheos, the Chaoines, and the Shianeses, and where the Masikota band came from.

4. Why a certain Cheyenne band, the Wotapios, and a certain Kiowa band, the Wetepahatos, carry the same Sioux name.

5. The identity of the proto-Arapaho bands on Lewis and Clark's map.

6. Who the Dotames were and why they disappeared from maps after 1805.

7. Why the Cheyennes were consistently bracketed with two other bands in the early documents.

8. Why the Chongasketons (allegedly the Sissetons) and the Wetepahatos (allegedly the Kiowas) were found together with the Cheyennes on the Minnesota River about 1766.

9. Why the Cheyennes call the Assiniboines "Hohe."

10. Why the Cheyennes are usually found contiguous to the Chongasketons and the Oudebatons on the early maps.

11. Why there has been confusion about the term "Dog People" as applied to the Cheyennes.

12. How the Wahpetons and the Oudebatons (alleged to be the same people) can be found on the same map.

13. How the Sissetons and the Chongasketons (also alleged to be the same) can be mentioned independently in the same narrative.

14. Why the Kiowas and the Wetepahatos were said by Lewis and Clark to speak different languages.

15. Why Mooney said that Nimousin must be a "misprint."

16. Why the names Sutaio and Sisseton appear in history at the same time that Chongasketon disappears.

Notes

Abbreviations Used in Notes

BAE   Bureau of American Ethnology
BIA   Annual Reports of the Commissioner of Indian Affairs
MS.   manuscript
NAA   National Anthropological Archives, Smithsonian Institution, including
       manuscripts from the Bureau of American Ethnology
OHS   Oklahoma Historical Society

Chapter One

1. These romantic trends apparently began with Montaigne and Aphra Behn and continue to the present. See Behn 1967, 127–208; Montaigne 1948, 150–58; Lévi-Strauss 1966; Diamond 1974; and Levy-Bruhl 1966.

2. The debates with and among the structuralists supply the best examples of imaginative patterns that have little to do with the material world. See Lévi-Strauss 1963, 1976; Needham 1974. Gluckman, of course, has analyzed conflicts, but his are always resolved within the existing structure (Gluckman 1955).

3. Bale 1981a,b; O'Reilly 1982.

4. Berthrong 1963, 1976, and elsewhere.

5. Powell 1969, 1981, and elsewhere.

6. Murdock and O'Leary 1975, 5:62–69; Powell 1980; Dockstader 1957. Also see "Cheyenne" in Hodge 1907.

7. Nespor 1984.

8. Needham 1929, 10.

9. See "The Ornithology of Cheyenne Religionists," *Plains Anthropologist,* in press.

10. Michelson MS. 2704, NAA.

11. Lowie 1915, 598; also see Lowie 1917.

12. Petersen 1964, 1968, 1971.

13. See first-page story in the *Kiowa Indian News* (Carnegie, Oklahoma), 9, no. 13 (November 1981).

14. Petersen 1968, 38.

15. Moore 1980a.

16. Fried 1975. Earlier discussions of these problems are in Helm 1968. Fried's most recent pronouncement is in Fried 1983.

17. Boas 1940; Lowie 1947; Harris 1968.

18. Richard Adams apparently agrees with these sentiments; see Adams 1975, 227.

19. Two good surveys on the origins of the national question in Marxist theory are Herod 1976 and Connor 1984. The classic works are Luxemburg 1976; Lenin 1960a, 1:631–87; and Stalin 1975.

20. Malinowski 1922.

21. Patterson 1981, 115–16, 122–23.

22. Stalin 1975, 18–28, 227–28; Lenin in Bhowal 1970, 1–4.

23. Emerson 1960, 102–3.

24. Mooney 1979, 229.

25. For present practice, see part 83, title 25, *Federal Register* 41, no. 171 (5 September 1978). For the history of these definitions see Prucha 1962 and Gibson 1980.

26. UNESCO 1953; Kothari 1971; Deng 1971.

27. Kotok 1971; Shevtsov 1982; Russell 1977.

28. Llewellyn and Hoebel 1941, 110–31.

29. Moore 1981b, 8–12.

30. In Cheyenne tradition, their exclusive right to buffaloes is symbolized by the yellow appearance of buffaloes (birth hair) and Cheyennes (vernix) at birth. As they expanded territory in the nineteenth century, the Cheyennes successively performed pipe rituals that legitimated the incorporation of new territory. See Moore 1974b, 163–64.

31. Llewellyn and Hoebel 1941, 132–68.

32. Harris 1968, 643–53.

33. Miller and Steffen 1977.

34. Wolf 1982; Herod 1976.

35. Steward 1948, 1955; Steward and Faron 1959; Carneiro 1981, 38–39.

36. White 1959a; Carneiro 1981; Sahlins and Service 1960; Service 1971; Harris 1968, 634–87. Of all these attempts to create an evolutionary taxonomy of social and political "types," I find Gertrude Dole's perspective the most useful. Her stages allow for variation and development across the supposed "barrier" separating tribes from states. See Dole 1968.

37. Lubbock 1889; McLennan 1970; Spencer 1967.

38. Snow 1959.

39. In this regard it is interesting that the major proponents of the "stimulus" theory of tribal formation were all classmates at Columbia University about 1950—Fried, Service, Sahlins, Wolf, and also Eleanor Leacock, Sidney Mintz, and Marvin Harris.

40. Boas 1896.

41. Fried 1967, 173.

42. Fried 1983.

43. Fried 1975, 98.

44. For example, the Middle Missouri palisaded village sites are all very similar architecturally, although we know that many different ethnic and linguistic groups occupied these villages. See Will 1924 and Wood 1967.

45. Moore 1974a, 1981a.

46. Cole 1931, 413.

47. Dorsey 1905.

48. Dorsey 1925, 60–119, 403–15.

49. Dorsey 1929, 150.

50. The book has been republished; see Dorsey 1972.

51. Dorsey 1931, 235.

52. Grinnell 1900, 21.

53. See Moore 1987.

54. Moses 1984. Mooney's bibliography was published with his obituary (Mooney 1922).

55. Mooney 1896.

56. Bass 1954; Mooney 1922.

57. Mooney 1907, plate XII.

58. Hoebel 1980; Moore 1981a.

59. Llewellyn and Hoebel 1941, viii.

60. Hoebel 1980; Moore 1974a, 1981a.

Chapter Two

1. The manuscripts of Albert S. Gatschet, J. N. B. Hewitt, and Ben Clark are deposited in NAA. These ethnographic accounts are earlier than or contemporary with the work of the "classic ethnographers"—Mooney, Dorsey, and Grinnell— but the manuscripts were never published.

2. I have selected for analysis in this chapter only complete band lists attributed to particular Cheyenne informants. Therefore I have excluded the list appearing in Ben Clark's Smithsonian manuscript, and also the unattributed lists and diagrams from Dorsey 1905 and Mooney 1907.

3. Mooney 1907; Grinnell 1962, 1:86–101; Eggan 1937, 35–95; Moses 1984, 161.

4. Mooney 1907, 405.

5. See the *Oxford English Dictionary*, 1933 ed., s.v. "Angle."

6. Petter's major publications are listed in volume 5 of *Ethnographic Bibliography of North America*, ed. George P. Murdock and Timothy J. O'Leary (New Haven, Conn.: Human Relations Area Files Press, 1975). Petter's dictionary, published in pieces over several years, I will cite as Petter 1915.

7. Blue Horse's allotment is listed on the copied and recopied allotment lists maintained by the government, such as those at Concho Agency, Bureau of Indian Affairs, Concho, Oklahoma. Rising Fire's narrative is in Barrett 1913, 96–97.

8. A brief biography of Barrett is recorded in Marable 1939.

9. Grinnell 1962, 1:98; Mooney 1907, 412; Petersen 1964, 157–58.

10. Bureau of Indian Affairs, *Cheyenne and Arapaho Agency* (Washington. D.C.: Government Printing Office, 1882), 56.

11. Powell 1980, xxvii–xxxi.

12. Little Chief drawing #11/1706, Museum of the American Indian, New York City. There is still some question about the identity of the artist for this drawing. If, as my colleague Candace Green suggests, someone from a southern band made this drawing, it does not, of course, support my generalization.

13. Truman Michelson's MS. 3218, NAA, describes tipi etiquette and spatial arrangements in some detail.

14. Birth years have been established from published sources, field notes, and early censuses, as noted on table 2.

15. Grinnell MS. 334, Southwest Museum, Los Angeles, Calif.; Michelson MS. 2822, NAA.

16. Several computer programs were used for analyzing "clusters" of bands and patterns of exclusion and co-occurrence of pairs of bands, but the mathematical results added little to what was already apparent by inspection.

17. Moore 1974a, 1981a.

18. Bent 1968, 338.

19. Lévi-Strauss 1963, 132–63.

20. Grinnell 1962, 1:90; Mooney 1907, 402 ff.; Dorsey 1905, plate xix.

Chapter Three

1. This discussion is summarized from Siebert 1967 and from "Siouan Family" in Hodge 1907. Papers delivered to a recent conference in St. Paul, chaired by Elden Johnson, indicate that some Plains societies were preadapted by an earlier residence on the prairies of southeastern Minnesota. Politically speaking, "Dakota" refers to all the Northern Sioux of this region except the Assiniboines. The Teton Dakotas, comprising the Oglalas, Brulés, Sans Arcs, Blackfeet, Miniconjous, Two Kettles, and Hunkpapas, call themselves "Lakota" because they speak a different dialect.

2. Ossenberg 1974. It may be, however, that the "Arvilla Complex" will not hold up as a viable taxon (Ray Wood, personal communication).

3. Jefferson 1917. Gary Moulton of the Center for Great Plains Studies is now editing a new edition of the Lewis and Clark journals, to be published by the University of Nebraska Press.

4. Hague 1887.

5. Cutright 1976. See Ronda 1984 for a discussion of Lewis and Clark's ethnographic methods. Also see articles in the special volume of the *Journal of the Washington Academy of Sciences* 44, no. 11 (November 1954).

6. Thwaites 1905, 6:80–83, 100. Thwaites added information from other sources, properly marked. Clark's original information is noted as either "same as," "do," or "ditto."

7. Thwaites 1905, 6:100.

8. Grinnell 1962, 1:31. The other most likely tribal identification, Arapaho, is not encouraged either by Scott 1907 or by Mooney's article "Arapaho" in Hodge 1907.

9. Quaife 1916; Osgood 1964.

10. Osgood 1964, 181.

11. Quaife 1916, 169.

12. Will and Spinden 1906, 188. Ronda comments at length on the difficulty of the linguistic situation; Ronda 1984, 116–17.

13. This is according to Preston Bell, an accomplished Atsina sign talker, and Edward Red Hat, the late Cheyenne arrow keeper.

14. Kennard 1936, 32.

15. Will and Spinden 1906, 210.

16. Quaife 1916, 149–50; Hosmer 1917, 1:109, 147, 177, 179, 190; Abel 1939.

17. Riggs 1893, 193.

18. Clark 1885, 59.

19. Abel 1939, 102, n.10.

20. Hoistah says six hundred lodges in Barrett 1913, 97, and Captain Clark, in 1816, revised his estimate of total population upward to two thousand, in his "A report of the names and probable number of the Tribes of Indians in the Missouri Territory, St. Louis, November 4, 1816" (manuscript, Missouri Historical Society, St. Louis).

21. Clark 1885, 98.

22. Kennard 1936; Will and Spinden 1906, 209–19; Hollow 1970. Also see "Travels in the Interior of North America, 1832–1834." by Maximilian, Prince of Wied, in Thwaites 1906, 24:234–61.

23. Riggs 1893; Wood 1971; Hyde 1956, 1961, 1973. Other ethnohistorical sources are listed under the appropriate tribes in Murdock and O'Leary 1975, vol. 5.

24. Riggs 1893, 155–64; Buechel 1970; Hassrick 1964, chap. 1.

25. It is not generally appreciated that the Atsina-Arapaho separation was very recent. See Scott 1907 and Trenholm 1970, 10–19. Mooney did not agree that the "Pauuch" were Atsinas. See "Allakaweah" in Hodge 1907.

26. The best expression of these general problems and principles is still found in Bryce 1893.

27. See Mooney's article "Kiowa Apache" in Hodge 1907.

28. Fisher 1812; Abel 1939, 154.

29. Mooney in Hodge 1907, 1:328.

30. My thanks to Lyle Redbird, a member of this band, for explaining that as a prefix, north is *nao-*, not *nota-* as I originally thought.

31. La Salle's observations are recorded in Margry 1879, 2:54. Also see Wedel and DeMallie 1980, 116.

32. Especially see the map notes in Tucker 1942; Wood 1983; and Karpinski 1931. Also see Henry 1900.

33. Phillips 1961, 2:223–44.

34. Jablow 1951, 10; Holder 1970; Powell 1969, 1:19–25.

35. See Wedel 1962, fig. 2; also Will and Hyde 1917; Blakeslee 1975.

36. Baker 1936.

37. Perrin du Lac 1807, 62–63. Most of Perrin du Lac's information, though accurate, seems to be plagiarized from other sources (Abel 1921). I quote him here in the hope that he has preserved some information that is otherwise lost.

38. Nasatir 1952, 1:379.

39. Nasatir 1952, 1:301.

40. Nasatir 1952, 1:304.

41. Abel 1939, 151–58.

42. See "Siouan Family" in Hodge 1907; Riggs 1893.

43. Mayhall 1962, 10; Swanton 1922, 398–414.

44. Hickerson 1970.

45. Petter 1915; Buechel 1970.

46. Carver 1956, 79–80, 1976, 99–100.

47. Nasatir 1952, 1:739.

48. Carver 1976, 100.

49. It is not among the bands listed in Riggs 1893, 163.

50. Williamson 1902, 244–45.

51. Hennepin 1903, 1:225.

52. Wheat 1954. The Spanish map is reproduced in the atlas accompanying Thwaites's edition of the Lewis and Clark journals (Thwaites 1905, vol. 8, map 2). All these maps have been rigorously criticized by Wood 1983, who feels that there are only two sources for all this information, Antoine Soulard and Truteau.

53. Grinnell 1962, 1:4.

54. The Hennepin map is on p. 25 of Karpinski 1931; the Franquelin map is cataloged under 1697 in the "Check List of Manuscript Maps," Newberry Library, Chicago, Illinois; the Joliet information is reproduced in *Macalester College Contributions,* ser. 1, no. 10 (1890): 224. Wedel 1974 has an excellent discussion of these maps and mapmakers and a reproduction of the Franquelin map.

55. Coyote, Michelson MS. 3218, NAA; White Bull, Michelson MS. 2704, NAA.

56. Delanglez 1941, 133–40. Franquelin's 1697 map says "Nation des hommes forts" (Newberry Library), but Hennepin's 1698 map says "Nations de Forts" (Karpinski 1931, atlas, 25).

57. Delanglez 1941, 136; Williamson 1902, 52, 247; Hennepin 1966, 203.

58. Lahontan 1703, 230–31.

59. "Relation officielle de l'éntreprise de Cavelier de la Salle, de 1679 à 1681," in Margry 1879, 1:481.

60. Carver 1976, 100.

61. Mooney 1907, 406.

62. See Coronelli 1688 map in Karpinski 1931, atlas, 22.

63. Williamson 1902, 16.

64. Hodge 1907.

65. See Grace Nute's introduction to Hennepin 1938.

66. Michelson 1913, 234. Hollow and Parks 1980, 78, say that Michelson noted Ojibwa as closest to Cheyenne, but they do not cite the passage in Michelson. Teeter 1967 and Goddard 1967 both reserve judgment on the precise genetic relations of these languages. Also see Goddard 1972.

67. Wood 1971; Grinnell 1918; Bushnell 1922; Riggs 1893, 194.

68. Smith 1981.

69. Hyde to Grinnell, 1 October 1917, Southwest Museum Archives, Los Angeles.

70. Smith 1981. Information on possible Cheyenne bands is on pp. 42–66, 104–14, 120, and 126. My thanks to Susan Peterson for her help in translation from French.

71. Senex 1721 map in Karpinski 1931, atlas, 36.

72. "Arikara" in Hodge 1907.

73. Lehmer 1970, 117; Weakly 1971. The actual tree-ring data, sent to me by Jeffrey Dean of the University of Arizona, indicates a significant wet period beginning about 1745.

74. Wood 1971; Grinnell 1918; Holder 1970, 90–97.

Chapter Four

1. Dorsey 1905, 2:xiii.

2. This is according to Joe Antelope, recent keeper of the sacred arrows, a descendant of DeForest Antelope.

3. Lt. Heber Creel's Ethnology Notebook D, Gilcrease Archives, Tulsa, Oklahoma.

4. Dorsey 1905; Grinnell 1907, 1908, 1971.

5. Cooper 1939.

6. Michelson's field notes are in NAA.

7. Michelson 1932.

8. Michelson MS. 2822, NAA; typed version is MS. 2704, NAA. Michelson interviewed two persons named White Bull; one was also called Ice. To avoid confusion, this second White Bull will be cited only as Ice; the other will be cited as White Bull.

9. MS. 2822. Michelson recorded the name of this story as "Holy Head of the Eaters." I have renamed it "Sacred Leader of the Eaters" to avoid confusion with another story called "The Rolling Head."

10. Michelson MS. 2796, NAA.

11. Powell 1969, 1:15.

12. Grinnell 1962, 1:336–58; Dorsey 1905, 1:12–15.

13. Michelson MS. 2822, NAA.

14. Grinnell 1908, 297.

15. Abel 1939, 131.

16. Michelson MS. 2796, NAA.

17. Clark MS. 3449, p. 35, NAA.

18. Kroeber 1900, 163.

19. Grinnell 1907; Michelson MSS. 2822, 2811, 2704, NAA; Grinnell 1962, 1:86–95; Mooney 1907.

20. Albers 1985, 15–30.

21. Acting Commissioner of Indian Affairs to Superintendent of Cheyenne and Arapahoe Indian School, 7 June 1907, CAA microfile no. 18, OHS.

22. Doris Duke Oral History Collections, Western History Collections, University of Oklahoma, interviews T-152, T-256-1.

23. Michelson MS. 2811, NAA.

24. Michelson MS. 2811, NAA.

25. This was a bone of contention among Grinnell, Mooney, and others. See Mooney 1907 and "Cheyenne" in Hodge 1907.

26. Moore 1974a.

27. Llewellyn and Hoebel 1941; Grinnell 1962, 1:86–101.

28. Llewellyn and Hoebel 1941, 67–131.

29. Michelson MS. 2704, NAA.

30. Michelson MS. 2704, NAA.

31. Michelson MS. 2704, NAA.

32. Michelson MS. 2704, NAA.

33. Michelson MS. 2704, NAA.

34. Michelson MS. 2704, NAA.

35. Michelson MS. 2822, NAA.

36. Michelson MS. 2822, NAA.

37. Michelson MS. 2811, NAA.

38. Michelson MS. 2822, NAA.

39. Grinnell 1918.

40. Ben Clark MS. 3449, NAA. The parentheses are preserved from Clark.

41. Iron Shirt's remark is in Michelson MS. 2822, NAA, and Coyote's narrative is in Michelson MS. 3218, NAA.

42. Bent 1968, 323.

43. Mooney MS. B, NAA.

44. Karpinski 1931, atlas, 29.

45. Marquette's Map of the Upper Mississippi Valley, 1673–1674, Archives, St. Mary's College, Montreal, Quebec.

46. Karpinski 1931, atlas, 18.

47. Lewis and Clark in Thwaites 1905, 6:94.

48. Parker 1976, 100, 137–38.

49. Abel 1939, 239.

50. Abel 1939, 104.

51. Lewis and Clark in Thwaites 1905, 6:99.

52. Lewis and Clark Ethnographic Chart, Archives of the American Philosophical Society, Philadelphia.

53. See "band" in Petter 1915; Mooney 1907, 406, Grinnell 1962, 1:95–96.

54. Roy and Kathryn Bull Coming, Ed and Minnie Red Hat, John Black Owl.

55. Buechel 1970, "Siyota," 464.

56. Cal Fast Wolf, Newberry Library, Chicago, personal communication.

57. Walker 1980, 269–70.
58. Grinnell 1962, 1:93–94.
59. Nasatir 1952, 2:739.

Chapter Five

1. See Preface to the *Critique of Political Economy* (Marx 1962, 362–64) for a succinct statement of Marx's theory of history and *The German Ideology* (Marx and Engels 1976, 35–38) for a short statement concerning the role of the individual in history. Also see Lenin 1960b, 159–61.

2. Service 1968. Marvin Harris has provided a literate though muddled discussion of these issues (1979, 160–64).

3. Ritzenthaler 1978, 743; Mooney 1928, 13, 26.

4. Danzinger 1979, 26–28. According to the map by Michelson and Swanton (Michelson 1913), the Cheyennes were historically situated less than two hundred miles from the Kickapoos, Sacs, and Foxes.

5. William Clark, entry 675, Population Figures 1800–1853, Records of the Civilization Division, Bureau of Indian Affairs, Record Group 75, National Archives, Washington, D.C.

6. Schoolcraft 1847, 518–24.

7. Schoolcraft 1847, 518–24.

8. Nasatir 1952, 2:706, 759–60.

9. Coues 1965, 1:144.

10. Reports to the Commissioner of Indian Affairs, 1840–60.

11. Report to the Commissioner of Indian Affairs, 1878, 54.

12. Mooney 1928, 13.

13. Dobyns 1976.

14. Moore 1987.

15. Major works on the fur trade are Chittenden 1935 and Phillips 1961.

16. Margry 1879, 2:54. This is my own rather literal translation. The Chaa were not themselves Cheyennes, as some have thought. See Wedel and DeMallie 1980, 116.

17. Carver 1956, 110–11; Smith 1981, 52.

18. Nasatir 1952, 1:299.

19. Thwaites 1905, 6:83–88. This is a combined figure for the "Kanzas," "Ottoes," "Missouries," "Mahar" (Omaha), "Osarge" and "Poncare," who were allied against the Tetons in this period. The figure excludes the Quapaws, who were not part of the alliance.

20. Dobyns 1966, 1983; Trimble 1987; Moore 1987.

21. Wood 1971.

22. This range is from Smith 1972, 28.

23. Lehmer and Wood 1977, 88.

24. Bowers 1965, 484–87.

25. Abel 1939, 152–58.

26. Nasatir 1952, 1:301.

27. Thwaites 1905, 6:100.
28. Jablow 1951.
29. Sunder 1965, 52; Phillips 1961; Chittenden 1935.
30. Patricia Albers, Anthropology Department, University of Utah, unpublished manuscript entitled "Sharing the Land," coauthored with Jeanne Kay.
31. Grinnell 1910, 1956; Mooney 1907, 371.
32. Grinnell 1956, 6–44.
33. Phillips 1961. 2:395–98.
34. Bent 1968, 58–60.
35. Ed Red Hat, Harvey White Shield, and Charlie Weston were the last members of the "Horse Bundle Lodge."
36. Bent 1968, 68.
37. Ruxton 1950, 1951; Garrard 1955.
38. Ruxton 1950, 252.
39. BIA 1847, 848–53.
40. Greg Campbell, Anthropology Department, University of Oklahoma, unpublished manuscript.
41. Hafen 1930, 49.
42. Hamilton 1960, 9.
43. Garrard 1955, 50.
44. Hickerson 1962; also see Hickerson 1970.
45. Schoolcraft 1851, 367–68.
46. Wilson 1917.
47. See Burgess, Johnson, and Keammerer 1973.
48. Bushnell 1922, 86–87, 166–67, 178–79.
49. My thanks to Rebecca Bateman for redrawing these site plans.
50. These site plans are from Will 1924, 314, 317, 324. Also see Bushnell 1922 and the *River Basins Survey Papers* published by BAE.
51. Smith 1972, 3–20.
52. Blakeslee 1975, 219–28; Lehmer and Wood 1977.
53. Bowers 1965, 10–25, 64–79.
54. Wied 1976; Wilson 1917.
55. Griffin 1977; Bowers 1950, 23, 1965, 29.
56. Wilson 1917, 7.
57. Goble and Goble 1972.
58. Ware 1960, 230.
59. From letter on display at Fort Larned Museum, Kansas. Skirmishes with firewood details are in Ware 1960, 60, 70, 127, 191, 230, 237, 255. Also see *Records of Engagements with Hostile Indians, 1868–1882* (Fort Collins, Colo.: Old Army Press, 1972).
60. Ben Clark MS. 3449, p. 54, NAA.
61. Moore 1982.
62. Ware 1960, 234–35.
63. DEVRES 1980.
64. Eckholm 1975; Openshaw 1974.

65. Graves 1919, 9, 16.
66. Heizer 1963.
67. Moore 1982.
68. Michelson MS. 2704, NAA.
69. Personal communication based on current work.
70. Kranz and Linder 1973; Hawley et al. 1981; Eiselin 1943.
71. Davis 1979.
72. Kenner 1969, 24–27; Wedel 1962, 113–15; Buskirk 1949, 30–43.
73. Mathews 1961, 449–51.
74. Hyde 1951, 232.
75. Grinnell 1962, 1:30.
76. Nespor 1984, 128–36.
77. This is confirmed by modern informants.
78. Nespor 1984.
79. BIA 1876.
80. BIA 1889, 1892.
81. BIA 1892.
82. Abel 1939, 97–98.
83. This difference between summer and winter wood is according to modern informants.
84. Wells 1965.
85. Ware 1960, 41–42; also see pp. 60, 70, 127.
86. Anderson 1982; Dix 1964.
87. Pyne 1982, 71–83.
88. Ware 1960, 356.
89. This was the unanimous opinion of soil conservation agents and local residents I interviewed in 1981–83.
90. Pyne 1982.
91. Tomelleri 1983.
92. Custer 1962, 35, 240.
93. Dykes 1960, 215.
94. German 1927.
95. Grinnell 1956, 65.
96. Berthrong 1963, 318–44.
97. This information came out in narratives collected for the Black Hills claim. See Moore 1981b, n. 36.
98. Carroll 1978, 147.
99. For a critical evaluation of Pike and other early accounts, see Küchler 1972; Lawson and Stockton 1981; and Hart and Hulbert 1932.
100. Webb 1931, 319–452.
101. Custer 1962, 11.
102. Grinnell 1956, 40; Berger 1983; U.S. War Department 1917, 61; Hyland 1976, 97–101; Devereux 1979, 148–49; U.S. War Department 1931, 14–15.
103. *Water Atlas of the United States* (Port Washington, N.Y.: Water Information Center, n.d.).

104. Interviews with local residents, 1981–83.

105. Skaggs 1978.

106. Archer and Bunch 1953, 199, 208, 223.

107. Osborn 1983; Carroll 1973, 126.

108. Redrawn from *Soil Survey of Kiowa County, Colorado* (Washington, D.C.: Soil Conservation Service, U.S. Department of Agriculture, 1980).

109. Redrawn by the author from the original in the Western Historical Collections, University of Colorado, Boulder.

110. Ware 1960, 341–42.

111. Hart and Hulbert 1932, 117.

112. Abert 1966, 85; also see Abert 1848, 110.

113. Ruxton 1950, 272.

114. BIA 1864.

115. Custer 1962, 7.

116. Ewers 1955, 43–44.

117. Latham 1962, 17–18.

118. In addition to soil surveys, I used *A Guide to Range Site Condition Classes and Recommended Stocking Rates* (Washington, D.C.: Soil Conservation Service, U.S. Department of Agriculture, 1977).

119. Calculations in that paper were based on Hoelscher and Woolfolk 1953; Stoddart, Smith, and Box 1975; Kranz and Linder 1973; Barbalace 1974; and Burgess, Johnson, and Keammerer 1973.

120. Levy 1961.

121. Barrett 1913.

122. Peden 1972; Morgan 1980.

123. Bent 1968, 129.

124. One informant said that the windbreaks were not necessary when lodges were made of buffalo skins instead of canvas.

125. Ewers 1955, 129–47.

126. Ewers 1955, 24.

127. Bent 1968, 158.

128. Garrard 1955, 56.

129. The census is from the Indian Archives, OHS. I have not included mules in my figures, since there were very few. I have also not included orphans and schoolchildren in calculating the mean, since none owned any horses.

130. See BIA 1868–90.

131. Ewers 1955, 24–26.

132. Holder 1970, 104–5.

133. Michelson MS. 2704, NAA.

134. Carroll 1978, 241.

135. Hoig 1961, 154–60. Also see the *Record of Engagements with Hostile Indians within the Military Division of the Missouri from 1868 to 1882* (Washington, D.C.: Government Printing Office, 1882), 14–21.

136. Differentiating properly between quantitative and qualitative phenomena has been a fundamental necessity in Hegelian and Marxist philosophy, as it should

be for all social sciences. See Shirokov 1978, 211–355; Hegel 1929, book 1; Marx 1975, 53–58; Selsam 1962, 92–97.

Chapter Six

1. Kluckhohn and Leighton 1962, 109–11.
2. Doris Duke Collection, Western History Collections, University of Oklahoma.
3. See Moore 1984 for a fuller discussion of this census.
4. Michelson MS. 3218, Coyote.
5. Lee to Haury, 6 May 1886, Darlington Letterpress Books, vol. 13, CAA roll 14, OHS. Also see Berthrong 1976, chap. 5.
6. Gatschet MS. 54, p. 183, NAA.
7. Ruxton 1950, 273.
8. Mooney "Sketchbooks," NAA
9. MS. 4452A, p. 80, NAA.
10. Berthrong 1976, 63; Capt. Jessie Lee to S. S. Haury, 11 November 1885, Cheyenne and Arapaho Agency Files, OHS; "List of Beef Bands at Cantonment, I.T.," 1 March 1886, Cheyenne and Arapaho Agency Files, OHS.
11. Bent to Miles, 15 November 1876, Cheyenne and Arapaho Agency Files, OHS.
12. Ruxton 1951, 180.
13. Chittenden 1935; also see Mooney, MS. D, for comments of Alights on a Cloud concerning Mexicans in the Black Hills.
14. "Mapa Geografico del Gobierno de la Nueva Granada o Nuevo Mexico" por D. Juan Lopez, Num. 124 in Carpeta II of *Cartografía de Ultramar, Atlas.* Another Spanish reference to Cheyennes (Flechas Rayadas) is in the Spanish Archives of New Mexico, Twitchell no. 2056. My thanks to Tom Kavanaugh for finding this reference.
15. Bent 1968, 83.
16. *Sand Creek Massacre Investigation Report,* Senate Executive Document no. 26, 39th Cong., 2d sess. (Washington, D.C.: Government Printing Office, 1865), 2:153.
17. Brown 1959, 11.
18. Both articles are in Albers and Medicine 1983; also see Leacock 1981.
19. Bent 1968, 41–48, 72–73, 293–95.
20. My informants, including council chiefs, claim it is incorrect to say that warfare decisions were left to the soldier societies only when the council could not decide about peace and war. In fact, referring the question to the societies was itself a declaration of war. See Hoebel 1960, 47–48.
21. Llewellyn and Hoebel 1941, 89.
22. Bent 1968, 41–48.
23. Mooney MS. 2213, NAA.
24. Bent 1968, 272–73.

25. Bent 1968, 64–67. Some accounts say that Black White Man was not himself a Negro, but was merely named after a Negro at Bent's Fort.

26. Grinnell 1962, 1:39–40; Bent 1968, 33.

27. Grinnell 1900, 72.

28. Problematic for the Cheyennes was the status of some Crow captives in 1831. See Grinnell 1956, 31, and Llewellyn and Hoebel 1941, 132–68.

29. Abert 1851, 6.

30. *Missouri Republican* (Independence, Mo.), 2 October 1849.

31. *Sand Creek Massacre Investigation Report*, 2:144–45 (see note 16 above); Carroll 1973, 135.

32. Bent 1968, 177.

33. Bent 1968, 159.

34. Bent 1968, 159, 177, 337–38; Doris Duke Collection, Western History Collections, University of Oklahoma, interview T-84, pp. 8–9.

35. Bent 1968, 337–38; Moore 1974a.

36. Bent 1968, 164–222.

37. Grinnell 1956, 155.

38. Berthrong 1963, 224–44.

39. Grinnell 1956, 264–65.

40. Llewellyn and Hoebel 1941, 146–48.

41. Grinnell 1956, 45–62.

42. Bent 1968, 74.

43. Bent 1968, 78–79.

44. Bent 1968, 339.

45. Hyde 1951, 303–23.

46. Custer 1962, 125.

47. Hayden 1863, 277.

48. Grinnell 1956, 49.

49. Carroll 1978, 140–47.

50. Berthrong 1963, 343.

51. Miles to Hoag, March 1873, Cheyenne-Arapaho Correspondence, National Archives.

52. Bent 1968, 315.

53. Ben Clark to Col. Mizner, Cheyenne-Arapaho Correspondence, National Archives. By this time "chiefship" had been somewhat redefined; see Moore 1974a. 1974a.

54. *Sand Creek Massacre Investigation Report*, 2:144–45 (see note 16 above).

55. Custer 1962, 126–27.

56. Moore 1974a.

57. Moore 1974a.

58. Gearing 1962.

59. Swanton 1946, 181.

60. According to Roy Bull Coming and Harry White Horse, a modern headsman of the Fox Soldiers.

61. Creel MS, Gilcrease Museum, Tulsa, Oklahoma.

62. Nespor 1984, chap. 4.

63. Report to the Commissioner of Indian Affairs for 1885.

64. Maps are in the Bourke Collection, Joslyn Art Museum, Omaha, Nebraska. A similar symbol was borrowed for the frontispiece of Grinnell 1961.

Chapter Seven

1. Twelfth United States census schedules, National Archives.

2. Comments on the 1880 census are in Moore 1984, 292–94.

3. Moore 1980a,c.

4. Nespor 1984, 186–220.

5. Berthrong 1976, 118–20.

6. Doris Duke Oral History Collection, Western History Collections, University of Oklahoma, interview T-143.

7. Doris Duke Oral History Collection, Western History Collections, University of Oklahoma.

8. My thanks to Donald Berthrong for sharing his copy of the letter.

9. This information is summarized from a report I prepared for the Southern Cheyenne Research and Human Development Association in 1978.

10. Berthrong 1976, 165–70.

11. Gibson 1980, 519–20; Prucha 1975, 202–3.

12. Long 1823, 174–86.

13. This same mechanism is discussed for the Lugbaras in Middleton 1960.

14. Fowler 1898, 57–59.

15. Grinnell 1956, 49–50.

16. Mooney 1979, 228–29.

17. Grinnell 1962, 1:94–95.

18. Bent 1968, 323.

19. Petter 1915, s.v. "band."

20. Abert 1848, 438.

21. Bent 1968, 294.

22. See "capture list," microfilm CAA-2, Indian Archives Division, Oklahoma Historical Society.

23. Winter count of Chunky Fingernails, Western History Collections, University of Oklahoma.

24. A photographic history of Mennonite activities is entitled "Seventy-five Years of General Conference Mission Work among the Cheyenne and Arapaho Indians in Oklahoma"; a copy is in the El Reno, Oklahoma, Public Library.

25. Berthrong 1976, 267, 250–56.

26. Powell 1969, 77–82.

27. Indian-Pioneer Papers, 7:296, Western History Collections, University of Oklahoma.

28. Grinnell 1956, 414–27.

29. Both Ives Goddard (1978) and Wayne Leman (personal communication)

doubt that a Sutaio dialect can be identified on phonetic grounds alone. It may be a case of a distinct social group with only an alleged phonetic difference.

30. Gatschet MS. 54, NAA.

31. Michelson MS. 3218, NAA.

32. Michelson MS. 2811, NAA.

33. Mooney 1907, 405; Petter 1915, s.v. "band."

34. Bent 1968, 243, 253.

35. Ben Clark MS. 3449, NAA; George Bent to George Hyde, 25 April 1906, Yale University Library.

36. Mooney 1907, 405; Petter 1915, s.v. "band" under "Eseomhetaneo"; J. N. B. Hewitt MS. 893, NAA.

37. Moore 1984.

38. Mooney 1907, 405.

39. Mooney 1979, 152–72; Jablow 1951.

40. Riggs 1893, 168–94; Grinnell 1962, 1:1–46.

41. Phillips 1961, 2:395–429.

42. Lavender 1954, 114–33.

43. Bent to Hyde, 8 October 1908, Coe Collection, Yale University Library.

44. They are specified as participants in the 1838 attack on the Kiowas, the last band to arrive. See Grinnell 1956, 50.

45. Bent 1968, 97, 339; Grinnell 1962, 1:95–101.

46. Bent 1968, 97.

47. Original survey maps are on file at the Oklahoma Department of Libraries, Oklahoma City.

48. Of course affines who were not Sand Creek descendants continually married into these bands. But since at least one parent in these bands was a Sand Creek descendant, all the children would be also.

Chapter Eight

1. Grinnell 1962, 1:90–92.

2. Mooney 1907, 408–9.

3. Bent to Hyde, 29 November 1912, Coe Collection, Yale University Library.

4. Mooney MS. C, NAA; Gatschet MS. 61, NAA; Creel MS, book D, p. 105, Gilcrease Museum, Tulsa, Oklahoma; Michelson MSS. 2822, 2811, NAA; Abert 1845, 6.

5. Mooney MS. 2213, NAA.

6. Hoebel 1980; Moore 1981a; Conrad 1983.

7. Moore 1987.

8. Moore 1980a.

9. Mooney MS. B, NAA.

10. Mooney MS. B, NAA.

11. Mooney MS. B, NAA.

12. Mooney MS. D, NAA.

13. Mooney MS. D, NAA.

14. Mooney MS. B, NAA.
15. Mooney MS. D, NAA.
16. Michelson MS. 2822, NAA.
17. Mooney MS. 2213, NAA.
18. Mooney MS. 2213, NAA.
19. Michelson MS. 2822, NAA.
20. Mooney MS. C, NAA.
21. Creel MS, book D, p. 103, Gilcrease Museum, Tulsa, Oklahoma.
22. Michelson MS. 3220, NAA.
23. Llewellyn and Hoebel 1941, 186.
24. Mooney MS. D, NAA.
25. Moore 1981a.
26. Mooney MS. 2531, NAA.
27. Llewellyn and Hoebel 1941, 207.
28. Llewellyn and Hoebel 1941.
29. Gatschet MS. 61, NAA.
30. Sand Creek genealogies.
31. Bent 1968, 37–38.
32. My thanks to Robert Nespor for digging out these letters and reports from the Indian Archives, OHS.
33. Grinnell 1961, 219–21.
34. Grinnell 1971, 129–31.
35. Randolph 1937, 133–40, Grinnell 1961, 87–104.

Chapter Nine

1. Rivers did not use this notation in his best-known ethnography and theoretical work. See Rivers 1914, 1967.
2. Morgan 1871.
3. Moore 1980b.
4. Stern 1931, 73–99; Resek 1960, 72–104.
5. White 1959b.
6. White 1959b, 93–97; Lavender 1954, 169; Lecompte 1978, 61, 223.
7. Hayden 1863.
8. Petter, n.d., 8.
9. John S. Smith MS. 43, NAA; Schoolcraft 1847, 3:446–59.
10. Gatschet MS. 54, NAA.
11. Creel MS, Gilcrease Museum, Tulsa, Oklahoma.
12. J. N. B. Hewitt MS. 893, NAA.
13. Petter 1952.
14. See Robert Redfield's introduction to Eggan 1937.
15. Radcliffe-Brown 1965.
16. Gregg and Williams 1948; Asad 1979.
17. Mrs. Vinnie Hoffman, 17 November 1981.
18. Everett Yellowman, Summer 1983.

19. Fletcher and La Flesche and Claude Lévi-Strauss, among others, have similarly departed from orthodoxy to emphasize certain points. Fletcher and La Flesche 1911; Lévi-Strauss 1967, 325–45.

20. The Sand Creek genealogies tend to show classificatory relationships before allotment in 1892, when heirship records were begun by the Bureau of Indian Affairs, and biological relationships afterward, when births were more carefully recorded. Nevertheless, the "social fertility" of the council chiefs is evident.

21. Petter 1915, 1952, 18–19; Gatschet MS. 54, NAA; Hewitt MS. 893, NAA.

Chapter Ten

1. According to modern arrow priests.
2. Provinse 1937; Oliver 1962; Bailey 1980.
3. Personal communication, December 1983.
4. Lubbock 1889.
5. Stern 1949, 340; Steward 1955, 51.
6. Campbell 1984.
7. Berthrong 1976, 47, 115.
8. Remington 1889, 542.
9. Newcomer 1974.
10. These kinds of historical processes are seen by Soviet scholars as part of "ethnogenesis." See Bromley 1983, 31–68; Dragadze 1980; Humphrey 1984.

Linguistic Appendix

1. Fouche 1961; Dobson 1968.
2. Petter 1915, 228; Alford and Leman 1976, 19; Mooney 1907, 361; Grinnell 1962, 1:3.
3. Alford and Leman 1976, xv; Petter 1952, 1.
4. Fouche 1961, 3:567–68.
5. Carver 1976, 216.
6. Williamson 1902, 100, 112.
7. Carver 1976, 100, 137–38; Carver 1956, 79–80.
8. Tucker 1942, plates V, VI, and XIV. For other examples of the "8" literation, see "Ottawa" in Hodge 1907.
9. Lahontan 1703, 230–31.
10. "Noms des nations qui habitent an nord," by Aubert de la Chesnaye, 1697, in Margry 1879, 6.
11. Franquelin 1697, Newberry Library, reproduced in Wedel 1974.

References

Abel, Annie Heloise
  1921 Truteau's description of the Upper Missouri. *Mississippi Valley Historical Review* 8 (1–2): 149–79.
  1939 *Tabeau's narrative of Loisel's expedition to the Upper Missouri.* Norman: University of Oklahoma Press.
Abert, J. W.
  1845 *Report of the secretary of war.* Senate Executive Document no. 23, 30th Cong. Washington, D.C.: Government Printing Office.
  1966 *Western America in 1846–1847: The original travel diary of Lieutenant J. W. Abert.* San Francisco: John Howell.
Adams, Richard N.
  1975 *Energy and structure.* Austin: University of Texas Press.
Albers, Patricia
  1985 Pluralism in the native Plains, 1570–1870. Unpublished manuscript, Department of Anthropology, University of Utah.
Albers, Patricia, and William James
  1986 Historical materialism vs. evolutionary ecology. *Critique of Anthropology* 6 (1): 87–100.
Albers, Patricia, and Beatrice Medicine
  1983 *The hidden half.* Washington, D.C.: University Press of America.
Alford, Dan K., and Wayne Leman
  1976 *English-Cheyenne student dictionary.* Lame Deer, Mont.: Bilingual Education Program.
Anderson, Roger C.
  1982 An evolutionary model summarizing the roles of fire, climate, and grazing animals in the origin and maintenance of grasslands: An end paper. In *Grasses and grasslands,* ed. James Estes, Ronald Tyrl, and Jere Brunken, 297–308. Norman: University of Oklahoma Press.
Archer, Sellers G., and Clarence E. Bunch
  1953 *The American grass book.* Norman: University of Oklahoma Press.

Asad, Talal
1979 British social anthropology. In *Toward a Marxist anthropology*, ed. Talal Asad, 367–76. The Hague: Mouton.
Bailey, Garrick
1980 Social control on the Plains. In *Anthropology on the Great Plains*, ed. W. Raymond Wood and Margo Liberty, 153–63. Lincoln: University of Nebraska Press.
Baker, O. E.
1936 Atlas of American agriculture. Washington, D.C.: U.S. Department of Agriculture.
Bale, Karen A.
1981a *Little Flower's desire*. New York: Zebra Books.
1981b *Sweet Medicine's prophecy*. New York: Zebra Books.
Barbalace, Roberta Crowell
1974 *An introduction to light horse management*. Fort Collins, Colo.: Caballus.
Barrett, Stephen M.
1913 *Hoistah, an Indian girl*. New York: Duffield.
Bass, Althea
1954 James Mooney in Oklahoma. *Chronicles of Oklahoma* 32 (8): 246–62.
Behn, Aphra
1967 *Oroonoko and other prose narratives*. Edited by Montague Summers. New York: Benjamin Blom.
Bent, George
1968 *Life of George Bent*. Edited by George Hyde. Norman: University of Oklahoma Press.
Berger, Joel
1983 Ecology and catastrophic mortality in wild horses. *Science* 220: 1403–4.
Berthrong, Donald J.
1963 *The Southern Cheyennes*. Norman: University of Oklahoma Press.
1976 *The Cheyenne and Arapaho ordeal*. Norman: University of Oklahoma Press.
Bhowal, P. C., ed.
1970 *Selections from V. I. Lenin and J. V. Stalin on national colonial question*. Calcutta: Calcutta Book House.
Blakeslee, Donald J.
1975 *The Plains interband trade system*. Ann Arbor, Mich.: University Microfilms.
Boas, Franz
1896 The limitations of the comparative method of anthropology, *Science* 4: 901–8.
1940 *Race, language and culture*. New York: Free Press.
Bowers, Alfred W.
1950 *Mandan social and ceremonial organization*. Chicago: University of Chicago Press.
1965 *Hidatsa social and ceremonial organization*. Bureau of American Ethnology Bulletin 194. Washington, D.C.: Government Printing Office.

Bromley, Julian
1983 *Ethnic processes.* Vol. 3. *Soviet ethnographic studies.* Social Sciences Today. USSR Academy of Sciences.
Brown, Seletha
1959 *Rivalry at the river.* Longmont, Colo.: Ferguson.
Bryce, James
1893 The migrations of the races of men considered historically. In *Annual report of the board of regents of the Smithsonian Institution,* 567–87. Washington, D.C.: Smithsonian Institution Press.
Buechel, Eugene
1970 *A dictionary of the Teton Dakota Sioux language.* Pine Ridge, S.D.: Red Cloud Indian School.
Burgess, Robert, W. Carter Johnson, and Warren R. Keammerer
1973 *Vegetation of the Missouri River floodplain in North Dakota.* Office of Water Resources Research Project no. A-022-NDAK, Department of the Interior. Washington, D.C.: Government Printing Office.
Bushnell, David I.
1922 *Villages of the Algonquian, Siouan, and Caddoan tribes west of the Mississippi.* Bureau of American Ethnology Bulletin 77. Washington, D.C.: Government Printing Office.
Buskirk, Winfred
1949 Western Apache subsistence economy. Ph.D. diss., Anthropology Department, University of New Mexico.
Campbell, Gregory R.
1984 The epidemiological consequences of the Northern Cheyenne removal to Indian Territory. Paper presented at Plains Conference, Lincoln, Nebraska.
Campbell, Lyle, and Marianne Mithun
1979 The languages of native America. Austin: University of Texas Press.
Carneiro, Robert L.
1981 *The chiefdom: Precursor of the state.* In *The transition to statehood in the New World,* ed. Grant Jones and Robert Kantz. Cambridge: Cambridge University Press.
Carroll, John M.
1973 *The Sand Creek Massacre.* New York: Sol Lewis.
1978 *General Custer and the Battle of the Washita: The federal view.* Bryan, Tex.: Guidon Press.
Carver, Jonathan
1956 *Travels through the interior parts of North America, in the years 1766, 1767 and 1768.* Minneapolis: Ross and Haines.
1976 *The journals of Jonathan Carver.* Edited by John Parker. St. Paul: Minnesota Historical Society Press.
Chagnon, Napoleon, and William Irons, eds.
1979 *Evolutionary biology and human social behavior.* North Scituate, Mass.: Duxbury Press.

Charlevoix, P. F. X., S.J.
    1900 *History and general description of New France.* New York: Francis P. Harper.
Chittenden, Hiram M.
    1935 *The American fur trade of the Far West.* 2 vols. New York: Press of the Pioneers.
Clark, W. P.
    1885 *The Indian sign language.* Philadelphia: L. R. Hamersly.
Cole, Fay-Cooper
    1931 Obituary of George Dorsey. *American Anthropologist* 33: 413–14.
Connor, Walker
    1984 *The national question in Marxist-Leninist theory and strategy.* Princeton: Princeton University Press.
Conrad, Lawrence
    1983 Comment. *Plains Anthropologist* 28 (100): 141–42.
Cooper, John M.
    1939 Truman Michelson. *American Anthropologist* 41: 281–85.
Coues, Elliott, ed.
    1965 *New light on the early history of the Greater Northwest.* 2 vols. Minneapolis: Ross and Hines.
Crisp, D. J., ed.
    1964 *Grazing in terrestrial and marine environments.* Oxford: Bartholomew Press.
Custer, George A.
    1962 *My life on the Plains.* Norman: University of Oklahoma Press.
    1977 Custer's original Battle of Washita reports. *War Chief* 11 (2): 1–10.
Cutright, Paul R.
    1976 *A history of the Lewis and Clark journals.* Norman: University of Oklahoma Press.
Danziger, Edmund J.
    1979 *The Chippewas of Lake Superior.* Norman: University of Oklahoma Press.
Davis, Irvine
    1979 The Kiowa-Tanoan, Keresan and Zuni languages. In *The languages of native America,* ed. Lyle Campbell and Marianne Mithun, 390–443. Austin: University of Texas Press.
Delanglez, Jean
    1941 *Hennepin's description of Louisiana.* Chicago: Institute of Jesuit History.
Deng, Francis M.
    1971 *Tradition and modernization.* New Haven: Yale University Press.
Devereux, Frederick L.
    1979 *The cavalry manual of horse management.* New York: A. S. Barnes.
DEVRES
    1980 *The socio-economic context of fuelwood use in small rural communities.* Washington, D.C.: Bureau for Program and Policy Coordination, U.S. Agency for International Development.
Diamond, Stanley
    1974 *In search of the primitive.* New Brunswick. N.J.: Transaction Books.

Dickemann, Mildred
1979 Female infanticide, reproductive strategies, and social stratification: A preliminary model. In *Evolutionary biology and human social behavior,* ed. Napoleon Chagnon and William Irons, 321–73. North Scituate, Mass.: Duxbury Press.
Dix, Ralph L.
1964 A history of biotic and climatic causes within the North American grassland. In *Grazing in terrestrial and marine environments,* ed. D. J. Crisp, 71–89. Oxford: Bartholomew Press.
Dobson, E. J.
1968 *English pronunciation, 1500–1700.* 2 vols. Oxford: Clarendon Press.
Dobyns, Henry F.
1966 Estimating aboriginal American population: An appraisal of techniques with a new hemispheric estimate. *Current Anthropology* 7: 395–416.
1976 *Native American historical demography: A critical bibliography.* Bloomington: Indiana University Press.
1983 *Their number become thinned.* Knoxville: University of Tennessee Press.
Dobyns, Henry F., ed.
1987 *The web of disease.* Forthcoming.
Dockstader, Frederick J.
1957 *The American Indian in graduate studies.* Contributions, vol. 15. New York: Museum of the American Indian.
Dole, Gertrude
1968 Tribe as the autonomous unit. In *Essays on the problem of tribe,* ed. June Helm, 83–100. Seattle: University of Washington Press for American Ethnological Society.
Dorsey, George A.
1905 *The Cheyenne.* 2 vols. Anthropological Series, vol. 9, nos. 1 and 2. Chicago: Field Columbian Museum.
1925 *Why we behave like human beings.* New York: Harper.
1929 *Hows and whys of human behavior.* New York: Harper.
1931 *Man's own show: Civilization.* New York: Ribbon.
1972 *The Cheyenne Indians: The Sun Dance, Wyoming.* Glorieta, N.Mex.: Rio Grande.
Dort, W., and J. K. Jones, eds.
1970 *Pleistocene and Recent environments of the central Great Plains.* Lawrence: University of Kansas Press.
Dragadze, T.
1980 The place of "ethnos" theory in Soviet anthropology. In *Soviet and Western anthropology,* ed. Ernest Gellner, 161–70. New York: Columbia University Press.
Dykes, J. C.
1960 *Great western Indian fights.* Lincoln: University of Nebraska Press.
Eckholm, Erik P.
1975 *The other energy crisis: Firewood.* World Watch Paper no. 1. Washington D.C.: Worldwatch Institute.

Eggan, Fred
    1937   The Cheyenne and Arapaho kinship system. In *Social anthropology of North American tribes*, ed. Fred Eggan. Chicago: University of Chicago Press.
Eiselin, Elizabeth
    1943   A geographic traverse across South Dakota. Ph.D. diss., University of Chicago.
Emerson, Rupert
    1960   *From empire to nation*. Boston: Beacon.
Estes, James, Ronald Tyrl, and Jere Brunken, eds.
    1982   *Grasses and grassland*. Norman: University of Oklahoma Press.
Ewers, John C.
    1955   *The horse in Blackfoot Indian culture*. Bureau of American Ethnology Bulletin 159. Washington, D.C.: Government Printing Office.
Ferris, Robert G., ed.
    1963   *The American West*. Santa Fe: Museum of New Mexico Press.
Fisher, William
    1812   *New travels among the Indians of North America*. Philadelphia: James Sharan.
Fletcher, Alice C., and Francis La Flesche
    1911   *The Omaha tribe*. Annual Report of the Bureau of American Ethnology, vol. 27. Washington, D.C.: Government Printing Office.
Fouche, Pierre
    1961   *Phonetique historique du Français*. 3 vols. Paris: C. Klincksieck.
Fowler, Jacob
    1898   *The journal of Jacob Fowler*. Edited by Elliott Coues. New York: Francis P. Harper.
Fowler, Loretta
    1982   *Arapaho politics, 1851–1978*. Lincoln: University of Nebraska Press.
Fried, Morton H.
    1967   *The evolution of political society*. New York: Random House.
    1975   *The notion of tribe*. London: Cummings.
    1983   Tribe to state or state to tribe in ancient China? In *The origins of Chinese civilization*, ed. David Keightley, 467–93. Berkeley: University of California Press.
Garfield, Viola, ed.
    1961   *Symposium: Patterns of land utilization and other papers*. Seattle: University of Washington Press.
Garrard, Lewis H.
    1955   *Wah-to-yah and the Taos Trail*. Norman: University of Oklahoma Press.
Gearing, Fred
    1962   *Priests and warriors*. Memoir 93. Washington, D.C.: American Anthropological Association.
Gellner, Ernest, ed.
    1980   *Soviet and Western anthropology*. New York: Columbia University Press.
Geraghty, James J., et al.
    1975   *Water atlas of the United States*. Port Washington, N.Y.: Water Information Center.

German, Catherine
  1927 *Girl captives of the Cheyennes.* Los Angeles: Gem.
Gibson, Arrell Morgan
  1980 *The American Indian.* Toronto: D. C. Heath.
Gilbert, William H., Jr.
  1937 Eastern Cherokee social organization. In *Social anthropology of North American tribes,* ed. Fred Eggan, 285–338. Chicago: University of Chicago Press.
Gluckman, Max
  1955 *Custom and conflict in Africa.* Oxford: Blackwell.
Goble, Paul, and Dorothy Goble
  1972 *The Fetterman fight.* New York: Pantheon.
Goddard, Ives
  1967 *Notes on the genetic classification of the Algonquian languages.* Bulletin 214. Ottawa: National Museums of Canada.
  1972 Historical and philological evidence regarding the identification of the Mascouten. *Ethnohistory* 19 (2): 123–34.
  1978 The Sutaio dialect of Cheyenne: A discussion of the evidence. In *Papers of the Ninth Algonquian Conference,* 68–80. Ottawa: Carleton University.
Graves, Henry S.
  1919 *The use of wood for fuel.* Bulletin no. 753. Washington, D.C.: U.S. Department of Agriculture.
Gregg, Dorothy, and Elgin Williams
  1948 The dismal science of functionalism. *American Anthropologist* 40 (4, part 1): 594–711.
Griffin, David E.
  1977 *Timber procurement and village location in the Middle Missouri subarea. Plains Anthropologist* Memoir 13.
Grinnell, George B.
  1900 *The Indians of to-day.* New York: Duffield.
  1902 Social organization of the Cheyennes. *Transactions of the International Congress of Americanists.*
  1907 Some early Cheyenne tales. *Journal of American Folklore* 20 (78): 169–94.
  1908 Some early Cheyenne tales, II. *Journal of American Folklore* 21 (82): 269–320.
  1910 Coup and scalp among the Plains Indians. *American Anthropologist* 12: 296–320.
  1918 Early Cheyenne villages. *American Anthropologist* 20 (4): 359–80.
  1956 *The fighting Cheyennes.* Norman: University of Oklahoma Press (originally published 1915).
  1961 *Pawnee, Blackfoot and Cheyenne.* New York: Charles Scribner's Sons.
  1962 *The Cheyenne Indians.* 2 vols. New York: Cooper Square (originally published 1923).
  1971 *By Cheyenne campfires.* Lincoln: University of Nebraska (originally published 1926).

Gurvich, Israel
  1981 Present-day ethnic processes among the peoples of Siberia. In *Ethno-cultural processes and national problems in the modern world,* 160–76. Moscow: Progress.
Hafen, LeRoy R.
  1930 The W. M. Boggs manuscript about Bent's Fort, Kit Carson, the Far West and life among the Indians. *Colorado Magazine* 7 (2): 45–69
Hague, Arnold
  1887 An early map of the Far West. *Science* 248: 217–18.
Hamilton, W. T.
  1960 *My sixty years on the Plains.* Norman: University of Oklahoma Press.
Harris, Marvin
  1968 *The Rise of anthropological theory.* New York: Crowell.
  1979 *Cultural materialism.* New York: Random House.
Hart, Stephen H., and Archer B. Hulbert
  1932 *Zebulon Pike's Arkansaw journal.* Denver: Colorado College and Denver Public Library.
Hassrick, Royal
  1964 *The Sioux.* Norman: University of Oklahoma Press.
Hawley, A. W. L., D. G. Peden, H. W. Reynolds, and W. R. Stricklin
  1981 Bison and cattle digestion of forages from the Slave River lowlands, Northwest Territories, Canada. *Journal of Range Management* 34 (2): 126–30.
Hayden, F. V.
  1863 Contributions to the ethnography and philology of the Indian tribes of the Missouri Valley. *American Philosophical Society Transactions,* n.s., 12: 274–320.
Hegel, George W. F.
  1929, *Science of logic.* 2 vols. New York: Macmillan.
Heizer, Robert F.
  1963 Domestic fuel in primitive society. *Journal of the Royal Anthropological Institute of Great Britain and Ireland* 93: 186–94.
Helm, June, ed.
  1968 *Essays on the problem of tribe.* Seattle: University of Washington Press for American Ethnological Society.
Hennepin, Louis
  1903 *A new discovery of a vast country in America.* Edited by Reuben Gold Thwaites. Chicago: McClurg (originally published 1698).
  1938 *Description of Louisiana.* Minneapolis: University of Minnesota Press.
  1966 *Description of Louisiana.* New York: John Shea, Readex Microprint (originally published 1880).
Henry, Harrise
  1900 *Découverte et évolution cartographique de Terre Neuve et des pays circonvoisins, 1479–1501–1764.* London: H. Stevens.

Herod, Charles C.
1976 *The nation in the history of Marxian thought.* The Hague: Martinus Nijhoff.
Hickerson, Harold
1962 *The Southwestern Chippewa.* Memoir 92, vol. 64, no. 3, pt. 2. Washington, D.C.: American Anthropological Association.
1970 *The Chippewa and their neighbors: A study in ethnohistory.* New York: Holt, Rinehart and Winston.
Hodge, Frederick W., ed.
1907 *Handbook of American Indians north of Mexico.* 2 vols. Bureau of American Ethnology Bulletin 30. Washington, D.C.: Government Printing Office.
Hoebel, E. Adamson
1960 *The Cheyennes.* New York: Holt, Rinehart and Winston.
1980 On Cheyenne sociopolitical organization. *Plains Anthropologist* 25: 161–69.
Hoelscher, Clark E., and E. J. Woolfolk
1953 *Forage utilization by cattle on northern Great Plains ranges.* Circular no. 918. Washington, D.C.: U.S. Department of Agriculture.
Hoig, Stan
1961 *The Sand Creek Massacre.* Norman: University of Oklahoma Press.
Holder, Preston
1970 *The hoe and the horse on the plains.* Lincoln: University of Nebraska Press.
Hollow, Robert C.
1970 A Mandan dictionary. Ph.D. diss., University of California, Berkeley.
Hollow, Robert C., and Douglas R. Parks
1980 Studies in Plains linguistics: A review. In *Anthropology on the Great Plains,* ed. W. Raymond Wood and Margo Liberty, 68–97. Lincoln: University of Nebraska Press.
Hosmer, James K., ed.
1917 *History of the expedition of Captains Lewis and Clark.* Chicago: McClurg.
Huddleston, Lee Eldridge
1967 *Origins of the American Indians.* Latin American Monographs, no. 11. Austin: University of Texas Press.
Humphrey, Caroline
1984 Some recent developments in ethnography in the U.S.S.R. *Man* 19: 310–20.
Hyde, George E.
1951 *The Pawnee Indians.* Norman: University of Oklahoma Press.
1956 *A Sioux chronicle.* Norman: University of Olahoma Press.
1961 *Spotted Tail's Folk.* Norman: University of Oklahoma Press.
1973 *Red Cloud's folk.* Norman: University of Oklahoma Press.
Hyland, Ann
1976 *Endurance riding.* North Hollywood, Calif.: Wilshire.

Jablow, Joseph
  1951 *The Cheyenne in Plains Indian trade relations, 1795–1840.* Monograph 19. New York: J. J. Augustin for American Ethnological Society.
Jefferson, Thomas
  1917 Life of Captain Lewis. In *History of the expedition of Captains Lewis and Clark,* ed. James K. Hosmer, xli–lvi. Chicago: McClurg (originally published 1813).
Johnson, Elden, ed.
  1974 *Aspects of Upper Great Lakes anthropology.* Minnesota Prehistoric Archaeology Series, no. 11. St. Paul: Minnesota Historical Society Press.
Jones, Grant, and Robert Kantz
  1981 *The transition to statehood in the New World.* Cambridge: Cambridge University Press.
Karpinski, Louis C.
  1931 *Bibliography of the printed maps of Michigan.* Lansing: Michigan Historical Commission.
Keightley, David, ed.
  1983 *The origins of Chinese civilization.* Berkeley: University of Calif. Press.
Kennard, Edward
  1936 Mandan grammar. *International Journal of American Linguistics* 9 (1): 1–43.
Kenner, Charles L.
  1969 *A history of New Mexican–Plains Indian relations.* Norman: University of Oklahoma Press.
Kluckhohn, Clyde, and Dorothea Leighton
  1962 *The Navaho.* Garden City, N.Y.: Doubleday.
Kothari, Rajni
  1971 Variations and uniformities in nation-building: Introduction to regional variations in nation-building. *International Social Science Journal* 23 (3): 339–54.
Kotok, Victor
  1971 The development of national state system in the USSR. *International Social Science Journal* 23 (3): 371–83
Kozlov, Vasili, and Julian Bromley
  1981 Present-day ethnic processes in the intellectual culture of the peoples of the USSR. In *Ethnocultural processes and national problems in the modern world,* 19–38, 244–69. Moscow: Progress.
Kranz, Jeremiah J., and Raymond Linder
  1973 Value of Black Hills forest communities to deer and cattle. *Journal of Range Management* 26 (4): 263–65.
Kroeber, A. L.
  1900 Cheyenne tales. *Journal of American Folklore* 13 (50): 161–90.
Küchler, A. W.
  1972 The oscillations of the mixed prairie in Kansas. *Erdkunde* 26 (2): 120–29.

Lahontan, Armand
1703 *New voyages to North-America.* London: H. Bonwicke.
La Salle, Cavelier de
1680 Lettre du découvreur à un de ses associés. In *Découvertes et établissements des Français dans l'ouest et dans le sud de l'Amérique Septentrionale, 1614–1754,* ed. Pierre Margry. Paris: Maisonneare.
Latham, Hiram
1962 *Trans-Missouri stock raising.* Denver: Old West (originally published 1871).
Lavender, David
1954 *Bent's Fort.* New York: Doubleday.
Lawson, Merlin P., and Charles W. Stockton
1981 Desert myth and climatic reality. *Annals of the Association of American Geographers* 71 (4): 527–35.
Leacock, Eleanor
1981 *Myths of male dominance.* New York: Monthly Review Press.
Lecompte, Janet
1978 *Pueblo, Hardscrabble, Greenhorn.* Norman: University of Oklahoma Press.
Lehmer, Donald J.
1954 *Archeological investigations in the Oahe Dam area, South Dakota, 1950–51.* Bureau of American Ethnology Bulletin 158. Washington, D.C.: Government Printing Office.
1970 Culture and culture history in the Middle Missouri Valley. In *Pleistocene and Recent environments of the central Great Plains,* ed. W. Dort and J. K. Jones, 59–71. Lawrence: University of Kansas Press.
Lehmer, Donald J., and W. Raymond Wood
1977 Buffalo and beans. In *Selected writings of Donald J. Lehmer,* ed. W. Raymond Wood. Reprints in Anthropology, vol. 8. Lincoln, Nebr.: J&L Reprints.
Lenin, V. I.
1960a *Selected works.* 3 vols. Moscow: Foreign Languages Publishing House.
1960b What the "Friends of the People" are and how they fought the Social-Democrats. In *Collected works,* 1: 129–332. Moscow: Progress.
Lévi-Strauss, Claude
1963 *Structural anthropology.* Vol. 1. New York: Basic Books.
1966 *The savage mind.* Chicago: University of Chicago Press.
1967 *The elementary structures of kinship.* Boston: Beacon (French ed. 1949).
1976 *Structural anthropology.* Vol. 2. New York: Basic Books.
Levy, Jerrold E.
1961 Ecology of the south plains. In *Symposium: Patterns of land utilization and other papers.* ed. Viola Garfield, 18–25. Seattle: University of Washington Press.
Levy-Bruhl, Lucien
1966 *The "soul" of the primitive.* Chicago: Henry Regnery.

Llewellyn, Karl N., and E. Adamson Hoebel
    1941 *The Cheyenne way.* Norman: University of Oklahoma Press.
Long, Stephen H.
    1823 *Account of an expedition from Pittsburgh to the Rocky Mountains.* Philadelphia: H. C. Carey and I. Lea.
Lowie, Robert H.
    1915 Oral tradition and history. *American Anthropologist* 17: 597–99.
    1917 Oral tradition and history. *Journal of American Folklore* 30 (116): 161–67.
    1947 *Primitive society.* New York: Liveright.
Lubbock, John
    1889 *The origin of civilization and the primitive condition of man.* New York: Appleton
Luxemburg, Rosa
    1976 *The national question.* New York: Monthly Review Press.
McLennan, John F.
    1970 *Primitive marriage.* Chicago: University of Chicago Press (originally published 1865).
Malinowski, Bronislaw
    1922 *Argonauts of the western Pacific.* New York: E. P. Dutton.
Marable, Mary
    1939 *Handbook of Oklahoma writers.* Norman: University of Oklahoma Press.
Margry, Pierre, ed.
    1879 *Découvertes et établissements de Français dans l'ouest et dans le sud de l'Amérique Septentrionale, 1614–1754.* Paris: Maisonneare.
Marx, Karl
    1962 Preface to the *Critique of political economy,* In *Selected works,* 1: 361–65. Moscow: Foreign Languages Publishing House.
    1975 Difference between the Democritean and Epicurean philosophy in general. In *Collected works,* vol. 1. New York: International.
Marx, Karl, and Frederick Engels
    1976 The German idealogy. In *Collected works.* 5: 19–539 New York: International.
Mathews, John J.
    1961 *The Osages.* Norman: University of Oklahoma Press.
Mayhall, Mildred
    1962 *The Kiowas.* Norman: University of Oklahoma Press.
Metcalf, George
    1960 *Star Village.* Bureau of American Ethnology Bulletin 185. Washington, D.C.: Government Printing Office.
Michelson, Truman
    1913 Preliminary report on the linguistic classification of Algonquian tribes. *Annual Report of the Bureau of American Ethnology* 28: 221–90.
    1932 The narrative of a southern Cheyenne woman. *Smithsonian Miscellaneous Collections* 87 (5): 1–13.

Middleton, John
  1960 *Lughara religion*. London: Oxford University Press.
Miller, David H., and Jerome O. Steffen
  1977 *The frontier*. Norman: University of Oklahoma Press.
Montaigne, Michel de
  1948 *The complete essays of Montaigne*. Translated by Donald Frame. Stanford: Stanford University Press.
Mooney, James
  1896 The ghost-dance religion and the Sioux outbreak of 1890. *Annual Report of the Bureau of American Ethnology* 14: 641–1110.
  1907 *The Cheyenne Indians*. Memoir 1. Washington, D.C.: American Anthropological Association.
  1922 Obituary. *American Anthropologist* 24: 209–14.
  1928 The aboriginal population of America north of Mexico. *Smithsonian Misscellaneous Collections* 80 (7): 1–40.
  1979 *Calendar history of the Kiowa Indians*. Washington, D.C.: Smithsonian Institution Press (originally published 1898).
Moore, John H.
  1974a Cheyenne political history, 1820–1894. *Ethnohistory* 21 (4): 329–59.
  1974b *Religious symbolism among the Cheyenne Indians*. Ann Arbor, Mich.: University Microfilms.
  1980a Aboriginal Indian residence patterns preserved in censuses and allotments. *Science* 207: 201–2. Addendum in 8 February issue.
  1980b Morgan's problem: The influence of Plains ethnography on ethnology of kinship. In *Anthropology on the Great Plains*, ed. W. Raymond Wood and Margo Liberty, 141–52. Lincoln: University of Nebraska Press.
  1980c Ethnology in Oklahoma. *Papers in Anthropology* 21 (2).
  1981a Evolution and historical reductionism. *Plains Anthropologist* 26 (94, pt. 1): 261–69.
  1981b *The Cheyennes in Moxtavhohona*. Lame Deer, Mont.: Northern Cheyenne Tribe.
  1982 The dynamics of scale in Plains Indian ethnohistory. *Papers in Anthropology* 23 (2): 225–46.
  1984 Cheyenne names and cosmology. *American Ethnologist* 11 (2): 291–312.
  1987 Structured dispersion: A Cheyenne response to epidemic disease. In *The web of disease*, ed. Henry Dobyns, forthcoming.
Morgan, Lewis H.
  1871 *Systems of consanguinity and affinity of the human family*. Smithsonian Contributions to Knowledge, vol. 17. Washington, D.C.: Smithsonian Institution Press.
Morgan, R. Grace
  1980 Bison movement patterns on the Canadian plains: An ecological analysis. *Plains Anthropologist* 25 (88): 143–60.

Moses, L. G.
  1978 James Mooney and the peyote controversy. *Chronicles of Oklahoma* 56 (2): 127–44.
  1984 *The Indian man.* Urbana: University of Illinois Press.
Murdock, George P.
  1949 *Social structure.* New York: Free Press.
Murdock, George P., and Timothy J. O'Leary
  1975 *Ethnographic bibliography of North America.* 5 vols. New Haven, Conn.: Human Relations Area Files Press.
Nasatir, Abraham P.
  1952 *Before Lewis and Clark: Documents illustrating the history of the Missouri, 1785–1804.* 2 vols. St. Louis: St. Louis Historical Documents Foundation.
Needham, James G.
  1929 *A handbook of the dragonflies of North America.* Springfield, Ill.: Charles C. Thomas.
Needham, Rodney
  1974 *Remarks and inventions.* London: Tavistock.
Nespor, Robert
  1984 The evolution of the agricultural settlement pattern of the Southern Cheyenne Indians in western Oklahoma, 1876–1930. Ph.D. diss., Anthropology Department, University of Oklahoma.
Newcomer, Peter
  1974 The Nuer are Dinka. *Man* 7 (1): 5–11.
Oliver, Symmes C.
  1962 *Ecology and cultural continuity as contributing factors in the social organization of the Plains Indians.* University of California Publications in American Archaeology and Ethnology, no. 48. Berkeley: University of California.
Openshaw, Keith
  1974 Wood fuels in the developing world. *New Scientist* 61 (883): 271–72.
O'Reilly, Jackson
  1982 *Cheyenne raiders.* Wayne, Pa.: Banbury Books.
Osborn, Alan J.
  1983 Ecological aspects of equestrian adaptations in aboriginal North America. *American Anthropologist* 85 (3): 563–91.
Osgood, Ernest S.
  1964 *The field notes of Captain William Clark.* New Haven: Yale University Press.
Ossenberg, N. S.
  1974 Origins and relationships of Woodland peoples: The evidence of cranial morphology. In *Aspects of Upper Great Lakes anthropology,* ed. Elden Johnson, 15–39. St. Paul: Minnesota Historical Society Press.
Parker, John
  1976 *The journals of Jonathan Carver.* St. Paul: Minnesota Historical Society Press.

Patterson, Thomas C.
1981 *Archaeology: The evolution of ancient societies.* Englewood Cliffs, N.J.: Prentice-Hall.
Peden, Donald George
1972 The trophic relations of *Bison bison* to the shortgrass prairie. Ph.D. diss., Colorado State University, Fort Collins.
Perdue, Theda
1979 *Slavery and the evolution of Cherokee society, 1540–1866.* Knoxville: University of Tennessee Press.
Perrin du Lac, François Marie
1807 *Travels through the two Louisianas.* London: Richard Phillips.
Petersen, Karen Daniels
1964 Cheyenne soldier societies. *Plains Anthropologist* 9 (25): 146–72.
1968 *Howling Wolf.* Palo Alto, Calif.: American West.
1971 *Plains Indian art from Fort Marion.* Norman: University of Oklahoma Press.
Petter, Rodolphe
1915 *English-Cheyenne dictionary.* Kettle Falls, Wash.: Mennonite Mission.
1952 *Cheyenne grammar.* Newton, Kans.: Mennonite Publication Office.
n.d. *Einiges aus meinen Missionserfahrungen in den vergangenen Jahren.* N.p.: N.p.
Phillips, Paul C.
1961 *The fur trade.* 2 vols. Norman: University of Oklahoma Press.
Phillpotts, Bertha Surtees
1913 *Kindred and clan in the Middle Ages and after.* Cambridge: Cambridge University Press.
Powell, Peter J.
1969 *Sweet Medicine.* 2 vols. Norman: University of Oklahoma Press.
1980 *The Cheyennes: Maheo's people.* Bloomington: Indiana University Press.
1981 *People of the sacred mountain.* 2 vols. New York: Harper and Row.
Provinse, John H.
1937 The underlying sanctions of Plains Indian culture. In *Social anthropology of North American tribes,* ed. Fred Eggan. Chicago: University of Chicago Press.
Prucha, Francis Paul
1962 *American Indian policy in the formative years.* Lincoln: University of Nebraska Press.
1975 *Documents of United States Indian policy.* Lincoln: University of Nebraska Press.
Pyne, Stephen J.
1982 *Fire in America.* Princeton: Princeton University Press.
Quaife, Milo M.
1916 *The journals of Captain Meriwether Lewis and Sergeant John Ordway.* Madison: State Historical Society of Wisconsin.

Radcliffe-Brown, A. R.
   1965 *Structure and function in primitive society.* New York: Free Press (originally published 1952).
Randolph, Richard
   1937 *Sweet Medicine.* Caldwell, Idaho: Caxton Printers.
Remington, Frederic
   1889 Artist wanderings among the Cheyennes. *Century Magazine,* August. Reprinted Seattle: Shorey Book Store, 1970.
Resek, Carl
   1960 *Lewis Henry Morgan: American scholar.* Chicago: University of Chicago Press.
Riggs, Stephen R.
   1890 *A Dakota-English dictionary.* Contributions to North American Ethnology, vol. 7. Washington, D.C.: Department of the Interior.
   1893 *Dakota grammar, texts, and ethnography.* Contributions to North American Ethnology. Washington, D.C.: Department of the Interior.
Ritzenthaler, Robert E.
   1978 Southwestern Chippewa. In *Handbook of North American Indians,* ed. William C. Sturtevant, 15: 743–59. Washington, D.C.: Smithsonian Institution Press.
Rivers, W. H. R.
   1914 *Kinship and social organization.* London: Constable.
   1967 *The Todas.* Oosterhout Netherlands: Anthropological Publications (originally published 1906).
Ronda, James P.
   1984 *Lewis and Clark among the Indians.* Lincoln: University of Nebraska Press.
Russell, Maud
   1977 National minorities in the Peoples' Republic of China. *Far East Reporter,* March 1977.
Ruxton, George F.
   1950 *Ruxton of the Rockies.* Norman: University of Oklahoma Press.
   1951 *Life in the Far West.* Norman: University of Oklahoma Press.
Sahlins, Marshall D.
   1958 *Social stratification in Polynesia.* Seattle: University of Washington Press.
Sahlins, Marshall D., and Elman R. Service, eds.
   1960 *Evolution and culture.* Ann Arbor: University of Michigan Press.
Schoolcraft, Henry R.
   1847 *Historical and statistical information respecting the history, condition and prospects of the Indian tribes of the United States.* Philadelphia: Lippincott, Grambo.
   1851 *Personal memoirs of a resident of thirty years with the Indian tribes on the American frontiers.* Philadelphia: Lippincott.
Scott, Hugh L.
   1907 The early history and the names of the Arapaho. *American Anthropologist* 9: 545–60.

Sellers, Roy Wood, V. J. McGill, and Marvin Farber, eds.
1949 *Philosophy for the future.* New York: Macmillan.
Selsam, Howard
1962 *What is philosophy?* New York: International.
Service, Elman R.
1962 *Primitive social organization.* New York: Random House.
1968 The prime-mover of cultural evolution. *Southwestern Journal of Anthropology* 24: 396–409.
1971 *Cultural evolutionism.* New York: Holt, Rinehart and Winston.
Shevtsov, Victor
1982 *The state and nations in the USSR.* Moscow: Progress.
Shirokov, M.
1978 *Textbook of Marxist philosophy.* Chicago: Proletarian (originally published 1937).
Siebert, Frank T., Jr.
1967 *The original home of the proto-Algonquian people.* Bulletin 214, Contributions to Anthropology: Linguistics I (Algonquian). Ottawa: National Museums of Canada.
Skaggs, Richard H.
1978 Climatic change and persistence in western Kansas. *Annals of the Association of American Geographers* 68 (1): 73–80.
Smith, G. Hubert
1972 *Like-a-Fishhook Village and Fort Berthold, Garrison Reservoir, North Dakota.* Anthropology Papers 2. Washington, D.C.: National Park Service.
1981 *The explorations of the La Vérendryes in the northern plains, 1738–43.* Edited by W. Raymond Wood. Lincoln: University of Nebraska Press.
Snow, C. P.
1959 *The two cultures and the scientific revolution.* Cambridge: Cambridge University Press.
Spencer, Herbert
1967 *The evolution of society.* Edited by Robert Carneiro. Chicago: University of Chicago Press.
Stalin, Joseph
1975 *Marxism and the national-colonial question.* San Francisco: Proletarian.
Stern, Bernhard J.
1931 *Lewis Henry Morgan, social evolutionist.* Chicago: University of Chicago Press.
1949 Some aspects of historical materialism. In *Philosophy for the future,* ed. Roy Wood Sellers, V. J. McGill, and Marvin Farber. New York: Macmillan.
Steward, Julian H.
1948 The circum-Caribbean tribes: An introduction. In *Handbook of South American Indians,* 4: 1–41. Bureau of American Ethnology Bulletin 143. Washington, D.C.: Government Printing Office.
1955 *Theory of culture change.* Urbana: University of Illinois Press.

Steward, Julian H., and Louis C. Faron
  1959 *Native peoples of South America.* New York: McGraw-Hill.
Stoddart, Laurence A., Arthur D. Smith, and Thadis W. Box
  1975 *Range management.* 3d ed. New York: McGraw-Hill.
Sunder, John E.
  1963 The decline of the fur trade on the Upper Missouri, 1840–1865. In *The American West,* ed. Robert G. Ferris, 128–37. Santa Fe: Museum of New Mexico Press.
  1965 *The fur trade on the Upper Missouri, 1840–1865.* Norman: University of Oklahoma Press.
Swanton, John R.
  1922 *Early history of the Creek Indians and their neighbors.* Bureau of American Ethnology Bulletin 73. Washington, D.C.: Government Printing Office.
  1946 *The Indians of the southeastern United States.* Bulletin 137. Washington, D.C.: Bureau of American Ethnology.
Teeter, Karl V.
  1967 *Genetic classification of Algonquian.* Bulletin 214. Ottawa: National Museums of Canada.
Thornton, Russell
  1987 *As snow before the summer sun.* Norman: University of Oklahoma Press.
Thwaites, Reuben Gold, ed.
  1905 *Original journals of the Lewis and Clark expedition, 1804–1806.* 6 vols. New York: Dodd, Mead.
  1906 *Early western travels.* 32 vols. Cleveland: Arthur H. Clark.
Tomelleri, Joe
  1983 Woody vegetation along the Arkansas River in western Kansas during the nineteenth century. Hays, Kans.: Department of Biology, Fort Hays State University.
Trenholm, Virginia C.
  1970 *The Arapahoes, our people.* Norman: University of Oklahoma Press.
Trimble, Michael
  1987 Cycles of infectious disease on the Upper Missouri: A preliminary chronology and case study. In *The web of disease,* ed. Henry Dobyns, in press.
Tucker, Sara Jones
  1942 *Indian villages of the Illinois country.* Scientific Papers, vol. 2. Springfield: Illinois State Museum.
UNESCO
  1953 *Interrelations of culture.* Paris: UNESCO.
U.S. War Department
  1917 *Manual for stable sergeants.* Washington, D.C.: Government Printing Office
  1931 *Cavalry marches and camps.* Special Text no. 161. Washington, D.C.: Government Printing Office.
Wake, C. Staniland
  1889 *The development of marriage and kinship.* London: George Redway.

Walker, James R.
   1980 *Lakota belief and ritual.* Lincoln: University of Nebraska Press.
Ware, Eugene F.
   1960 *The Indian War of 1864.* New York: St. Martin's Press.
Weakly, Ward F.
   1971 Tree-ring dating and archaeology in South Dakota. *Plains Anthropologist* 16 (54), Memoir 8.
Webb, Walter Prescott
   1931 *The Great Plains.* New York: Grosset and Dunlap.
Wedel, Mildred M.
   1974 Le Sueur and the Dakota Sioux. In *Aspects of Upper Great Lakes anthropology.* ed. Elden Johnson, 157–71. St. Paul: Minnesota Historical Society Press.
Wedel, Mildred M., and Raymond J. DeMallie
   1980 The ethnohistorical approach in Plains area studies. In *Anthropology on the Great Plains,* ed. W. Raymond Wood and Margo Liberty, 110–28. Lincoln: University of Nebraska Press.
Wedel, Waldo
   1962 *Prehistoric man on the Great Plains.* Norman: University of Oklahoma Press.
Wells, Philip V.
   1965 Scarp woodlands, transported grassland soils, and concept of grassland climate in the Great Plains region. *Science* 148: 246–49.
Wheat, Carl I.
   1954 *Mapping the Transmississippi West.* San Francisco: Institute of Historical Cartography.
White, Leslie A.
   1959a *The evolution of culture.* New York: McGraw-Hill.
   1959b *The Indian journals, 1859–62.* Ann Arbor: University of Michigan Press.
Wied, Prince Maximilian of
   1976 *People of the first man.* New York: E. P. Dutton.
Will, George F.
   1924 *Archeology of the Missouri Valley.* Anthropological Papers, vol. 22, part 6. New York: American Museum of Natural History.
Will, George F., and George E. Hyde
   1917 *Corn among the Indians of the Upper Missouri.* Lincoln: University of Nebraska Press (reprint, n.d.).
Will, George F., and H. J. Spinden
   1906 *The Mandans.* Peabody Museum Papers, vol. 3, no. 4. Cambridge: Harvard University.
Williamson, T. S.
   1902 Who were the first men? *Collections of the Minnesota Historical Society* 1: 16–246.
Wilson, Gilbert L.
   1917 *Agriculture of the Hidatsa Indians: An Indian interpretation.* Studies in the

Social Sciences no. 9. Minneapolis: University of Minnesota (J&L Reprints, 1977).

Wolf, Eric R.

1982 *Europe and the people without history.* Berkeley: University of California Press.

Wood, W. Raymond

1967 *An interpretation of Mandan culture history.* Bureau of American Ethnology Bulletin 198. Washington, D.C.: Government Printing Office.

1971 *Biesterfeldt: A post-contact coalescent site on the northeastern plains.* Washington, D.C.: Smithsonian Institution Press.

1983 *An atlas of early maps of the American Midwest.* Scientific Papers, vol. 18. Springfield: Illinois State Museum.

Wood, W. Raymond, and Margo Liberty, eds.

1980 *Anthropology on the Great Plains.* Lincoln: University of Nebraska Press.

Index